Sebastian Zug

The Gift of Water

Forum Politische Geographie

Herausgegeben von Paul Reuber

Schriftleitung: Martin Müller

Band 11

www.politische-geographie.de

LIT

Sebastian Zug

The Gift of Water

Bourdieusian capital exchange
and moral entitlements
in a neighbourhood of Khartoum

LIT

Cover Photo: Neighbours take water from a tap located in a hole, Khartoum, December 2010, S. Zug

Published with the support of Fribourg University, Switzerland

Bibliographic information published by the Deutsche Nationalbibliothek
The Deutsche Nationalbibliothek lists this publication in the Deutsche Nationalbibliografie; detailed bibliographic data are available in the Internet at http://dnb.d-nb.de.

ISBN 978-3-643-90452-2
Zugl.: Fribourg, Univ., Diss., 2013

A catalogue record for this book is available from the British Library

©LIT VERLAG GmbH & Co. KG Wien,
Zweigniederlassung Zürich 2014
Klosbachstr. 107
CH-8032 Zürich
Tel. +41 (0) 44-251 75 05
Fax +41 (0) 44-251 75 06
E-Mail: zuerich@lit-verlag.ch
http://www.lit-verlag.ch

LIT VERLAG Dr. W. Hopf
Berlin 2014
Fresnostr. 2
D-48159 Münster
Tel. +49 (0) 2 51-62 03 20
Fax +49 (0) 2 51-23 19 72
E-Mail: lit@lit-verlag.de
http://www.lit-verlag.de

Distribution:
In Germany: LIT Verlag Fresnostr. 2, D-48159 Münster
Tel. +49 (0) 2 51-620 32 22, Fax +49 (0) 2 51-922 60 99, E-mail: vertrieb@lit-verlag.de

In Austria: Medienlogistik Pichler-ÖBZ, e-mail: mlo@medien-logistik.at
In the UK: Global Book Marketing, e-mail: mo@centralbooks.com
In North America: International Specialized Book Services, e-mail: orders@isbs.com
e-books are available at www.litwebshop.de

Contents

Index of figures ix

List of abbreviations xi

Acknowledgments xii

Preface xiii

1 Introduction 1

2 Water Access, the Local Scale, and Moral Geography 7

    2.1. Political Ecology of Water. Public, Private, and the Community 8
        2.1.1. Analysing Power Relations 8

    2.2. Political Ecology is Normative 11
        2.2.1. Piped Water Infrastructure in the Urban South. Technological Superiority 13
        2.2.2. The Neoliberalization of Water Pipes 16
        2.2.3. The Revival of the Local and the Community 21

    2.3. From Analysing Policy to Analysing Consumers Choices: Locating the Gift 27
        2.3.1. Multiplicity. The Constrained Choice of Water Strategies 29
        2.3.2. A Typology of Water Transfers between Neighbours 31
        2.3.3. Water Gifts. A Review of Scientific Literature 33
        2.3.4. A Framework to Analyse Water Gifts: Conditions for Water Solidarity between Neighbours 36

    2.4. Developing Water Gifts within the Waterscape 40
        2.4.1. The Scale of Waterscapes 41
        2.4.2. The Biography of Water Drops. Circulation and Transformation 46
        2.4.3. The Moral Waterscape. Between Interest and Altruism 53

3 Social Action between Morality and Interest. Extending Bourdieu's Theory of Practice 61

    3.1. Introduction: Waterscapes in Light of Bourdieu's Theory of Practice 61

    3.2. Morality in Bourdieu's Behaviour and Theory 68

  3.2.1. Bourdieu's Moral Authority. Critique by a Scholar 68
  3.2.2. Is There a Moral in Bourdieu's Work? Ignoring the
      Actors' Critical Capacity and the Charge of
      Economism 72
  3.2.3. Moral Capital, the Acknowledgement of Being Good 79
  3.2.4. Anchoring Bourdieu in Moral Philosophy 83

 3.3. The Possibility of Disinterestedness in the Economy of
    Symbolic Goods. A 'Conventional' Reading of Bourdieu 87
  3.3.1. The Uncertainty of Returns. Gifts and Time 87
  3.3.2. Transactions in Multiple Fields. Perceived
      Disinterestedness by Gift Recipients 89
  3.3.3. Accidental Disinterestedness. The Habitus as a
      Product of History 92

 3.4. The Capital of Moral Entitlement. The Negation of
    Reciprocity 94

 3.5. Reconsidering the Actor's Critical Capacity 102

 3.6. Using Boltanski to Justify Disinterestedness:
    Conceptualizing the Social beyond Power 107
  3.6.1. Critical Sociology versus Sociology of Critique 107
  3.6.2. Justification: the Antithesis of Interest 109
  3.6.3. Integrating Justifications and the Economy of
      Symbolic Goods 113
  3.6.4. Rendering the Model Precisely 118

 3.7. Conclusion: from a Perfect to an Imperfect Economy of
    Symbolic Goods 124

4 Doing Research in Greater Khartoum and Methodology 129

 4.1. Access to the Field and Scientific Cooperation 130

 4.2. Research Methods for Analysing Square 11's Waterscape 135

**5 Fragmentation. A Recent History of Urban Development
and Water Supply in Greater Khartoum 143**

 5.1. A Short History of Greater Khartoum and Dar Alsalam
    Square 11 143
  5.1.1. The Urban Transformation of Greater Khartoum and
      Migration 143
  5.1.2. The Study Area Dar Alsalam Square 11 148

5.2. Fragmentation of the Water Network at the Scale of the City 154
  5.2.1. Water Resources and Water Production 156
  5.2.2. Water Distribution in Greater Khartoum: a Network
         Perspective 157
  5.2.3. Network Access: a Question of Social Class 160

5.3. Fragmentation among Neighbourhoods with Similar
     Socio-Economic Characteristics 162
  5.3.1. A Water History of Square 11: Transformation of a
         Non-Connected Area into a Connected One............................162
  5.3.2. Tracking Fragmentation by Tree Canopy 166
  5.3.3. Explaining Differences in Water Network
         Performance...169
  5.3.4. Lobbying for Square 11. Negotiating Fragmentation...............171

5.4. Fragmentation Inside Square 11 176
  5.4.1. The Spatial-Temporal Development of Tree Canopy
         and Water Supply 176
  5.4.2. Topography, Network Design, and the Possibility of
         Managing Water Distribution Inside Square 11 179
  5.4.3. Local Perceptions about Water Justice in the Square...............183

6 **Milking the Network. People's Struggles for Scarce
  Network Water**..187

6.1. The Scales of Heterogeneity. Fragmented Supply and
     Unequal Access..187

6.2. Appropriation of Pipes through Technical Adjustments...................193
  6.2.1. Pipe Manipulations 195
  6.2.2. Suction Pumps..202
  6.2.3. Conclusion 204

6.3. Spatial Heterogeneity as a Result of Water Access Inequality............205
  6.3.1. Analytical Framework for Household Tap
         Performance...206
  6.3.2. Area A: Pumping Water to those who can Easily
         Access Water without Pumps 211
  6.3.3. Area B: Maximum Water Inequality..214
  6.3.4. Area C: the Frontier between High and Low
         Performance...215
  6.3.5. Area D: Accessing Water by Lowering the Tap under
         Difficult Conditions...216

    6.4. Conclusions 218
        6.4.1. Constructing the Neighbourly Waterscape beyond
             Network Supply. From Water to 'Waters' 218
        6.4.2. Locating Appropriations in the Moral Waterscape of
             the City 225

7 Accessing the Neighbour's Tap. The Gift of Water 229

    7.1. Classifying Water Biographies by Economic Costs 230
        7.1.1. The Economic and Social Costs for Making Gifts 231
        7.1.2. The Benefits of Receiving Gifts 238
        7.1.3. The Overall Economics of Different Biographies of
             Water 241

    7.2. Gifts between Close Friends. Supplying Water by Hose 245
        7.2.1. The Social Embeddedness of Water Supply by Hose 245
        7.2.2. Compensation for Water Supply by Hose 251
        7.2.3. Explaining Supply by Hose in the Economy of
             Symbolic Goods 254

    7.3. The Entitlement to Water. Accessing the Neighbour's Water
        is a Right 255
        7.3.1. The Social Embeddedness of Bucket Supply 256
        7.3.2. The Minimal Obligation to Grant Access to Water 260
        7.3.3. Justifying Water Gifts to People who do not
             Reciprocate 262

    7.4. Water Gifts – a Universalistic Explanation 263

8 Conclusions 275

    8.1. The Gift of Water and Decommodification. Social Practice
        between Moral and Interests 277

    8.2. The Gift of Water and the Community. A Local Basic
        Lifeline Concept 279

    8.3. The Gift of Water and the City. Social Welfare and the
        Negative Aspects of Solidarity 281

Bibliography 285
Appendix: List of Interviews 308
Summary 311
Zusammenfassung 314

Index of figures

Fig. 1: A Conceptual Framework to Analyse Water Gifts 36
Fig. 2: Uncertainty of Return in Gift Transactions 88
Fig. 3: Different Reciprocal Constellations 90
Fig. 4: The Capital of Moral Entitlement (Non-Reciprocal True Disinterestedness) 99
Fig. 5: The Internalization of Reason from the Meta-Pragmatic Register into the Economy of Symbolic Goods 120
Fig. 6: Mutual Production of Imperfection in the Economy of Symbolic Goods and the Meta-Pragmatic Register 122
Fig. 7: Complicity of Economic Transfers in the Morally Influenced Imperfect Economy of Symbolic Goods 126
Fig. 8: Research Plan 131
Fig. 9: Khartoum and Omdurman 144
Fig. 10: Settlement Structure and Services in Dar Alsalam Square 11 149
Fig. 11: Tea Stall Used as Popular Committee Office and Old Water Tower 154
Fig. 12: Water Infrastructure in Square 11 and Neighbouring Squares 165
Fig. 13: Tree Canopy and Topography of Square 11 and Neighbouring Squares 168
Fig. 14: A Group of KSWC Staff Closing a Valve in a Manhole 175
Fig. 15: The Development of Tree Canopy in Square 11 (2006-2012) 177
Fig. 16: Internal Fragmentation of Square 11's Network Supply 177
Fig. 17: Daytime Water Flows on Day 1 180
Fig. 18: Daytime Water Flows on Day 2 180
Fig. 19: Nighttime Water Flows 181
Fig. 20: Conceptualizing Water Supply and Water Access 190
Fig. 21: Water Pressure and Flow 196
Fig. 22: KSWC Standard Pipe Installation 198
Fig. 23: Standard Water Tap with Good Pressure 198
Fig. 24: Maximum Manipulated Installation 199
Fig. 25: Optimized and Regular Connection 200

Fig. 26: Makeshift Closure of Hole in 4 Inch Pipe 200
Fig. 27: Tap below the Surface 201
Fig. 28: Suction Pump 203
Fig. 29: Generator Operated Suction Pump 203
Fig. 30: Water Access and Supply Inequality: the Heterogeneity of
    Tap Performance 209
Fig. 31: Water Pressure Measurements in Area A 212
Fig. 32: Water Pressure Measurements in Area D 217
Fig. 33: Multiplicity of Water Access Strategies 221
Fig. 34: Quantification of Water Access Strategies 223
Fig. 35: Water Vendor with Donkey Cart 232
Fig. 36: Typical Spatial Arrangement of a Plot in Square 11 235
Fig. 37: Water Biographies in Square 11 243
Fig. 38: Gift Transfers by Hose in Area A 246
Fig. 39: Gift Transfers by Hose in Area B 249
Fig. 40: Gift Transfers by Bucket in Area B 256
Fig. 41: Gift Transfers by Bucket in Area C 258
Fig. 42: Water Taps on Public Ground in Area D 261
Fig. 43: Example of a Justification: Questioning the Validity of the
    Moral Entitlement to the Neighbour's Tap 271
Fig. 44: A Classification of Water Transfers by their Embeddedness
    in Capitalism 278

List of abbreviations

GIS	Geographic information systems
GPS	Global positioning system
IMF	International Monetary Fund
KSWC	Khartoum State Water Corporation
NGO	Non-governmental organization
NCP	National Congress Party
SDG	Sudanese Pound (1 SDG = 0.315 EUR, average exchange rate between August and December 2010)
UN	United Nations
WAMAKHAIR	Water Management in Khartoum International Research Project

Acknowledgments

This book is not only the result of an individual endeavour but it is also built on varying 'gifts' from many individuals, to whom I would like to express my gratitude: to Professor Olivier Graefe from Fribourg University for his excellent guidance of my PhD thesis, his reflections on my work and the freedom he gave me to follow my own ideas; Dr. Olivier Ejderyan for continuous intensive discussions on social theory; Professor David Blanchon for inviting me to the Université Paris Ouest Nanterre and the exchange of ideas; Professor Gregor Dobler and Professor Benedikt Korf for two discussions which strongly influenced my reflections; Dr. Alex Loftus and Professor Elísio Macamo for their valuable comments; the Commission for Research Partnerships with Developing Countries (KFPE), the Swiss National Science Foundation (SNSF), and Fribourg University for financing my field research in Khartoum, my visit to Paris, and this publication; as well as Ly Lan Dill for proof reading.

I am strongly indebted to the residents of Dar Alsalam Square 11, and several other locations in Khartoum, who volunteered their time and answered my often very personal questions with a remarkable openness; to Osman Elfathi Osman and Amar Numeri Nasr who went above and beyond translating; to Mohammed Abdul Wahed and Tango Bullen who assisted me in the field; to Abdalla Mohammed Adlan and Abdalla Altayeb for surveying Square 11 and supporting my research when I had already left Khartoum.

Many people assisted in creating a desirable atmosphere provided during the times when the computer was switched off. These include Katharina; my family from Weilersbach and Rombach; my friends; Bernd and Corinne Fleischer, the Royaume de la Gâité, and Emilie Lavie, who hosted me on different continents; my fellow PhD students in Khartoum Luisa Arango, Laure Crombé, Salma Abdalla, and Anne-Sophie Beckedorf; and finally all human and physical geographers in Fribourg, who created an incredible social environment.

Preface

Within this remarkable piece of work Sebastian Zug makes the bold claim that the "water pipe paradigm" distracts researchers from other modes of water provision and from understanding water within a historically and geographically specific moment. Such a simple and yet astonishing claim foregrounds the author's exploration of the water gift as a fundamentally important relationship established between residents of low-income settlements in the global South. As someone still, perhaps, distracted by the piped water paradigm, this claim, and the book in general, challenges some of my taken-for-granted understandings of water provision. It forces me to confront my own biases and those of the field in which I work - urban political ecology. The book sets a new benchmark for theoretically informed, empirically grounded political ecological research in the global South and I very much hope it will be discussed, debated and built upon in future.

The book presents the findings from a period of intensive field research in Khartoum; however it reads the empirical findings through a set of theoretical perspectives that have been ignored and overlooked in political ecology. The author knows the sub-field of urban political ecology intimately and his review of contemporary debates is both engaging and informative. Already hinting at what is to come, Zug is particularly sensitive to the non-economistic roots of research in urban political ecology, even while he is critical of the distractions of the water pipe. The truly innovative work comes in the next chapter where the author begins to consider Bourdieu's theory of practice as a way of conceptualising the non-economic water transfers he had witnessed from his time spent researching in Khartoum. Rather than contenting himself with a simple application of Bourdieu's writings to urban political ecology, the author seeks to extend Bourdieu's theoretical project through work on morality and in conversation with neo-Hobbesian frameworks and writings in pragmatic sociology. Deeply complex theoretical debates are conveyed lucidly and elegantly. The climax to this chapter presents a framework that seeks to understand what Zug refers to as an imperfect economy of symbolic goods, one that lies between market and moral-based justifications.

The book is not, however, a work of philosophy and the author seeks to extend, challenge, and experiment with the theoretical framework he has laid out through considering the detailed empirical research that he has conducted in Khartoum. His chosen site for research clearly posed challenges of its own and it is a testament to the tenacity and doggedness of the author that such interesting stories of neighbourly water transfers are able to emerge. By focussing on one small square of a site-and service scheme on the outskirts of Khartoum, the author is able to narrate a convincing and engaging story of how different water transfers develop between different residents depending not only on their perceptions of one another but also on moral codes, religious interpretations and both interested and disinterested positions. At times, the book becomes like a handbook on urban water provision in the global South as the researcher joins both municipal engineers and neighbours in seeking to rectify low pressure supplies in one part of Square 11, without reducing the flow to others. Astonishingly, Zug makes the claim that 58% of those not supplied by the network, consume water from their neighbours. Given that the Khartoum case is unlikely to be exceptional, it seems remarkable that such transfers are only receiving, in this work, the attention they deserve.

When the author turns to debates on the right to water, the book acquires a new pitch. Challenging the simplistic roots of "culture-based" claims to altruism, the book suggests that "the religious rule that defines water as a commons is primarily a religious translation of the universal right to water". Yet again, the author shows how considering the water gift challenges dominant conceptions within the political ecology of water, while also demonstrating how taking water gifts seriously might speak to broader claims around the right to water. Throughout the book, the author sustains a detailed theoretical argument that is innovative and clearly articulated. As with the best of geographical scholarship, the text works through such a theoretical debate in relation to a rich empirical analysis: the researcher becomes one of the lay plumbers working the margins of networked and non-networked water supplies. Zug's bold, revelatory argument around the water gift will contribute much to the understandings of both urban political ecology and of the politics of water. He provides us with fundamentally new understandings of the starting points through which we might engage in struggles to democratise access to water, building from a new conceptualisation of the social and from new understandings of how people work together to access this most fundamental resource.

Alex Loftus, King's College London, September 2013

1

Introduction

In 2010 the United Nation's General Assembly (2010) recognized "the right to safe and clean drinking water and sanitation as a human right that is essential for the full enjoyment of life and all human rights". Declaring water a human right legally transforms the basic need into an entitlement. The UN resolution is a specific juridical reformulation of the 'universal right to water' into international law. Such a law has already been codified on different levels, such as constitutional and legal amendments in more than 100 countries (Bakker 2013: 257), in different religious laws (e.g. Larson 2011; Pradhan and Meinzen-Dick 2010), and in long-established community arrangements of collective water management (e.g. Benda-Beckmann, Benda-Beckmann, and Spiertz; Boelens, Getches, and Guevara-Gil 2010). Consequently, the UN's declared human right to water is only one point of reference – albeit a widely discussed one (e.g. Bakker 2007; Biswas, Rached, and Tortajada 2008; Gleick 1999; Gupta, Ahlers, and Ahmed 2010; Hemson 2008; Sultana and Loftus 2012) – to justify people's entitlement to the water required to satisfy everyday consumption needs. This book contributes to the debate on the water rights of individual households – not by focusing on the efforts and responsibilities of governments and public or private corporations; but by analysing the social redistribution of water from water-rich households to their water-poor neighbours.

Governmental implementation of the right to water has not only been made an important topic in national and multinational policy debates but also in critical scholarship. This focus is motivated by persistently high inequality in water access in the global South in general and urban Africa in particular. The "modern infrastructural ideal" (Graham and Marvin 2001) of access to tap water is far from achieving a spatially comprehensive and socially inclusive coverage. In 2010, only 34 % of Sub-Saharan urban households were connected to piped water networks with taps directly on their premises (UNICEF and WHO 2012: 56). Social scientists – especially 'political ecologists of water', a central reference of this book – focused on understanding how the social stratification in network water access is produced and embedded in power relationships (e.g. Gandy 2008; Loftus 2007; Swyngedouw 1997). The significant actors within such a perspective are policy makers as well as the public and private water corporations who provide water under the formers' policy. The scale of analysis is the 'waterscape of the city'. Policies are made for this waterscape and within it; they are influenced by global trends like neoliberalism, and under support and pressure from international monetary institutions and donors. From such a perspective, the right to water partially regulates the interface between water providers and their customers.

The social science debate focuses on the economic and political construction of water access of only 34% of the urban population. The access of the remaining 66% of households is mostly presented as merely signifiers of inequality. This majority represents those who are deprived of cheap, comfortable access to water network.

A comprehensive understanding of the systems under which the 'deprived' have access to water is rare. The only exception is a small group of scholars analysing what they call 'informal' water supply systems or small-scale independent water providers, like that of water vendors (e.g. Collignon and Vézina 2000; Kjellén and McGranahan 2006; Kariuki and Schwartz 2005). As for network supply, the households obtaining water from these providers are hardly conceptualized beyond their function as consumers of the water suppliers. The social transaction described is an economic one where the vendors ensure water access, but are motivated by income creation rather than by satisfying people's social welfare.

I will argue in this book, that urban dwellers have a wider array of possibilities to access water with acceptable quality standards than simply as customers of water providers. Making these empirically based claims requires shifting the perspective from describing supply – the service of water production and transport – to studying people's daily water practices. The goal of such an approach is to reveal how individuals satisfy their consumption from what they define to be possible water sources. The case study area was defined as one of Khartoum's peri-urban neighbourhoods with a weak performing water network. After studying this area, along with other locations around the city, it became clear that households access water without payment from water vendors as well as from their neighbours' purchased water. Consuming free water is not a quantitatively negligible practice. On the contrary, it is a strategy that is regularly applied by many households and which even covers the full water consumption of a portion of them.

In these transfers, water recipients do not act like customers, since they do not pay for the service. Rather, accessing free water requires an active change of water's economic status in the potential donor's home. The flow of water to the final consumer can be described as a 'biography of things' (Kopytoff 1986). In such a biography, water is not decommodified in a long-term political process, as debated for example for processes of marketization in urban political ecology of water. In contrast, in their biography, water drops are transformed at different stages in *everyday* flows. A drop of water originating from a natural resource, which is nothing more than H_2O flowing in the Nile or stored in an aquifer, is first moved into a commodity state (Appadurai 1986) by those adding value to it through extraction, purification, and transport. So that this water can be given free of charge from a donor to a recipient, it must be moved out of the commodity state. This economic transformation generates costs for those granting others free access to the water they purchased. For a determination of the logic of these transformations the described water practices must be analysed on a very local scale, which I have termed the 'neighbourly waterscape'. By focusing on this scale, households are not considered merely as water consumers; but as actors actively shaping the waterscape by taking on the role of provider, as well as by negotiating the conditionalities of water transfers. Valorising the consumer in the analysis conforms to the demand of certain anthropologists to extend the focus of political ecology of water to reconstruct the subjective meaning embedded into water (e.g. Baviskar 2003; Mosse 2003; Strang 2004).

In this research, free water transfers from the 'water-rich' and water vendors to the 'water poor' are conceptualized under the notion of the gift. This notion was made popular by Marcel Mauss (1966 [1923]) and has been heavily debated since. The principal ambiguity of the explanation of the gift is the relevance of interested and disinterested motivations; hence whether gifts are reciprocal or generous (Verhezen 2009: 85). To understand free water transfers, the social relation between the donor and the recipient of the water gift must be reconstructed, just as the social framework in which the transaction takes place. Such a reconstruction requires understanding people's motivations to transform the commodity of water into a gift.

This tension between the different motivations of gifts is theoretically elaborated through the opposition of Pierre Bourdieu's theory of practice (1977

[1972]) with Luc Boltanski's work on justification (Boltanski and Thévenot 2006 [1991]). Bourdieu's relational approach to the social helps translate political ecology's focus on power relations to the local scale, the 'neighbourly social field'. "Flows of water" can be reconstructed as "flows of power" (Swyngedouw 2004). Bourdieu represents those approaches to the gift that highlight reciprocity. In the 'economy of symbolic goods', received gifts are either compensated by counter gifts, or they lead to symbolic indebtedness, which positively modifies the donor's social position and negatively influences that of the recipient. Disinterested behaviour in Bourdieu's approach is paradoxically only possible when actors have an interest in acting disinterestedly, hence if they are compensated for being good.

Boltanski is one of the scholars (e.g. Alexander 1995; Caillé 2001 [1994]; Sayer 1999) who criticised Bourdieu's 'social reductionist' or 'economistic' explanation of social practice. Boltanski argues that people can ground their action in what he calls in his later work a 'meta-pragmatic register'; but they do not always necessarily do so (Boltanski 2011 [2009]). "In certain situations, justifiable and universalizable agreements are possible, [which] are capable of resisting their denunciation as simple power relations under the veil of relations of justice" (Boltanski and Thévenot 2000: 212). If actors consider a universal right to water applicable in a specific situation, they can act without striving for profit maximization.

This research follows a dual approach. First, it makes use of Bourdieu's and Boltanski's conceptualizations of the social to understand water gifts in Khartoum. Second, based on empirical findings, it elaborates how interested and disinterested motivations can be brought together within a single theoretical framework by supplementing Bourdieu's theory of practice with Boltanski's 'meta-pragmatic register' as an alternative mode of action. Critically analysing Bourdieu's conceptualization of morality, and proposing an adjustment of his theory to allow morality to infiltrate everyday practice, addresses the economistic critique of the theory of practice without completely rejecting the theory itself. Bourdieu's central concept of the habitus provides a substantial basis for the mediation between morals and interests within particular social fields. I will propose to transfer his 'perfect' economy of symbolic goods into an 'imperfect' one in the following pages.

Besides suggesting an enhancement of Bourdieu's theory of practice, I aim to contribute to scientific debates in urban political ecology of water and urban studies of Khartoum. Based on the water practices observed in Khartoum, there seems to be a gap in political ecology of water concerning scholarship on free water transfers. Only research in other cities will show whether the substantial prevalence of water gifts in Khartoum is exceptional or whether the gift plays an equally important role elsewhere. As a foundation of a comparative approach between different cities, I will elaborate the social, spatial, and economic factors that favour the emergence of water gifts. Making the gift of water an independent topic is not a romanticising anthropological excursus on the solidarity of people in the global South, detached from the unequal production of network water supply on the scale of the city. Rather, these very local processes subtly influence the formulations of water policy. As such, water gifts are only one of the many elements that need to be understood, even if the 'only' aim is to understand 'waterscapes on the scale of the city'.

Although Greater Khartoum belongs to the five most populated agglomerations in Africa (UN DESA 2012), there has been very little research in recent decades. Analysing water gifts provides insights into the social organization beyond the flow of water between donor and recipient. It shows how social relations are formed between households originating from throughout Sudan, who accidentally became neighbours through imposed urban planning measures.

Organization of the Book

This book starts with an overview of political ecology of water with a focus on determining the relevance of considering households as actors who shape the waterscape, rather than merely as water consumers (chapter 2). Shifting the focus from a political ecology of the city to a political ecology of 'neighbourly' and 'moral waterscapes', allows setting the scale and thematic focus required for a conceptualization of water gifts. Using analyses of social science literature on water as a foundation, I demonstrate that the water gift has so far elicited little interest from social scientists as a water access strategy. In the third chapter, I briefly outline the theory of practice as a possible theoretical framework for political ecology followed by an in depth analysis of Bourdieu's conceptualization of disinterestedness and morality. After determining the possibilities of integrating disinterestedness under a conventional reading of Bourdieu, I will unravel some of his assumptions step by step. Extending the Theory of Practice with Boltanski's 'meta-pragmatic register' allows the integration of theoretical reasoning and historical habitualisation of morals into the Theory of Practice.

After a presentation of the methodology of the empirical study (chapter 4), three chapters discuss the empirical case. Chapter 5 gives a general introduction to water supply in Khartoum and presents the fragmentation of network water supply at different scales. Chapter 6 turns the focuses on the households and reveals direct neighbours have different yet successful strategies to access water supplied by the public water corporation. Fragmentation of supply in combination with heterogeneity in access provides the contexts of water inequality in which redistribution of water by gift transfers takes place. In chapter 7, two types of water gifts are presented. One is explained within Bourdieu's 'economy of symbolic goods', whereas the other justifies the moral extension of his theory.

2

Water Access, the Local Scale, and Moral Geography

Making the gift of water the central topic of this research was not a decision taken behind a desk. Rather, it was the result of an explorative investigation of water access strategies of households in various locations in peri-urban Greater Khartoum. In very spontaneous motorbike rides throughout the peripheries of the agglomeration during a period of several weeks, short interviews were conducted in various locations that I felt were very interesting in terms of understanding the peri-urban waterscape. There were a number of possibilities for people to access free water. Operators of water towers, who sell water to water vendors, always allow people to fill their buckets for private use free of charge, regardless if the tower is publicly or privately operated. Similarly, people obtain water from companies that produce water for other purposes, like a chicken farm and a stone quarry neighbouring the informal settlement Nifasha (western Omdurman). The farm allows people to access water used for watering a hedge around their premises. Along the irrigation pipes, the company installed several water taps to facilitate access. The stone quarry allows people to take water from a tap in the garden of the employee's accommodations. Water gifts are not restricted to transfers from water producers to individual households. People, who purchase water for their own consumption, frequently become water donors. Water is either carried in buckets or pumped through garden hoses from the 'water-rich' to the 'water-poor'. Observing these transfers in several of the peri-urban neighbourhood stresses the need to take the phenomenon into consideration for an all-encompassing understanding of water in Greater Khartoum.

The scientific debates on urban water supply barely notice these transfers. When the transfers are mentioned, they are hardly scientifically developed. I will argue that incorporating water gifts is crucial for an understanding of water in the empirical context of peri-urban Greater Khartoum. This chapter will contextualize the gift within scientific debates on water, focusing on the political ecology of water. In 2.1, I will present the major topics of political ecology of water, like the public-private divide at the city scale, which will be important in understanding processes at smaller scales where gift transfers stand in opposition to market-based supply of water. In the past few years, debate has opened up concerning the community as an actor in water supply yet it does not acknowledge the relevance of water gifts. In order to integrate the gift, subchapter 2.2 will argue for supplementing political ecology with a consumer cantered perspective. Under such a perspective, the gift can be conceptualized as one element of the 'urban waterscape'. After a review of the limited existing research on water gifts, I will present a framework to analyse water gifts that will take into consideration economic, spatial and social phenomena. In subchapter 2.3, the term 'waterscape' from political ecology will be extended into a scalar term and will be combined with the biography of things, to conceptualize (de)commodification processes – which are at the centre of political ecology of water – not over the long term, but as a transformation of water in everyday practice. Water gifts cannot be understood as a purely economic phenomenon wherein the donor is a supplier and the recipient a customer. By referring to moral geography and defining a 'moral waterscape' (2.4), other motivations than interest can be reconsidered. The chapter will conclude with the elaboration of research questions (2.5).

2.1. Political Ecology of Water. Public, Private, and the Community

2.1.1. Analysing Power Relations

A group of Anglo-Saxon, neo-Marxist scholars (e.g. Swyngedouw 2004; Bakker 2003a; Budds 2009; Kaïka 2003; Linton 2010; Loftus 2009; Gandy 2008) dominate the debate on urban water management in human geography. Under the label 'urban political ecology of water' they critically analyse the socio-nature of water supply, hence the flow of water in a social system. Swyngedouw's The City as a Hybrid: On Nature, Society and Cyborg Urbanization (1996) can be seen as the founding text that set the stage for the group's work, moving political ecology into urban contexts while strongly anchoring it in Marxist thought. Within such an approach, water is taken "as the entry point" to "reconstruct and hence theorize the urbanization process as a political ecological process" (Swyngedouw 1996: 76). Water, consequently, becomes the object of research, embedded into a wider social context.

Marx, Nature, and Society

Swyngedouw strongly argues "that Marxism still has a place not just in maintaining geography as a vibrant and exciting discipline, but – perhaps most importantly – in contributing to the production of a truly humanising geography" (Swyngedouw 1999a: 92). He criticises however the fact that many Marxist scholars in Anglo-Saxon geography restrict their work to a

> particular form of structural-economistic Marxism [ignoring or marginalizing] a whole generation of Marxist writings that came from an entirely different trajectory. Throughout the century, culture, ideology, language, psycho-analysis, gender and everyday life have been and still are an integral and important part of historical materialist perspectives (Swyngedouw 1999a: 97).

Véron (2006: 2094) summarizes the situation by stating that urban political ecology of water is moving beyond an orthodox Marxist approach, signified for example, by the work of Kaïka (2003) and Swyngedouw, Kaïka, and Castro (2002) on the 'discursive production' of scarcity.

While opening up Marxism for non-economistic readings, Swyngedouw strongly argues for a return to Marx's historical materialism, criticising that "most sociology including Marxist sociology" concentrated "on the labour process as mere social process" leading to "the over-emphasis on the social relations under capitalism" while ignoring "the material and socio-physical metabolic relationships", resulting "in a partial blindness in the social sciences of the twentieth century to questions of political ecology and socio-ecologic metabolisms" (Swyngedouw 2006: 28). Swyngedouw's work can also be considered eco-Marxist writings, which notably include the work of Castree (1995).

Swyngedouw puts Marx's notion of metabolism[1] at the core of his approach to conceptualizing the relationship between the social and the natural rather

---

[1] Marx borrows the term of metabolism from the agricultural chemist Justus von Liebig, and uses it not as an analogy to describe social processes, but "in an ontological manner in which human beings, like society, were an integral, yet particular and distinct, part of nature" (Swyngedouw 2006: 25).

than between only the social and the economic.[2] He argues that already for Marx "this socio-natural metabolism [...] is the foundation of and possibility for history, a socio-environmental history through which the nature both of humans and nonhumans is transformed" (Swyngedouw and Heynen 2003: 904). Nature in political ecology does not only exist as a social construction (e.g. Swyngedouw 2006: 7); "while nature provides the foundation, the dynamics of social relations produce nature's and society's history" (Swyngedouw 2004: 16). Through metabolic circulation[3], natural objects (including biological human beings) become socially relevant, while retaining material significance. The resulting hybridity is underlined by Swyngedouw (e.g. 1996: 66) when he refers to Donna Haraway's (1991) notion of "cyborgs" and Bruno Latour's (1993) "quasi-objects". This approach allows political ecologists to avoid both, "the extremes of environmental determinism and social constructivism [...] by focusing instead upon the internal, mutually constitutive relationships within and between humans and non-human entities" (Loftus 2007: 43).

The city itself is conceptualized as a socio-natural hybrid. Consequently, "urbanization is primarily a particular socio-spatial process of metabolizing nature, of urbanizing the environment" (Swyngedouw 2004: 8). This urban hybrid is set together by "myriad processes that support and maintain social life, such as, for example, water, energy, food, or computers, always combine society and nature in infinite ways" (Swyngedouw 1999b: 445). Swyngedouw aims to understand the city as such, but rather than analysing all metabolisms, he focuses on the flows of water.

> Just as the investigation of the circulation of money and capital illustrates the functioning of capitalism as an economic system, I aim to demonstrate that the circulation of water – as a physical and social process – brings to light wider political economic, social, and ecological processes (Swyngedouw 2004: 3).

To reconstruct the water supply system and consequently the urbanization process, the metabolisms of water need to be understood in their present flows and through the history of their constitution. The complexity of such a reconstruction is illustrated by Swyngedouw (2004: 18) stating that

---

2 A similar approach was chosen by Foster (2000).
3 The notion of circulation is stressed by Swyngedouw in relation to metabolisms. He frequently compares metabolisms with the double circulation of blood in the vascular system of the human body (e.g. Swyngedouw 2004: 31).

> Drinking tap water combines the circulation of productive, merchant and financial capital with the production of land rent and their associated class relations; the ecological transformation of hydrological complexes and the biochemical process of purification with the libidinous sensation and the physiological necessity of drinking fluids; the social regulation of access to water with images of clarity, cleanliness, health, and virginity.

Though political ecological research claims to take materiality seriously, their research does not necessarily emphasize the reconstruction of physical metabolisms as much as it does social ones. Political ecology of water remains a social science and due to the Marxist foundation its focus is set on unveiling the political construction of water under capitalism, making power a central category.

> [The] multiple metabolisms of water are structured and organized through relations of power, socio-natural power, that is, relations of domination and subordination, of access and exclusion, of emancipation and repression. These social power relations become embedded in the flow and metabolisms of circulating water (Swyngedouw 1996: 76).

2.2. Political Ecology is Normative

Urban water supply is a fruitful field for Marxist critique of capitalism, since water supply systems – especially, but not exclusively, in the cities of the South – are characterized by obvious inequality in access. While the rich tend to receive high quantities for low prices – sometimes even directly or indirectly subsidized – the formal networks do not even reach many poor neighbourhoods.

Political ecology takes a twofold perspective on water. First, the social reality of inequality is empirically deducted: "urban political ecology attempts to tease out who gains from and who pays for, who benefits from and who suffers from particular processes of socioenvironmental change" (Swyngedouw and Heynen 2003: 910). In water supply this perspective mainly reveals the social inequality inherent in water supply systems.

This perspective is the basis for "the political program of political ecology", which aims on enhancing "the democratic content of socio-environmental construction by means of identifying the strategies through which a more equitable distribution of social power and a more inclusive mode of the production of nature can be achieved" (Heynen, Kaïka, and Swyngedouw 2006: 12). Thus, the critique of empirical inequality translates into a critique of the socio-political production of this inequality. Through their work, political ecologists of water take strong positions in this debate. They are critical in the sense of 'critical' theory of the Frankfurt School and Bourdieu's 'critical' sociology, or as Robbins puts it: "political ecology represents an explicit alternative to 'apolitical' ecology" (Robbins 2012: 14).

The two perspectives analyse two different actors: the (potential) consumers and the policy maker. The latter and the decisions they make circle back and result in the situation analysed in the first perspective. While the first perspective is mainly descriptive serving as a justification for political claims and is in much research assumed rather than empirically deducted, the second perspective is the sphere of political ecology's scientific creativity. It allows political ecologists to influence non-scientific actors (national politicians, international institutions, water supply companies and their lobbyists, national and international NGOs, anti/alter-globalization movements including consumers as activists, and other politically conscious actors), who themselves controversially and ideologically discuss the same topics as the scientific narratives, defining water between common and commodity, between human right and scarce resource, between luxury product and basic need. Political ecologists are actors in the policy debates, not in the sense that they elaborate policy recommendations and actively cooperate or advise governments and water companies, but because they raise and offer critiques on water policy.[4]

In political ecology, the claim for distributive justice is not a utopian debate on a 'right to water' in absence of means to implement it. Rather, it is always discussed within the framework of the restrictions posed by normative claims, which are notably anchored in resources. Water supply needs to be financed, which especially includes the construction and operation of physical infrastructures, and the utilization of natural resources. This requires taking into consideration ecosystems and their sustainability.

---

4 Their political involvement therefore strongly differs from some of the French water scholars (e.g. Sylvie Jaglin and Bernhard Barraqué), who actively advise political and economic actors.

2.2.1. Piped Water Infrastructure in the Urban South. Technological Superiority

Inequalities in access are political ecologists' empirical justification for criticizing water supply management in cities of the South. These inequalities can be assumed to be prevalent in any of these cities, but to different extents. It is not the mere access to water that is in question, but the quantity and quality of water people can access, and the labour and financial costs that arise for the consumers.

The Piped Network Paradigm

A widely accepted consensus (recent exceptions will be discussed later) in the narratives of political ecology is – often implicitly – to divide water supply technologies along the lines defined by the United Nations to measure indicator 7c of the Millennium Development Goals, which aims to "reduce by half the proportion of people without sustainable access to safe drinking water and basic sanitation" (UNICEF and WHO 2012: 1). Access to drinking water is measured both for rural and urban areas by the percentage of people with access to what the UN calls an 'improved' water source. The UN (UNICEF and WHO 2012: 33) defines whether or not people have an improved source not by the measurement of the quality and quantity of water consumed, but assumes this to be reflected by the technology that is used to access water. The improved water sources relevant in urban areas are all related to pipe infrastructure, which includes the most propagated category 'pipe into dwelling, yard or plot', and as second class acceptable technical solutions "public taps" or "standpipes".[5] From the moment an intermediary actor (UN's category: "cart with small tank or drum") is in-between water production and the consumer, the water source is classified as unimproved, just like "surface water". Sultana (2012) argues that also "critical geographical scholarship" often focusses only on "large-scale infrastructures, such as urban piped networks, connected meters, dams, and irrigation systems" while "smaller-scale water infrastructures and stand-alone technologies that are not

---

[5] For completeness, other improved sources, as defined by the UN are "tube wells", "boreholes", "rainwater collection", "protected springs", and "protected dug wells", which however, are generally not predominant urban technologies although they can certainly be found especially in peri-urban areas. Other unimproved sources are tanker trucks, as well as "unprotected springs and wells". "Bottled water" is a special category because the UN assumes that bottled water is only a supplementary water source rather than the primary one.

in a connected or reticulated system, such as individual tube wells, have not received the same level of attention".

The argument underlying the superiority of the pipe strongly follows the modernization paradigm, in which developing countries are assumed or encouraged to replicate the development path of European countries. Gandy (2004: 373) has outlined the development of the 'bacteriological city' in Europe, where "the urban ideal of the fully connected metropolis emerged as a powerful symbol for modernity in the wake of the chaotic and disconnected nineteenth-century city". This ideal incorporated scientific results from epidemiology and its emergence was made possible thanks to technological advances, as well as the appearance of municipal managerialism. Together with sanitation systems the networks of purified water assure the metabolic circulation of water. "The development of the bacteriological city – with its integrated technological networks — rested on a widely held misconception that all cities would ultimately conform to this model" (Gandy 2004: 368). As we will see later, with the example of Greater Khartoum, this was not the case for large parts of urban population in the South. Even if Gandy argues that under growing neoliberalism in the last decades, water is no longer a citizen's right (Gandy 2004: 371), the technological ideals of the bacteriological city, including the superiority of the network, remain widely accepted, while alternatives to the paradigm are only taken into consideration as second best options. While "the term drinking water [has become] synonymous with tap or piped water" in European languages, "the piped water paradigm has settled itself at the heart of local political debates and has become a main recipient of international aid" (Braadbaart 2009: 79, 81).

The Economic Superiority of the Network

Beside the public health argument, an economic argument supports the superiority of the network. Water from a pipe network tends to be much cheaper than water from other commercial sources, which might require walking for long distances or payments to water vendors. While the health argument can be contested since in many cities water from taps does not necessarily fulfil drinking water standards and is a potential source of waterborne diseases[6], the economic argument as well as the increased comfort of having a tap is evident.

---

6 Collignon and Vézina (2000: 49) argue that "the quality of water provided by independent providers is practically the same as that of water from the mains, where it is drawn."

Comparing the price per unit of water supplied through the formal and the informal system has become a standard component of analysing urban water supply. Probably starting with his research on Abidjan, Saint-Vil (1983: 483) demonstrated that people accessing water from water vendors pay a higher price per unit than those connected to formal piped systems. In the case of Abidjan, the price was five times higher. Swyngedouw (2004: 139), in his research on Guayaquil, even found prices that were 200-300 times higher and Mitlin (2004: 329) summarized several studies with price differentials ranging somewhere between Abidjan and Guayaquil. While the upper class generally has access to water from the network, hence, cheap water provision, the poor must purchase water at high costs, aggravating the consumption discrepancies between different socio-economic spheres of society. In Windhoek for example, several rich households with swimming pools and tropical gardens consume roughly 600 to 800 litres per person and day, while a person in the informal settlements consumes on average only 20 litres (Niemann and Graefe 2006: 32), knowing that every additional litre consumed must be compensated by reduced consumptions of other goods.

Connecting the poor to the formal networks is therefore seen as a contribution to poverty reduction and to public health, not only because of the assumption that tap water is healthier, but also due to increased consumption. The informal water supply systems on the contrary are seen as an unwanted obstacle in the development process, delivering expensive water with low standards.

The strongly growing market of bottled water or purified water in containers in cities in the South further enforces inequality. Unlike water in most European countries, where the success of bottled water is strongly attached to lifestyle and marketing (e.g. Gleick 2010; Wilk 2006), bottled water in developing countries is also related to more serious health considerations. Not only 'unimproved' water sources but also tap water does not necessarily fulfil national, international, or the consumer's quality standards. Purchasing water from bottles becomes an option, at least to replace the water consumed by the human body. Since unit prices are much higher than for any other water source, bottled water is only accessible for those who can afford it. Access to water by standards proclaimed in the bacteriological city is not only denied to those who are not connected to the network, but also to those who receive water of inferior qualities from their taps and cannot afford to supplement with bottled water.

My objective is not to question the normativity of the water pipe paradigm. In the case of Greater Khartoum, people want to have piped water in their house, and their aspirations are in line with those of the policy makers and political ecologists. However, as long as this paradigm is not put into practice and households remain disconnected or poorly served, the paradigm itself distracts the researchers' perspectives from other modes of water provision, and thus the understanding of water in a particular place.

2.2.2. The Neoliberalization of Water Pipes

The piped water paradigm in discourses from the local to the global is also very prevalent in the political ecology of water. An empirical justification based on health analyses and even the adverse economics of the so-called informal providers is not necessarily required in empirical research, and the justification of the normative claims of political ecologists are mostly taken for granted. This was especially true up until the early 2000s and the narratives therefore hardly asked if the pipe water infrastructure was the only possible solution. Rather, research was restricted to analysing why people do not have access to the 'networks'. Accordingly, the most prominent field of analysis was centred on the analysis of different institutional arrangements in water supply.

Objects and Subjects of Water Narratives Until 2000

Within political ecology of water, the best policy to manage water is extensively debated. In this debate past, present, and probable future policies and their implementation are analysed. From the 1980s to the early 2000s, water research concentrated on three types of actors and two 'spheres of impacts'. A first category of actors are the 'policy makers'. This group does not only include the immediate political actors within countries that determine a water framework of a country or a city, but also those who try to influence these policies in different ways. The international monetary institutions, namely IMF and the World Bank, pushed significantly for the reform of the water sector in many countries. The second group are national or international, social, environmental, or profit motivated lobbyists (e.g. World Water Council with the World Water Forum, United Nations with their Millennium Development Goals, scientific discourse, and international non-governmental organizations) who frame the international opinion on water and influence the decisions of policy makers. Sudan for example implemented neoliberal reforms in the water sector without the monetary institutions imposing any structural adjustments. Instead, it followed general international trends (Beckedorf 2011: 19). The third group of actors are the 'implementers', who construct and maintain infrastructure as well as manage and bill water flows. The group is comprised of a very heterogeneous group of public and private actors, who implement the water policy of a certain country or city, more or less in line with policy framework.

The political ecology debate analyses two spheres influenced by water policy: the social and the natural. The interrelation with nature is one of the key elements of political ecology's core definition. It also determines political ecology's fields of application as those in which a social relation exists with nature. As a natural element, water is a prime example of such a relation. Water needs to be obtained from a source that can be a river, the sea, a lake or an aquifer and after human consumption, it returns to nature. Through human water consumption and other activities, these water sources and the related ecosystems always experience more or less significant transformations.

Political ecology's water narratives focus very much on governing water at the policy level. Potential consumers were generally not considered as actors directly shaping water networks but as voiceless beneficiaries or as those deprived of water supply policy and its implementation. Physical access, the price paid, and the quality of water received allow comparing water indicators with other social indicators and determining water inequality, the main social benchmark for judging water supply systems from the perspective of a critical political ecology. To understand water from this perspective, the only requirements were an analysis of the political economy of water management on the scale of the water network and a description of consumer impact; rather than understanding water related processes on the scale of the consumers or those processes launched by the consumers as actors on other scales.

The Dominant Debate. Public versus Private

The conceptualization of consumers as passive beneficiaries in these narratives is strongly related to the dominance of policy dialogues. By affirming that "Water has an economic value in all its competing uses and should be recognized as an economic good" (UN International Conference on Water and the Environment 1992), the UN's Dublin Statement on Water and Sustainable Development in 1992 underlined a policy shift in water management from the "municipal hydraulic paradigm" to "market environmentalism" (Bakker 2010b: 35)[7]. This shift is strongly reflected in the dominant discussion in the literature on water provision since the 1980s: the correct role of the private sector (Loftus 2009: 955).

For most of the 20th century the municipal hydraulic paradigm has remained relatively uncontested[8].

> Strong normative claims were [...] made in favour of government involvement. Justifications [...] included the symbolic and cultural importance of water as a (partially) nonsubstitutable resource essential for life; its strategic political and territorial importance; the intense conflicts that arise over the use of a flow resource required to fulfil multiple functions (agricultural, industrial, drinking-water, ecosystem health); and the need in industrialized, urbanized societies to mobilize large volumes – invariably at a high cost relative to the economic value generated (Bakker 2010b: 34).

Despite these ambitious objectives, the UN determined the state of water provision for consumers to be one of the major obstacles to development. The 1980s were thus declared the 'international drinking water supply and sanitation decade', with a focus on providing "safe water and sanitation for all by 1990" (Hemson 2008: 17).

Although unprecedented amounts of bilateral aid and multilateral finance were directed towards water supply projects (Bakker et al. 2008: 1892), this funding "was biased towards ambitiously large-scale, capital-intensive, centralized hydraulic projects" (Bakker 2010b: 76), with disappointing results (e.g. Budds and McGranahan 2003; Schwartz 2008: 49). The public sector failure was no longer solely attributed to a lack of investments. Rather, "the main

---

[7] The term market environmentalism refers to a paradigm in water governance, which is implemented by a set of different reforms that include privatization, private sector participation, commercialization, deregulation and decentralization (for an overview, see Bakker 2010b: 37). In the practitioners' debate on water policy, but also partially in the scientific one, the term privatization – which is only one reform among others – is often used to describe any set of reforms under market environmentalism, even if it does not contain privatization (in its narrow sense of ownership of infrastructure from public to private sector actors) in a particular location (e.g. Castro 2008: 65). Instead of privatization, I will use the term private sector participation, which includes not only the transfer of infrastructure to private companies, but also simply the participation in management of water infrastructure. To describe all reforms under market environmentalism (including reforms inside a public body like commercialization, which are related to management practices rather than to actors), I will use the term neoliberalization of water.

[8] France is an exception. Private sector participation was relevant through the 20th century (e.g. Pezon 2011)

lesson learnt was that concentrating on the technical aspects of service provision is, in itself, unlikely to improve the provision of water services" (Schwartz 2008: 50). The municipal hydraulic paradigm had not fulfilled its normative expectations. International policy discourse, which strongly incorporated the neoliberal agenda, assumed public water corporations did not perform in an economically sustainable manner. Consequently, the water sector was opened up more and more for private investments. Through structural adjustment programmes, the World Bank and the International Monetary Fund have put strong pressure on governments of low and middle-income countries to implement neoliberal reforms in the water sector (Budds and McGranahan 2003: 91), thus transforming citizens into customers (Bakker 2003b: 42).

It was the high contestation of the role of multinational corporations in water management that made it such a dominating topic in political ecology as well. Towards the end of the 1980s, multinational corporations started to enter water markets in the global South, which comprised of a handful of global players[9], only. The proponents of neoliberal reforms[10] assumed that private sector participation would solve the problem of urban water supply for several reasons. The multinationals would relieve the governments from the burden of investments, and driven by profit expectations, they would extend the networks to the edges of the cities. Based on the experiences of the preceding decades of government stewardship over the water sector, the private sector was promoted as more efficient and less corrupted. The environment became another central topic in the argument, mainly based on the assumption that full paying consumers would be economically motivated to reduce the consumption of 'scarce' water.

Under neoliberalism, water ethics are significantly altered: "Economic equity (the 'benefit' or 'willingness-to-pay' principle) displaces social equity (the 'ability-to-pay' principle) in water pricing" (Bakker 2010b: 37). However, since the networks were expected to deliver much cheaper water per unit than the

---

9 The water sector is divided between a hand full of European companies with the two French companies, Suez and Veolia, holding over two-thirds of all private water operations in the world (Hall 2006: 179). In 2006, private companies operated water services in only 9.5% of Middle Eastern/North African cities and in 19.4% of Sub-Saharan cities with over 1 M inhabitants. The estimations for smaller cities are much lower (Lobina and Hall 2008: 90).

10 The arguments of proponents of water provision have been analysed in several papers: Araral (2009); Bakker (2007); Budds and McGranahan (2003); Castro (2008); Hall and Lobina (2007); and McGranahan, Mitlin, and Satterthwaite (2008).

wide-spread water vendors already present, private sector participation was expected to be a win-win situation. It was anticipated that it would be profitable for companies and reduce the burden of water costs for the poor consumers while increasing water quality and comfort due to the extension of networks. Proponents of neoliberal reforms increasingly argued that neoliberalism would insure the human right to water, shifting from neoliberal economic rhetoric to an ethical egalitarian one (e.g. Bakker 2010b: 150).

In the 1990s and early 2000s, the advantages and disadvantages of private over public sector water management were intensely discussed. This debate, especially in human geography, later concluded that the participation of multinational corporations in the management of water supply in most cities of the global South had failed (e.g. Budds and McGranahan 2003; Castro 2007, 2008; Hall and Lobina 2006, 2007; Prasad 2006; Swyngedouw 2009). Hall and Lobina (2006) argue that the new connections achieved by the multinational corporations are insignificant and even fell behind the progress made in the preceding decade, in which performance was paradoxically used as a justification for the private sector.[11]

Arguments, that were previously raised against private sector participation, are now supported by empirical findings and certain financial institutions have even started officially acknowledging the limitations of the private sector (Bakker 2007: 440). The multinational corporations have failed, both, in economic and in social terms. Beyond a general critique of neoliberalization, water has two features that make it even more difficult to fully privatize. Its bulkiness, which leads to high transportation costs, does not allow for direct competition with the construction of multiple pipes to each house. Rather, competition is restricted to obtaining concessions. Secondly, water is a basic need, which puts a high moral pressure on the water provider. Accordingly, water was rarely fully privatized, instead public-private partnerships were established, which gave the governments the leeway to regulate private companies and impose conditionalities on their business. This however, allowed or

---

11 In the latest progress report for the Millennium Development Goals, the UN announced the target of "reducing by half the proportion of people without sustainable access to safe drinking water and basic sanitation" was reached 5 years ahead of schedule, despite the fact that improved sources in urban Sub-Saharan Africa stagnated at 83% between 1990 and 2010 and the relative number of households with on-site pipes even declined from 43% to 34% (UNICEF and WHO 2012: 55). Consequently, worldwide achievements in general and in Sub-Saharan Africa in particular, are due to improvements in rural not urban areas, where private sector participation was concentrated. The UN figures should not be interpreted as a sign of the success of water privatization.

required governments to subsidize companies to provide water to the urban poor (Bakker 2003b: 38). This unclear, permeable border between private and public also allowed the companies to renegotiate contracts and claim subsidies. "Almost half of the projects have seen contracts renegotiated, generally on terms more favourable to multinational companies to secure their continued interest" (Hemson 2008: 38). This along with support from multilateral financial donors (Bakker 2008: 237), strengthened the economic profitability of the company; but these aspects stand in opposition to the expectation of the private sector's economic interdependence. Despite it all, profits were insufficient to satisfy the multinationals, who consequently, lost interest in engaging in water concessions (e.g. Bakker 2010b: 97; Swyngedouw 2009: 38). Resignation led to confessions, such as the following from one of SAURs chief executives: "[The false] belief that any business must be good business and that the private sector has unlimited funds [...] The scale of the need far outreaches the financial and risk taking capacities of the private sector" (cf. Budds and McGranahan 2003: 1007). Investments have declined since the early 2000s and many companies have even pulled out of existing contracts (e.g. Hall and Lobina 2004: 271; Page 2005: 302). The policy makers' pro-poor expectations did not materialize either. Instead, on the basis of the evaluation of several empirical cases, Castro (2007: 765) suggests that "these policies have actually reinforced existing inequalities".

2.2.3. The Revival of the Local and the Community

Water policy in the 1980s and 1990s was mostly synonymous with the establishment of piped water infrastructure. This was also due to the fact that "the uneven levels of connectivity in developing countries had been widely perceived as a temporary phenomenon to be overcome through ambitious efforts at urban planning and reconstruction" (Gandy 2004: 368). In such a situation, policy making was restricted to negotiations at the scale of the city, hence, between politicians, private companies, funding institutions, and engineers; a sphere where water consumers were considered as beneficiaries in a top down approach.

There are basically two alternative types of water supply in which actors on a local scale take charge: local private and community-based solutions, which can also sometimes operate in cooperation. Community water management is understood as water management by local actors, which is not based on business objectives, but on the collective action of water consumers organizing their own water supply. Consequently, management options on the local scale can be roughly differentiated by their motivation to provide water. Although local water supply solutions were always – and in absence of water delivery from public and private water corporations, had to be – widespread, they were long overlooked as an alternative in the policy dialogue. In this section, the for-profit water supply will be outlined briefly as a central mode of water supply in the global South. Thereafter, the emergence of the commodity perspective in water management will be presented.

Local Water Supply by Private Actors

Local, for-profit water supply is most commonly labelled an 'informal' water supply. The term 'informal' must be viewed critically here, as it is as imprecise as 'community water supply'. First, 'informal' is only defined in opposition to 'formal'. However, it is used in narratives mainly to describe for-profit actors rather than consumer-established systems, which can be simultaneously non-profit and informal.

In urban practices, these 'informal' water entrepreneurs sometimes produce water themselves, for example by operating tube wells; they resell water obtained from the formal network (water kiosks); or they transport water from formal or informal sources to consumers. Water vendors, who use bicycles, tricycles, and carts (hand-pushed, animal drawn, or motorized) to transport water (e.g. Kjellén and McGranahan 2006: 11), are very common in most African cities and are a highly visible element in urban waterscapes. In some places, small-scale independent providers install their own networks to supply those who are not connected to the main network (Trémolet and Binder 2010: 7). Access to water from all these systems tends to be more expensive than through centralized networks.

Local for-profit water supply has a long tradition in developing countries. It has also been partially discussed in scientific literature, even though much less so than formal water management (e.g. Cairncross 1990; Kjellén and McGranahan 2006; McGranahan et al. 2006; Solo 1999; Verdeil 2003; Whittington et al. 1989). The sector is to a certain degree the local equivalent of multinational corporations in that it is a local capitalist response to water scarcity. Similar to water companies cutting connections, water vendors can also stop supplying people who do not pay or who exceed credit limits that have been granted to them. Both are motivated to invest money and/or labour in water supply, predominantly due to their income/profit expectations. Like multinational corporations, for-profit 'informal' water suppliers can also become regulated since they operate in a social sphere rather than under perfect market conditions. Prices can be kept low through social sanctions by community members, which can be external to the economic transaction. The vendors are also members of the community and must therefore defend their social reputation. These types of water entrepreneurs emerge from within the community, mainly as a reaction to local water scarcity because of an insufficiently developed 'formal' water supply. Like private water network companies, vendors can justify their business with consumers' need for their services and not merely with their egotistical interests. There are, however, significant differences between the two types of water supply, which are not restricted only to the different scales and the social embeddedness of actors. Water distributed by water vendors is much more easily controlled by the market than network water, since customers can choose their water vendor, while they can never choose their particular network provider.

Non-network water supply is a prerequisite for urban growth in many African cities, considering that people extend urban residential zones in locations where the basic need for water can be satisfied. The 'informal' systems emerge where potential markets exist. Inversely formulated, urban extensions can emerge only where water can be made accessible. By delivering water to areas that planners had not designated as residential, water vendors contribute to a 'people driven land management' and interfere in strategies of planned urban development. In absence of alternatives, consumers are even willing to accept these systems' comparatively high water costs and certain quality restrictions.

The high tolerance for low technology supply systems in many cities in Africa is a necessary acknowledgement that these systems are highly required, despite the disadvantages – notably the costs for consumers. These systems do not fulfil the piped water paradigm, but policy makers tend to assume they are temporary solutions, which allow them to maintain the paradigm. There is nothing "particularly contradictory about a water strategy that aims to get vendors to provide improved water (and sanitation) services to the urban poor in the short run, and to drive vendors out of business by way of providing better utility services in the long run" (Kjellén and McGranahan 2006: 22). Formalization is a strategy to better control these providers in order to improve the quality of the delivered water and to influence price regimes. In

Greater Khartoum, water vendors are to a certain degree under the control of government institutions that license carts and barrels used for water transport. They require vendors varnish the interior of the barrels formerly used to carry oil. The different degrees of 'formality' in these systems calls even further into question the term 'informal' when describing water vendors.

The Revalorization of the Community in Practice and Policy

Just like local, for-profit water supply, community managed water supply was not invented by policy makers; rather, it is a reconceptualization. For a long time, communities cooperated in achieving joint water access, which could be rather complex in technical, social, and managerial terms, as for example in detail elaborated for irrigation systems (e.g. Geertz 1972; Lansing 1987; Wittfogel 1957). Thus, community management existed long before development agencies started promoting communities as central elements of successful development.

The community perspective in development studies was strongly encouraged by the participatory models of the 1970s and 1980s, including Robert Chambers' (1986) 'Participatory Rural Appraisal', which made civic participation and ownership a criteria for successful development (Sultana 2009: 347). Focus was, however, mainly placed on rural areas (e.g. Page 2003: 485) whereas community management of water in urban areas was much less discussed and propagated. Proponents of the public and the private paradigm of urban water management aimed at achieving universal coverage of urban dwellers through centralized network infrastructure, which did not require taking into consideration the community as an actor.

Around the turn of the century, when both the municipal hydrological paradigm and market environmentalism had failed, the potential function of the community in urban water supply was reconsidered. Throughout the entire process of questioning the previous two paradigms, the communities themselves played an important role.

By political activism, consumers entered the policy debate. The most prominent case was the Bolivian city Cochabamba (e.g. Hoffmann 2010; Lobina 2000), where people heavily protested against price hikes in early 2000 after the government gave a multinational corporation a 40-year-concession for operating the city's water supply system. The protests were successful and the government ceased the contract and once again placed water under municipal control. Referring to the case of Cochabamba has become 'state of the art' in literature about the failure of the neoliberalization of water supply and especially for the relevance of public resistance to water privatization. In activist movements, it became a heroised symbol for successfully fighting the influence of private companies in the water sector. As such, public protest in Cochabamba and elsewhere[12] did not only affect the management of local water distribution systems, but also the international debate on water management in general. It became an argument, promoted in activist literature (e.g. Olivera and Lewis 2004; Shiva 2002) and documentaries and it became accessible to a global public interested in politics.

Public protesters, hence, earned a voice in the water management debate. While protests only rarely led to contract cancellations or expropriations of the multinationals, they still "posed serious challenges to the public legitimacy of private companies" (Bakker 2010b: 97). The objectives of activists were not only directed against neoliberalism, but

> At the core of their vision of 'alternative' water supply management is the notion of 'community'. Appeals to the 'water commons', calls for 'water democracy', and campaigns for the 'remunicipalisation' of water supply are examples of the central role which community plays in the vision of anti-privatisation activists (Bakker 2008: 236).

Local Actors in the New Local Water Paradigm

In contemporary policy dialogues, strong emphasis is put on the role of local, for-profit actors in water supply. In the past several years, community concepts involving private sector participation, also labelled 'public-private-community partnerships', have argued for cooperation with local private actors rather than with multinational water corporations. These concepts foresee the private sector participation of small scale providers in the construction or management of physical infrastructures. They have become a widely discussed development alternative (e.g. Allen, Dávila, and Hofmann 2006b; Franceys and Weitz 2003; Jaglin and Bousquet 2011; Kjellén and McGranahan 2006; Sansom and Bos 2008; Schwartz and Sanga 2010).

Public water towers in Greater Khartoum have come under private management in the past years, where small companies lease a water tower and sell the water to water vendors. Furthermore, within the pipe water paradigm, private

---

12 For an overview, see Lobina and Hall (2007) and Swyngedouw (2005)

ownership of water does exist. In certain African cities, physical assets including small networks like in Cotonou are privately owned or management contracts for piped water are established (Collignon and Vézina 2000: 33, 62). Schwartz and Sanga (2010) present an example of a delegated management model in the Kenyan city Kisumu. Ten metered water connections are contracted out by the public water corporation to one member of the community, who is charged by a 'master-meter' and resells water to water kiosks, who then sell it to the households around their house.

Community participation in these partially NGO promoted and subsidised systems, differs in various conceptions, and can, as in the Kenyan case, include the choice of community members as contractors or the constitution of water committees that contribute to the selection and regulation of entrepreneurs (Schwartz and Sanga 2010). Jaglin's and Bousquet's notion of 'community-based privatization' illustrates that assumed benefits of private involvement are at the centre of the concept. These systems "are a vehicle for the introduction of market principles (purchase of water on volume consumed, constitution of renewal provisions, keeping of operating accounts, subcontracting and purchase of services from the competing private sector, etc.)" (Jaglin and Bousquet 2011: 171). In these community-based systems, water prices tend to be higher than those charged for water from the formal network, since mini-networks cannot achieve economies of scale (Jaglin and Bousquet 2011: 183) and intermediary actors, like in the Kenyan contract system, need to be paid by the consumers for their services (Schwartz and Sanga 2010). Coupled with the risk of "cherry-picking of profitable or otherwise attractive cities, neighbourhoods, and regions" (Bakker 2008: 245) and the practical absence of cross-subsidizing at the scale of the city (Jaglin and Bousquet 2011: 183), the impact on water justice is highly questionable.

In these management forms, community can play a role but the concept is mostly based on entrepreneurs, hence located in a capitalist setup. This is far from the visions of the anti-privatization activists, who called for "communal or collective water ownership" that would turn water into a "commons" (Bakker et al. 2008). Cooperatives are the prime governing entities that allow management of water infrastructure from within the community, partially with NGO support. However, management and ownership of infrastructure is in the hand of "a community water committee – a representative body, often elected, which makes both the everyday and long-term plans for the water supply in a particular community, often through discussion with an external adviser" (Page 2003: 485). Cooperatives operate thanks to the social coherence of its members and mutual social control as well as on the feeling of ownership, which is based on the actors' dual identity as both consumer and supplier in the same system. Bakker (2008: 246) questions whether cooperatives really are a sustainable solution for urban water supply, claiming instead that

> much of the literature on collective, community-based forms of water supply management tends to romanticise communities as coherent, relatively equitably social structures, despite the fact that inequitable power relations and resource allocation exist within communities.

Basing herself on the example of 'post-privatization Cochabamba', she draws the conclusion that cooperatives can even lead to the "fragmentation of the water supply system, creating two tiers of services [the cooperatives and the public network] with vastly unequal levels of state support" (Bakker 2008: 239).

2.3. From Analysing Policy to Analysing Consumers Choices: Locating the Gift

Regardless of whether or not community conceptions are a solution for water supply in developing countries, the discussion about these systems has enriched the debate on water management in general, because it questions the focus of analysis on water policy along the private/public divide. Instead, these discussions reinforce research on water management on the community level, with the justification, that understanding processes on the community level and promoting them can be a path to achieve the humanistic goals of political ecologists. Taking the 'community scale' into consideration is not this scale's 'new invention'; but a shift in the perspective of researchers and policy makers. The fundamental contribution of the debate to the discourse is that consumers are transformed from objects (who are negatively affected by absent or malfunctioning water supply) into subjects (who actively interfere in the flow and politics of water beyond consumption).

This research benefits from the opening up of the debate for community action. However, it is not primarily interested in analysing which responsibilities can be attributed to the community to improve the water supply situation.

Instead, it focuses on the role it already plays today, and how people's everyday water practices contribute to the production of waterscapes from the house to the city. These practices are not merely restricted to people's predictable reaction to given water supply scenarios. Their supply strategy choices are also informed by the specific social contexts in which these practices are embedded. Up-scaling processes do not necessarily need to take a publicly visible form, such as protests, but can be hidden within the people's appropriation of water infrastructures, by which water becomes channelled in ways which were not defined by the policy. People do not only technically interfere in water infrastructure, but they also develop their own supply concepts.

I am suggesting in this book that we should temporarily shift the perspective on water supply in cities in the South from a top-down to a bottom-up approach. This does not aim to promote a participatory development paradigm, but rather, to take people's practices with presently existing water supply strategies as a starting point to holistically construct water supply beyond policy. This shift of perspective requires stepping back – at least temporarily – from political ecology's normative objective of capitalist critique. However, three justifications can still be given for doing so in a political ecological framework.

(1) An analysis of water from a consumer perspective allows a more holistic description of water access strategies. By introducing 'water gifts' between different local actors, a dual consumer identity can be highlighted. From the perspective of the public water provider they remain ordinary consumers, whereas from the perspective of the 'water-poor', they become alternative suppliers. In the 'waterscape of the city', gifts contribute to the redistribution of water. They directly interfere in the manifestation of urban water inequality, hence in the normative benchmark of political ecology of water.

(2) Taking into consideration all possible supply options in a neighbourhood goes beyond a mere description of these options; it allows developing a 'political ecology of the neighbourhood'. Here, access to different supply options is closely related to the distribution of economic wealth, but also to the political and social relationships of individual households, which affect their individual choice of water supply strategies and the outcome of such choices. Water gifts can change local power structures and stabilize social hierarchies inherent in a 'neighbourly social field'. As such water gifts are highly political.

(3) This approach supplements the policy perspective rather than replacing it. The relevance of local processes can finally be determined in terms of the

functionality of water supply policies, which are not restricted to the active interaction of local actors with the system, through protest, refusal of payment, or illegal connections but also indirectly for example through the satisfaction of water supply through alternative means. Turning the perspective towards 'ordinary people' is a contribution to the political ecology of water and its normative goal of understanding and questioning water inequality.

The proposed approach has strong conceptual roots in political ecology, which already demands a holistic analysis of the multi-scalar field of water supply (e.g. Norman, Bakker, and Cook 2012; Swyngedouw and Heynen 2003). My approach is nothing more than the translation of this claim into research practice.

A bottom-up approach in analysing water supply examines the multiple options people have to satisfy their water need rather than focusing on how one particular form of water supply provides water to a specific location. In section 2.2.1, I will review the multiplicity of water supply options from literature, and will then conceptualize the set of neighbourly water transfers (2.2.2), that comprise the gift of water. After reviewing the literature on water gift transfers (2.2.3), I will develop a framework under which water gifts can be analysed.

2.3.1. Multiplicity. The Constrained Choice of Water Strategies

Bakker (2010b: 123) asks the question: "Are the poor really thirsty?" In her research in Jakarta, she wonders why "members of poor households (when asked) rarely mention lack of water as their primary concern [although] they are depicted as desperately needy of water in policy documents". Certain households with the possibility to connect to the network even choose not to do so. Those who are not yet connected or cannot legally have a connection, because they have no permanent tenure rights, do not form popular political movements to campaign for basic services. They prefer consuming expensive water from water vendors, and the richer neighbours' privately operated deep tube wells. Bakker's (2010b: 124) primary explanation for consumers' satisfaction with expensive water is "that the idea of cleanliness among [local] communities is 'based on culture and tradition,' rather than bacteriological criteria". Like dirty water from shallow hand-dug tube wells, the network water is perceived as unhealthy because of the odour of residual chlorine.

The first important result from Bakker's example is that people have a choice of different water sources. This choice, however, is constrained but not restricted to several aspects such as water availability. The perspective must therefore differ from perspectives of international institutions such as the UN, under which households are classified according to the 'best' water supply they have access to, rather than their real water supply (e.g. UNICEF and WHO 2012). The choice of water is not an absolute one, in which households select that type of locally available water that best fits their needs. Their choices are much more complex, leading in many urban settings to single households consuming water from multiple sources. In Bakker's example of Jakarta, 61% of the sample households used more than two sources (Bakker et al. 2008: 1903). In African cities the use of multiple sources is also very common, like in three Ugandan towns (49% - 74%; Howard et al. 2002: 68) and in Egbeda, Nigeria (89%; Oyedotun 2012: 5). Multiple water sources are on the one hand a result of insufficient stability of the primary source. Networks in many African cities are characterized by frequent cuts and low pressure. On the other hand, people purchase different 'waters' for different purposes. While more expensive water might be used for human consumption, cheaper water is used for construction or cleaning (e.g. Verdeil 2003: 444).

The second important insight gained from Bakker's example in Jakarta is that we have to look from the consumer perspective at water sources to understand the consumer's choice of water rather than deducing their preferences using policy makers' expectations including the superiority of the network. Collignon and Vézina (2000: 17) criticise water experts for analysing the choice of water mainly by cost, distance, availability, and ease of access and forgetting subjective factors such as the water's taste and clarity and maintaining good relations with neighbours. This list of subjective factors will need to be substantially extended by analysing the preferences in the empirical reality of specific places, where potential water sources are not merely a material economic construction, but also a social one. One of the most obvious examples of such a social construction is bottled water in the countries of the North. People have access to cheap, highly convenient network water in their homes that is always available right where it is needed and which overall, conforms to high quality standards. In comparison, bottled water is much more expensive, costing time and energy because it must be purchased in a shop and carried home. Furthermore, it is not necessarily of any better quality, or even taste. Despite these factors bottled water is a big business. The demand for this water has been inscribed in the consumer's habitus and drinking bottled water for many goes without saying. For Wilk this demand for bottled water is an "exceptionally clear example of the power of branding to make commodities a meaningful part of daily life. […] Today marketers recognize that goods have magical powers that have nothing to do with 'needs', and they have become magicians who transform mundane and abundant things into exotic valuables" (Wilk 2006: 305).

A household's water strategy, which can consist of one or several supply options, is framed by availability, subjective preference, and constraints. Availability is not only physical availability, but also socially produced physical limitations of individual households to access certain types of water. Household members can choose only those options that are available or which they can make available at a specific moment and within a certain distance around their home. These options include water taps, stand pipes, public wells, water vendors, openly accessible sources like lakes, rivers, and irrigation canals, as well as possible individual investments such as illegal connections to the network to steal water, gutters to collect rainwater from the roof, and private installations to access groundwater like hand pumps. The options at a household's disposition are therefore very different from the debated potential options of various forms of infrastructure under different management at the policy level. Households evaluate available options based on their preferences, which include aspects like taste, colour, quality, comfort; but also in reference to their cultural and religious concepts. Whether they can really access their preferred options depends on individual constraints, which include economic abilities, but also their relationship to those who provide water.

The empirical case of Greater Khartoum – as we will see in the empirical chapters – revealed that many water-poor households consume water that other, water-rich households had purchased, from a pipe network, but also occasionally from water vendors. Neighbourly redistribution of water, is taken into consideration in water policies and partially also by scholarly literature. However there are serious gaps in the literature, at least if we consider Greater Khartoum to be a typical rather than a particular case.

2.3.2. A Typology of Water Transfers between Neighbours

Water transfers between neighbours are not restricted to gift transfers. Three principle types can be differentiated: for-profit, associative, and free transfers. The work of Verdeil (2003) can be used to illustrate the tree types, since they are – unlike in Greater Khartoum – all prevalent in one single city, Metropolitan Cebu in the Philippines.[13]

In Metropolitan Cebu, water is metered. Giving water to neighbours therefore leads to direct costs for the household. In the for-profit model not only the costs of water from the network are claimed from the neighbour, but it is brought under an accumulation of capital, which increases the price of water on average by nearly 700% (Verdeil 2003: 347). Water transfers to neighbours become a business just as home delivery of water by mobile vendors. These for-profit transfers are common and they are reported for other urban contexts (e.g. Sri Lanka: Nauges and Berg 2008: 545; Uganda: Tumusiime and Njiru 2004: 227; Mozambique: Zuin et al. 2011). Keener, Lunego, and Banerjee (2010: 9) deduce from a survey with government officials that re-selling of water by household is common practice in more than 70% of the largest cities of 24 African countries. These transfers are sometimes prohibited, mostly tolerated, or even legalized (Collignon and Vézina 2000: 31). The policy-promoted counterparts to these water supply options, developed completely by the community, are labelled in scientific literature as 'water kiosks'. They exist in public-private-(community) arrangements like in South Africa (Loftus 2006b: 1032) and Kenya (Whittington, Mu, and Roche 1990).

In addition to reselling water, Verdeil describes – but in much less detail – two other neighbourly water transfers. In the second type of transfer, several neighbours cooperate to jointly access one tap. While one person makes the contract with the water corporation, the costs are shared among all households (Verdeil 2003: 338). The logic underlying this arrangement is that of a little 'association' from the perspective of the users, because the members jointly organize and manage their water access, at least from the tap onward, while the water in the tap turns into a club good, to which all actors have access, and which is protected against overuse by the social relations among the actors. The very small number of actors can strongly contribute to the successful management of this 'commons', as developed by Elinor Ostrom (1990). Müller and Mitlin (2007: 432) give an example of such a system in Windhoek, where sharing a tap is part of a wider arrangement of several households sharing a plot, which is a plot that is designed for one household, only.

---

[13] Other supply options in her case are the network, hand pumps, services of water vendors with tricycles or standpipes.

While the association model is still very much connected to the economic value of water, because efforts are made to share costs fairly – even if this does not necessarily mean that everybody pays exactly what he or she consumes – the third type consists of free transfers that seem to be distinct from economics. In Verdeil's (2003: 337, 346) example, free transfers are only accessible to households with family ties. They make up only slightly more than 10% of total water flows between neighbours. The negation of the economic in the transfer leads to a gift relationship, which Verdeil mentions in passing when she refers to a "broader 'agreement' regarding life in a group" (Verdeil 2003: 337; own translation). It is these arrangements that must be analysed in more depth, especially to allow an understanding of water transfers in Greater Khartoum, where transfers without financial compensation or contribution are the only empirically observed transfers among neighbours.

2.3.3. Water Gifts. A Review of Scientific Literature

The term 'free water' is itself a metaphor for different conceptualizations of transfers, which are strongly elaborated under the notion of the gift. Water gift analysis is more complex than the mere description of a flow of water between a donor and a recipient, without financial compensation as in a market transaction, or material compensation as in barter. A 'gift of water' is not restricted to a uni-directional flow of water but it is a complex process embedded both in the relation between the two transaction partners and in the context in which the transfer takes place.

Marcel Mauss's essay on the gift (1966 [1923]) is the central reference point of the debate.

> Much of our everyday morality is concerned with the question of obligation and spontaneity in the gift. It is our good fortune that all is not yet couched in terms of purchase and sale. Things have values which are emotional as well as material; indeed in some cases the values are entirely emotional. Our morality is not solely commercial (Mauss 1966 [1923]: 63).

This citation presents in a nutshell the tension inherent in gift transactions. Is the gift nothing more than an interested transaction just like a market exchange guided by reciprocity, which merely hides the interestedness of the gift? Or can a gift transfer be entirely based on non-interested motivation, allowing altruism or the pure gift? While some authors acknowledge that pure gifts are possible without reciprocity (e.g. Singer 1993), others tend towards an economistic reading of the gift as we will later see in detail with the work of Pierre Bourdieu. Understanding the logic of the gift, requires reconstructing if and how interests are involved as a motivation for gifting.

Free water transfers are hardly developed in water literature. Most overview literature on the water sector ignores this category, with the exception of a DFID publication (Allen, Dávila, and Hofmann 2006a) on peri-urban water supply, which integrates "water gifts" as one supply option among the commonly known ones. Also in case studies, even the mere description of these transfers – as with Verdeil – is very rare and authors hardly explain the function and the genesis of these transfers but rather limit themselves to mentioning their existence: they state that people "beg for water" (Loftus 2005: 196), "borrow water" (Bond and Dugard 2010: 10) or "collect water from neighbours with private connections for which they may [or may not] pay a fee" (Whittington et al. 2002: 3). The quotes indicate that water transfers that are not paid for take place, but they are not made a topic. The reader interested in these relations is left with simple questions. Is borrowed water paid back by equivalent water or money or is compensation indirect or even inexistent? What are the criteria that make people pay a fee or not? And how does gifting change the social relations between the donor and the recipient and between both of them and society?

The conceptualisation of a gift under the notion of reciprocity reveals the gift as only appearing to be free; because in reality, they are produced or not according to economic logic. In a case study of Cape Town's township Khayelitsha, where non-paying households were cut off from the network, Xali (2002) discovered that 89% of those cut off 'requested' and received water from their neighbours for free. The solidarity cannot be taken for granted and some neighbours even locked their taps, because of the "fear that they will end up paying more money for water and may themselves end up as victims of water cutoffs" (Xali 2002: 114). Many of the 'water-poor' in that situation were reluctant to take water and they preferred to try to clear their debts or to install illegal connections as soon as possible. "Water cutoffs diminished their dignity by making them request water from neighbours" (Xali 2002: 107). Xali portrays the 'requested' gift of water as a material benefit – since cut-off households receive water – but contrasts these benefits with negative impacts for the recipient. "The gift narrows the distance between the giver and receiver because it is a form of sharing, yet it widens the social distance between them because the receiver is now indebted to the giver. The gift can, simultaneously or sequentially, be an expression of generosity and/or an act of violence" (Verhezen 2009: 32). In order to maximize the satisfaction of personal interests, a successful strategy for potential recipients can be to avoid requesting gifts and instead, buying water. Equally, for potential donors, not giving water, which might reduce social reputation, can be economically rational if the gift transfer involves high financial and/or social costs. Motivation to give, can – but does not necessarily need to be – explained by such a balancing of interest.

The costs involved in water gifts do not necessarily make water gifts a temporal solution in times of crises, which people need to prevent. Rather, water gifts can have a positive and desirable function within a social system. Amiraly (2009: 255; own translation) analyses water gifts between neighbours in Chennai, where water flows take the form of a reciprocal gift:

> In an Indian society, where relationships to others are highly valued, giving and receiving follows precise codes. What is received from the donor – in this case, the water – will be returned by the recipient at another moment, in a different way, to free himself from the debt and allow the reproduction of the gift relationship.

Amiraly highly values the social function of the water gift, as an integral part of neighbourly solidarity, which transcends even caste and family boundaries (Amiraly 2009: 252). Water gifts can become an element in the construction of social relationships between people, both as a means of breaking boundaries and consolidating ties.

Why are water transfers not strongly reflected in literature? Interestingly, while completely ignoring free neighbourly water flows, Keener, Lunego, and Banerjee (2010: 9) argue that 'for-profit' neighbourly transfers are ignored in the debate, since "households usually 'hide' in the surveys the fact that they buy water from their neighbours because household water resellers often are not listed in the established categories of household surveys". Their methodological critique can be directly turned against their own statistical survey with empirical evidence from Greater Khartoum. Collected data suggests that in Greater Khartoum, water taken from neighbours is never paid for, while Keener, Lunego, and Banerjee (2010: 7) classify Khartoum's water supply under the notion 'household reseller', which implies a financial transaction.

Shortcomings in quantitative surveys are not a sufficient argument to conclude that water gifts are ignored, since even qualitative field research does not intensively consider water gifts. More empirical evidence of free water transfers would be required to argue that these transfers have been overlooked or even ignored because of assumed policy irrelevance of said transfers.

2.3.4. A Framework to Analyse Water Gifts: Conditions for Water Solidarity between Neighbours

In order to understand water gifts they must be analysed within a particular empirical reality. In this book, I suggest a conceptual framework that distinguishes between the economic, spatial, and social factors that enable water gifts. This separation allows us to analyse the conditions that enable gifts from very different viewpoints.

The perspective on the 'cost of the gift' and on 'spatial heterogeneity' are closely related to the primary water supply options people have in a particular location like water taps, hand pumps, or water vendors. The incurred expenses due to the purchase of water by a potential donor from these primary sources strongly affect the overall cost of a gift, and consequently the burden created by the gift for the donor. Heterogeneity of water access refers to the access to the primary source of water. Only when 'water-poor' and 'water-rich' live in proximity do water gifts become reasonable.

The spatial and economic conditions provide the basis on which the gift can be analysed as a 'social transaction' between a donor and a recipient. Analysis needs to focus on the relationship between the donor and the recipient on the one hand, and the moral concepts to which actors relate these gifts on the nother hand. Only by combining all three elements – the spatial, the economic, and the social – can gifts truly be understood, beyond a mere description.

Fig. 1: *A Conceptual Framework to Analyse Water Gifts*

The Costs of the Gift

The costs involved in water gift transactions are produced by the donor's purchase of water from a water provider and the costs embedded in the transaction between the donor and the recipient. Transaction costs include the physical transportation of water from a donor to the recipients. Hoses, water pumps and other technical equipment for transporting water must be bought and maintained, or physical labour has to be invested to carry water in buckets or jerrycans. In some countries, water transfers between neighbours are illegal (Collignon and Vézina 2000: 31), which creates a cost based on the risk of punishment. Beyond transport related costs, gift transactions can negatively impact the donor's privacy and is time-consuming. Costs of water gift transactions are not restricted to the donor, but can be partially shouldered by the recipient through labour for transportation and social indebtedness to the donor in a gift economy. Consequently, even if a recipient takes water free of charge from a neighbour, this water is not free of cost and can even be more expensive than purchasing water from a different source.

While the recipient can bear costs in the gift transaction, the costs of water purchases are always the responsibility of the donor – otherwise the transaction would not be a gift but an economic transaction. The price of water in current water policies is often not guided by the market, but regulated mostly in order to subsidize water for the poor. Depending on the particular tariff arrangement and the accounting system of the water provider, different costs for water are incurred. The difference can be illustrated by Amiraly's (2009) Chennai case presented above, where the water company is considering replacing the present flat rate billing system by a metered system, which would turn water from a 'partial' commodity into a full one. While water beyond personal need is not charged in the present system, gifting water after the introduction of a meter would increase the water bill of the potential donor.[14] Consequently, the cost of solidarity involved in gifting increases. Amiraly fears that the introduction of water meters would lead to a decrease in water gifts and consequently weaken the positive social function he assumes these gifts to have. He turns this argument of social deterioration into a direct argument against the water corporation's plan to install water meters: "What seems disturbing in the case of Chennai is the willingness to introduce a tool that

---

14 A similar point is made by Trémolet and Hunt for neighbourly transfers unrelated to gifts. They argue that with the introduction of water meters, the profitability of the for-profit water vendors decreases (Trémolet and Hunt 2006: 17).

weakens the ties of solidarity between users, despite the fact that these ties constitute a response to deficiencies of supply services" (Amiraly 2009: 256; own translation).[15]

Even though flat rate tariffs are more likely to encourage water gifts, the gifts do not only take place under such favourable conditions. This is empirically highlighted in examples where free water flows between neighbours under a metered system, such as Xali's (2002) case of Cape Town. In this example, the reluctance of would-be water donors can be related to the economic conditions of the transfer in a metered system, but transfers still take place. The same holds true for Amman, where despite water metering 19% of households partially rely on their neighbours for their water consumption (Iskandarani 2002: 44). Even under an economic conceptualization of the gift, such transfers can still be more beneficial to both transaction partners than if the water-poor household purchased from water vendors. The savings realized by consuming the neighbour's cheap network water instead of expensive vendor water can be shared between the two transactions partners within the gift economy, financially benefitting both partners.

In Khartoum, water is supplied exclusively under a flat rate tariff, which provides favourable conditions for accessing water. Banerjee and Morella (2011: 132) provide an overview of 84 water utilities in Africa. In only 18% of these utilities, water is not at all metered. However, in 54% of cities that have introduced water metering, less than 70% of households are actually metered. If we assume that water corporations start installing water meters in areas of high volume consumers, a high proportion of those urban poor connected to the network are charged a flat rate tariff and experience similar economic conditions for water gift transfers than those households studied in Khartoum. The impact of the different tariff systems on the prevalence of water gifts would need to be evaluated with a comparative approach in countries where both systems are prevalent.

---

15 The particular type of tariff arrangement in metered systems can further affect water prices. With block tariffs, many water utilities introduced a billing system which is opposed to economic market logics, especially the idea of economics of scale (e.g. Boland and Whittington 2000). The more water people purchase, the higher the unit price. The system leads to a cross-subsidization from high to low-volume consumers. Sometimes the first block is free of charge (basic lifeline). For water solidarity, the system further discourages sharing water with neighbours, because of the risk that personal tariffs increase or in case of a basic lifeline tariff, additional water is no longer free.

Spatial Heterogeneity of Water Access

The cost of water transaction is only one factor when considering the probability of water gifts; spatial configurations are also important. Gifting water requires heterogeneity. If all neighbours in an area have a good access to conventional water sources, gift transactions are unlikely, because people do not need water. The same holds true if all household suffer from water shortage, because the cost of gifting scarce water is very high. From an economic point of view the best conditions for water gifts arise if one partner has abundant water sources, whereas the other partner has severe problems in accessing water at reasonable prices. In such a constellation, low costs of giving are opposed to high benefits of receiving, leading to an overall social benefit of the transaction. However, in order for the 'water-rich' and the 'water-poor' to exchange water, a highly local heterogeneity needs to exist so that water can be transported. As for other publicly accessible water sources like wells and standpipes, the household's distance can make these other sources of free water too expensive, due to the time and labour involved in carrying. For water gifts by garden hose or pipe the distance between donor and recipient is even more spatially restricted. Infrastructural costs as well as technical limits (pressure is inversely proportional to the distance) and property rights (e.g. if the hose needs to travel across land which belongs neither to the donor nor the recipient) further restricts these systems.

Heterogeneous spatial configurations can be produced through the water network's techno-natural differences and variable socio-economic capacities, which allow only some neighbours to connect to networks. Heterogeneity is inscribed into space either in the form of a patchwork within a neighbourhood or along the social or technological borders of the city. Bousquet (2010: 148) reports that in colonial Nairobi, people came from an informal settlement to beg for water from the homes of the white settlers, who were supplied by a clean drinking water network. Not only does the proximity of neighbourhoods with different economic status enable water gifts, but water gifts can also occur between neighbourhoods with very similar socio-economic characteristic's, if one neighbourhood is connected to the network while the other is not. Heterogeneities also occur on the short term, especially when networks are interrupted and certain households run temporarily out of supply, while others still have plenty of water stored in tanks or barrels.

The Embeddedness of the Gift in a Social Framework

In a practical context, much more is required than merely favourable spatial and economic constellations. Billionaires pass beggars on the street without giving. Just as gifts do not necessarily take place when conditions are favourable (the billionaire), they can take place under unfavourable conditions. This was the case when a comparatively poor house owner insisted on purchasing a bottle of water for me, a rich European researcher, who came to his house for an interview. Just as with any other gift, water gifts need to be analysed in the wider social framework in which they take place while taking the particular social relationship into consideration. The conceptualization of the social embeddedness of water gifts lies at the core of this book and is developed in chapter 3.

2.4. Developing Water Gifts within the Waterscape

In the previous chapter, the multiplicity of water supply options was presented and the gift as one option among them was exemplified. Water gifts are embedded into practices and regulatory frameworks in a specific social field, which is located on a very local scale. Beside the donor and the recipient, other actors can be indirectly involved, for example by acknowledging the moral value of a particular gift. The actors render gifts possible through the different meanings they attribute to water, which partially refer to regulatory frameworks outside the specific field of action. However, the materialization of the gift is not only embedded in a social environment, but also in wider economic and material relationships. As water gifts need to be taken into consideration to understand the functioning of a water network, the water network and alternative water supply sources such as water vendors, also need to be analysed to reconstruct the logics of water gifts.

With the terms 'waterscape' and 'hydrosocial cycle', the political ecology of water offers two conceptual perspectives to locate water gifts in a framework that goes beyond the material interaction between a donor and a recipient and the social explanations of this transaction. Instead, water gifts can be related to the socio-natural production of water in the city as well as to the production of the city itself. While the term 'hydrosocial cycle' suggests a process-oriented perspective on water flows, the 'waterscape' reflects a status quo of water at a specific scale. In the following two sections, I will start by developing the terminology of the waterscape in relation to scale before contrasting the hydrosocial cycle with the concept of the biography of things.

2.4.1. The Scale of Waterscapes

The term 'waterscape' was introduced by Swyngedouw (1996: 76), who defined it as

> a liminal landscape [...] where the cyborg character of the transgression between society's nature and nature's society is perpetually emptied out, filled in again, and transformed. This circulation of water is embedded in and interiorizes a series of multiple power relations along ethnic, gender and class lines. These situated power relations, in turn, swirl out and operate at a variety of interrelated geographical scale levels, from the scale of the body upward to the political ecology of the city to the global scale of uneven development.

Swyngedouw's definition stresses the mutual constituency of the natural and the social and the processes inherent in the waterscape that bring these two elements together.

From Landscapes to Waterscapes

'Waterscapes' are a combination of 'water' and 'landscapes', both in the construction of the term and in its utilization as a scientific concept. The term 'waterscape' is to be seen as a metaphor. The Oxford Dictionary of English (2010) defines a 'waterscape' as "a landscape in which an expanse of water is a dominant feature", like a landscape dominated by lakes. However, it can also refer to landscapes where water is not at all visible on the surface. That waterscapes can be barely visible is underlined by Swyngedouw with the notion of 'liminal' in his definition. The waterscape instead is a perspective on any space; by making water the element of interest, it is made 'visible'.

The term 'landscape' itself is very ambivalent as Henderson (2003) outlined in his review of the different conceptualizations of the term. In his classification, the term – as it is used in political ecology – can be attributed to the category of an "epistemological landscape". This landscape perspective is based on a socio-spatial dialectic: "One simply can't know society without knowing its spaces, and one can't know social space without knowing the social relations that constitute it. The two are mutually constitutive" (Henderson 2003: 198).

Based on a 1970s Marxist tradition, this landscape perspective does not analyse 'traditional' landscapes and their decline, nor does it neutrally analyse the change of social space as in other concepts of landscape. Rather, it questions inherent social inequalities. "Thus, very particular social relations tend to be invoked, those formed around the major axes of social difference and struggle: class, race, ethnicity, gender, and sexuality" (Henderson 2003: 190).

The term 'waterscape' always implies a perspective that demarcates an empirical object in space. Just as in photography, in which the artist selects both the object and how close to crop the background, the political ecologist selects a specific waterscape, be it a city like Durban (Loftus 2006a), a nation state like Spain (Swyngedouw 1999b), or a specific river basin like that of La Ligua in Chile (Budds 2008). The description of a 'waterscape' can only represent a snapshot or a version of reality. The 'waterscape' contains the everyday natural, social, and technical processes linked to water, hence the rain, the evaporation, the purification, the flows and consumption, the daily struggles, the shortages, the showers, the leakages, the payment, and the theft, as well as the related material manifestations, like the network, the tap, the bathroom, the bucket, and the trees.

The objective of political ecology goes beyond describing the specific waterscape based on how it is observed at a single moment in time. Loftus (2007: 55) argues that "the waterscape is produced relationally and historically". Consequently, the explanation of a waterscape requires analysing the interrelations that influence its constitution and which can be partially located outside the waterscape. Additionally, although a waterscape is situated in a specific moment in time, it needs to be analysed within the historical processes in which it was created. This includes considering the power relations that are continuously at work. Thus, a waterscape or a landscape is not "a fixed record of power but one which is constantly changing and being shaped by new political interests, connections, and constituencies" (Mosse 2003). Even if an analysis of a waterscape does not focus on history, historical processes cannot be ignored.

I interpret the notion of the 'waterscape' as a concept that highlights the multiple facets that water incorporates. The notion questions both mono-disciplinary approaches to understanding water, which do not take into consideration the social, technical, or natural aspects into consideration, and the water pipe paradigm under which non-network water flows tend to be ignored.

The Meaning of Water

A reconstruction of a waterscape within a framework of 'political ecology' needs to analyse the inequalities inherent in the waterscape at a given moment on the one hand and the elements that produced these inequalities on the other hand. Only the combination of these two elements allows a Marxist critique of the system directed towards the power structures underlying the waterscape. It is the specific empirical context in which a waterscape is rooted that determines the processes, actors, and artefacts which need to be included in the analysis. The understanding of the waterscape therefore needs to be instrumental rather than completely holistic.

The priorities chosen by political ecologists of water – who are mainly geographers – to analyse waterscapes, have been criticized by anthropologists. Baviskar (2003: 5052) denounces the fact that political ecology "tends to unitary analyses that distil meanings down to the economic 'last instance', rendering resources as sources of only profit and subsistence, and not social life" and claims to treat "identities, interests and resources, not as pre-determined givens, but as emergent products of the practices of cultural production". She represents several anthropologists in the water debate, including Mosse (2008: 943), who argue that social science literature has almost entirely ignored that "institutions of water management in Africa are socially embedded and ritually authorized". Strang (2004: 245) highlights the fact that human interactions with water are permeated by the meanings of water: "water as the spirit, as life, as social, connective substance, as wealth and power, as generative source and regenerative sea, as nature, id, emotion and unconscious".

Baviskar's anthropological critique of political ecology of water needs to be both taken seriously and put into perspective. Political ecologists of water consider the meaning produced in the utilization of water as an element to understanding water supply systems. One example is the historical analysis of water within urbanization processes in the establishment of the 'modern European city' (e.g. Gandy 2004; Kaïka 2004; Swyngedouw 1996). When water supplies entered the house, hygiene practices changed and "the new de-odorized urban body, embodying quite literally a new civic, modern-urban ideal, carried by an urban bourgeoisie that was becoming quickly self-confident of its new role, became re-odorized in new ways, expressing cultural distinction and power differentiation" (Swyngedouw 1996: 78). These new practices were inscribed both physically – with the construction of public and private baths – socially, by making bathrooms a symbol of wealth and social distinction, and bodily hygiene a class distinctive feature. Similarly the actors' attribution of meaning to water was intensively examined in works that analyse the social construction of water scarcity (Kaïka 2003). The notion of everyday practices stresses the connection between "grand political economic considerations and the seemingly banal, taken-for-granted act of turning on a tap" (Ekers and Loftus 2008: 713).

The meaning attributed to water by social actors is only taken into consideration when they are assumed to matter for the wider understanding of the functioning of the waterscape; rather than attributing scientific value to the mere description of any water practice or water ritual. The crucial challenge, however, is to determine what really matters. It is only by considering the actors' cultural representations of water that we can determine their importance – both for individual water practice and for the entire waterscape. Ultimately, a waterscape that extends beyond politico-economic reconstruction will allow a more global understanding of water in its various dimensions. "Water connects domains of life such that the water used in one will affect the water used in others, and if the notion of system suggests more integration of these domains than is warranted, perhaps 'connectivity' might be a better term for what we seek to define" (Orlove and Caton 2010: 402). To grasp the functioning of a waterscape with its multiple interconnections of nature, things, and actors, the consumer's attribution of meaning is not only a peripherally interesting anthropological excurse, but it is also relevant in explaining the waterscape as such. Moral values influence the decision-making of policy makers, in the construction and operation of water infrastructures. Likewise the consumers' 'willingness to pay' or the 'willingness to steal' water can be influenced by specific, local interpretations of the social meaning of water. Consequently, even if the political ecology of water aimed only to understand power relationships, it still requires a comprehensive understanding of the social meaning carried by water.

Understanding the gift of water is a prime argument for the need to take cultural constructions of water into consideration. The multiple supply options inherent in the cities of the South centrally constitute elements of the waterscape. Water networks can at least be partially explained by market logic, with an analysis of people as economic agents. By definition, gift transactions cannot be understood from the viewpoint of market exchanges, but only from the underlying social framework. The attribution of meaning to water ultimately enters the waterscape not only as a ritual practice, but as an everyday transaction that affects the inequality of water access.

Thinking the Waterscape on Multiple Scales

Depending on the perspective taken on water in the reconstruction of an urban waterscape, the relevance of gifts and everyday practices differ. In analysing a city, water gifts are relevant, but they are only one element among many others. Furthermore, they are an element located on a scale that is often not spotlighted, especially when the network is debated. When the perspective is however shifted to a local scale like in this research, the gifts appear much more prominent. As a central water access strategy it should not be ignored. Both perspectives focus on the description of a waterscape, but a waterscape on different scales.

The scale of a waterscape is not a given. A waterscape can be defined by a researcher based on administrative criteria like a city or a neighbourhood, on 'natural' boundaries like the watershed[16], or technical definitions like the limits of a network. Regardless how a waterscape is defined, it is an artificial delineation of a study object, which can never contain all the elements relevant to its understanding. A landscape painting captures the landscape at a scale selected by the painter. The elements in the painting are however related to processes not presented in the painting, either, because they are so little, that they are not visible on the specific scale, or because they depend on elements outside the frame. The same holds true for water. "The circulation of water combines political and economic power at the international, national, regional, and local levels with a social and economic struggle for the control over and appropriation of water" (Swyngedouw 2004: 2). Looking at water at any scale requires linking it to those struggles on other scales.

Depending on the researcher's spatial definition of the waterscape – in other words, his perspective – elements of the waterscape appear with different relevance. In case studies in political ecology of water either one waterscape or several non-overlapping waterscapes on a similar scale are defined. In order to benefit from different scalar perspectives, I suggest analysing different waterscapes within the same case study. By this, I do not refer to independent waterscapes, like that of two different cities, but to waterscapes that are contained within other waterscapes. Hence, the same areas can be analysed on different methodological scales. The waterscape of a city contains waterscapes of individual neighbourhoods, and is itself contained in the waterscape of the

---

16 Definitions based on natural boundaries are not necessarily defined outside of the social sphere, but as Molle (2009: 492) stresses these definitions are also "political and ideological constructs".

whole country. The waterscape of a neighbourhood is physically and socially related to the waterscape of the city and vice versa. The advantage of such an approach is that very local processes can be analysed in much more depth and the functioning of water supply can be determined. A local waterscape can then be placed in relation with 'the bigger picture'.

To understand the everyday water practices in the case study area in Greater Khartoum, waterscapes at different scales, nested within each other, will be used. In the 'waterscape of the city' (Greater Khartoum, built area ca. 600 km²) policies are defined and investment decisions are taken. The 'waterscape of the interconnected networks' (northern Dar Alsalam, 14 km²) is technologically defined as the neighbourhoods in which the individual networks are connected together to a larger network. The 'waterscape of the neighbourhood' (Square 11, 0.8 km²) is an administrative unit, which is reflected in the spatial organization of housing, administrative responsibilities and the design of the network. In the neighbourhood several 'neighbourly waterscapes' (0.004-0.008 km²) will be analysed that contain only a few households each. The analysis of each of the scales requires a different perspective, since each focuses on different actors (such as politicians or children carrying water), different objects (water treatment plants or buckets), and debates (on policies or pressure in a particular tap). A gift transaction is carried out within the 'neighbourly waterscape', but the gift of water is never disconnected from the other waterscapes.

2.4.2. The Biography of Water Drops. Circulation and Transformation

Waterscapes emerge from the history of water in a particular place, and this history is formed by a social relation between nature and society. It is this interaction that is at the core of political ecology. How is the molecule H_2O[17] transferred into water? How much 'nature' remains a part of water? And how much agency is to be attributed to water? To answer these questions, procedural concepts including the hydro-social cycle and socio-natural metabolisms were brought forward by political ecologists to grasp the hybrid character of water. In this section, I will use the biography of things to supplement political ecologic concepts of transformation with a clearly defined concept of socio-economic transformation.

---

17 The metaphor H_2O is used by Illich (1986) in distinction to 'water', to express that water is not restricted to nature but that it is a "stuff" created by society.

Circulating Water in the Hydrosocial Cycle and in the Urban Metabolism

The hydro-social cycle is on the one hand inspired by the notion of the hydrological cycle and on the other hand it is a fundamental critique of the concept. Linton (2010) develops a history of the hydrological cycle, in which he "treats the hydrological cycle as a hydrosocial phenomenon [in the sense of a social construction of scientists], albeit one that represents water in a way that erases its own social content" (Linton 2010: 107). The critique against the hydrological cycle consequently is directed against ignoring the social dimensions of water flows. "The flows of water on the earth's surface, moreover, are radically affected by people: In the Northern Hemisphere, some 80% of river discharge is regulated, or controlled, by dams". With this statement, Linton (2010: 229) underlines that the "very nature of the circulation of water on earth […] has to be described in social as well as hydrological terms". The hydrosocial cycle is the social extension of the hydrological cycle, which still incorporates water circulation. The total amount of water remains constant and it circulates through natural processes such as evaporation, rain, and discharge on and below the surface. This circulation is altered by human activity through dams, pipe systems, irrigation facilities, and other interactions with water. The hydrosocial cycle describes singular phenomenon, but specific elements of this circulation can be described and analysed within a waterscape, like the flow of water from an aquifer through pipes to the consumer.

The notion of circulation is also central in Swyngedouw's concept of a socio-natural metabolism, which, in opposition to the hydrosocial cycle, is not a global phenomenon but references a city: "Modern urbanization or the city can be articulated as a process of geographically arranged socio-environmental metabolisms" (Swyngedouw 2006: 34). He compares the city with a living organism, and the blood circulating through the body with the water supply network. "Metabolic circulation, then, is the socially mediated process of environmental, including technological, transformation and trans-configuration, through which all manner of 'agents' are mobilized, attached, collectivized, and networked" (Swyngedouw 2006: 32). While the metabolism or the metabolic circulation grasps the city as an entity, metabolic transformations are the processes within the circulation that transfer both H2O and 'social' water through the city.

Both the terms of 'metabolism' and 'hydrosocial cycle' focus on the interface between the social and the natural, and both take a procedural perspective, although they define the object differently. Metabolism remained mainly a theoretical concept in the narratives used by Swyngedouw to conceptually integrate nature and society with Marxism. The hydrosocial cycle is much stronger when applied as a framing concept for empirical work than in the detailed reconstruction of the individual metabolic transformations of water that occur during the circulation of water in a socio-natural environment.

How Ecological is Political Ecology?

Political ecology in general and political ecology of water in particular is not as 'ecological' as the term would suggest. Walker (2005: 74) presents an overview of political ecology and argues that in the 1980s and 1990s political ecology strongly examined biophysical ecological change. Thereafter, the political became more important and "in much contemporary political ecology the 'concerns of ecology' […] become primarily questions of power, struggle and representation, while the connections of these struggles to the biophysical environment remain unexamined" (Walker 2005: 78). Political ecology of water is much in line with later political ecology, and biochemist or biophysical processes are hardly analysed (among others: Bakker 2010a; Loftus 2009; Swyngedouw 2004).

Rather than developing a critique of political ecology of water, I suggest using terminology cautiously. Depending on the empirical case studied, socio-natural transformations can be much less important than the socio-economic transformation. Consequently, the socio-natural production of water should not be overemphasised by stressing the hybridity of water. For example, this holds true for the analysis of the neoliberalization of water supply management, where processes like commodification alter mainly the economic rather than the physical properties of water. Just as the people's attributing of meaning to water has to be closely analysed if it interferes with the functions of the waterscape, the chemical and physical transformations of water need to be considered if they have significance for the analysed phenomena in the waterscape. Only then, does natural science need to be taken into consideration to understand the materiality of water.

The gift of water is primarily a topic that does not require examining physical transformations.[18] In the analytical framework of the gift presented above

---

18 In contrast to explaining gift transactions, 'spatial heterogeneity' that produces the 'water-poor' and the 'water-rich' requires taking into consideration gravity and mechanical engineering of water networks. In combination with social processes the performance of particular tap is pro-

(2.2.4), I have developed three elements – social transaction, cost of the gift, and spatial heterogeneity – which need to be studied in order to explain the gift. The mere process of gifting water is hardly related to physical processes.[19] The gift is negotiated between the 'water-rich' and the 'water-poor' in a 'social framework' that takes into consideration the 'costs of the gift'. The transformation in the process is a socio-economic one. Water that was produced for the market is made free of charge by the 'water-rich' for the 'water-poor'.

Analysing water in a hydrosocial cycle or in a socio-natural metabolism is valuable to stress the relevance of natural processes in the production of the waterscape. However, to analyse gift transfers, focusing on the socio-economic transformation allows a better grasp of the production of gifts.

The Biography of Things. A Process-Oriented Perspective on Commodification

In this book, I have therefore chosen to introduce a different process-oriented concept that focuses solely on the socio-economic transformation of water. I will apply Appadurai's (1986) and Kopytoff's (1986) 'biography of things', which I have adopted as the 'biographies of water drops'. The terminology combines the process-oriented perspective embedded in the notions of metabolic circulation and hydrosocial cycle with commodification processes, which are redefined against their use in political ecology.

Not every 'thing' is automatically a commodity; it must be made into one through social processes. Marx states that "to become a commodity, a product must be transferred to someone else, whom it will serve as a use value, by means of exchange" (Marx 1962 [1867]: 55). It is the embeddedness of objects in the market that defines whether a thing is a commodity or not. Its value can be expressed in monetary terms.[20] If objects are not traded on the

---

duced. For the analysis of inequality in water access, I will consequently refer to natural science perspective on water. In addition to mechanical engineering, I will analyse tree canopy as an indicator for heterogeneity in water access.

19 The physical transformation is restricted to the change of spatial location of the water in the process.

20 Also in barter transactions we can speak of commodification because things are directly exchanged with each other, but the exchange value is still clear for both transaction partners. In line with Carrier, goods in these transfers are commodities. "The objects are alienated from the transactor: they are not especially associated with each transactor, nor do they speak of any past or future relationship between transactors. Instead, such objects are treated solely as bearers of abstract value or utility" (Carrier 1995: 20).

market, they are not commodities. 'Commodification' is the altering of an object's commodity status. "'Commodification' refers, literally, to the extension of the commodity form to goods and services that were not previously commodified" (Jackson 2002: 96), hence which had use value only. Jackson's definition describes commodification as a change of a 'type of thing'. Examples are the shift of elderly care from the family house to nursing homes, or the commodification of water in a city through marketization. Commodification consequently refers to the entire society. With the notion of the biography of things, the focus is significantly different. It is directed towards the change of a 'specific thing', like a single drop of water.

The difference between a 'type of thing' and a 'specific thing' in political ecology can be illustrated by the work of Page (2005), with whom I have a diverging interpretation of the concept of a biography of things. He presents a "commodity biography of water in twentieth century Tombel" (Cameroon) where water "first became a commodity in the 1940s. It was partially decommodified in the 1960s, was recommodified in the 1980s and decommodified again in the 1990s". Referring to the biography of things allows Page to highlight that "commodification is transient and reversible" (Page 2005: 295), which is very much in line with water research in the 2000s, when the participation of multinational corporations was increasingly considered failed interventions, and alternatives – including less commodified systems – became a new option. Page explicitly states for his work that decommodification "does not refer to a particular item or quantity of water, but water in general in a particular place" (Page 2005: 295).

Page's biography focuses more on the management of water than the biography I aim to describe. In his original conceptualization, Kopytoff has 'specific things' in mind. He presents the example of stamp collecting, "where, one may note, the stamps are preferably cancelled ones so there is no doubt about their worthlessness in the circle of commodities for which they were originally intended" (Kopytoff 1986: 80); the stamps were given a second life. A 'biography of stamps' does not analyse how used stamps in general were variously defined as a valuable collectible – in the sense of a commodity – or a worthless piece of paper, but rather, it looks at how a particular stamp shifts between being and not being a commodity. The processes, which can be described within a biography of things – be it water, a hut or a car –, links the material thing with its social and economic attribution of value in a specific situation, within everyday practice. Like the hydrosocial cycle, which can be used to analyse specific socio-natural metabolic transformations of water at different stages in their circulation, the biography of water can analyse how water is socially and economically transformed. This alternative perspective on processes of commodification and decommodification is one of the added-values of analysing the biography of water drops. Since specific drops of water are analysed symbolically, the heterogeneity of the waterscape can be described in more detail. Different biographies of water drops can be presented and compared. By following the biography beyond the flow from the source to the consumer, the water gift can be integrated in such a biography of water in the sense of an additional life phase of the same water drop.

To keep the terminologies clear, two process-oriented definitions of commodity transformations need to be distinguished. I suggest using the terms 'commodification' and 'decommodification' as they are used in political ecology of water, where it refers, in Page's acceptation of the term, to the movement (rather than necessarily a complete transformation) of the totality of water in a social system towards or away from the logic of the market, through the introduction of water meters for example. In the Social Life of Things, Appadurai (1986) uses these terms[21] slightly differently. Commodification does not refer to the type of thing, but to the society. "To the degree that many or most things in a society [qualify as commodities], the society may be said to be highly commoditized" (Appadurai 1986: 16). Accordingly, 'decommodification' and 'commodification' for him are processes that change the functioning of the social system. In both approaches the perspective is set on an aggregated scale, generalizing the relevance of market logics within the social system or a water supply system.

For the transformation of things in movement within the biography of things, Appadurai, develops a different terminology by defining "commodity phases of the social life of any thing" (Appadurai 1986: 13). Within the transformation, things are "moving in and out of the commodity state" (Appadurai 1986: 13). Consequently, over a longer term, water in a city can be more or less commodified, while everyday water moves in and out of the commodity state.

From an economic perspective moving something out of the commodity state involves certain costs. Henderson (2004) analysed the passage of food items

---

21 Appadurai terms it slightly differently as '(de)commoditization'. The terms are used simultaneously in the discourse, while '(de)commodification' is predominantly used.

that were produced for the market, but which are obtained by a food bank for free distribution to those in need. When entering the food bank, goods are stripped of their commodity identity. The costs for it are shouldered by those redefining the thing, hence, those who support the food bank in kind or with money. Through that, these food items "gain a new life, constituted by a complex set of mediations and surrogate movements, and they gain this life precisely at the point where Marx says the life of the commodity should end" (Henderson 2004: 490). Removing the commodity identity is not an automatic process; it requires a motivation – a social or political commitment – which works against the logic of the market.

Water flowing between neighbours follows a very similar trajectory to that of cans distributed from a food bank to the poor. The social life of water gifts is one phase of certain water drops in their biography. Providers produce water and transfer the natural resource into the social sphere. They add value in form of extraction, treatment, and transportation and shift water into the commodity state when they deliver it to customers against payment. Through consumption, some water moves out of the commodity state, reflecting a typical commodity lifecycle. Other water, however, experiences further economic transformation, hence, an extension of its biography. It becomes a gift.

The Biography of Water in the Waterscape

By disconnecting the biography of water from the hydrosocial cycle and the metabolic circulation, it is easier to focus on specific aspects of water transformation in the city. The biography of a water drop concentrates on particular flows of water in the city rather than on the totality of water in a city (metabolic circulation) or within an extensive natural phenomenon (hydrological cycle). This restriction is achieved by conceptualizing water flows as linear and not circular. A biography of water starts with the 'birth' of water (e.g. the extraction of the water from an aquifer) and ends with its 'death' (when it leaves the social space). It consequently does not necessarily require analysing water within major socio-natural systems, which is at the centre of circular concepts. Nevertheless, specific biographies of water can be seen as an integral part of the circulation of water if one aims on understanding the whole city. Proposing two different perspectives on water in the city – the procedural concept of the biography of water and the spatial concept of waterscapes – is only an analytical differentiation between two things that are deeply entwined. First, the biography of water links processes found outside of the waterscape to the waterscape in question. For example, a 'waterscape of a neighbourhood' can only be explained when not restricted to water processes inside the particular waterscape. It requires taking external ones into consideration, like water policy made in the 'waterscape of the city', and water production in the 'waterscape of a water treatment plant'. Second, within a single waterscape, different biographies coexist. The waterscape therefore allows the analysis of how a particular biography of water is influenced by other biographies. The decrease of water consumption from a particular source cannot exclusively be explained from within its biography. It requires understanding the alternative supply options available to people in their waterscape.

2.4.3. The Moral Waterscape. Between Interest and Altruism

The goal of my research is to make sense of social processes related to water in a particular area. In this subchapter, I will relate the term 'waterscape' to moral geography and define the term 'moral waterscape' to link the water debate to moral philosophy.

'Doing philosophy' is not the end goal of this research. Philosophy serves as a tool in a geographical approach that pushes the discipline's boundaries, both in methodological and theoretical questions. Making the gift of water a central topic, requires a detailed analysis of gifts beyond the mere assertion that transfers take place, that are not directly compensated by money flows. It is the relations between the donor and the recipient that need to be reconstructed. In these relations, material elements, like return gifts, can play a role. An economistic reading of the gift assumes a norm of reciprocity, which integrates seemingly free transfers in hidden economic transactions. The more we ignore such a reading, the more we have to specifically analyse the motives of each actor and the more likely we will be to touch on topics of morality. Regardless of whether we believe the stories people tell about their reasons for offering gifts, these explanations are value laden, containing notions of good, right, and just.

To understand the role of gifts in a waterscape, but also other modes of transfer, we have to analyse how the gifts materialized in the waterscape in the form of water transfers but also through the related accumulation of power. We also need to explain the functionality of a gift on the basis of an economic, social, and moral reality. In this subchapter, I will discuss how geography and philosophy are valuable elements for my empirical research.

Moral Geography

Morality and ethics are not only topics restricted to philosophy and theology. Human geography touches morals in two very distinct ways. First, it analyses the social in which morality can be a crucial element. Second, by performing a geographical analysis beyond a mere description of the world, the researchers evaluate social processes based on their moral convictions. "There have been times when the positive appeared to dominate the discipline. This was the case during the 'quantitative revolution' of the 1960s and the subsequent era of geography as 'spatial science'" (Smith 2000: 2). However, researchers' morality strongly influenced geography in the past decades. Radical, critical, feminist, and post-colonial geographies question distribution, gender, racism, and other social phenomena on the basis of a normative framework.

The 'moral turn in geography', which Smith (1997) proclaimed, does not refer to the emergence of a normative underpinning of the work of many geographers. It was rather the acknowledgment that geographers were conceptually engaging more powerfully with moral philosophy on a theoretical level in the 1990s by "rethinking traditional questions of moral philosophy through the geographer's conceptual lens of space" (Dyer and Demeritt 2009: 48). This acknowledgement was coupled with a call for further intensification.

The 'moral geographic perspective', or moral geography as a sub-discipline, consequently analyses moral geographies in the sense of a study object.

> The ideas covered by the term 'moral geographies' [...] help us to analyse the taken-for-granted relationship between geographical ordering of the world and ideas about what is good, right and true. They reveal how central geographical objects (space, place, landscape, etc.) are to the ordering of seemingly natural expectations about who and what belong where and when (Cresswell 2005: 132).

'Caring at a distance' (e.g. Korf 2007; Silk 2004) is one of the topics in the field, in which the geographical concept distance affects people's morality regarding solidarity. A prime example is international chains of aid connecting potential donors to 'distant strangers' rather than to people directly, socially connected in face-to-face relationships. We will also touch on the topic of distance, both social and geographical, for water gifts in Greater Khartoum. To conceptualize the interplay between morals, gifts, and water, I want to highlight the inverse process, the inscription of actors' morality into the material world. Before I develop the terminology of the 'moral waterscape', I will clarify central terminologies and perspectives under which morality can be analysed in philosophy, in order to contextualize my project.

Moral, Ethics and the Division of Moral Inquiry

Across the various disciplines and among different authors, there is no consistent delineation between the definitions of the terms 'morality' and 'ethics' (e.g. Sayer 2010b: 164; Lee and Smith 2004: 2). For the purpose of this research I will follow Lee and Smith (2004: 2):

> We distinguish between ethics as moral theory, and morality as practical action. Thus ethics, as the subject of moral philosophy, involves reflection on moral values, their origin, meaning and justification. Morality refers to what people believe and what they do in pursuit of, or merely as a reflection of, their own conceptions of the right and the good.

Three levels of ethical investigation can be distinguished in moral philosophy. While descriptive ethics 'describe' the morals of actors; normative ethics discus how one should act, hence the morals themselves; and in meta-ethics, concepts are defined to grasp morality. My research is situated mainly on the descriptive and the meta-ethical level. Bourdieu's (e.g. 1990 [1980]) theoretical approach to morality is the core of the third chapter, where the relation of interest and morals will be analysed in gift practices. The definition of gifts in social theory can be considered a meta-ethical debate.

Radical geography including political ecology of water is strongly normative. Thus for example, the work presented here criticizes inequality in water access, though it is not given a central role in the argumentation. Concepts in water policy debates, like the right to water, and convictions that water has to be treated as a private or a common good, strongly reflect these claims. Olson and Sayer (2009: 182) criticize that "radical or critical geographers are still very much engaged in work that is normative, but there is currently little incentive professionally to appraise or evaluate the reasons behind particular normative positions". Hence rather than developing their own moral concepts, the geographers normative values are taken for granted and are applied as a guiding framework for their work.

Analysing gift transactions encourages expanding this perspective beyond the socio-economics of the transaction and relates the transaction to moral frameworks. The research perspective consequently requires incorporating descriptive ethics. I do not aim to incorporate the understanding of water flows into philosophy, but rather, to consider people's morals as a constitutive element of social action. By taking a descriptive perspective, geographers leave the terrain of most philosophers and move into an anthropological investigation of moral values in a specific local context. The approach consequently is more a geography of moralities, taking 'morality' as a noun rather than moral geography with 'moral' as an adjective. Differently formulated moral geographies are "thick descriptions of moral features of place" (Proctor 1999: 7). In analysing a waterscape in an urban context, morality affects action on different scales. On the scale of the city, morality influences the decisions of policy makers who might take inspiration from international discourses like on development and locally, people's everyday practice can be guided by morality.

Making the local the starting point of moralities assumes on a meta-ethical level that what is good and what is bad is not universal. This perspective is discussed under the notion of relativism. "The character of 'moral' discourse in our own time and place may be radically different from that of other times and places. In order to understand moral statements, one must therefore situate them historically and geographically" (Driver 1992: 25; cited in: Smith 2000). Under relativism, the only entry point to understanding the morality of the everyday is empirical research approaching morality through the analysis of morally informed action and/or moral convictions in a particular place.

Deriving the Moral Waterscape

Morality is observable on two levels; firstly, the practices themselves – the everyday moralities – and secondly more indirectly through the results of moral behaviour. The term 'landscape' encompasses both spheres by combining the physical with the social. If the social is moral, the resulting landscape is a moral landscape. Proctor (1998: 193) argues that "ideology transforms habitat into a moral landscape, a geographical embodiment of the good". Setten (2004) empirically develops a case for a Norwegian agricultural landscape. She contrasts farmers' agricultural practices with agricultural policies and shows that moral concepts like environment, ecology, biodiversity, and aesthetics are materialized and how they change the landscape. Policy makers for example give value to maintain a 'traditional landscape' including dry-stone walls. "Sanctioning present landscapes through a preference for the past demonstrates the moral power of planning" (Setten 2004: 409).

The concept of moral landscape can also be applied to the waterscape. The waterscape, as Swyngedouw formulates is a "liminal landscape" (Swyngedouw 1996: 76). The inscription of social values does not necessarily need to be as visible as the stone walls in Norway. However, in a 'moral waterscape', moral concepts can affect for example the connectivity of households to various types of water supply. The morality in the waterscape can be subject to change, just as any other element in the waterscape. The formulation, consolidation, and modification of moral frameworks are partially dependant on the flows of water and the flows of power.

A 'moral waterscape' does not imply that the waterscape functions completely on morality, but that morality is one attribute of the waterscape. In this sense I would even claim that any waterscape is a 'moral waterscape', to different degrees, incorporating different moralities of different social actors. The waterscape of a city in which water gifts are an integral element of water supply is one example where morality impacts water flows significantly; but it is not the only one.

Formulation of Research Questions

The scientific interest of research in Greater Khartoum was not defined prior to the project. It was continuously developed and inspired by empirical reality. The only research question developed before going to the field roughly stressed the scalar perspective:

1. *How do households ensure their water needs under an unaccomplished modern ideal of full water supply with tap water?*

This first research question requires approaching water supply and access in Greater Khartoum on a rather small scale, defined as the 'waterscape of the neighbourhood'. Hence, right from the beginning, my research aimed to see water primarily from the perspective of consumers. This thus contrasts with much of the work done by most political ecologists of water, who focus on the political economy of policy-making (e.g. Beckedorf (2011) for the case of Greater Khartoum). In the explorative phase of the research, the answer to this question was a mere description of water access strategies of households, who are not properly supplied by a water network. The description of the waterscapes was only seen as a step in resolving the question. To understand the particular waterscape, social practice needs to be explained. To move from a descriptive to an analytical approach, additional research questions were defined that aim to explain particular processes, which create the observed water practices.

In the selected neighbourhood, nearly all households are connected to a water network, however, a large proportion of households do not receive water from their connection. Under the assumption that households prefer access to tap water over other supply options, the heterogeneity of water access needed to be explained, leading to the second research question:

> 2.   *How is uneven access to network supply produced?*

To explain inequality in water access, the 'waterscape of the neighbourhood' needs to be explained in relation to processes on different scales, while taking into consideration the combination of social, political, natural, and technological processes. A first element of the research question analyses the investment decisions of the Khartoum State Water Corporation (KSWC). It thus relates the water network to the institution that is responsible for it and considers the particular network not as an independent unit but embedded in the context of a set of connected networks. Second, the network itself is a dependant technological artefact; it is operated in a particular natural environment. Here the analytical focus will be mainly on the topography, which physically alters pressure regimes in the network. Third, the performance of a tap is not only related to water delivery, but also to its accessibility. Consequently, heterogeneous access to the network needs to be explained as a combination of top-down and bottom-up processes.

Under heterogeneous network performance, people need to supplement water directly using other options that generate different costs. The spatial ordering of people with different access; combined with the costs of water for potential donors; as well as the cost of water from alternative suppliers, like water vendors; provides the framework in which gift transactions take place. For a deeper understanding of water gift practices, two research questions were developed that engage with the water gift's social dimension.

> 3.   *Under which social constellations between the donor and the recipient do water gifts take place?*
>
> 4.   *What is a donor's motivation to give water to recipient?*

With these two questions, the gift is approached from an empirical standpoint. Describing the social relationship between the donor and the recipient allows specific gift transfers to be embedded into the relational social framework. Here the assumption is that accessing water gifts differs depending on the relationship between the donor and a recipient. By analysing different actors and their motivations to gift water, empirical data is linked to the discussion of altruism, hence to what extent water gifts are compensated – thus, motivated by interest – or based on the donor's morality – understood here as the negation of interest.

In addition to the four empirical research questions, one theoretical research question will be analysed. To explain water gifts, the empirical data needs to be embedded within social theory. In this research I will apply Bourdieu's theory of practice. However, the application will lead to contradictions between my empirical data and his theory. Consequently, I will adjust the theory of practice based on the following 'theoretical' research question:

5. *How can different motivations of water gifts be conceptualized within Bourdieu's theory of practice?*

The development of this question will be the central theme of the next chapter.

3

Social Action between Morality and Interest. Extending Bourdieu's Theory of Practice[22]

3.1. Introduction: Waterscapes in Light of Bourdieu's Theory of Practice

This research uses political ecology of water as a particular perspective on water practices in Greater Khartoum. To understand how individual household's daily practices contribute to producing waterscapes at different scales, the political ecology perspective needs to be supplemented with a theoretical approach that conceptualizes the individual's active engagement with a waterscape. To conceptualize water practices with a focus on the 'neighbourly waterscape', the work of the French sociologist Pierre Bourdieu, known as the theory of practice, offers a valuable starting point. The scope of this book does not allow for a detailed introduction to the theory of practice; I am assuming the reader has a general knowledge of its basic concepts.[23] The following introduction will very briefly present the theory of practice, recalling only those concepts that will be further explored in the following subchapters. It will also show the convergence between the theory of practice and the political ecology of water.

---

22 Central ideas of this chapter have been published in Zug (2013)
23 In the last decades, numerous introductions to Bourdieu's work have been written. Among them: Jenkins (1992), Barlösius (2006), Rehbein (2006), and Swartz (1997).

Fields of Application of the Theory of Practice

The theory of practice goes back to Bourdieu's early research in Algeria in the 1960s (e.g. Bourdieu 1977 [1972]). Despite being trained as a philosopher, Bourdieu strongly engaged in empirical research and stressed that "the deepest logic of the social world can be grasped only if one plunges into the particularity of an empirical reality, historically located and dated, but with the objective of constructing it [...] as an exemplary case in a finite world of possible configurations" (Bourdieu 1998 [1994]: 2). Later, he transferred and further developed his empirical-based theoretical views in various social 'fields' in a French context, which included the scientific field (Bourdieu 1997), the field of literature and arts (Bourdieu 1996 [1992]), and the political field (Bourdieu 2000).

His theories are widely used beyond French sociology and his work has transcended disciplinary borders. His concepts are not only intensively applied in social anthropology and sociology; but also in marketing, media studies, literature, education, and cultural studies, amongst others (e.g. Silva and Warde 2010). Painter argued in 2000 (246) that "Bourdieu is one of those social theorists whom geographers cite frequently, but rarely engage with in any depth". Since, the reception of Bourdieu's theory as a central social framework to understanding social interaction in geography has strongly intensified, both in German and Anglo-Saxon geography (e.g. Dirksmeier 2009).

Bourdieu and the Political Ecology of Water

In political ecology of water, few authors apply the theory of practice to empirical cases beyond a handful of selected concepts like habitus and symbolic violence (exceptions are Cochran and Ray 2009; Eichholz et al. 2012; Graefe 2006, 2010; Mehta 2005; Zimmer and Sakdapolrak 2012). No studies were found in which the theory is applied to drinking water in an urban setting. Applying Bourdieu to urban political ecology of water contributes to opening political ecology beyond the analysis of water as an element in capital accumulation. Such a perspective is crucial in conceptualizing gifts, as they are defined by the absence of a payment.

Political ecology and the theory of practice both focus on revealing power to better understand society, before transferring this understanding to a critique of power. Ekers and Loftus argue that political ecology of water applies two perspectives to power. The realist conception considers that power "can be held and deployed", giving certain actors "the power to make water flow or not flow through cities" (Ekers and Loftus 2008: 701). The second perspective is relational: "In the rich empirical studies there is a clear appreciation of how power circulates through social-hydraulic landscapes in decentralised and taken-for-granted manners. In this respect, power is an *effect* of a myriad of relations, not something that can be held" (Ekers and Loftus 2008: 700).

The theory of practice can be applied as a theoretical foundation for the relational approach to power. The relational understanding of the social is strongly developed in Bourdieu's conceptualization of space. He argues that

> directly visible beings, whether individuals or groups, exist and subsist in and through difference; that is, they occupy relative positions in a space of relations which, although invisible and always difficult to show empirically, is the most real reality [...] and the real principle of the behaviour of individuals and groups (Bourdieu 1998 [1994]: 31).

Bourdieu's Conceptualization of the Social

The notion of social space is strongly developed by Bourdieu. He conceives of it as a sphere in which people are relationally ordered according to the capital they have accrued. The notion of capital is not restricted to a Marxist conception of capital; rather, Bourdieu extends it to encompass social, cultural, and symbolic capital that function as the "set of actually usable resources and power" (Bourdieu 1984: 114). Social position consequently does not depend only on economic wealth, but also on social relations, education and prestige. Bourdieu assumes a relationship between the actors' "social positions [...], dispositions (or habitus), and position-takings (*prises de position*), that is, the 'choices' made by the social agents in the most diverse domains of practice, in food or sport, music or politics, and so forth" (Bourdieu 1998 [1994]: 6). Consequently, Bourdieu correlates lifestyle, with a person's history, which includes among others socialization and education in particular social environments. This history is inscribed in the body of the actor (Bourdieu 1990 [1987]: 191) by the habitus; a concept defined by Bourdieu as "systems of durable, transposable dispositions, structured structures predisposed to function as structuring structures" (Bourdieu 1990 [1980]: 53).

Social action, informed by the habitus, takes place in different social fields, which can be considered as "closed, separate microcosms" (Bourdieu 2000 [1997]: 19) within social space. Like in social space, each field orders people according to their endowments of capitals. However, the value of various forms of capitals is determined within the field; what is valuable in one field can prove to be worthless in another.

Social Fields and Waterscapes

The concept of fields allows analysis to focus on particular social spheres. In my reflections, I will concentrate on two social fields, the urban field of water supply and the 'neighbourly social field'. The urban field of water supply is strongly related to the 'waterscape of the city' in political ecology. Social power is unequally distributed across scales between consumers and political actors, and companies, and between different actors on the same scale. The materialization of the 'city's waterscape' – including the existence of a network in a particular area – can be understood as the result of power relations between these actors.

The 'neighbourly social field' does not cross over into different scales like the field of water supply does. However, it is equally internally stratified by social actors striving for capital, positions, and power. Defining a 'neighbourly social field' should not be confused with people living in a particular neighbourhood with borders that have been externally defined by researchers or administrators. Instead "the boundaries of the field can only be determined by empirical investigation" (Bourdieu and Wacquant 1992: 100). Bourdieu defines the 'social field' from within, while its "limits are at the point where the effects of the field cease" (Bourdieu and Wacquant 1992: 100).

The limits of a 'neighbourly field' are determined by the social interaction of a particular actor with people living in spatial proximity. In a person's 'neighbourly field', everyone with whom she or he interacts becomes a member, regardless of their actual feelings, be it friendship or animosity. The neighbourly field is socially defined. However, since, households are more likely to accidentally meet people living close by then people in streets further away, the neighbourly field tends to be spatially concentrated around the household and blurs as its spreads further out. A household's particular social activity consequently defines the limits of his 'neighbourly field'. The fields of direct neighbours, therefore, do not necessarily comprise the same people but they tend to strongly overlap in the spatial centre. In everyday practice, a stranger can enter the 'neighbourly field' of a particular person by interacting with him or her; however, the stranger's position in the field will be marginal if the interaction is restricted to a single encounter.

The 'neighbourly social field' is not congruent with the 'neighbourly waterscape'. The 'neighbourly waterscape' describes all the water access strategies used by neighbours and the underlying processes. Of these strategies only gift transactions are negotiated in the neighbourly field. Water purchases from the network and from water vendors[24] are not the result of interactions between neighbours, but embedded in the interaction between a consumer and a provider.

The Economy of Symbolic Goods

Bourdieu conceptualizes social practice inside the fields as an economy. However, under his extended definition of capital, he does not restrict such practices to monetary exchange but introduces the 'economy of symbolic goods'. The 'economic economy'[25] and the 'economy of symbolic goods' follow similar principles. Flows of goods or services are conceptualized as exchange.

In an economic economy, the exchange rate is directly reflected by the price paid for a good. "This consensus regarding the exchange rate is also present in an economy of symbolic exchanges, but its terms and conditions are left implicit" (Bourdieu 1998 [1994]: 96). In Bourdieu's approach, water given from one neighbour to another is compensated by a material or symbolic good returned at another moment in time. By exchanging capital, actors improve their social position in the field. It is through observation of such processes that Bourdieu directly links social interaction with power.

Altruism, Camouflaged Interests, and Logical Logic

The 'economy of symbolic goods' is the motor of social interaction and interest is the fuel for acting within this economy. Consequently, Bourdieu refuses altruism as an explanation for gift-giving, even when donors and/or recipients state that a gift was donated disinterestedly. Bourdieu is very critical of people's explanations of the social world. He argues,

---

24 An exception is water delivered by a vendor to a closely related neighbour.
25 Bourdieu uses this term to denote the conventional economy, hence exchange based on economic capital only.

[actors] successfully perform what they (objectively) have to do only because they believe that they are doing something different from what they are actually doing; because they are actually doing something different from what they believe they are doing; and because they believe in what they believe they are doing (Bourdieu 1988 [1984]: 207).

Since people do something different than what they believe they are doing, the scientist needs to search for the underlying rationality, which Bourdieu calls the 'logic of logic' in opposition to 'practical logic', which the actors assume to be underlying their practice. By that he excludes moral reasons as motivation for social action as well as disinterestedness as a result of moral acts.

Bourdieu severely reduces processes in the social world to interests. This approach allows Bourdieu to describe social practice in a very coherent way with simple terminology. However, this comes at the cost of ignoring the moral side of human beings, who can act according to their conviction of what is good or right. He acknowledges morality – a severely underdeveloped category in his thought – only as a relative social structure. Acting according to one's morals is only possible if it is better compensated than acting immorally. With this construction of morality, Bourdieu strongly opposes Kantian deontology, in which moral acts are based on the actors' conviction of 'doing the right thing', regardless of whether or not they are compensated for the action. The reduction of social reality is therefore due to the restrictive relational conceptualization of the social, in which Bourdieu "identifies the real not with substance but with relationship" (Bourdieu 1987: 3).

In the following subchapters, I will present a critique of Bourdieu's theory of practice. My aim is not to dismiss his theory, but rather to adjust it in such a way as to integrate morality. Although, the theory of practice incorporates many elements of grand theory, Bourdieu himself was very reluctant to postulate it as a closed theoretical system (Barlösius 2006: 8). If we apply Bourdieu's own argument concerning the need for empirical grounding of scientific thought, it is clear that his theory can and needs to be adjusted to and for empirical findings. My proposed adjustments were motivated by the analysis of gift transactions in Greater Khartoum's 'neighbourly waterscapes'. In the empirical chapters, the findings are not only presented to understand local water transactions, but also to ground the critique and adjustments I propose in my theoretical elaborations.

Criticising and Developing the Theory of Practice

Especially in France, social scientists have a very ambivalent relationship with Bourdieu's theory, which is not conducive to a constructive development of his approach. Lahire complains: "In France, Bourdieu's sociology is either hated (even ignored) or worshipped. If we overlook the former totally negative attitude, we may note that adoration is not appropriate to scientific life" (Lahire 2011 [2001]: 4). Instead, "critically debating Bourdieu's approach should not be seen as a weakening but as the one and only possibility of taking the approach seriously" (Celikates 2006: 73, own translation).

By considering both my empirical results and the critiques of other authors about the central weaknesses of Bourdieu's theory, I have attempted to constructively enter into an empirical-theoretical dialogue that transforms Bourdieu's (perfect) 'economy of symbolic goods' into an 'imperfect economy of symbolic goods'. This imperfect economy considers that 'market' interactions can be undertaken by actors for moral reasons. This is perhaps easier with a German-speaking scientific background than a French one. In Germany, Bourdieu has become one of social science's most quoted authors in the recent past (Gemperle 2009: 1). However, his thought has not been systematized into a general sociological theory (Hillebrandt 2009: 47) that would require a clear positioning in the scientific field for or against it.

Outlook

The following elaborations are strongly guided by confronting the terms 'interest' and 'disinterest'. Disinterestedness is defined here as social action that does not satisfy one's own interests. Hence, disinterested acts produce a capital loss for the person performing said actions. Subchapter 3.2 will critically present the concept of morality in Bourdieu's theoretical project. This in turn will allow the classification of his approach within moral philosophy. The interested function of morality will be expressed by introducing 'moral capital' as a specific type of social capital. Sub-chapter 3.3 will show that even under a very restrictive understanding of Bourdieu's concepts, disinterestedness can emerge due to the uncertainty of return, the actor's embeddedness in multiple social fields, and the sluggishness of the habitus. By introducing a 'capital of moral entitlement' (3.4), imperfection is introduced into the 'economy of symbolic goods' by considering that actors can be morally motivated to act disinterestedly. The critique of Bourdieu's approach will thus translate into an improvement of the theory. In subchapter 3.5, I will outline entry points for morality into the theory of practice and in 3.6, Luc Boltanski's work is consulted to develop a concrete concept of how morality and disinterestedness can be understood as joint processes in the theory of practice. The chapter concludes (3.7) with an outline of an 'imperfect' economy of symbolic goods.

3.2. Morality in Bourdieu's Behaviour and Theory

Bourdieu's theory of praxis is not intended to be a central contribution to moral philosophy, and it is not. Bourdieu does not integrate the concept of morality into the theory of practice. Nevertheless, the theory of practice can be interpreted within moral philosophical debates. The objective of this subchapter is to search for the moral in Bourdieu's work.

Before analysing Bourdieu's theory itself (3.2.2), developing the notion of 'moral capital' (3.3.3), and showing convergence between theory of practice and Gauthier's *Moral by Agreement* (3.3.4.), I will present a short digression (3.2.1) on the morality of Bourdieu himself. This approach is justified by Bourdieu's own work in which he claims for reflexivity. Scientific reflexivity urges researchers to critically analyse their own cognition and to reconstruct the relational structure of the scientific community (Hark 2009: 204). Bourdieu's work shows a trajectory from studying the other to studying the self. After anthropological investigations in Algeria (Bourdieu 1977 [1972]), and an elaboration of social classes in France, he turned to academia, the field in which he was active himself (Bourdieu 1988 [1984]), and finally in his last published book *Sketch for a self-analysis* (Bourdieu 2007 [2002]), he became his own object of study. By analysing Bourdieu's own actions as a critical scholar, I will attempt to uncover the moral foundation of his thought, which cannot be explained with the theory of practice alone.

3.2.1. Bourdieu's Moral Authority. Critique by a Scholar

Bourdieu's sociology is often labelled 'critical sociology'. This classification, alongside Bourdieu's own understanding of critical sociology, is very helpful to denote the relevance of 'the moral' in Bourdieu's actions as a scholar. Critical sociology is not to be confused with critical rationalism, where the researcher has to be critical in order to reject theories; instead, it expresses being critical of social phenomena (Rehbein 2006: 70).

The term critical sociology reflects 'critical theory', the theoretical program of the Institute for Social Research at the University of Frankfurt, connected to authors like Theodor W. Adorno, Max Horkheimer, and Herbert Marcuse.[26] It is the notion of being 'critical' which is central to both approaches and their closeness in that regard can be demonstrated by their joint focus on social inequalities, the way they have addressed these inequalities, and even how they articulate them for a non-scientific public. Bauer and Bittlingmayer (2000: 280, own translation) argue that in both early critical theory and critical sociology, the ruled perceive the established order as normality in the sense that reality "is perceived by the actors as self-evident. Therefore overcoming this reality seems be beyond the actor's ability to desire and to think". Oppressed actors do not understand the logic of oppression, but rather actively contribute to its reproduction (Bauer and Bittlingmayer 2000: 280). Social scientists instead have the capacity to construct the 'logic of logic', hence, revealing the adverseness of a social system, which creates a moral obligation to act. Both critical theorists and Bourdieu have fulfilled these obligations and criticized social and political actors of their time, predominantly those connected to capitalism.[27]

Bourdieu's own political activism and his position towards the involvement of intellectuals in politics changed during his career.

> In his early writings, he argues that there should be a clear separation between sociology as a science and politics as distinct arenas of struggle [...] because sociologists were not philosophers or moralists who were called to offer prophetic insights on all the important issues of the day (Swartz 2004: 337).

Despite his reservations, Bourdieu entered the political arena very prominently in 1995[28] when he "increasingly emerged as a symbolic figure for critics of

---

26 In retrospect Bourdieu stated that "one of my first reflexes as a young sociologist was to constitute myself against a certain image of the Frankfurt School" (Bourdieu and Wacquant 1992: 192). However, he acknowledges similarities between the two schools of thought: "I've always had a pretty ambivalent relationship with the Frankfurt School: the affinities between us are clear, and yet I felt a certain irritation when faced with the aristocratic demeanour of that totalizing critique, which retained all the features of grand theory, doubtless so as not to get its hands dirty in the kitchens of empirical research" (Bourdieu 1990 [1987]: 19).

27 The Frankfurt school most prominently brought forward a critique of the conservative establishment's capitalism in post-war West Germany.

28 To a much less visible degree, Bourdieu was already politically active in the 1980s when he joined protests with Michel Foucault; through his support for the French comedian and actor, Coluche, during the latter's heavily debated presidential bid; and through his advisory role as educational expert preparing reports for France's Socialist government. However, compared to

globalisation [...] and was almost automatically made the kind of major intellectual he had never wished to be" (Joas and Knöbl 2011 [2004]: 4). Swartz (2004: 341) explains Bourdieu's move towards political activism by changes in scientific and political fields as well as changes of Bourdieu's position within these fields. Through his publications and position as professor at the prestigious Collège de France, Bourdieu, over the years, had built up much scientific credibility. This symbolic capital – to use his own terminology – made it possible for his voice to be heard. With the deaths of Jean-Paul Sartre in 1980 and Michel Foucault in 1984, the most visible French public intellectuals of their time, a gap emerged that Bourdieu could fill. In addition to these external aspects, dissatisfaction with the political situation of the time was a core motivation for Bourdieu. Bourdieu was always politically oriented towards the left; however he became increasingly dissatisfied with the changes in the Socialist government's political agenda. He criticised the influx of market oriented reforms and their subsequent reductive effects on the welfare state, partially amplified by neoliberal intellectuals egging on public opinion.

When public employees demonstrated against cuts in social security programs, Bourdieu joined and stood as the emblematic figure of these movements in the eye of the media (Fuchs-Heinritz and König 2005: 309). His following publications became much more populist, directly confronting neoliberal politics. The title of an anthology of various interviews and short texts, *Acts of Resistance: Against the Tyranny of the Market* (Bourdieu 1998), illustrates his position. Furthermore he vigorously urged intellectuals to publicly oppose neoliberalism, strongly expressing his ideas in a discussion with the left-wing German writer Günter Grass: "The power of rulers is not only economic, but also intellectual. Therefore one has to speak out to re-establish a joint utopia, because one of the abilities of neoliberal governments is to kill utopias, to make utopias appear outdated" (Grass and Bourdieu 1999: own translation).

Bourdieu had always been critical. It was the way he framed his political goals that changed in the 1990s when he stepped into the spotlight. In 1993, a few short years before he became the leading French political intellectual, he published *The Weight of the World: Social Suffering in Contemporary Society* (Bourdieu 1999), which can be seen as an attempt to provide empirical proof of the negative impact of globalization (Joas and Knöbl 2011 [2004]: 4). As such, it is a justification for his later political commitment; grounded in an analysis of the

---

the public presence of Sartre and Foucault during the same period, as well as his own commitment after 1995, this early activism is rather negligible (Swartz 2004: 334).

empirical world, rather than in philosophical thought alone. Although, he did not transform his earlier research into arguments in the media, all of his research was 'critical', and the choice of research topics had always been "guided by moral and political considerations: inequality, suffering, and domination" (Swartz 2004: 338). When Bourdieu undertook his first empirical research project in Algeria in the late 1950s (Bourdieu 1979 [1965]), he demonstrated that the pre-colonial mode of social organization functioned adequately, thereby questioning the French colonial program (Robbins 2007: 81). Schultheis (2007: 111) even presumes that Bourdieu's personal confrontation with the manifestation of social suffering triggered his shift from philosophy to social research. *Homo Academicus* (1988 [1984]) and *Masculine Domination* (2001 [1998]) are two other significant titles from different periods that criticise the structure of French society through the empirical reconstruction of exclusion from the educational system and gender related symbolic violence.

From the very start, Bourdieu's scientific project aimed to unmask hidden relations of power in order to raise awareness amongst his readers, including those in power, about the situation of the oppressed and excluded. Neoliberalism, which he defined as "the utopia of unlimited exploitation" (Bourdieu 1998: 94), increasingly became Bourdieu's declared enemy. He assumed associations, unions, parties, as well as a strong national or supranational state were the players that could still prevent this utopia from coming true by constructing "a social order which is not governed solely by the pursuit of selfish interest and individual profit" (Bourdieu 1998: 105). Underlying this dismissal of neoliberalism is Bourdieu's knowledge of the empirical reality he generated through his research. This reality however, is a morally valued reality. Criticising a political regime, a cultural praxis, or an individual action requires at least a basic defined moral concept. "In a manner reminiscent of Plato, Bourdieu attaches a universal moral project, the creation of a just society, to a scientific one, the search for truth" (Kauppi 2000: 18). The minimal moral vision of a just society is the basic requirement for criticising the impact of capitalism, to state that capitalism is to be questioned because it makes certain people suffer. It is only because Bourdieu's sociology has such a moral underpinning that it qualifies as critical in the sense of critical theory.

3.2.2. Is There a Moral in Bourdieu's Work? Ignoring the Actors' Critical Capacity and the Charge of Economism

Bourdieu's personal acts and thought is very normative; morality is defined and fashioned from Bourdieu's standpoint as an observer of the real world. He makes moral sense from his empirical observations. Bourdieu acted according to his individual morality by publicly criticising what he perceived was wrong in French society, with the goal of achieving a better society. The analysis of Bourdieu's morals in the preceding section was predominantly descriptive, in terms of who he was as a man and an intellectual, rather than being intrinsically normative, because Bourdieu's morality was not judged but described.[29] I will continue with this descriptive approach, but shift from his morality to the role of morality in his theoretical construction of social capital. Accordingly, I present an interpretation of the second order of an individual's morality. Following Smith's (1997) call for a moral turn in geography, morality is not only to be described, but its role in constructing the social needs to be taken seriously. The perspective, therefore, explicitly considers the meta-ethical level. Bourdieu's theoretical conceptualization of morality is analysed and contrasted with other approaches in moral philosophy. An interpretation of his moral conception will allow us to develop a theoretical framework within which we can grasp morality as part of the empirical reality analysed in Greater Khartoum.

The Logical Logic. Bourdieu's Justification for Ignoring Morality

Bourdieu was strongly criticised by various scholars for neglecting morality in his conceptualization of society (e.g. Alexander 1995: 130; Boltanski 2011 [2009]: 20; Ignatow 2009: 99; Lamont 1992: 5; Sayer 2010a: 89; 2005; Lempert 2010: 211; Honneth 1986 [1984]). Alexander (1995: 190) argues that "while Bourdieu may embody universalism in his concrete practices, he cannot explain universalism in a theoretical way". Alexander refers to a discrepancy between what I defined as Bourdieu's personal morality and his theorization of social action.

While Bourdieu's political acts are grounded in reason-based morality, he does not acknowledge that actors have the same capabilities and rather "drives the instrumental reduction of action – practice as profit-seeking – into every

---

[29] A normative or prescriptive approach would require the questioning of Bourdieu's values, which does not figure in either my personal or scientific goals.

realm of social life" (Alexander 1995: 157). At least concerning the relevance of morality in individual behaviour, Bourdieu is much closer to older critical theory than to more recent generations of theoretical thought from Frankfurt. Axel Honneth developed a theory of recognition (Honneth 1997), in which he assumes that people are driven by social struggles over the recognition of moral values (cf. Hartmann 2008: 110). Jürgen Habermas's discourse ethics follows a similar path. Habermas departs from a Kantian categorical imperative (Kant 1870), but he sets it within a dialectical context, where a norm is universalized if all participants of a practical discourse come to an agreement on the validity of the norm through a process of communicative justification (Habermas 1987: 76).

> From the perspective of Habermas, Bourdieu's approach is objectivistic and philosophically naive. Bourdieu wants to exclude the problems of lifeworld, subject, and social rules from sociology, in order to allow an objectivist – or more precisely a relationally constructive approach (Rehbein 2006: 76, own translation).

Rehbein argues that the differences between Bourdieu and Habermas are partially rooted in different epistemological objectives. Habermas searches for a prototype of an emancipated society that can be used as a basis to formulate his critiques, while Bourdieu applies science to an empirical reality, which Habermas in turn does not sufficiently consider. Bourdieu defends his belief that actions cannot be motivated solely by conscious moral intentions and directly contradicts Habermas when he accuses the latter of ignoring that,

> cognitive interests are rooted in strategic or instrumental social interests, that the force of arguments counts for little against the arguments for force (or even against desires, needs, passions and, above all, dispositions), and that domination is never absent from social relations of communication (Bourdieu 2000 [1997]: 65).

In order to follow social norms, people need a motive that is not bound in the norm itself but in profitable exchange of capital. People will only comply with a norm if they benefit more from following it than acting against it. The struggle for positions in the social field depends on the acquisition of relevant capital and safeguarding previously acquired capital. Following the norm can be motivated by sanctions, which are only functional if they reduce a person's capital endowment when he or she acts 'immorally'; for example by negatively impacting the person's social reputation in terms of symbolic capital. Alternatively to sanctions, acting morally can be motivated by capital gains if we assume that society rewards people who comply with norms.

Bourdieu states that an individual's explanations of his own acts should not be accepted as a valid explanation of social reality.

> Perhaps the subtlest pitfall lies in the fact that agents readily resort to the ambiguous vocabulary of the rule, the language of grammar, morality and law, to explain a social practice which obeys quite different principles. They thus conceal, even from themselves, the true nature of their practical mastery as learned ignorance (*docta ignorantia*), that is, a mode of practical knowledge that does not contain knowledge of its own principles (Bourdieu 1990 [1980]: 102).

Consequently, morality only exists in the 'practical logic' of actors and not in the scientific explanation of social action. Bourdieu uses the gift as a prime example for such a dual truth. The gift is on the one hand "experienced (or intended) as a refusal of self-interest and egoistic calculation, and an exaltation of gratuitous, unrequited generosity. On the other hand it never entirely excludes awareness of the logic of exchange" (Bourdieu 2000 [1997]: 191). For individuals, it is not impossible to recognize the real underlying logic, but in most cases they underpin personal self-deception made possible by collective self-deception in order to maintain "the sincere fiction of disinterested exchange" (Bourdieu 1977 [1972]: 171).

Ignoring Morality as a Result of Positioning in the Scientific Field

Equally, theory is always a matter of choice. Not considering the individual's moral capacity is a simplification of reality that can be criticised, but which also allows Bourdieu's theory to be internally coherent at the cost of not being all-embracing. On the one hand, this choice is based on scientific reasoning. On the other hand, the scientist is also restricted by struggles for recognition and positions in the social field. Recognition in the scientific field is attributed to scientists developing innovative ideas rather than those echoing existent thought.

Even though Bourdieu was strongly influenced by Claude Lévi-Strauss, he emancipated himself by redefining structuralism within the 'economy of symbolic goods', thus establishing himself as an independent theorist in the scientific field. Honneth (1986 [1984]: 56) argues that

> [Bourdieu] seems to have torn down a principal pillar of the Lévi-Straussian theoretical edifice: the classification systems natives use to order their reality are no longer to be regarded as the products of an automatic logic of the human mind, but are to be understood as the results of the utility-oriented strategies of social groups.

By explaining social practice through an analysis of people's utility oriented strategies, Bourdieu is not replacing structuralism with rational choice theory, which he strongly criticizes.

> This narrow, economistic conception of the 'rationality' of practices ignores the individual and collective history of agents through which the structures of preference that inhabit them are constituted in a complex temporal dialectic with the objective structures that produced them and which they tend to reproduce (Bourdieu and Wacquant 1992: 123).

Although the individual follows an economic logic, "the Bourdieusian concept of strategy should not be understood as a choice, subjective and rational, but as a feel for the game: a practical sense, emanating from a system of dispositions" (Poupeau 2000: 77). This feeling for the game is mainly unconscious. It is "an intentionality without intention which functions as the principle of strategies devoid of strategic design, without rational computation and without the conscious positing of ends" (Bourdieu 1990 [1987]: 108). The actors in the game follow an unconscious economic logic rather than moral values embedded in the structure of their respective societies.

Including morality, as defined by Kant as an action independent from strategic self-interest, into his framework would question the consistency of the 'economy of symbolic goods'. However it would also allow economically imbalanced social action and by doing so it would question Bourdieu's break with the structuralism of Lévi-Strauss's sociology. Arguing strongly for the relevance of interest in social interaction allowed Bourdieu to position himself against Lévi-Strauss; but it also developed the theoretical construction of interest that dominated his work. By considering morality in more depth in his later work, Bourdieu would have incessantly questioned his earlier stance against Lévi-Strauss. Hence, one can speculate that an insufficient consideration of morality was not only a theoretical choice, but also a result of the constellations in the scientific field. Interestingly enough, reconsidering individual morality allowed his student, Luc Boltanski, to emancipate himself from Bourdieu, his teacher, as we will see later.

Caillé's Critique of Ignoring Morality

One of the most concrete critiques of Bourdieu's treatment of individual reason is formulated by Alain Caillé. He is one of the leading members of the

Mouvement anti-utilitariste dans les sciences sociales and criticises the theory of practice for being utilitarianist (e.g. Caillé 1994).

Utilitarianism is based on the ideas of the 18th century philosopher Jeremy Bentham, who connected morality to the "principle of the greatest happiness of the greatest number" (Bentham 1839 [1789]: 272). Selfish, individual, maximization of profit, which is assumed in utilitarianism, is set in opposition to social welfare, which is the summed-up utility of all people affected by an action. It is morally good to strive for action if the overall welfare effect is positive, regardless of one's individual profit. Bentham's philosophy is an applied philosophy, in which he argued for policies aiming to increase overall welfare.

> Given actual inequality ('is'), the concept of equality ('ought') put forward by Bentham [...], does not entail equality of treatment. Thus, Bentham wished both to change existing laws (and in particular the attitude of legislators) in order to afford equal considerations to the interest of [disadvantaged groups like] women, and to insert clauses in the existing legislation, in order to give special protection to [them] (Boralevi 1984: 11).

Bourdieu's social project can only partially be classified as utilitarian. Although he analyses society under the primate of profit seeking, and he himself questions the consequences, such as symbolic violence and social exclusion, as acting against the greatest happiness of the greatest number, he does not foresee any elements through which society could enforce the principle of maximum happiness against the individual's striving for power despite negative effects on social welfare, hence, acting morally good in the sense of utilitarianism.

Caillé charged Bourdieu's approach of economism (e.g. Caillé 1981, 1994, 2006). He places Bourdieu among those sociologists who use rational choice theory widely "to explain not only what is going on on the market, and through monetary exchanges, but any kind of social behaviour: learning, wedding, religious belief, love or crime etc." (Caillé 2006: 1). This charge of economism was also often directed at Bourdieu's theoretical project by other scholars (e.g. Alexander 1995; Favereau 2001). Caillé, however, does not restrict his critique to Bourdieu's theoretical work; he transforms it into a very personal critique. He links Bourdieu's ideas to rational choice theory and argues that the related "enlargement of the traditional scope of economic science has been the intellectual and ideological prelude and the starting point to neoliberalism which is nowadays triumphing as well in academic economic science as in the real world" (Caillé 2006: 1). The subtle message of this statement is that Bourdieu's theoretical objectives negatively materialized in the real world when judged according to Bourdieu's personal, moral convictions.

Bourdieu strongly rejected economic readings and rather interpreted his work as being opposed to the reduction of all human practices to economics (Bourdieu and Wacquant 1992: 115). He offers two key arguments to separate his approach from neoclassical theory. First, he claims to "break with the economism that leads one to reduce the social field, a multi-dimensional space, solely to the economic field, to the relations of economic production, which are thus constituted as co-ordinates of social position" (Bourdieu 1985: 723). This is accomplished by the introduction of non-economic forms of capital (in the classical sense): symbolic, social, and cultural capital. Second, he calls upon the construction of "a realist definition of economic reason as an encounter between dispositions that are socially constituted (in relation to a field) and the structures, themselves socially constituted, of that field" (Bourdieu 2005 [2000]: 75). By introducing the habitus as a moderator between structure and agency, he distances himself from the homo economics, and pushes rationality into the unconscious sphere. The critique of Caillé however is not directed towards these attempts of defence. Rather, it questions Bourdieu's assumption that social action is a result of profit maximization.

By comparing Bourdieu's early works with later ones,[30] Caillé tries to demonstrate the "impossibility of leaping from the axiomatics of interest to the thought of generosity" (Caillé 2001 [1994]: 24). I will argue differently. With his comparison, Caillé highlights the habitus as an entry point to integrate morally motivated action into the work of Bourdieu. Pure disinterested actions, or Caillé's version of moral actions state that people "must obey to the moral law that in principle wants to know nothing about interest, but demands that they exclusively act out of duty" (Caillé 2001 [1994]: 23). Bourdieu only accepts disinterested action if it is paradoxically motivated by interest. He uses the gift to explain the double truth of the act of giving. "The interval between gift and counter-gift is what allows a relation of exchange that is always liable to appear as irreversible, that is, both forced and self-interested,

---

30 Caillé's benchmark between Bourdieu's early and late works was a text first published in 1989 as *Intérêt dans le Désintéressement* (Cahiers de Recherche, Group de Travail sur la Socialisation), which was later integrated into *Practical Reason* (Bourdieu 1998 [1994]).

to be seen as reversible" (Bourdieu 1990 [1980]: 105). For the actor – with one side of the truth – a gift may appear disinterested; but if we determine the logic behind it, it is nothing more than an exchange of both economic and symbolic capital in form of acknowledgement through gratitude. Caillé summarizes that "within the system of the early Bourdieu, nothing is lost, nothing is created" (Caillé 2001 [1994]: 25).

Bourdieu – motivated by a perceived critique of his use of the term 'interest' – introduces the alternative term 'illusio' in order to detach his work from economist readings (Bourdieu and Wacquant 1992: 116). "In fact, the word interest initially meant very precisely what I include under the notion of 'illusio', that is, the fact of attributing importance to a social game, the fact that what happens matters to those who are engaged in it, who are in the game" (Bourdieu 1998 [1994]: 77). 'It matters' means that people have an interest, or, differently formulated, a desire to act within the specific game. In the theory of practice it is the dispositions which generate action; people have internalized how to act in specific situations. Hence, the habitus "permits us to understand that there are disinterested forms of behaviour which do not have as a principle the calculation of disinterestedness, the calculated intention to surmount calculation or to show that one is capable of surmounting it" (Bourdieu 1998 [1994]: 87).

It is this argument that earns momentary acknowledgement by Caillé when he admits that "Bourdieu's thought has evolved considerably" (Caillé 2001 [1994]: 27); despite the fact that Caillé directly qualifies the statement by asking: "Is there really a second Bourdieu? A Bourdieu after Bourdieu?" and finally giving the answer himself: "It seems doubtful" (Caillé 2001 [1994]: 27). This contrasted statement in Caillé's acknowledgement follows a turn in Bourdieu's argumentation, in which he softens his previous statements.

> Without doubt the social universes within which disinterestedness is the official norm are not necessarily governed throughout by disinterestedness: behind the appearance of piety, virtue, disinterestedness, there are subtle, camouflaged interests; the bureaucrat is not just the servant of the state, he is also the one who puts the state at his service [...] (Bourdieu 1998 [1994]: 87).

For Caillé, it is these interests that "close the lid on the question [Bourdieu] had just opened" (Caillé 2001 [1994]: 27) and which lead back to the early Bourdieu who argued with interest in disinterestedness. I agree with the gist of Caillé's critique, but differ in my appreciation of several aspects. There are gaps in Bourdieu's theory to recognise disinterestedness, caused notably by his denial of the existence of the individual's critical capacity, which I will elaborate in subchapter 3.4. However, even within Bourdieu's framework, there are possibilities to integrate disinterestedness without introducing a critical capacity. We will examine this in subchapter 3.3 as we look at individual reasoning about what is moral and what is not.

Conclusion

Bourdieu's opposition to morality as a motivation for action is a result of his personal and scientific trajectory and a more or less conscious positioning within the scientific field. Ignoring the individual's moral capacity can be understood as a as a result of how his theoretical thought came into being. The critical question is whether this simplification is appropriate or whether it is an oversimplification of the specific social reality being studied. This question must be answered in light of the empirical material analysed and the researcher's interest in comprehending different social spheres. My empirical study will reveal limitations in the capacity of Bourdieu's theory to explain phenomenon such as water flows between neighbours; this precise situation opens up the debate in terms of the possibilities of reintegrating morality within Bourdieu's framework. Although Bourdieu opposed any thoughts of integrating morality, such an approach is possible, since his theory is not in total conflict with individual reasoning.

3.2.3. Moral Capital, the Acknowledgement of Being Good

Even if Bourdieu's approach to morality in general is very limited, his conception of morality can be expressed by applying his terminology. Incidentally, Bourdieu mentions the notion of ethical disposition, however without fully elaborating on its modes of function and even less on its genesis. In this section I will interpret the meaning of the term and develop a 'moral capital' that allows for the description of morality as an element in an interest-based economy.

Ethical Disposition. Bourdieu's Attempt to Conceptualize Morality

In several of his books, Bourdieu mentions the term 'ethical disposition' in reference to honour (Bourdieu 1977 [1972]: 165), as means of distinction of artists (Bourdieu 1984: 261), or as a unifying force in a family, which "incline[s] its members to identify the particular interests of individuals with the collective interests of the family" (Bourdieu 1998 [1994]: 70). One of the rare texts in which Bourdieu directly confronts his economy of the social with moral philosophy is *A paradoxical foundation of ethics*, a 1991 conference, reprinted in the annex of *Practical Reason* (Bourdieu 1998 [1994]). This short text clarifies the notion of ethical disposition, even though, it is not explicitly explained there either.

Bourdieu once again elaborates on the relevance of personal interest for social action and the impossibility of true disinterestedness, but this time he explicitly analyses the relation between a social group's rules and the individual's action. He argues that a social group is defined or constituted by a set of universal rules and membership to the group requires an acknowledgement of these rules. Compliance to the rules has positive impacts on capital endowment: "Groups always reward conduct that conforms universally (in reality, or at least in intention) to virtue [of the specific group]. They particularly favour real or fictitious tribute to the ideal of disinterestedness, the subordination of the *I* to the *us*, or the sacrificing of individual interest to the general interest" (Bourdieu 1998 [1994]: 142). Bourdieu upholds the idea that the rules of the field do not determine social action (Bourdieu 1998 [1994]: 141). Consequently, violating the rules of a field is possible. The individual would however not be rewarded for complying with the rule but rather sanctioned for violating it. Such behaviour still follows a practical sense in the case where the 'immoral' action leads to individual benefits that are higher than the loss caused by non-compliance to the rule.

In Bourdieu's theory, practical reason, which leads to individual action, is centrally based on the habitus. This habitus is formed of different dispositions and contains those that urge the actor to comply with the field's rules; all the while informing the individual on how to judge his or her own and others' action as good or bad. It is these dispositions which Bourdieu has in mind when he uses the term ethical dispositions and that I call here a set of distinct moral dispositions[31]. Bourdieu's argumentation of interest in disinterest is clear: following a moral disposition is compensated through acknowledgement. I suggest introducing the notion of 'moral capital' as a subcategory of

---

31 In keeping with my differentiation between ethics and morality (Section 4.1.2), I consider Bourdieu's 'ethical dispositions' to be moral dispositions, since they are an element of social practice rather than a reference to the scientific discipline.

symbolic capital to grasp this acknowledgement as a substantial part of Bourdieu's capital transfers.

The Moral Capital

In literature several attempts were made to introduce a 'moral capital'. Generally, 'moral capital' is defined as something a person accumulates through moral action (Kane 2001; Ruonavaara 1997; Sherman 2006; Swartz 2010; Valverde 1994). Sherman (2006) elaborates this argument for an impoverished community in California, where young people invest in their 'moral worth' by acting according to the local moral framework. Their actions, when perceived by other members of their community, then become 'moral capital', and finally, they obtain an advantage through access to the few available jobs. Defining alternative capital within Bourdieu's framework does not contradict his thought. Many authors have done so, including Bourdieu himself. Most of these new capitals, such as political capital (Bourdieu 1998 [1994]: 15), educational capital (Bourdieu 1988 [1984]: 45), linguistic capital (Bourdieu 1991: 18) are field-specific variants that can be linked back to the four basic types of capitals.

The introduction of 'moral capital' into the 'economy of symbolic goods' follows a very conventional reading of Bourdieu. Instead of radically altering his thought, it situates the ethically related social action more clearly as a form of symbolic capital. Bourdieu defines symbolic capital as

> an ordinary property (physical strength, wealth, warlike valor, etc.) which, perceived by social agents endowed with the categories of perception and appreciation permitting them to perceive, know and recognize it, becomes symbolically efficient, like a veritable magical power: a property which, because it responds to socially constituted 'collective expectations' and beliefs, exercises a sort of action from a distance, without physical contact (Bourdieu 1998 [1994]: 103).

As such, symbolic capital has two different forms of genesis. First, it is a "meta-capital" (Bourdieu and Wacquant 1992: 114), in the sense that it is based on the acknowledgement of the endowment of other capitals: "Every kind of capital (economic, cultural, social) tends (to different degrees) to function as symbolic capital [...] when it obtains an explicit or practical recognition" (Bourdieu 2000 [1997]: 242). The symbolic valuation of any of these capitals is based on field inherent structures: a PhD title has a higher symbolic value on the job market than in the local football club.

Second, symbolic capital can be the acknowledgement of conduct in line with the rules of the social field. In his very early writing on male society in rural Algeria, Bourdieu elaborates on the notion of honour:

> The man of honour [...] is at once the virtuous man and the man of good repute. Respectability, the obverse of shame, is essentially defined by its social dimension, and so it must be won and defended in the face of everyone. Boldness and generosity [...] are the supreme values, whereas evil lies in weakness and pusillanimity, in suffering the offence without demanding amends (Bourdieu 1979 [1965]).

Honour is a symbolic capital in the context of Kabyle Society; it is a key element in ensuring one's social position. The individual is acknowledged as a man of honour if he acts honourably, that means if his actions are in line with the rules given by the Kabyle society. This can take the form of generosity, which is the acknowledgement of investing capital in form of a gift for example, or through specific modes of behaviour: "The man of honour is the man who faces up [...] who confronts others by looking them in the face" (Bourdieu 1979 [1965]: 128).

Only in this second form does a symbolic capital become a 'moral capital', because it does not judge the endowment of another form of capital, but rather the actions taken in accordance with the expectations of the social field, which is the society's moral framework that determines what is good and evil. A 'moral capital' consequently is defined as the part of symbolic capital that evaluates the quality of social acts against moral standards. A 'good' person inside a social field is a person in possession of 'moral capital'.

The notion of 'moral capital' helps to clarify why actors in a perfect 'economy of symbolic goods' act morally. Persons in possession of 'moral capital' can utilize this symbolic capital for their own benefit. If persons are perceived as trustworthy because of their moral acts, their 'moral capital' can transfer over into social capital, and evolve finally into material benefits. The accumulation of 'moral capital' can turn into social power, as in unreciprocated gift transfers: "The gift is expressed in the language of obligation. It is obligatory, it creates obligations, it obliges; it sets up a legitimate domination" (Bourdieu 2000 [1997]: 198).

A materially non-reciprocated gift leads to symbolic domination on two levels. If the recipient expresses his or her debt through gratitude towards the donor, the symbolic domination is internal to their relationship. The donor morally dominates the recipient, which directly affects the relative positions of both actors within their social field. If others recognize the donor's moral actions, the indebtedness can become disconnected from the relation between donor and recipient and begin to define one's belonging to social classes endowed with different levels of prestige.

3.2.4. Anchoring Bourdieu in Moral Philosophy

Bourdieu does not give his work an explicit moral and philosophical foundation, although approaches exist to which he could relate his conception of the social. Contemporary moral philosophy is dominated by three philosophical strands, which either refer to Utilitarianism, Kantian Deontology, or Hobbesian social contract theory (Steinfath 2003: 81). In this section I will link Bourdieu's moral philosophy to the work of David Gauthier (1986), who builds his morals of agreement on Hobbes. To better discuss Gauthier's Adjustments of Hobbesian thought, I will start with a brief introduction to Hobbes himself.

Hobbes: the Impossibility of Voluntary Disinterestedness

Similar to utilitarianism[32], Hobbes argues that "Individuals are taken to be instrumentally rational, that is, concerned with pursuing whatever means are necessary to the furtherance of their own ends" (Southwood 2010: 25). By that, he strongly contradicts Kant, who "assumes that we do not need to have wishes or interests in order to act morally, instead ethical convictions can be both motivation and reason" (Wolf and Schaber 1998: 41, own translation). In what Hobbes calls the natural condition of mankind everyone poses a risk to the life of the other: "If any two men desire the same thing, which nevertheless they cannot both enjoy, they become enemies; and in the way to their end [...] endeavour to destroy or subdue one another" (Hobbes 1651: 61).

Hobbes assumes that a better situation would be possible if people cooperated with each other. This would require that they agree to "constrain their conduct in certain ways so long as others do likewise. [Than] individuals attain better outcomes where each is better off than in absence of cooperation" (Southwood 2010: 25). Hobbes assumes that such a social contract, which would allow a transition from the natural state into a state of cooperation,

---

32 A moral sociology of the actor for Bourdieu could also be derived from Utilitarianism (but never from Kantian Deontology). This can be done by developing a shift from prescriptive to descriptive ethics. My choice to start with Hobbes is related to Gauthier's choice to do so.

cannot be accomplished by the inhabitants themselves. Instead leaving the adverse natural state requires ceding all their power to a sovereign. "In this contract, citizens must be fully subordinate to their sovereign. The sovereign himself can establish positive rights, which the citizens can only resist if their life is threatened. Civil law, to which the sovereign himself is not bound, replaces the subjects' morality" (Leist 2003: 4, own translation).

Gauthier's 'Morals by Agreement': the Social Benefit of Cooperation

A pure Hobbesian approach cannot describe Bourdieu's moral approach, since the interplay between habitus and the field in which Bourdieusian thought is grounded is incompatible with a sovereign, who dictates social structures. A much more productive adjustment, at least to understand Bourdieu's moral concept, is David Gauthier's neo-Hobbesian social contract theory, which he presents in his book *Morals by Agreement* (1986).

Gauthier adopts two key ideas from Hobbes. The first states that individuals act to increase their personal profits. Gauthier bases his approach on rational choice theory. In line with Hobbes, Gauthier opposes Kant by arguing that morals in society are a result of social interaction rather than of reason: "Morality does not emerge as the rabbit from the empty hat. Rather, as we shall argue, it emerges quite simply from the application of the maximizing conception of rationality to certain structures of interaction" (Gauthier 1986: 10).

Second, a society in which individual profit seeking is constrained by a social contract is beneficial for individual actors and therefore subjectively admirable. Gauthier, however, does not share Hobbes assumption that a sovereign is required to establish and maintain a beneficial society. Instead Gauthier argues, that paradoxically the individual's egotistical nature is already enough to maintain cooperation and to create mutual benefits. Cooperation therefore can be the result of self-determined, egotistical actors.

Gauthier argues against the persistence of Hobbes' gloomy natural state. Instead, he defends the possibility of a bottom-up progressive transition from a non-cooperative to a cooperative society. To allow cooperation to emerge, Gauthier argues with evolutionary theory. He divides people into two groups: a 'straightforward maximizer' searches to maximize "her satisfaction or fulfil her interest, in the particular choices she makes" (Gauthier 1986: 16). A 'constrained maximizer' in contrast looks for long-term benefits and bases "actions on a joint strategy, without considering whether some individual strategy would yield her greater expected utility" (Gauthier 1986: 167). The strategy of a 'constrained maximizer' is assumed to be superior: "The benefits of co-operation ensure that, in any given set of circumstances, each member of a group of reciprocal altruists should do better than a corresponding member of a group of egoists"[33] (Gauthier 1986: 188).

Lévi-Strauss explains such a benefit – without making it the only motivation – with an example of rituals of exchanging wine in little restaurants among strangers. The wine received in a small bottle with one's meal is poured into the glass of the neighbour at the table, who reciprocates by filling the glass of the donor with his or her own wine. "Each person in this revealing scene has, in the final analysis, received no more than if he had consumed his own wine. From an economic point of view, no one has gained and no one has lost. But there is much more in the exchange itself than in the things exchanged" (Lévi-Strauss 1969 [1949]: 59). The gift of wine is a means to initiate a conversation between the two, a way to make friends out of strangers. Though the exchange of economic capital was unprofitable, social capital was increased through the transaction.

In the Hobbesian natural state, cooperation could not emerge because 'straightforward maximizers' would exploit the 'constrained maximizers'. In the language of the gift, 'straightforward maximizers' would drink the gifted wine, without reciprocating by filling the glass of their counterparts, making cooperation a costly strategy rather than an evolutionary advantage. To prevent the risk, a 'constrained maximizer' can decide to not make gifts to people who they think will not comply with the rules of the gift. Instead, when confronted with an egoist, "she behaves [as well] as a straightforward maximizer, acting on the individual strategy that maximizes her utility given the strategies she expects the others to employ" (Gauthier 1986: 169). By excluding straightforward maximizers, a group of constrained maximizers can maintain the evolutionary benefit of cooperation. People can enter into the group if they prove to be trustworthy, by acting according to the moral framework of the society. In Gauthier's programme a transition from an egotistical to a cooperative society becomes possible from the moment a very small group of people starts cooperating.

---

33 The terminology "reciprocal altruist" is based on the evolution biologist Trivers (1971). It is to be understood as a synonym for constrained maximizer. Egoists refer to straightforward maximizers.

Gauthier and Bourdieu

Gauthier's strong focus on interests is only part of the reason why I have used his 'morals by agreement' as a moral underpinning of Bourdieu's 'economy of symbolic goods'; there is also a correspondence between their respective lines of argumentation.

Gauthier strongly echoes Bourdieu's concept of habitus by arguing for the relevance of dispositions in everyday practice. He argues that "the just person is fit for society because he has internalized the idea of mutual benefit, so that in choosing his course of action he gives primary consideration to the prospect of realizing the co-operative outcome" (Gauthier 1986: 157). Social action consequently is not guided by a rational computation of interests, but by the experience that supporting others will pay off. In the previously developed terminology, the disposition of being a 'constrained maximizer' is an ethical disposition. It is the acknowledgment of compliance with the social rule of short-term disinterestedness by other constrained maximizers, who will compensate the investment by including the person who complies morally into the reciprocal circle of cooperation with all the attached benefits. As a moral disposition, it is valued in one specific field, which we can roughly delimit as a local field of mutual cooperation. If we take a step back from absolute classifications, this is a field in which people who *tend to* constrain their immediate interests in favour of collective interests are endowed with 'moral capital', as opposed to those who are known to frequently default. The system is based on the assumption of a social framework that rewards good behaviour and in which the possibility of detection and exclusion of straightforward maximizers is inherent.

In both projects, interested and morally correct behaviour is connected to uncertainty and risk. For Gauthier, the disposition to act in line with morality is based on an individual's strategic choice as he or she calculates the probability of profitability of a transaction and of sticking to the local rules (Gauthier 1986: 42). Bourdieu offers similar arguments:

> The giver's undeclared calculation must reckon with the receiver's undeclared calculation, and hence satisfy his expectations without appearing to know what they are. In the same operation, it removes the conditions making possible the institutionally organized and guaranteed misrecognition (Bourdieu 1977 [1972]: 171).

Linking Bourdieu to Gauthier allows us to position Bourdieu's theory within moral philosophy. In their thoughts the definition of what is moral and what is not is practical rather than philosophical while social action is instrumentally rational rather than consciously based on reason. Morality can be derived by a researcher from observing social practice and its function analysed in terms of social practice. This very strong connection is achieved by binding together the very abstract concept of morality with the view of interest as reconstructable empirical phenomena. The strength of this approach in comparison to utilitarian, Kantian, and most other contract theoretical approaches like Rawls' (1971) renowned 'theory of justice' is that morality is to be derived from the empirical reality of practical interaction rather than being defined as an 'ought'. The rules of the field are the result of power struggles and as such they are specific in every field, rather than having universal claims. Morality therefore can be understood with sociological methods of observing a specific reality without having to enter into theoretical ethical debates, about what ought to be morally good. This assumption facilitates Bourdieu's construction of the 'economy of symbolic goods'.

3.3. The Possibility of Disinterestedness in the Economy of Symbolic Goods. A 'Conventional' Reading of Bourdieu

The theory of practice allows morality to be taken into consideration only when it correlates with interest. Consequently, disinterestedness requires an interested motivation. This subchapter will argue a different standpoint that postulates that it is entirely possible to follow Bourdieusian concepts, while being able to explain under certain limited constellations, that actors do act disinterestedly. Consequently, people accept a loss in capital based on practical rather than theoretical reasons.

3.3.1. The Uncertainty of Returns. Gifts and Time

The 'economy of symbolic goods' is more complex than a fully informed 'economic' economy, partially because return is less certain. Bourdieu's elaborations on time is his most acknowledged contribution to the gift debate (e.g. Osteen 2002: 24). He claims that even Mauss and Lévi-Strauss ignored the relevance of time between gift and counter gift (Bourdieu 1998 [1994]: 94). For him this interval is a key element in defining the gift: "The lapse of time that separates the gift from the counter-gift is what allows the deliberate oversight, the collectively maintained and approved self-deception, without which the exchange could not function" (Bourdieu 1990 [1980]: 105). It is this collective self-deception of the economic reality that makes the gift different from economic exchange. This difference, however, mainly manifests in the actors' 'logic of practice', rather than in the 'logic of logic', where the gift can be deconstructed as an economic exchange.

However, if Bourdieu is read carefully, there are slight differences in the economic logic. He argues, that

> the market of symbolic goods presents itself in the form of a system of objective probabilities of profit (positive or negative), or to use Marcel Mauss's phrase, a set of 'collective expectations' that can be counted on and that have to be reckoned with. In such a social universe, the giver knows, that his generous act has every chance of being recognized as such (Bourdieu 2000 [1997]: 193).

These probabilities are objective, because they are based on the field's logic, but they remain probabilities rather than certainties like in ordinary market exchange, where the price is negotiated and paid in direct exchange for the good.

The time gap therefore introduces an element of insecurity into the exchange. The individual (A) does not know if he or she will ultimately be compensated by a counter gift, nor whether the habitus of the transaction partner (B) acknowledges A's gratitude and attributes 'moral capital' to him or her. This holds especially true in societies that are characterized by heterogeneity, where the habitus of people are not completely adjusted. Additionally, unprofitable investments can result from the death of the recipient or if donor and recipient lose track of each other before reciprocation takes place, erasing the stored 'moral capital'. The loss in such a relationship is not a result of disinterested behaviour of the donor, but of a failure of the habitualized strategy, the feel for the game.

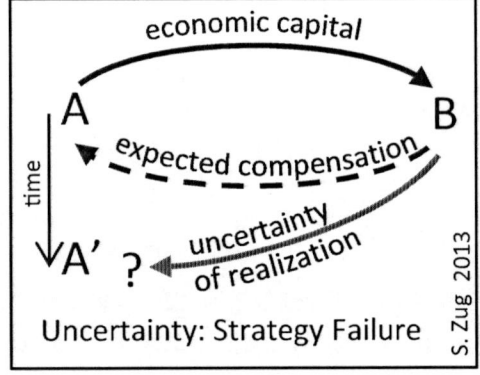

Fig. 2: *Uncertainty of Return in Gift Transactions*

3.3.2. Transactions in Multiple Fields. Perceived Disinterestedness by Gift Recipients

While uncertainty in a gift exchange distorts its economic reality, the heterogeneity of the different capitals involved can additionally affect the constellation of actors. The 'economy of symbolic goods' is not necessarily based on exchanges between two transaction partners within a single field, because it does not function with money that restricts economic transactions to an interaction between seller and buyer. The currency of symbolic capital can add other parties into the exchange, who are not involved in the material exchange, since acting according to the rules of a specific field can be acknowledged by the recipient, as well as by other members of society. In situations where a donor's action is acknowledged in a different field than the transactional field, it is not uncommon to witness a situation develop that encourages the donor to accept or even choose an unprofitable exchange from direct transaction partners. This can be explained by the existence of field specific reward strategies in secondary fields.

Rotary Clubs are an example of such a constellation. They allow us to reconstruct a Bourdieusian 'logic of logic', while accepting his primacy of interest as motivation for social action, and ignoring reason-based morality.[34] Let us assume a Rotarian supports a foreign student with a scholarship. The 'moral capital' attributed to the Rotarian by the gratefulness of the scholarship holder is disproportionally small when compared to his or her financial expenses. The donor's hidden interests, which extend beyond the flows between the two protagonists, can however be revealed. In his analysis on marriage systems, Lévi-Strauss (1969 [1949]: 178) determined two modes of reciprocity. So far in my elaborations, I have mainly concentrated on his first type – direct reciprocity – which restricts social exchanges to exchanges between one donor and one recipient. With generalized reciprocity, Lévi-Strauss introduced an exchange mode enacted among multiple actors, while maintaining the premise that a society's social structure makes people contribute in such a way that the exchange remains equal rather than exploitative. In generalized reciprocity, material flows follow a univocal circular reciprocity. Lévi-Strauss constructs these cycles in a very restrictive logic wherein they are destroyed if one party breaks the chain.

---

34 The example of Rotary Clubs is used to illustrate the logic with no basis in any empirical material.

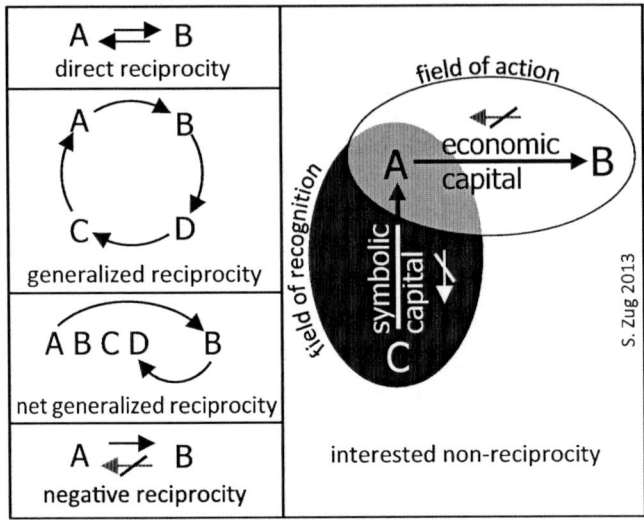

Fig. 3: Different Reciprocal Constellations

Ekeh (1974) relaxed the system by introducing a second type of generalized reciprocity, which he calls 'net' generalized reciprocity, in which the interaction takes place between the group and individual members. In order to benefit from the group, a person must reciprocate to the group. "The receipt of a benefit by any one party is regarded as a credit to that party by all other parties and therefore his reciprocation is regarded as a credit to all of them" (Ekeh 1974: 55). However, practical transfers happen between two specific actors. As a member of the social group, A supports B, who is also a member of the group. B then reciprocates to a different member in the group (D). There is reciprocity between the recipient and the group, however, for the moment not between the individuals. A lost, B reciprocated what he or shereceived, and D won. Individual reciprocity is ensured through a constant process of give and take, assuming equality in terms of the 'net' flows of all actors. However, defaulting renders the system dysfunctional.

The Rotarian example is difficult to understand within both logics of generalized reciprocity, because returns from the scholarship holder to the Rotarian's society are unlikely, especially if we assume that the former is from a developing country. Although the capital flows between the transaction partners are negative, we cannot conclude that the scholarship holder exploits the Rotarian based on negative reciprocity, defined as the attempt to get something for nothing with impunity[…]. Indicative ethnographic terms include 'haggling' or 'barter', 'gambling', 'chicanery', 'theft', and other varieties of seizure. […] The participants confront each other as opposed interests each looking to maximize utility at the other's expense (Sahlins 1996 [1978]: 195).

He or she is not exploiting because granting a scholarship is the Rotarian's decision; as opposed to the student pressuring the latter into action.

The given mode of exchange, which I will argue to be 'interested non-reciprocity', challenges the notion of reciprocity from within Bourdieu's theory. This is a paradox especially if we take into consideration that Bourdieu conceptualizes society based on interests, whereas structuralists like Lévi-Strauss (1969 [1949]: 55) state that the primary mode of generating practices is not restricted to interests, but also includes social norms. For the Rotarian, the transaction is not limited to donating money to the scholarship holder, since he or she is also active in 'elitist' fields in which the recipient is not a member. Disinterestedness towards the poor is a highly valued form of 'moral capital' within the Rotary Club and consequently is a precondition to becoming a recognized or even a leading Rotarian. Furthermore, outside the club, prestige can be accumulated by being identified as a club member by business partners, by friends, and neighbours.

This example demonstrates that from the perspective of the scholarship recipient the transaction not only appears disinterested, but is truly so because the Rotarian's interests are satisfied in other social fields by other social actors. For the Rotarian however, being good satisfies an interest (in the 'Rotary field', which is also the field of recognition) in disinterestedness (towards the scholarship holder), and can be a very profitable. The actor paying the price for the scholarship – spoken in the terminology of the economy of symbolic exchanges – is not the Rotarian but other Rotarians and people who acknowledge the scholarship giver as a good person by attributing 'moral capital' to him or her. They lose position in the elitist fields, which in turn pressures them into also investing 'altruistically' to keep pace with the scholarship giver. Attributing 'moral capital' to the scholarship donor is imposed upon them.

The complexity of social interaction and the multiplicity of actors either directly or indirectly involved, with different modes of valuating material transfers, allows, under certain constellations within the 'economy of symbolic goods', transfers of economic capital. These transfers are not balanced materially or symbolically between donor and recipient. Disinterestedness here is not a motivation, but an effect.

3.3.3. Accidental Disinterestedness. The Habitus as a Product of History

The previous two sections presented a reading of Bourdieu, in which the motivation of potential donors only exists in relation to interests – at least expected interest. Disinterestedness, as an expectation of loss in the moment of initiating a gift, does not underlie these transfers. However, if we focus our reading on Bourdieu's construction of the habitus, we can determine transactions in which the practical logic initiates an economic transfer despite an expected loss. Under certain circumstances, Bourdieu's theory offers the possibility of true disinterestedness in the real world. This disinterestedness is however not based on an actor's theoretical reason; it is a defect in the 'economy of symbolic goods'. I will argue in this section that Bourdieu's concept of the hysteresis effect allows disinterestedness to enter social action, but only as an accident of history produced by the habitualisation of past economic realities that do not reflect the economics of current games, rather than taking moral reasoning into consideration, which would allow intended disinterestedness.

In order to conceptualize this disinterestedness, the perspective must be shifted from the direct transaction between two actors to one between the actor and the social framework in which he or she acts. "Every established order tends to reproduce (to very different degrees and with different means) the naturalization of its own arbitrariness" (Bourdieu 1977 [1972]: 164). Bourdieu denotes our capacity of taking for granted the perceived social order as naturally self-evident as 'doxa' (Bourdieu 1977 [1972]: 166). However, there is a discrepancy between the 'logic of practice', in which the naturalization of the social structure takes place, and the scientist's awareness of this social construction within 'logical logic'. The researcher can affirm that the internalized structures do not necessarily reflect the objective structures in spite of the actor's perception. This leads to a discrepancy between social structure and social action.

Bourdieu uses the term hysteresis to capture this discrepancy as a temporal phenomenon connected to social change. Hysteresis describes the inertia of the habitus (Bourdieu 2000 [1997]: 162). Accordingly, the "practices generated by the habitus appear as ill-adapted because they are attuned to an earlier state of the objective conditions" (Bourdieu 1984: 109). Hysteresis occurs both on an individual and on a societal level. If an individual changes position in a social field, like "a nouveau riche, a parvenu or a déclassé" (Bourdieu 2005 [2000]: 86), his or her habitus does not necessarily become immediately equal to the habitus of people who have long held this social position. People internalize habitus within their body throughout their life. There will always be a delay before socially mobile people adjust to their new position, should this adjustment ever occur. Likewise, the change of the society's social setup can lead to hysteresis. Bourdieu refers to his own works on Algeria in the 1960s, when "peasants endowed with a pre-capitalist habitus were suddenly uprooted and forcibly thrown into a capitalist cosmos" (Bourdieu and Wacquant 1992: 130). During this period, the habitus of people had not yet adjusted to the new context and 'pre-capitalist' modes of social interaction continued to be practiced, although the investments that had been valuable in the previous system were no longer compensated.

The hysteresis effect leads to an 'accidental' disinterestedness. Disinterestedness, as a disadvantageous but voluntary economic transaction takes place, when the objective structure of the society or the position of a person in it changes, and the same action, which was previously profitable, becomes unprofitable. The actors continue this unprofitable action because they are used to doing it this way due to their habitus. The hysteresis effect internally contradicts with Bourdieu's interest-based analysis of disinterestedness, which is according to him only possible sociologically "through the encounter between habitus predisposed to disinterestedness and the universes in which disinterestedness is rewarded" (Bourdieu 1998 [1994]: 88). If we consider hysteresis, disinterestedness becomes possible not only in universes in which disinterestedness is rewarded, but also in those in which disinterestedness used to be rewarded.

If we acknowledge that the hysteresis effect is not a phenomenon of short term transitions, only, but one capable of spanning the development of generations, habitus motivated disinterestedness can be strongly entangled in a long-term development of a given society's moral framework. Nevertheless the habitus is subject to change; as is this moral framework. Previous modes of disinterestedness can become lost in a neoliberalizing world, but as long as the habitus preserves previously developed social values, it can maintain disinterestedness in certain spheres of social life. Bourdieu rightly argues with the existence of camouflaged interests, but this does not mean that social life is determined by interest alone. If we read Bourdieu in this way, the later Bourdieu opens up for true disinterestedness, because he withdraws from "nothing is lost, nothing is created" (Caillé 2001 [1994]: 25). Instead people act out of their habitus' dispositions. Benefits from the sum of that action can be awarded, but it is not necessary. A person's capital investment motivated by a moral disposition of the habitus can be much higher than the return of counter gifts, acknowledgement, or prevented sanctions. It is possible that individuals are aware of this functioning; but they do not need to be, since the habitus conceals the process.

With this argument, we maintain the basic moral grounding of Bourdieu's work. In principle people act according to their own interests, but since people do not necessarily question their habitus and the inherited dispositions developed far back in time – dispositions that might even have been objectified as religious laws – the habitus can make people behave against their own interest. They act according to the game, but the winner is not necessarily the one who follows the rules. Morality does not need to make people follow rules out of interest, but the rule itself can turn out to be the motivation to follow. We are not yet in a Kantian philosophy where people base their morality on reason, but where people simply do not question the obligation to follow rules. A moral rule, even when ill adapted to a person's interest, is followed as long as the habitus is sluggish enough to maintain it. Disinterestedness here is a historical accident.

3.4. The Capital of Moral Entitlement. The Negation of Reciprocity

The previous subchapters demonstrated that to a certain extent disinterestedness is possible even within the theory of practice. However, such a perspective remains very restrictive, postulating morality as a reason for acting since a person's disinterested actions are not the result of his or her choice but rather the result of processes in a given field. By confining morality to 'moral capital' we would have to classify ourselves as egoists in a world determined by individual profit seeking. We would have to also accept that we cannot break out even if we wanted, because any attempt to escape would satisfy our interests on another level. Following Adam Smith's approach to morality, 'moral capital' would immediately disqualify the protagonist from being moral at all, since "the diagnostic feature of moral commitments is that at the limit they are held regardless of whether the actor receives praise, indeed even in the face of disapprobation" (Sayer 1999: 413).

Bourdieu is obsessed with finding a purely 'empirical explanation' of the social, which he translates into his economic explanation. His argument that hidden interests can always be revealed in empirics holds up only under a cursory examination. While I do agree that somewhere, there does exist hidden interests for all disinterested action, this should not be mistaken for a sufficient reconstruction of a 'logical logic' of a complete economic transfer of symbolic goods.

Taking the 'economy of symbolic goods' seriously would explain behaviour as an interested disinterestedness only if it had a positive impact on the individual's field positions. The capital spent to signal being disinterested must at the very least equal the symbolic compensation expected, rather than assuming the minimal benefits will be sufficient to compensate for maximal costs. Bourdieu is incapable of explaining any capital flow based on a deliberately expected loss by a person.

In this subchapter, I will argue against Bourdieu and defend the possibility of disinterestedness based on theoretical reasoning, by placing moral arguments within the theory of practice. We are not theoretically bound to Bourdieu's limited perspective on morality, based on a Hobbesian understanding of morality. There is no reason not to confront Bourdieu's thought with the idea that individuals might in some instances aim – consciously or unconsciously, but in the 'logical logic' – to direct their activities towards the disinterested benefit of others, or according to what they perceive as right.

For the moment, the existence of morality is only an assumption that will be theoretically defended in subchapters 3.5, before being confronted with empirical evidence. The following sections will develop the effects of this assumption on the conceptualization of the 'economy of symbolic goods', which will lead us to a new capital: the 'capital of moral entitlement'. This new capital is purposely constructed according to Bourdieu's economic terminology. To a certain degree, it also functions like other capitals, even though it remains a paradoxical capital.

Bourdieu also developed capitals that were not mere reformulations of his ordinary capitals. One example is Bourdieu's suggestion of bodily capital. This form of capital is not produced solely by investment and exchange like economic, social, and cultural capital; rather, it is partially "a gift of nature" (Bourdieu 1984: 206), like beauty or a blow from destiny like cancer.

The Capital of Moral Entitlement

The 'capital of moral entitlement' – or in short 'moral entitlement' – strongly differs from 'moral capital'. While 'moral capital' is accumulated by the donor, the 'capital of moral entitlement' is available to the person in need. Defining a moral-based capital from the perspective of a potential gift recipient is rare in academic literature. Only Ruben Gowricharn (2004: 608) describes an empirical case in which the family members of Surinamese migrants, working in either the United States of America or the Netherlands, hold a "kind of moral capital" to receive remittances. Gowricharn, unfortunately, does not further elaborate this notion, which is exactly what I understand as a 'capital of moral entitlement'. This entitlement is one among others as defined by Amartya Sen (1983: 754): "Entitlements refer to the set of alternative commodity bundles that a person can command in a society using the totality of rights and opportunities that he or she faces". Moral entitlement is therefore the entitlement that refers to the moral framework of a specific society.

'Moral entitlement' is a notion developed by Benedikt Korf (2007) in his work on moral geography of aid transfers, with no basis in Bourdieu's work or the notion of capital. Korf argues that post-disaster aid after the Tsunami in the Indian Ocean in 2004 was not free. Instead, people had to pay a high price by acknowledging "generosity through the staging of gratitude" (Korf 2007: 368), which they expressed for example in theatrical performances, songs and dances for representatives of their donors. Since this gift of aid was not materially reciprocated, the donor wielded symbolic violence over the recipient or, – according to my terminology – the donor is compensated with 'moral capital' leading to the symbolic indebtedness of the recipient. "In unequal reciprocity relations as pertinent in global aid, this expected return for the gift is the acknowledgement of the current order" (Korf 2007: 368), and disaster victims become "passive recipients devoid of their status as fellow citizens on this planet" (Korf 2007: 367).

Korf moves from descriptive ethics of the 'is' to normative ethics of the 'ought', critically suggesting a shift in aid administration to avoid such humiliating effects. He proposes the establishment of a global emergency fund based on global taxation, which would separate aid from the generosity of the donor (Korf 2007: 376). All would be obliged to pay into this impersonal fund replacing current voluntarily donations that are direct reactions to specific disasters. But the most privileged would contribute stronger. Such a system "transforms a beggar or victim to a rightful claimant. Being a rightful claimant to support is something qualitatively very different than being a recipient that simply receives a gift from a generous person" (Korf 2007: 375). While paying into such an aid scheme is a duty rooted in international law, access to it becomes what Korf defines as a moral entitlement, "a claim which is independent of the generosity – and thus the virtuous acts – of the donor" (Korf 2007: 374).

On a meta-ethical level, Korf justifies the possibility of this shift in the moral regime of aid transfers with Onora O'Neill's differentiation between virtue and rights-based duties. O'Neill argues that both duties are possible motivations for social actions, rather than incompatible elements of different philosophical traditions, a differentiation she rejects as "historically anomalous and not well substantiated" (O'Neill 1996: 2). Present aid flows are virtue-based duties, which are weak because they are commendable but not obligatory. Hence, they produce 'moral capital' and embody interests as understood by Bourdieu or Gauthier. Under a global fund, the duties would be strong because they would be based on rights, making their fulfilment compulsory, independent from the interest of the respective donor, and in so doing, they would conflict with Bourdieu and Gauthier.

For Korf, the practical move from virtues to rights in aid is possible, but it requires the auxiliary construction of the global fund in its function of disconnecting recipient and donor and eliminating the symbolic violence produced by the recipients' failures to materially reciprocate. However, if historically, global morals had developed differently and world society had internalized the global right for decent living, the global fund would not be required. The same holds true if we shift into other contexts. If we take a village setting morality has a very different genesis and it is possible for both virtue-based duties and right-based duties to co-exist. Under these circumstances, true disinterestedness, based either on a socially enacted and accepted norm (Kant) or a utilitarian moral ideal of doing good, becomes a potential motivation for action.

Thinking Moral Entitlements in the Economy of Symbolic Goods

In Korf's fictive global fund, moral entitlement would exist as soon as the fund administration recognized a need. Since this moral entitlement exists through acknowledgement, it becomes a symbolic capital for disaster victims. However, while symbolic capital – the acknowledgement of one's endowment with ordinary capitals – and 'moral capital' – the appreciation of the way capital is invested in light of local moral concepts – are positive terms, the 'capital of moral entitlement' is generally negatively related to ordinary capitals, meaning the less capital persons own the higher their endowment with the 'capital of moral entitlement'. An example is, or at least used to be, the indisputable rule in buses that you give your seat to an elderly or handicapped person. The person qualifies for the seat because of low endowment of 'bodily' capital.

Depending on the situation and the social context, capitals of moral entitlement can materialize from the acknowledgement of low endowments of other capitals. Poverty as a result of low income or a disaster, as well as hunger or thirst, can be acknowledged as a persistent shortage of economic capital. People can also need specific goods at particular moments, independent of being poor in general. An example is a cyclist with a puncture; another cyclist passing by can help out with a spare tube. On these occasions, the shortage is based on a lack of opportunities at a particular moment in time. A spare tube can only be bought in a shop and not on the road. If the tube is given for free, the motivation can be attributed to a 'cyclists' moral codex'. It is also possible that the Bourdieusian non-economic, basic capitals are acknowledged as a 'capital of moral entitlement'. Special support can be granted to people with low qualifications (low cultural capital) and newcomers in a field in which they lack social ties (low social capital) can be introduced to other members of the field.

Having a 'capital of moral entitlement' at one's disposal (B) is a resource like any other capital. It can be used to obtain other capitals from the 'social market' to which the entitlement corresponds. A person (A), endowed with a specific economic capital, of which another person (B) is in need, can be requested to perform an economic transfer if the potential donor's (A) ethical dispositions acknowledge the endowment of the person in need (B) with the specific 'capital of moral entitlement'. Like other capitals, this gets spent by utilization. A poor neighbour (B) will lose some of his or her 'capital of moral entitlement' if his or her perceived dependency reduces because of the support received. The person will lose all endowments with 'capital of moral entitlement' for financial support if he or she receives a large donation, which changes the person's socially perceived status from poor to non-poor. The cyclist (B) who received a spare tube will not receive an additional one, because after receiving the first one the cyclist is no longer in need and therefore others (A) will not perceive him or her as entitled anymore.

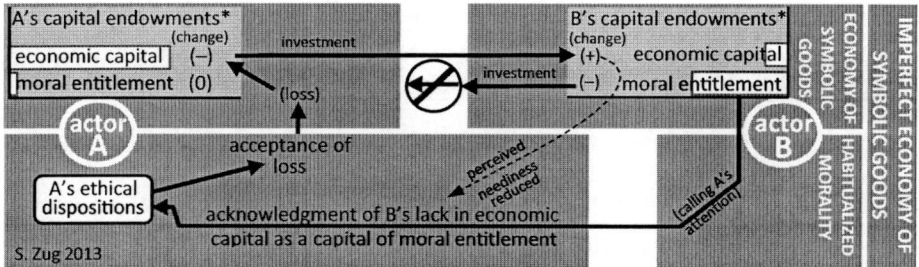

*moral capital is not affected; economic capital can be replaced in the model with flows of other ordinary capitals

Fig. 4: The Capital of Moral Entitlement (Non-Reciprocal True Disinterestedness)

In its function as perceived shortage, the utilization of the 'capital of moral entitlement' (B) leading to the transfer of economic capital (A→B), does not necessarily add any capital to the capital endowments of the donor (A) as required for a full economic transaction (A↔B). The recipient (B) invests the donor's (A) perception of him or her (B) being poor. Since the donor's (A) motivation is based on ethical dispositions, it is his or her moral duty accepting not being reciprocated (B←A). Consequently, the donor (A) experiences and accepts a loss of economic capital.

Being morally entitled to something is not a universal claim for everyone; furthermore, it is limited by material restrictions in the economy of symbolic good. If something like a cyclists' 'tube solidarity' existed, than the 'entitlement to the tube' is only valid if other cyclists have a spare tube. If everyone is poor, there is no one from whom they can claim financial support, even if there was an entitlement to support. Additionally, there can be restrictions in the definition of the moral disposition, which can exclude people constantly or temporarily from the entitlement. Take the example of someone who has internalized the morality that people begging on the street need to be supported by a small donation. However, in the particular person's definition black people can be excluded due to a racist morality. The person could also restrict donations to one person per day, satisfying his or her moral disposition with the first person met, and at the same time placing into perspective the entitlements of all other potential beneficiaries on that specific day.

The 'capital of moral entitlement' allows morality to interfere in the 'economy of symbolic goods' leading to the possibility of true disinterestedness, which is not compensated by hidden interests that can become possible explanations for social action. Accepting true disinterestedness certainly conflicts with a conventional reading of Bourdieu's 'economy of symbolic goods', but if we accept that perfect economies are only theoretical constructions, the 'imperfect economy of symbolic goods' allows us to stop ignoring the human capacity to allow their action to be guided by moral convictions.

The Habitualisation of Morality

The 'capital of moral entitlement' can be thought within the terminology of habitus and field, which Bourdieu binds together tightly as "two modes of existence of the social, [...] history made into a body and history made into a thing" (Bourdieu 1990 [1987]: 190). Individuals inherit disinterested dispositions through their socialization within their families and in fields that attach relevance to these dispositions. They can internalize these ethical dispositions like any other disposition. In the field, these ethical dispositions exist as moral structures, which can be implicit norms or customs as well as objectified social laws of a specific society. These structures are guidelines for daily social action on the operative level and at the same time, the reference standards to evaluate social practice, which also attributes 'moral capital' to people who act morally. Together with the individual's striving for interest, these ethical dispositions form the rules of the game. The field's moral structures determine which action is morally correct, and also whether a social action needs to be perceived as virtue-based or rights-based. If virtue-based, a capital transfer is compensated by 'moral capital'. If rights-based it is not, but rather forces the donor to accept an overall capital loss. Like other social structures, a society's moral structure and ethical dispositions mutually adjust to changes.

Since moral entitlements as capitals are defined within a social field, changes in the moral structure also change moral entitlements. What was previously a moral entitlement can become worthless, and what had no or low 'capital of moral entitlement' can become precious. The changes in employment policies in companies and public administration in South Africa are a very drastic example of changes in a moral framework. During Apartheid, the political system deprived black people of symbolic capital, whereas whites were assured high social status. The moral structure intentionally neglected the black population and it was legally objectified by the regime. Among many other restrictions, access to leading positions was denied to black people. When the ANC took over the government, the morality underlying government decisions was changed. In post-Apartheid South Africa, the colour black remains a symbol of the disadvantaged, the ones who lack economic capital due to historic reasons. A social stratification of society is no longer politically admired; instead, the new objective is to fight a situation perceived to be immoral. Consequently, the policy of 'affirmative action' transforms the colour black into an advantage on the labour market by morally favouring the employment in leading positions of those who had been historically disadvantaged. Under this new morality, the colour black still remains a symbol of low endowment of most ordinary capitals, but transforms into a moral entitlement in the hands of black job applicants. The example shows that changes in the moral structure and the related changes in the social practice informed by the habitus, also affect the valuation of 'capital of moral entitlement'.

Bourdieu repeatedly argues with masking social action under the veil of misrecognition, which makes a person feel acting disinterestedly, despite being guided by interest. With the 'capital of moral entitlement', Bourdieu's assumption that the intention of social action is always interested is loosened, but the motivation does not necessarily need to be replaced by conscious moral reasoning. We can – and for the moment I will do so – conceptualize an individual's morality to be exclusively the unconscious compliance with habitualized social norms. Regardless of a norms' arbitrariness, incomprehensibility, or even proven injustice, people comply because they have learned that this is what must be done. The strict replica of religious laws[35] could be brought under such a habitualized morality. Prayer rituals and dietary laws are not followed simply because people consciously concluded that it was the right or good thing to do, but also because it is what they were told to do, what they learned while becoming a member of the religious field. As long as rules are neither questioned, nor modified, nor newly established by members of the society, an individual's action is not based on reason, but on the habitus. It is only when an individuals' action is not fully determined by the habitus that their social action needs to be explained through a scientific reconstruction of the person's reasons.

---

35 The term religious law does not necessarily mean that the laws are exclusively developed from theological arguments, but they can be formed also from social history. In a dialectical process, a habitus is codified into a religious law and theological concepts are incorporated into the believer's habitus.

The Impact of the Capital of Moral Entitlement on Power

A 'capital of moral entitlement', thus conceived, stands in opposition to symbolic violence and 'moral capital'.[36] 'Moral capital' accumulated by generous individuals improves their positions relative to the positions of the other members within social space and especially relative to those members who benefit from their generosity; thus reproducing social inequality and hierarchies. Having symbolic power in a field allows actors to consciously and subconsciously initiate capital transfers in which they receive the highest return (Peter 2011: 19-20). Symbolic power is a precondition of economic exploitation of the lower classes.

The 'capital of moral entitlement' is explicitly constructed in a way that it does not lead to the accumulation of symbolic power for the donor, because it does not lead to gratefulness. Instead the poor receive certain possibilities for symbolic violence over the rich, since they can blackmail the rich with the image of poverty.

Since rights-based capital transfers are not motivated by interest, economic wealth is transferred from those with higher status to those with lower status without compensation. The total inequality in positions in the social field and especially in the ownership of economic capital can in theory become reduced in societies that have incorporated unconditional moral values of redistribution into their dispositions.

3.5. Reconsidering the Actor's Critical Capacity

In the passage of different modes of exchange in the past subchapters, I started from the interested and reciprocal symbolic exchange in a conventional reading of Bourdieu and moved to an extended reading by modifying the perfect economy. This was accomplished by finding within his framework ideas that contradict Bourdieu's work, which culminated with the assumption that social action does not necessarily need to be purely interest-based. Morality was argued as being a part of a habitus, hence, relevant as a motivation equal to interest, rather than in line with interest. Analytically, this perspective

---

36 This line of argumentation assumes moral values that are directed towards solidarity with people of lower classes. I will not take into consideration moral laws that oblige the poor to give to the rich.

allows us to argue exclusively within a 'logical logic'. Social interaction would now have to be reconstructed by determining the moral structure of a specific field, and not only the economic one. Analysing practices would remain within the sphere of social analysis. From observing social practice, conclusions can be drawn on the moral and economic structure of society and social practice can be explained accordingly. Subjective morality need not be debated, because individual morality merely reflects society's moral structure.

Opening up Bourdieu's thought with a habitualized morality is a response to the critique of economism, but it does not yet address the critique of Bourdieu's reductionist perspective on the capacities of the actor. The objective of this subchapter is to depict the arguments of the reductionist critique and to respond to it by assuming that morality is not only learned and replicated by social actors, but that actors can consciously reflect upon morality and consciously decide upon acting and also reshape their own moral dispositions through individual reasoning. Acknowledging the critical capacity requires questioning the centrality of the habitus for guiding – or to formulate it more controversially: determining – social action.

How Deterministic is the Habitus?

Deterministic readings of Bourdieu's theory, such as "structures produce habitus, which determine practices, which reproduce structures" (Bidet 1979 [1973]: 203; in: Bourdieu and Wacquant 1992: 137), are strongly rejected by Bourdieu himself: "circular and mechanical models of this kind are precisely what the notion of habitus is designed to help us destroy" (Bourdieu and Wacquant 1992: 137). Bourdieu argues instead, that "the immediate fit between habitus and field is only one modality of action if the most prevalent one ('We are empirical,' said Leibniz, by which he meant practical, 'in three quarters of our actions')" (Bourdieu and Wacquant 1992: 131). However, the fourth quarter of actions still remains connected to the habitus even if not directly so. In these situations the actors can consciously decide upon their action and especially in "times of crises, in which the routine adjustment of subjective and objective structures is brutally disrupted" (Bourdieu and Wacquant 1992: 131), they must do so. Bourdieu uses these non-empirical decisions as an argument against a deterministic habitus; but even these actions are not fully independent from the habitus. "Through the habitus, the structure of which it is the product governs practice, not along the paths of mechanical determinism, but within the constraints and limits initially set on its inventions" (Bourdieu 1990 [1980]: 55). Thus the habitus clearly defines the frame of action and makes creativity a restricted creativity.

People are not free to base their course of action on moral convictions, but unconscious habitualized action is replaced by "strategic calculation of costs and benefits, which tends to carry out at a conscious level the operations that habitus carries out in its own way" (Bourdieu and Wacquant 1992: 137). With or without utilizing the habitus, social action remains, complying with the interested rule of the game. "It is a world where behaviour has its causes, but actors are not allowed their reasons" (Jenkins 1992: 61). In conscious decisions, the economic 'logical logic', however can become clearer to people. Within the habitus, people can choose only the immediate implementation of an action and not between social actions with opposing economic effects. Through attributing a charge of determinism to Bourdieu, this does not imply that every single action is foreseeable, but that Bourdieu's "attempt to mediate between objectivism and subjectivism, structuralism and action theory, finally fails because of the predominance of social structures" (Celikates 2009: 72, own translation).

Several authors argue that social reality is reduced when social actors are exclusively conceptualized as consciously or unconsciously deciding to perform instrumentally rational behaviours (e.g. Alexander 1995; Celikates 2009; Jenkins 1992; Lahire 2011 [2001]; Sayer 2005; Sewell 1992).

> Neither Bourdieu nor many of his enthusiastic readers seem to understand what a multidimensional social theory actually requires; how individual action and its social environments can be interrelated without reduction; how ideal and material dimensions can be brought into play without sacrificing their autonomy and reducing one to the other (Alexander 1995: 193).

A comprehensive grasp of a 'logical logic' of empirical interaction, must on the one hand acknowledge – as requested by Bourdieu – that social reality is not necessarily what the individual perceives social reality to be, but additionally, it needs to take into consideration – what Bourdieu denies and what Alexander calls the "ideal dimension" – that people can act on conscious reasoning.

Alexander illustrates the weakness of Bourdieu's approach by applying his thought to political systems. Bourdieu produces an image of a vertical society, of society equated with stratification, with struggles dictated by scarcity and regulated by the egoism of supply and demand. There is no horizontality, neither cross-class solidarities nor national identities which provide opportunities for inclusion, much less any conception of an institutionalized ideal of civility or universalism (Alexander 1995: 187).

Bourdieu therefore lacks a way to distinguish in "moral or political terms, an authoritarian from a democratic order, an inegalitarian democracy from a more socially just one, or even a fascist society that strives for distinction from a totalitarianism of a leftist kind" (Alexander 1995: 187). Political movements – of which Bourdieu was a part – would then not be grounded on ideas of reformers, like Gandhi, Martin Luther King, Jesus, or Karl Marx but function merely as symbolic strategies designed to profit only these very social movement leaders (Alexander 1995: 192). The weakness of Bourdieu's conceptualization becomes obvious in his own analysis of political movements, at a time when he was already actively participating in them. Rather than explaining the workers movement in 1997 within his theoretical framework, he called it a "social miracle" (Bourdieu 1998: 88), indicating that even he had reached the empirical limits of the applicability of his own thought (Ejderyan 2009: 52).

The Habitus as the Entry Point for Morality into the Theory of Practice

Sayer argues, that the concept of habitus – the basic guiding element for people's action in Bourdieu's approach – "is a product of sociological disciplinary imperialism, reflecting the discipline's competition with and aversion to psychology and biology" (Sayer 2005: 50). He suggests keeping the habitus as a central concept and "moderat[ing] the claims made by Bourdieu for the explanatory power of the concept, and to supplement it with a recognition of the close relationships between dispositions and conscious deliberation, the powers of agency and mundane reflexivity, and by addressing actors' normative orientations, emotions and commitments" (Sayer 2005: 50). By "softening the unnecessarily sharp distinction between bodily and cognitive processes" (Ignatow 2009: 99) the habitus remains a very useful tool to demonstrate that motivations – both moral and economic ones – can become internalized into dispositions and make people act according to the structures of the field, while the underlying logic can become masked. At the same time, actors can consciously break out, not only by taking rational decisions – in the sense of the rules of the game – but they can act consciously disinterested, producing a 'practical logic' based on conviction. This subjective conviction becomes the motivation and the explanation in the 'logical logic', while the habitus loses its determining impact on social actors.

A Plea for the Actors Moral Capacities

Actors are not in a homogeneous world, they have the capacity to act in different fields and hence their habitus is also influenced by social activities in these various fields. Bourdieu himself acknowledges the existence of a "habitus divided against itself, in constant negotiation with itself and with its ambivalence, and therefore doomed to a kind of duplication, to a double perception of self, to successive allegiances and multiple identities" (Bourdieu 1999: 511; cited in: Sayer 2005: 26). In these situations, as well as when the outcome of an action is very unsure, people can neither trust their habitus, nor their consciousness based on their 'feeling for the game'. They must reflect and weigh the different options of acting against each other. It is precisely during these moments of uncertainty that a conscious reasoning must enter into action. If 'objectively' analysed, this reasoning can be in contradiction with the economic sense of the game, because the outcomes are not sufficiently clear, at the conscious and subconscious level, to make decisions. The actor's 'internal conversations' (Sayer 2005: 30) are important elements in resolving a specific situation and are important for its scientific reconstruction.

Acknowledging the reflexive capacity of the individual actor, would give the individual possibilities to consciously act in a specific moment against the learned dispositions of his habitus, but it would also allow the individual to actively interfere in the development of his or her own habitus. It is thus possible for the habitus to become an object of reflection, rather than the automatic result of the individual's trajectory.

An approach which considers moral motivations alongside interest renders the conceptualization of the social more complex and requires additional theoretical concepts to grasp the interconnectedness of social action's different motivations. However, proceeding thusly will also better grasp related weaknesses in Bourdieu's approach including the conceptualization of multiplicity, the contradiction of social structures and dispositions, as well as the conceptualization of social change. In this book, Luc Boltanski's conceptualizations will be consulted to theoretically allow lay normativity to enter the 'economy of symbolic goods'.

3.6. Using Boltanski to Justify Disinterestedness: Conceptualizing the Social beyond Power

Extending the 'economy of symbolic goods' with an actor endowed with critical capacities requires a conceptualization of the negotiation between interested and morally grounded action. Rather than only stating the possibility of moral action, I will develop a framework that also takes into consideration the historical genesis of society's moral structures.

I will refer to the work of Luc Boltanski, who allows such an integration. Even though his focus is on the critical capacities of actors, he does not deny the relevance of interest per se. Boltanski sees his work as "a bridge between the social sciences and moral philosophy" (Boltanski and Thévenot 2000: 208). As such it can be used to bridge the gap between the 'economy of symbolic goods' and the morality of actors. I will first elaborate on the differences between Boltanski's and Bourdieu's approach (3.6.1), and then proceed to present Boltanski's work on justification, which allows conceptualizing morality in social space (3.6.2). In section 3.6.3, I will present Boltanski's rough ideas of convergence between his and Bourdieu's concepts of the social, and finally I will develop a unification of the two programmes using Bourdieu's terminology (3.6.4).

3.6.1. Critical Sociology versus Sociology of Critique

Combining Bourdieu's theory with the work of Boltanski has a very special dynamic, since Boltanski collaborated very closely with Bourdieu in his early scientific career (e.g. Diaz-Bone and Thévenot 2010: 10). Since the late 1960s, Boltanski contributed to the work of Bourdieu's circle of scholars and finally between 1974 and 1976 they published joint articles, predominantly in Bourdieu's published journal *Acts de la Recherches en Sciences Sociales*; the most well-known being *La production de l'idéologie dominante* (Bourdieu and Boltanski 1976; cf. Bogusz 2010: 18-25). However, Boltanski should not be misinterpreted as a scholar following in Bourdieu's footsteps. Later, with his doctoral thesis, which was not supervised by Bourdieu, Boltanski left the close circle around Bourdieu.

> Factually, one can say that there are [...] two Boltanskis. The first used to be the dedicated, efficient and inventive collaborator of Pierre Bourdieu. [...] Boltanski called Bourdieu the boss – le patron, with no irony at all. [...] And there is another

Boltanski: the sociological master who seemed to reinvent sociology overnight in the late 1980s with his partner Laurent Thévenot, around the concept of justification. A new lexicon was created to give an account of radically new objects. A new style that associated original philosophical complicities with the refusal of the ideological commitment usually linked to critical sociology (Fabiani 2011: 401).

Philippe Corcuff (2003: 44) rightly demands Boltanski's approach be understood as radically post-Bourdieusian; just as one must take Bourdieu's approach as radically post-Marxist.

Boltanski's theoretical program forms, together with Bruno Latour's and Michel Callon's work in the sociology of science, French pragmatic sociology (Bénatouïl 1999: 380). Boltanski is oriented towards American Pragmatism that argues:

> While subjects coordinate themselves automatically and almost without reflection as long as there are no perturbations in their joint action, they only have to direct their attention toward hitherto routinely presumed cognitive and moral assumptions when such disruptions occur (Honneth 2010: 377).

Pragmatic sociology is a 'sociology of critique' in which the focus is put on the analysis of the individuals' questioning of the social. Morality becomes a feature of the subjects rather than embedded only in the scholars' critique of the social. As such, pragmatic sociology is strongly opposed to Bourdieu's critical sociology.

Pragmatic sociology is rooted in a critique of critical sociology. The centre of this critique is Bourdieu's conceptualization of the actor. Boltanski argues that Bourdieu conceptualizes the subject only as a "cultural dope" (Boltanski 2011 [2009]: 20) or as an agent rather than an actor, since being subject to structures, strips the subject of his critical capacities (Boltanski 2011 [2009]: 43).

For Boltanski, highlighting the critical capacity of the individual translates into a restriction of the critical self-conception of the social scientist:

> We have to give up the idea that we can have the last word by producing – and imposing on the actors – more powerful reports than the ones they themselves are able to produce; in other words, we have to abandon the way classical sociology has conceptualized the asymmetry between researchers and actors (Boltanski 2012 [1990]: 28).

His argument questions the conceptualization of the 'logic of logic' as the only valid and unveiled truth of the social and consequently the position of the scholar as the only legitimate critic of the social. By that he implicitly questions Bourdieu's political engagement on the basis that he reveals social hidden logics while ignoring the critical capacities of actors.

In his conception of sociology, Boltanski instead pushed for a sociology that tries to understand judgments of people as a constitutive element of the social.

> We take [people's] arguments seriously, along with the proofs they offer; we do not attempt to diminish or disqualify them by contrasting them with a more powerful interpretation. [...] Sociologists of critique [...] give up the possibility of basing their own interpretations on a stable form, one that could be constructed by exploiting the material resources at their disposal, a form of what classical sociologists commonly call 'social structure'; instead, they allow themselves to be guided by the stable forms that appear in the actors' accounts (Boltanski 2012 [1990]: 30).

Legitimate critique of the social becomes restricted to the critique that is developed by individuals and its possible scientific reconstruction.

3.6.2. Justification: the Antithesis of Interest

Boltanski is best known for his work on justification, which he developed with Laurent Thévenot. Justification can be considered the antithesis to Bourdieu's formulation of interest, since social practice based in a process of justification is the result of a negotiation between social actors about its moral correctness. This section will describe the broad outlines of the processes of justification as one possibility of social action among others.

The Functioning of Justification

Justification-based action only takes place in situations where people are in disagreement but want to come to a joint solution instead of solving the problem by force. Criticizing a person's actions as compared to 'how one should act' triggers the cycle of critique and justification, giving the counterpart the possibility to react and deliver arguments supporting his mode of action. In order for people to mutually agree on something, the relevant arguments must be presented and agreed upon. The cycle of critique and justification is an open process in which the actors refer to universal principles of equivalence. The universality of these principles does not mean that they are universally defined once and for all, since "the model does not posit any universals, [...] but poses universality as a horizon searched by agents" (Boltanski and Thévenot 2000: 210). Universality therefore is a social construction built up over time by the subjects themselves. They make certain principles universal. An individual's action can thus be based on these socially produced universal principles, rather than determined by interest or predetermined normative structures.

Since there are multiple universal principles that can be valid in the same situation, there are always several solutions to each dispute, even if all the actors involved agree on the universality of every single principle. Multiplicity is conceptualized by Boltanski and Thévenot by defining six different worlds (the inspired, the domestic, the civic, the market, and the industrial world, as well as the world of fame). Each world contains a polity[37], a system of justification, to which people can refer to in specific situations. The characteristics of each polity are developed from a philosophical work (St. Augustine, Jacques Bénigne Bossuet, Thomas Hobbes, Jacques Rousseau, Adam Smith, Claude-Henri de Saint-Simon), all of which subscribe to the principle of a common humanity. This is a prerequisite for the possible emergence of a joint agreement among social actors in opposition to slavery or other systems in which a decision is imposed on the social actors (Boltanski and Thévenot 2006 [1991]: 107). They therefore "set aside philosophies of either a realist or a critical bent that regard social order as emanating from power and domination in favour of constructions whose goal is to build equilibrium within the polity" (Boltanski and Thévenot 2006 [1991]: 13).

The main analytical term in their system is 'worths', which "are based on general principles of equivalence whose validity transcends the present situation, and they can thus be the basis for agreements that are acceptable to all, agreements oriented towards universality" (Boltanski 2012 [1990]: 48). Worth is a notion that is attributed to the status of things or persons. "For each world, it is possible to establish a *list of subjects*, most qualified by their state of worth (*unworthy beings* or *worthy beings*)" (Boltanski and Thévenot 2006 [1991]: 142). A worthy person is the head of a household in the domestic world, or a highly qualified worker in the industrial world. In opposition to Bourdieu's conceptualization of the field, worthiness in Boltanski's approach does not focus on people's efforts to achieve high positions, but on the discrepancy between what could be called de facto and de jure worthiness. The father of a family who does not care for his children properly does not fulfil the expecta-

---

37 Boltanski uses the French term 'cité' which is mostly translated to English as polity or city.

tions placed on him within the domestic world, leading to a discrepancy between the high worthiness of his position and the evaluation of his worthiness in daily practice.

The discrepancies between a perceived and the correct order of people and things allows for the criticism of the order, and consequently, of individual behaviour. In the industrial world, people are ordered according to the higher common principles: "efficiency of beings, their performance, their productivity, and their capacity to ensure normal operations and to respond usefully to needs" (Boltanski and Thévenot 2006 [1991]: 204). An employee who does not perform as expected can be questioned by the employer, hence, a contention arises.

> A contention will [...] originate in a challenge to the view according to which the prevailing situation is well ordered, and in a demand for a readjustment of worths. For example, a situation is not harmonious if in that situation the way a qualified operator works is not adapted to the capacities of his machine (Boltanski and Thévenot 2006 [1991]: 132).

A 'contention' that takes place exclusively in one polity – in this case the industrial one – can be solved by putting it to a 'test' in which the employee is given the possibility of defending her (or his) performance. The employee could argue that her low productivity is due to technical problems with the machine, which, if approved by the employer, would call into question the machine's worth, while re-establishing the employee's worth, by acknowledging a state of equilibrium between her position in the industrial world and her productivity.

During a cycle of critique and justification, people can also shift their arguments into a different polity, which is a significantly different process from a 'test'. Here people do not argue with the order of a particular world, but they question the 'validity of the test', in other words they question whether a particular situation belongs to the world to which it had been attributed so far (Boltanski and Thévenot 2006 [1991]: 216). Questioning validity is possible, because things and people can be attributed to different worlds. The authors give an example, which can be seen as a continuation of the previous example (Boltanski and Thévenot 2006 [1991]: 218). They describe a situation in which an employee gets fired for professional misconduct. This situation is based in the industrial world and should be solved in the industrial polity. As she is getting fired, the employee refers to a family photo on the employer's desk, implicitly requesting the employer not to fire her because of her family situation. The employee uses an argument that does not justify her performance in the industrial world, but instead, refers to a principle in the domestic polity. The decision to fire the employee therefore requires considering the contradictory worth of a single person, in the same situation, but in different polities.

From Boltanski's example, one can deduct three solutions to the problem, in which all involved parties agree on the decision taken. First, the employer fires the employee and the employee accepts because she agrees on her poor performance in the industrial world. Second, the employee does not get fired; since the employer acknowledges that her family situation morally justifies continued employment, even though the company could earn more economic benefits if the person were replaced. The notion of 'capital of moral entitlement' can be localized in this situation, since an argument convinces an actor to act disinterestedly. A third solution 'in justice' would require both parties find a compromise between polities, such as keeping the person employed, satisfying the domestic argument to a certain degree, but transferring her to another position with fewer responsibilities, thus reducing the impact of the employee's poor performance on company production.

Transferring Boltanski's Polities to a Non-French Context

The central idea, which helps create the framework of a morally inspired 'imperfect economy of symbolic goods', is that through the process of justification, people refer to universal principles of conduct. They are universal in that they are understood by the actors; however, they are at the same time neither singular nor deterministic; but rather, the result of social processes of negotiation. The six polities developed by Boltanski and Thévenot are a very open attempt to deduct modes for people's normative evaluations of practices from philosophy. Boltanski and Thévenot do not see these polities as the only possible ones and they went on to define other polities in later work.[38] They also explicitly state that the polities they developed refer only to a French context:

---

38 In *The New Spirit of Capitalism* Boltanski and Chiapello define a 'projective city' (city and polity are synonymous, both are translations of the original French term 'cite'), which refers to engagement and creativity within networks (Boltanski and Chiapello [1999]: 92). Lafaye and Thévenot define a 'cité verte', which refers to the environmental consciousness of people's priorities (Lafaye and Thévenot 1993).

> These models reflect the way the competence for justice that can be attested in our society today has taken shape; they cannot be extended to other societies or to other eras without a detailed analytical effort to test them against arguments developed by persons belonging to these societies, and against the situations in which these arguments could be mobilized, insofar as we have access to such information (Boltanski 2012 [1990]: 39).

Thus, analysing justifications and decision-making in a Sudanese society would require reworking the polities in depth or – even better – creating polities based on philosophies that guide the actions of Sudanese people. Such research would contribute to creating a new typology – a Sudanese model of justification. The objective of my research is not to develop a comprehensive system of all possible polities. Instead, my aim is to analyse a specific sphere of society – the 'neighbourly waterscape' – in which interests and reason jointly influence social action. Considering that Boltanski and Thévenot's polities are only based on an assumption of symmetry between philosophy and practice, I will not refer to these clearly defined polities. Instead, I will try to understand justification as a negotiation process between non-deterministic arguments that refer to different concepts. Furthermore, these concepts are perceived by the actors as universal, and can therefore be used as arguments. Therefore, the polities used will remain implicit. However, the work is a small contribution to the bottom-up development of these polities, which also acknowledges Honneth's critique of Boltanski's and Thévenot's way of determining the polities from philosophical texts. He argues that instead of finding

> the roots and prototypes of presently influential conceptions of social justice [...] in political philosophy, [...] a still more obvious approach would of course be to empirically identify the currently prevalent conceptions of just coexistence, be it through panel discussions, appropriately designed interviews or questionnaires (Honneth 2010: 380).

3.6.3. Integrating Justifications and the Economy of Symbolic Goods

Bourdieu's theory of practice and Boltanski's work on justification start with very different assumptions on the motivation for social action. While in Bourdieu's 'economy of symbolic goods', interests dominate social action, Boltanski argues that people adjust their actions to universal principles on which concerned actors agree, regardless of individual interest. Still I will argue in this section that a combination of both theories is possible and valuable to expand the theory of practice by integrating morality. Already in 1999, Bénatouïl called for such an approach and argued that "critical and pragmatic sociology can and should [...] exchange their conceptual tools" (Bénatouïl 1999: 391). However, as Susen recently remarked, a cross-fertilization hardly took place: "In the literature there is a profound gap, and little in the way of constructive dialogue, between Bourdieu's 'critical sociology' and Boltanski's 'sociology of critique'" (Susen 2011: 454), although Boltanski himself later pushed for such a dialogue in 2009 (Boltanski 2011 [2009]: XI).

The Regimes of Actions. Boltanski's Attempt to Formulate a Comprehensive Social Theory

Combining the theory of practice with Boltanski's justifications is possible, because Boltanski did not conceptualize justifications as the one and only mode in which action takes place. In his early work, Boltanski (2012 [1990]) conceptualized justification within the regime of justice. To this regime, he added the regimes of fairness, violence, and love, three alternative modes of action. Consequently, not all social action is based on the mutual process of agreeing on a higher principle. In the regime of violence, actors act in disagreement with their counterpart (Boltanski 2012 [1990]: 72), in the regime of fairness action is based on a tacit agreement (Boltanski 2012 [1990]: 69), and acting in the regime of love takes place in a peaceful situation in which people do not strive for equivalence (Boltanski 2012 [1990]: 114). Hence, not all regimes contain an active process of negotiation. The four different regimes are not stable in a society. "The idea of a universe operating wholly according to justice is as utopian as the idea of a universe totally given over to violence is dystopian" (Boltanski 2012 [1990]: 68). Instead, social action can be shifted between the different regimes.[39]

When conceptualizing the four regimes, Boltanski lays out a comprehensive theory of the social. However, his theory remained very partial because he mainly limited his elaborations to the regime of justice, while he hardly developed violence and fairness, the regimes closest to Bourdieu's work. In *Love*

---

39 E.g. if people question a common practice, the action is moved from the regime of fairness into the regime of justice, in which the practice is renegotiated. If actors neither confirm the old practice, nor agree on a new one, and people still act, this action is moved to the regime of violence. Action is moved from the regime of love to the regime of justice or violence, when people question the unconditionality of this love.

and Justice (Boltanski 2012 [1990]), their basic structures were only outlined. From then on, they served merely as a place holder for social activities that did not fit into the regime of justice, like when people acted either under an unquestioned, implicit agreement, or when they acted against each other without aiming for mutual understanding. Consequently, in his scientific work only a part of what he considered to be the social was finally conceptualized.

The Practical and the Meta-Pragmatic Register. Boltanski's Search for Synergy

In his recent book *On Critique* (2011 [2009]), Boltanski stresses the relevance of action that does not take place within the regime of justice. He substantially criticizes French pragmatic sociology, hence, the theoretical program which is a substantial part of his own work:

> The primacy given to pragmatism over structuralism then assumes the form of a quasi-ethics […]. It contrasts bad structuralism – macro, holistic, totalizing (even totalitarian), marred by 'legalism', ignoring the humanity of human beings and the modalities of their engagement in action – with good pragmatism, respectful of persons and the situations in which they interact, in the 'here and now', where they commit their capacities for invention, experimentation and interpretation to the search for a form of 'living together' (Boltanski 2011 [2009]: 53).

He argues that such a position leads to an "overestimation of the capacities possessed by actors to create meaning" (Boltanski 2011 [2009]: 54), which contradicts the multiplicity of regimes he developed in *Love and Justice*. He takes partial responsibility for this development by admitting, that

> these pluralist positions were not expressed with sufficient force (and were perhaps insufficiently clarified at the conceptual level) to prevent the framework presented in *On Justification* giving rise to re-appropriations which tend to employ it as if it made it possible to effect a closure on reality and hence render it in some sense calculable (Boltanski 2011 [2009]: 56).

Considering Boltanski's own scientific career, which includes his emancipation from Bourdieu, he makes a remarkable step in the scientific field: he argues for a unification of pragmatic sociology and critical sociology. He introduces a system that attributes social action to two registers: the 'meta-pragmatic register' and the 'practical register'. Bourdieu's work is given a pride of place within this framework because Boltanski constructs the 'practical register' explicitly from Bourdieu's 'theory of practice' (Boltanski 2011 [2009]: 62). The principle distinction between the 'practical' and the 'meta-pragmatic register' is the degree of reflexivity underlying the action. Reflexivity considers that "human beings are not content to act or react to the actions of others. They review their own actions or those of others in order to make judgments on them, often hinging on the issue of good and evil – that is, *moral judgments*" (Boltanski 2011 [2009]: 3).

The boundaries of Boltanski's early four regimes are reflected in the distinction of the two registers, without Boltanski explicitly clarifying the relationship between the old and new typology.[40] One could even argue that these new registers are replacing the four old regimes of action. The 'meta-pragmatic register' can be understood synonymously with the regime of justice that Boltanski pulled from his own publication *On Justification*. Justice however is no longer defined in opposition to love, fairness, and violence, in other words, the comprehensive framework Boltanski developed in *Love and Justice*. It has become defined in opposition to the 'practical register' alone. The absence of reflexivity is the element that distinguishes the 'practical register' from the 'meta-pragmatic register', and which also distinguished the regime of justice from the other regimes in Boltanski's old system.[41] The 'meta-pragmatic register' is however not just the ensemble of the regimes love, fairness, and violence; it is an alternative conception to distinguish non-reflexive action from a reflexive one, which for example completely ignores the possibility of social action being based on unconditional love.[42]

Although Boltanski grounds the 'practical register' in Bourdieu's theory, he does not acknowledge all of Bourdieu's assumptions. This is of fundamental importance, because by conceptualizing the actor bound to interests, the 'meta-pragmatic register' would be denied existence. However, Boltanski closely echoes some of Bourdieu's concepts. He argues that

---

40 The new classification uses the term 'register' instead of 'regime'. I assume he changed the terminology in order to express that these two registers, are not additional regimes, but rather, that they replace the former regimes. He is not completely consistent in the new use of the term 'register' and at one point, refers to a 'practical regime' (Boltanski 2011 [2009]: 65).

41 Whenever people reflect on their practice in these regimes they push action towards the regime of justice, e.g. when the fairness of social action is questioned, when people want to stop violence by starting a dialogue, or when love turns from unconditional *agape* into *philia* in the sense of friendship, which is "based on the recognition of reciprocal merit [implying] that friends must be equally able to evaluate another person's merits, and thus that they share a common knowledge about what constitutes worth" (Boltanski 2012 [1990]: 105).

42 Not insisting on love can be interpreted as a step towards Bourdieu, since the regime of love, is at least as contradictory with Bourdieu as justification, since it refers to the denial of any interest per-se.

> one of [the] important characteristics [of actions in the practical register] is that the people involved in the course of action act as if they more or less knew what was going on – what they are in the process of doing – and/or as if the others, or some others, in whom one can have confidence, knew it (Boltanski 2011 [2009]: 62).

What Bourdieu would call the rules of the game are in Boltanski's formulation 'tacit agreements', which strongly reflect the equivalence contained in the fairness regime. These agreements go beyond Bourdieu's habitus, because they can also be the result of "more or less stable states of mind, capable of giving rise to qualification and even, in public relations, of being extended into justifications" (Boltanski 2011 [2009]: 63). Boltanski does not use the term 'habitus', but rather refers to "habits" or "dispositions" (e.g. Boltanski 2011 [2009]: 81). First, this has to do with the absolute claims with which Bourdieu uses the term, which by definition excludes the possibility of a shift of action into a 'meta-pragmatic register'. Second, Boltanski rejects Bourdieu's idea of the habitus being generalized into a class habitus (Boltanski 2011 [2009]: 144).

Impact of the Rapprochement of the two Theories

With this new framework Boltanski aims on "providing tools that make it possible to reduce the tension between critical sociology and the sociology of critique. It therewith pursues an objective of pacification" (Boltanski 2011 [2009]: XI). From his own perspective the compromise requires stepping back from the work in *Love and Justice (2012 [1990])*, by defining the four regimes of action. However, he does not have to reformulate his central work on justification and the idea that social action can take place in different spheres. Beyond the theoretical advancement of the pacification, he can benefit in the scientific field, since he has emancipated himself from France's 'mainstream' pragmatic sociology.

Boltanski's plea is not restricted to pragmatic sociologists, but is also directed explicitly at critical sociologists. He argues,

> To be credible today, sociologies directed towards a metacritique of domination should draw the lessons of past failures and, taking heed of the different arguments that have just been developed, equip themselves with an analytical framework that makes it possible to integrate the contributions of what we have called the overarch-

ing programme, on the one hand, and the pragmatic programme, on the other (Boltanski 2011 [2009]: 44).[43]

The impact of such a compromise is significantly higher on the theory of practice than on Boltanski's own work. Integrating the 'meta-pragmatic register' always requires adjusting Bourdieu's assumptions, because it incorporates an element which Bourdieu assumes to be irrelevant in an explanation of the social, rather than an element he had simply not yet developed. A unification of the two theories does not only shift some activities from the 'economy of symbolic goods' into the 'meta-pragmatic register'. Rather, the 'economy of symbolic goods' itself is changed, since the people's habitus is produced by experience, regardless of the register in which practice takes place. A habitus influenced in the meta-'pragmatic register', consequently, will also change practices in the 'economy of symbolic goods'.

The convergence of the two theories and the required changes of the assumption provide the basis for allowing morality to 'infiltrate' into the 'economy of symbolic goods'. Consequently, Boltanski's suggestion constitutes a theoretical solution for the reductionist critique of Bourdieu's approach and a possibility to conceptualize the gift of water beyond economic exchange.

3.6.4. Rendering the Model Precisely

Thinking justification in relation to the 'economy of symbolic goods' requires elaborating an interface between the two registers, an example of which will be developed in this section. This section aims on developing such an interface. Since I aim to integrate Boltanski's conceptualizations of critique into Bourdieu, and not vice versa, I will consequently prefer Bourdieu's terminology over Boltanski's, and use Boltanski's terms only if Bourdieu has no equivalent. I consequently will replace the 'practical register' with Bourdieu's term '(imperfect) economy of symbolic goods'.[44]

---

43 Both the notion of 'sociologies directed towards a metacritique of domination' and the 'overarching program' are to be read as two metaphors for Bourdieusian critical sociology. 'Sociology directed towards a metacritique of domination' refers to Bourdieu's objective to criticize power asymmetries and 'overarching character' refers to the distance at which it holds itself from the critical capacities developed by actors in everyday situations (e.g. Boltanski 2011 [2009]: 43).

44 Boltanski's practical register, as the sphere where practice takes place, is nothing more than the economy of symbolic goods, but an economy of symbolic goods that is only a partial sphere of social interaction. Since the functions that Boltanski describes in the meta-pragmatic register are absent in Bourdieu's theory, Boltanski's terminology will be used to describe justifications of so-

Boltanski does not fully develop the interface between the 'meta-pragmatic register' and the 'economy of symbolic goods', since he sees the whole book as a "series of remarks" rather than as a "finished work" (Boltanski 2011 [2009]: IX). Nevertheless he elaborates some first basic terms, of which the notion of tolerance is of central interest. "To speak of tolerance means, roughly, that for as long as possible people turn a blind eye to the diversity of usages, to the differences between different ways of doing. These differences can be seen and known without being registered" (Boltanski 2011 [2009]: 63). The existence of this tolerance is not based on moral convictions of behavioural diversity, but related to the risk of being sanctioned oneself. Criticizing other's behaviour, which deviates from one's own expectation, can result in a counter critique which goes against the interest of the person, and reduces his or her willingness to criticize. Boltanski does not use the term 'interest', but 'tolerance' can be conceptualized as a conflict between the selfish behaviour to maximize individual interest – also in Bourdieu's sense as striving for positions and capital – and the individual's moral convictions. It is much easier to take moral action if one benefits oneself. The striving for interest in daily practice therefore stabilizes the action in the 'economy of symbolic goods'. However, the interests are not necessarily strong enough to restrict action to the 'economy of symbolic goods', it only works as long as "antagonisms remain below a certain threshold of tolerance" (Boltanski 2011 [2009]: 65). From the moment an actor has reached the own limit of tolerance for an action against a normative expectation, a critique is formulated towards the 'misbehaving' actor, thus triggering the process of critique and justification.

Developing Boltanski's integration beyond his elaborations allows developing a model of the relation between the 'economy of symbolic goods' and the 'meta-pragmatic register'. Most social interaction is located in the 'economy of symbolic goods', but action can be shifted to the 'meta-pragmatic register' in case of a conflict in the 'economy of symbolic goods', which the actors are willing to solve through arguments.

---

cial actors. Boltanski's two registers are hence referred to as the 'economy of symbolic goods' and the 'meta-pragmatic register'.

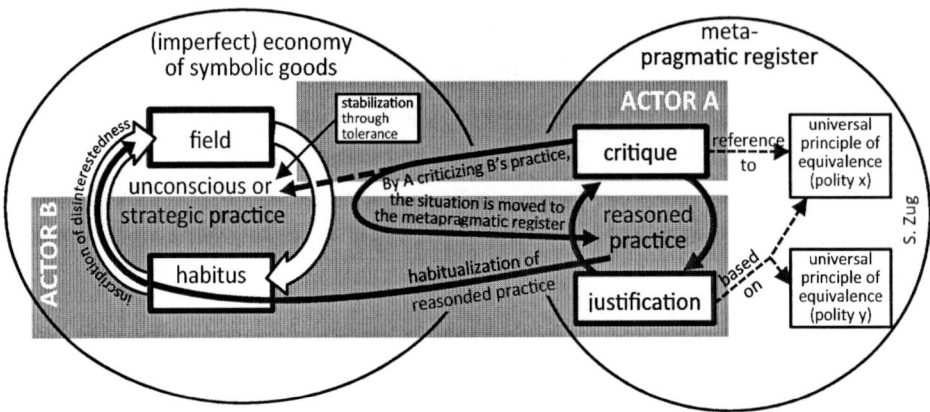

Fig. 5: The Internalization of Reason from the Meta-Pragmatic Register into the Economy of Symbolic Goods

The process is started by an actor A, who is discontent with the practice of the actor B. By formulating a critique, A moves the habitualized action of B from the 'economy of symbolic goods' into the 'meta-pragmatic register'. In the 'meta-pragmatic register', A justifies his or her critique with a universal principle of equivalence, and B justifies his or her action with the same principle or with a principle from another polity. If actors agree on the joint justification, social practice becomes reasoned practice. If the criticized actor B can convince the criticizing actor A that his or her actions are correct, A's habitus will be reinforced and the following actions of a similar nature can be brought back under an unchanged habitus in the economy of the symbolic goods. Correspondingly, if A's critique gets acknowledged by B, the new reasoned practice is superior to the previous habitualized one. However, after a while both actors can become increasingly used to this reasoned practice and, finally, take it for granted. People (A and B) stop consciously reasoning, which leads to a habitualisation of the agreement established in the most relevant polity and a shift of the situation from the 'meta-pragmatic register' to the 'imperfect economy of symbolic goods'.

Since habitus and field are mutually constitutive (e.g. Bourdieu 1990 [1987]: 190), the habitus of the individual actors becomes more and more incorporated into the structure of the field as rules of the game, which will consequently be unconsciously followed by the actors. This process makes the 'economy of symbolic goods' imperfect, because the new 'logical logic' is not entirely based on capital exchange, but it contains principles that are based on moral reason. It is this habitualisation of moral reasoned practice, which over time can disconnect individual reasoning of practice from practice itself.

Although social action is partially grounded in individual reason, the process of habitualisation can require the scientific reconstruction of social action as a 'logical logic'. People might just be able to argue, 'that this the way we do things', without being able to reconnect the practice (which contains moral elements rather than only interest-based ones) to the universal principles that defined the action way back in time, especially if the action is habitualized over generations. Reconstruction of the original universal principles in such a situation requires a multidisciplinary approach looking empirically on the practice and at the same time historically reconstructing the genesis of the interested but morally influenced habitus.

It needs to be underlined for this framework, that there is a difference between the rules of the game in the field and the socially constructed universal principles in the 'meta-pragmatic register'. The universal principles are reason-based; they are developed in a conscious and theoretical debate. The rules of the game reflect this moral framework, but they are not equal to it. Rather, they represent the practical compromise between interests and morals. Universal principles and the rules of the game therefore can be contradictory, which consequently is the precondition for critique. The difference can be seen as a similar restriction as hysteresis, which claims that the interested habitus can reflect interests that were relevant in the past only. The difference here is not only time but the multiplicity of polities and the continuous adjustments of reasoned practice with interest.

The Limits of Arguments: Imperfection in the Meta-Pragmatic Register

The developed frame demonstrates that arguments are valuable and that they can morally change the flow of action; however, critique and justification also remain actions that take place in a social framework in which people are not equal. Celikates[45] criticizes the fact that despite Boltanski's acknowledgement that not all actors have similarly strongly developed critical capacities, he does not explain "how these differences in the application of reflexive capacities develop and on what they are based" (Celikates 2009: 168). Celikates introduces the term 'structural deficit in reflexivity' which refers to the status in

---

45 All direct citations of Celikates are my own translations.

which actors "cannot grasp 'problematic' situations (e.g. unjust situations) […]; hence these situations are either not recognized or they are recognized, but they are not correctly understood, and therefore cannot be criticized" (Celikates 2009: 168). The terminology can help us to understand the impact of processes in the 'economy of symbolic goods' on the 'meta-pragmatic register'[46].

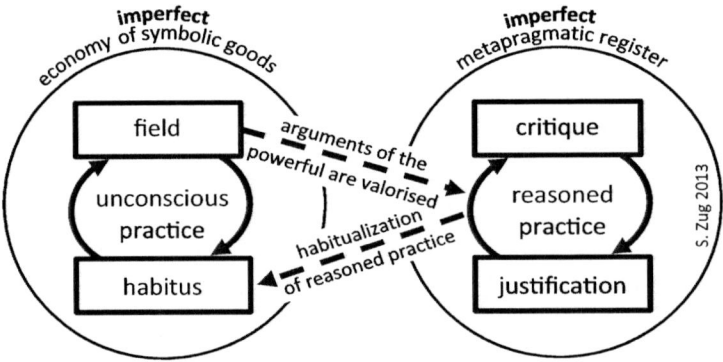

Fig. 6: Mutual Production of Imperfection in the Economy of Symbolic Goods and the Meta-Pragmatic Register

Celikates argues that although people are in principle 'capable' of reflecting on actions, they do not necessarily need to be 'able' in every situation to do so. "Failing to apply the technically existing ability to reflect can be caused by an insufficient training of the actor's capacity to do so, as well as by external or internal constraints (the absence of objective and subjective circumstances)" (Celikates 2009: 172). The insufficient capacity is reflected by a low endowment with cultural capital, in other words, not having learned how to develop arguments and how to effectively present these arguments in a discussion. Constraints can either be argued in line with the interests that make people 'tolerate' subjectively wrong behaviour in Boltanski's sense or the different endowment of actors with symbolic capital. In justification, the aim is that people agree on a solution in a given situation. People in these negotiations are, however, not necessarily equal, which affects the persuasive power of their arguments. A simple example is elders who are endowed with high

---

[46] Celikates analysed the complementarity of Bourdieu and Boltanski in the first part of his book, but later – when developing the term 'structural deficit in reflection' – focused on integrating critical theory mainly based on Habermas and Honneth with pragmatic sociology, which however, do not make his arguments any less valuable for my project.

quantities of symbolic capital that gives value to their arguments. Their negotiation power can be significantly higher when a solution in a 'meta-pragmatic register' is wanted, and other actors might happily accept their suggestion and perceive it as a just solution, not necessarily because they are convinced of the fairness of the elders' proposals but because they trust their critical capacities. Consequently, imperfection is mutually produced between the two registers and not only restricted to the 'economy of symbolic goods'. In the 'meta-pragmatic register' arguments have different values depending on the position of the person advancing the argument in the social field. Interests negotiated in the 'economy of symbolic goods', consequently, can – but do not necessarily need to have – an effect on reasoned practice.

Concluding Remarks

Conceptualizing the 'meta-pragmatic register' as a temporary alternative to the 'economy of symbolic goods' does not only allow us to integrate morality into Bourdieu's framework – which was already possible with the introduction of the 'capital of moral entitlement'. However, it sets the arguments on a stronger theoretical foundation, which also allows a historic perspective on the genesis of moral values in everyday practices. The morality inscribed into the habitus and the structure of the field can now be questioned by individuals on the local level in everyday situations, on the basis of reason. It can also be called into question by international movements like the environmentalist movement, who base their argumentation – as Lafaye and Thévenot (1993) have developed – on an emerging "green polity", which has increasingly been acknowledged as containing very important principles for correct behaviour. Alexander's critique of Bourdieu's thought (see 3.5; Alexander 1995: 192) is no longer valid for the 'imperfect economy of symbolic goods'. Under the adjustment, Gandhi, Martin Luther King, Jesus, Karl Marx, and 'the environmentalist movement' have the potential to become role models and their ideas have become guides that people can integrate into their daily practices.

3.7. Conclusion: from a Perfect to an Imperfect Economy of Symbolic Goods

The proposed adjusted 'economy of symbolic goods' is imperfect in two ways. First, it is assumed that it does not explain all situations in life, because some actions take place in the 'meta-pragmatic register'. Second, even if action takes place in the 'economy of symbolic goods', these transactions can reflect previous reasoning, which took place in the 'meta-pragmatic register' before being internalized into the habitus and the structure of the field. A morally influenced habitus therefore does not make people act according to personal interests only, but can lead to an imperfect economic transaction under acceptance of capital loss.

An economic transfer in such a constellation can be – but is not always – an investment in the economic sense, because it does not necessarily aim for profitability. I suggest seeing the introduction of moral reasoned behaviour as an adjustment of social theory to the complexity of social reality, which admittedly makes explaining society more complex, but also more realistic. Bourdieu himself took exactly such a step when he introduced the 'economy of symbolic goods' in opposition – among others – to rational choice. He supplemented ordinary capital transfers with 'more social' capitals, by relaxing materialistic assumptions. Introducing morality into Bourdieu's work should be seen as the continuation of a process he had initiated; it is 'simply' the reduction of certain, more economic assumptions, namely the dictate of interestedness.

The Duality of Morals and Interests in Every Action

The developed model is an attempt to bring two sides (interest and morality) together. It is explicitly not to be understood as either/or, in the sense that registers exist independently from each other. The interdependence is not only reflected in the 'imperfection' of the 'economy of symbolic goods', but equally in the 'meta-pragmatic register', which is influenced by field-based 'structural deficits in reflection'. Hence, the approach requires using the notion of the gift, not as a one-dimensional phenomenon but under a wider definition, which considers both manifest interest as well as their denial.

I have strong reservations concerning Jacques Derrida's deconstruction of the gift. He argues a gift cannot exist at all, because "from the moment the gift would appear as a gift, as such, as what it is, in its phenomenon, its sense and its essence, it would be engaged in a symbolic sacrificial or economic structure that would annul the gift in the ritual circle of the debt" (Derrida 1992 [1991]: 23). The donor's slightest feeling of goodness or the recipient's feeling of gratitude would already be enough to transform the transaction into an economic one.

We must detach ourselves from the idea of *pure* gifts that underpins Derrida's analysis. Impure gift transactions are those transactions that take place in an 'imperfect economy of symbolic goods', hence, in-between the market and moral-based motivations. It is this in-between category that we must maintain to understand the multiplicity of reasons for social actions. Impure gifts contain certain interests of actors, but these interests are not fully balanced. "In 'fair trade', moral and ideological considerations such as social justice and environmental sustainability are an ethical premium or a market advantage which adds value to the final product" (Fridell 2006: 83). Consequently, the customer is willing to pay more than the market price for a good. This transaction is still an economic transaction, since the consumers pay for the good. In addition, they pay a bonus, for which they will not be compensated. This holds true if we assume they do not do it for others to see and to give themselves a good conscious, only. It is some consumers' moral dispositions that make them accept the loss of the price difference between a fair and a 'non-fair' trade banana, and which grants the farmers their moral entitlement. The transfer is partial disinterested within an imperfect 'economy of symbolic goods'. The compensation of a material transaction in absence of payment or barter can comprise a variety of transfers of different capitals rather than only a single one, since it is embedded in a complex society.

A Model of the Imperfect Economy of Symbolic Goods

The following graph presents a very simplified and idealized schema of an impure gift transaction, which aims to explain the functionality of the transfer. In no way is it a claim that it would be empirically possible to gather the relevant data and to calculate the profitability of social action. Rather, it should help to understand how human practice is related to different types of motivations, hence how the different conceptualizations of the gift in the previous subchapters relate to each other. The graph is restricted to practice taking place in the 'imperfect economy of symbolic goods'; hence it depicts only those situations in which people's morally extended habitus is the main driver of social action, rather than conscious reasoning.

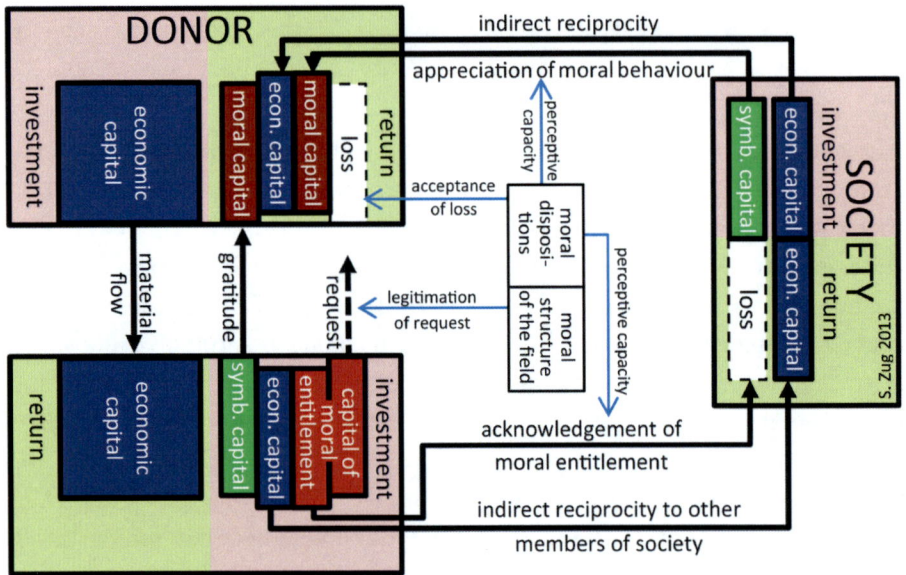

Fig. 7: Complicity of Economic Transfers in the Morally Influenced Imperfect Economy of Symbolic Goods

The basic assumption of a 'perfect' economy of symbolic goods is profitability: the donor as well as the recipient expect – consciously or subconsciously – to receive at least the equivalent of the capital that was or will be invested. Profit is possible for both transaction partners, since the value of an exchanged good can be higher for the recipient than for the donor. Gauthier (1986: 187) would call this the evolutionary advantage of cooperation. For the sake of simplified reading the graph does not take profit into consideration, but shows a situation where investments of all participating actors are internally balanced with returns, which is the minimal precondition to initiate a gift exchange under the assumed absence of uncertainty and mutual acceptance of the transfer, hence, absence of violence.

The logics of the gift take hold of a situation from the moment an actor transfers economic capital to another actor without payment or any form of formal contract. The transfer modes developed in the previous subchapters assumed that gifts are pure. Under a virtue-based moral structure, being grateful is a form of repayment with symbolic capital, which turns into 'moral capital' for the donor, because it attests having acted in conformity with a virtue, although he or she is not formally obliged to do so. The resulting moral superiority of the donor can be annulled after a return of an equal amount of economic capital. Under a rights-based moral structure of the field, the perfect economy becomes imperfect, in the most extreme sense, since in order to receive economic capital, an investment of 'capital of moral entitlement' is needed, which does not materialize for the donor at all because of being predisposed to accept loss by his or her ethical dispositions (which are the internalized codes of conduct related, but not equivalent to conscious reason in the 'meta-pragmatic register'). In both cases indirect constellations are possible, where a third actor is involved in the transfer, as in the example of the Rotarian (3.3.2) who is doing good (economic capital) for one person and being compensated in another field with 'moral capital'.

The habitus, which is the guiding principle of any action in the 'economy of symbolic goods', has incorporated two elements into the 'imperfect' economy of symbolic goods: first, the interested rules of the game, which aim at maximizing profit, and second, disinterested rights-based moral principles which grant moral entitlements. In practical moments, both elements come into play and guide people's actions as a unit. Recipients can respond to the same gift by being grateful to the donors (symbolic capital → moral capital), and at the same time, being only partially grateful, knowing that they themselves sometimes support people with a similar transfer of 'moral capital'. Donors can also count on other members in society, when in need (indirect reciprocity). The gratefulness of recipients can be further reduced if donors have at least partially internalized that what they are doing is worth it because it relates to something they assumes to be good or right. In the donors' capital endowment this element leads to a loss, because the recipients only pay with 'capital of moral entitlement', which cannot be turned into positive capital for the donors. If moral entitlement is used for a transaction, it is not necessarily the donor who must pay the loss, but it can also be a third person or a group of persons that acknowledge both the recipient's moral entitlement and also that the donor is fulfilling this entitlement. The donor therefore gains 'moral capital' in the form of appreciation of other members of society. In this case other actors bear the cost, because they lose relative positions in the social field, by transferring 'symbolic capital' to the donor.

In the following chapters this extended approach of Bourdieu's theory of practice will be used to analyse a 'neighbourly waterscape' in Greater Khartoum based on the results of my empirical research.

4

Doing Research in Greater Khartoum and Methodology

Greater Khartoum belongs to those cities that research has generally overlooked in recent decades. Davies and Abu Sin's (1991) collective work on the *Future of Sudan's Capital region* attempted to shed light on multiple urban topics, but it remains an exception. In the decades since, research on the city has been rare and the few published works (e.g. Denis 2005; Gertel 1993; Lavergne 1995; Pantuliano et al. 2011; UN Habitat 2009) merely provide a general overview rather than a detailed study of the city.

The same holds true for the analysis of water supply in the city. Very few authors conceptualized water supply in Khartoum with a focus on the social embeddedness of water (Cairncross and Kinnear 1992; Gadir 2006; Nègre 2004). The lack of research both on urban development in the city and on water management is not necessarily an obstacle, but it requires tackling research with a very explorative approach. In-depth elaboration of water in the city was the goal of the *Water Management in Khartoum International Research Project* (WAMAKHAIR, 2008-2012), a collaboration between the Ahfad University for Women in Khartoum and several French, German, and Swiss universities. Water was the unifying interface between the work of several researchers from different scientific backgrounds, who focus on various processes in the 'waterscape of the city' or in waterscapes at smaller scales within the city. Analysing water reveals social, economic, and political processes that contribute to the understanding of the city and its socio-spatial transformations beyond the flows of water. This book is based on my PhD research within WAMAKHAIR. Other theses developed in the same framework have already been defended (Arango 2009; Beckedorf 2011; Crombé 2009).

4.1. Access to the Field and Scientific Cooperation

Doing Research in Sudan

That research did not cover Khartoum more intensively in recent decades is not because the city does not provide interesting research topics. Instead, it can be assumed – especially for non-Sudanese researchers – that this is related to the country's difficult political situation. Long civil wars in South Sudan (1983-2005) and Darfur (since 2003), a referendum in January 2011, and the resulting independence of South Sudan the following July, have created a difficult political context for doing research. The Sudanese government, led by Omar al-Bashir since the 1989 military coup has been severely isolated by the international community. The situation was exacerbated by the opening of a case against Al-Bashir at the International Criminal Court in 2008. Al-Bashir was accused, convicted, and an arrest warrant was issued for him concerning war crimes and crimes against humanity in March 2010 and for genocide in July 2010 (e.g. Mills 2012). Sudan's reaction – expelling thirteen international humanitarian aid organizations on the day the first warrant was issued – illustrates the tense relations Sudan entertains with the international community (e.g. Sheffield 2013: 173).

Empirical research took place over nine months, divided into five visits between February 2009 and December 2010. This was a period when political topics were dominated by both the case against Al-Bashir and the preparations of the referendum. The tense political situation can be assumed to be one of the major elements contributing to the difficulty of 'cooperation' with the Sudanese government. Granting a foreign researcher access to the field does not directly benefit the government's agenda, especially since research tends to lead to a critique of the government. Considering Sudan's complicated international relations, successfully accessing the field would have required networking and negotiations with local partners, the ability to negotiate with government officials, and a fair amount of luck to be in the right place at the right time. Ahfad, the cooperation partner university, was fully in charge of negotiations with the government concerning all research formalities. In the political field of Khartoum, this rather small University can be assumed to have much less negotiation power than well-established universities, such as the Khartoum University in the city centre.

	Date	Weeks	Research
1	02/09 – 04/09	11	Explorative research in Greater Khartoum. Research in Mandela. 4 weeks prohibited to work.
2	10/09 – 12/09	8	Research in Mandela
3	01/10 – 03/10	8	No research permission
4*	08/10 – 09/10	4	Research in Dar Alsalam Square 11
5*	11/10 – 12/10	4	Research in Dar Alsalam Square 11
(6)	(11/11)	0	No visa granted

*phases during which the case study presented in this thesis was actually undertaken.

Fig. 8: Research Plan

In retrospect, conducting research in the first phase by relying solely on a research agreement with the Khartoum State Water Corporation (KSWC) and a short letter by the Ahfad University while employing a Southern Sudanese research assistant[47] might have been naïve, given the political situation. After a month of general exploration of agglomeration's peripheries by motorbike, the informal settlement Nifasha in the western peripheries and Mandela, a camp for the internally displaced in the south of Khartoum, which was in the process of formalization, were selected as case study areas. The objective at this stage was investigating the relationship between water and land ownership. After two weeks of intensive work in Mandela, my passport was confiscated and I was neither allowed to work nor to leave the country for nearly one month. When I extended my visa, my profession was accidentally or purposely designated "lawyer" in Arabic, leading to the accusation that I might investigate human rights violations in the camp under the cover of a geography student. The problem was resolved for the second research phase, which allowed me to continue explorative research in Mandela, resulting finally in a quantitative survey with 200 respondents. The third research phase was scheduled at the same time as the first arrest warrant against al-Bashir was issued and the aid agencies were expelled. The governmental Humanitarian Aid Commission was not only responsible for organizing the expulsion processes, but also for issuing research permits for my working areas. For two months, I waited for a permit to continue research in Mandela and to launch the second case study in Nifasha, the informal settlement in western Omdur-

---

47 If I had worked with a northern Sudanese research assistant loyal to the Sudanese government instead, it would have facilitated contact with Sudan's government during that particular political situation.

man. Despite continuously investing in my social capital by following the local principles of 'paying gratefulness' with days of waiting in offices, having tea, and 'entertaining' the administrators in the Humanitarian Aid Commission, access to Mandela and Nifasha was denied.

The high probability of no longer being able to access the old field areas nearly led me to abandon the research in Sudan. The study had been designed in three steps, starting with an explorative qualitative research phase, followed by a quantitative descriptive one, which finally set the stage for an in-depth understanding of particular waterscapes through qualitative interviews. The data generated in the first seven months of my stay in Khartoum became worthless, since the questions that had emerged from the quantitative study (phase 2) could no longer be interpreted in the light of people's subjective sense (phase 3), making the data superficial. The material generated in Mandela and Nifasha are only referred to in this book as side notes.

I once again received a one month visa to go to Sudan in August 2010. However, I no longer relied on being allowed to continuing research in my previous research areas; in the end, I never was allowed to return to these areas again. One of the key findings in Mandela, Nifasha, and the explorative phase in the peripheries was the importance of free water transfers in Khartoum. I turned this topic into the central focus of my research, dropping the issue of the relationship between land and water, which is much more sensitive politically.

To continue research, I selected a third area where water gifts were also prevalent. This choice was highly restricted, because with my previous experience and my file with the secret service, the area had to be politically non-sensitive. Dar Alsalam Square 11 fulfilled this criterion. The neighbourhood is formal and therefore no research permit from the Humanitarian Aid Commission is required, unlike the internally displaced camps and informal settlements. Square 11 is distant from other camps and the proportion of Southern Sudanese is comparatively low, which was important since tensions were expected to rise with the upcoming independence of the South.

In the new area, I greatly emphasized my willingness to cooperate with government institutions. Very early on, I established contact with secret service officers responsible for the area, who agreed to my research and whom I regularly informed about most of my activities. Officers of the public water corporation were not contacted from the bottom-up, but rather from the top-down. These conditions were the necessary compromise in order to continue doing research. Movement was restricted to a rather small area and possible topics to be discussed were limited. Consequently, I did not discuss the actors' political affiliations, the role of party politics for water provision, and topics related to ethnicity[48], although they might have added another layer to the waterscape analysis in Square 11. With the exception of an accusation of spying, which I disproved[49], no major problems arose with government.

Social Power and the Project

A second month-long field visit was allowed shortly after the first one. A final third visit was planned for late 2011. However, the application for a visa failed mainly because of the difficult situation which resulted in the Sudanese partner university losing interest in the cooperation. The theoretical approach developed in chapter 3, combining interests and reasons for action in different polities, can be applied to the WAMAKHAIR project itself. The group of researchers can be understood as a social field, in which actors are ordered by their capital endowment. This endowment includes not only acknowledgement of their particular scientific qualifications including academic titles (cultural capital), but also the social capital of project partners.

The Sudanese partner university was strategically placed in this game, since it was the sole interface with government institutions for several European researchers, including myself. Being in the position to organize visas and research permits, they had the power to render research possible or condemn it to failure. The release of my confiscated passport was only possible thanks to the university's commitment in the early phases of the project and their negotiations with the secret service. However, this commitment later dissipated. This change can at least be partially explained through an analysis of power games within the project and the actors referencing different polities to justify their choices.

The choice of arguments used to justify particular practices was influenced by the different contexts in which the project's researchers had been socialized.

---

[48] Ethnicity was discussed only if it was made a topic by my respondents. I only directly asked for home regions, rather than for people's ethnic group.

[49] While performing differential GPS measurements, for which we installed a tripod on a roof of a house, I was accused by the local political elite of tapping the mobile phone network and was brought to secret service officers, who wanted to confiscate the technical equipment. The situation was finally resolved when security officers I knew were asked for help.

The hypothesis I wish to submit here, is that the project partners did not agree on the relevance of what Boltanski would call the 'domestic world'. The Sudanese project partner pushed for employment of a PhD student, who was also a relative of the leading Sudanese researcher in the project and the university president. One of the European research partners agreed to the proposal and financed and supervised the PhD student. However, after a while the student's scientific performance was evaluated as insufficient. The argument from the domestic polity was in conflict with arguments in the industrial polity. The PhD student needed to perform adequately to be deemed 'worthy' enough to hold the position in the 'industrial world'; this was not the case according to the European research partner's performance evaluation.

Despite the discontent, the European partner maintained the work contract and supervision, which can be explained by the interests embedded in the 'economy of symbolic goods'. Ending the contract would have led to a contestation of polities, hence the argument that performance in the 'industrial world' is more important in this particular situation than the social situation of the Sudanese PhD student in the 'domestic world'. Because of the powerful position of the Sudanese counterpart in the field, the continuation of the supervision and the 'tolerance' of the student's lack of adequate performance in the 'industrial world' was the 'price to be paid' to continue research in Sudan. When this particular European project partner had completed most of its field research, it was no longer dependant on the administrative services of its Sudanese partner. With the Sudanese project partner losing its relational power, the European partner's freedom to act increased. The mismatch of worths in the industrial world was no longer 'tolerated' and the employment and supervision of the Sudanese PhD student was terminated. The Sudanese project partner was discontent because the European project partner had shifted the situation from the 'domestic world' to the 'industrial world' without attempting a consensus in the 'meta-pragmatic register'. Therefore the relationship was shifted into what Boltanski (2012 [1990]) would have called a 'regime of violence' in his early work. The situation sharply deteriorated the project's cooperation and negatively impacted my relationship to the Sudanese project partner, since I was perceived as related to the European partner supervising the Sudanese PhD candidate. This is one possible reason why the visa for the last research trip could not be organized.

From the start, working with the project was difficult. Only small groups of people within the project managed to transfer their relationship into a cooperative mode, as Gauthier (1986) would have understood it. They behaved like 'constrained maximizers', knowing that disinterested actions would benefit them over the long term. This form of cooperation between individuals was beneficial for me and other involved actors. However, the whole project never managed to enter this mode. This was clearly illustrated by the widespread absence of sharing secondary data and students' finalized research work among all project members, as well as unsolved 'territorial struggles' in demarcating case study areas, and 'ownership' struggles of research topics. Consequently, the 'evolutionary benefit' of cooperating, hardly materialized. The constant need to navigate the project's exacerbated tensions made work very difficult, draining time and energy. Accordingly, the research was not simply a challenge in terms of understanding particular waterscapes. Rather, access to the country and the field was a struggle with government institutions and a challenge due to the complex power relations in the social field of WAMA-KHAIR. Since I could not fully defend my stakes against the different actors of these power games, much more time, money, and energy were spent in Khartoum than intended. This is demonstrated in my choice to base my elaborations only on the two last research phases (8 weeks), when I had spent a of total nine months in Khartoum. Of the other seven months (phase 1-3, Figure 8), only about three months are completely lost because I was barely allowed to work. The work accomplished during the other four months exploring different peripheral areas and conducting research in Mandela allowed me to build up a sizeable body of knowledge about water access in the city beyond the particular case study area Square 11. Being able to deduce the relevance of water gifts for everyday water practices would have not been possible without these research phases. Basing this book on a rather small case study, however, gave me the chance to very deeply analyse this particular waterscape.

4.2. Research Methods for Analysing Square 11's Waterscape

When research was shifted from Mandela to Square 11, methodology had to be pragmatically adjusted, since the research was always at risk of been stopped again by the government. The three step research design was replaced by an integrated inductive method in which a qualitative approach was used in order to analyse social action. Statistical data was gathered in passing, rather than in a separate step. The social science perspective was supplemented with a technological analysis of the neighbourhood's particular water network.

A qualitative research design as used here aims primarily at making sense of the empirical reality, from within this reality. A central principle in a qualitative methodology therefore is 'openness'. This includes methodologies that allow actors' subjectivity to be expressed and accessing the field with no predefined assumptions (e.g. Lamnek 2005: 20). Complete openness is an ideal of qualitative research, which can never be fully achieved. Whenever researchers enter a field, their perspectives are influenced by previous research, everyday knowledge, and theoretical readings. Being influenced by Bourdieu's conceptualization of society with 'interested' actors was a particular perspective that guided my analysis of gift transactions. This perspective was sensitive towards reciprocal returns for seemingly free transfers of water. Openness in my research is thus understood as making empirical results an underpinning to question theoretical concepts and finally adjusting them to social reality, rather than vice versa.

Openness towards the field is exemplified by a circular research design that "forces the researcher to permanently reflect on the whole research process and on particular steps in the light of other steps" (Flick 2009: 92). Data obtained from the field is interpreted and then integrated into the next research step, where it is confronted with the same or other actors in that particular field. Glaser's and Strauss's concept of 'theoretical saturation' helps determine the end of research, which is not predefined, for example by a specific number of interviews.

> Saturation means, that no additional data are being found whereby the sociologist can develop properties of the category. As he sees similar instances over and over again, the researcher becomes empirically confident that the category is saturated. He goes out of his way to look for groups that stretch diversity of data as far as possible, just to make certain that saturation is based on the widest possible range of data in the category (Glaser and Strauss 2009 [1967]: 61).

It is clear that in this research, the point of theoretical saturation was not fully reached. Research would have benefited from a third field visit to Square 11, in which the developed ideas could have been exposed to additional actors and consolidated by conducting more detailed interviews with previous respondents. However, the data gathered is sufficient to carefully interpret everyday water gift practices.

Selection of Case Study Areas within Square 11

Square 11 was selected as a case study area due to the prevalence of water gift transactions and government restrictions as explained above. In order to receive an overview of the entire square, an explorative study was conducted in which households living in different sections in the square as well as elite inhabitants and actors working in water supply were interviewed. This first analysis offered a rough description of the elements of the local waterscape, the household's access strategies, and the spatiality of access to the network. Based on this information four case study areas within the square were intentionally selected; each area forming a 'neighbourly waterscape'. In all these waterscapes, gifts were prevalent, but the technology to transport the gifts differs. All households in these clusters were interviewed.[50]

The primary aim of qualitative research is not a generalization of results, but an in-depth understanding of processes in a particular area. Thus, the analysis of these four case studies does not claim to represent all of Khartoum or Dar Alsalam. Every case study area is jointly created by individual households who maintain an array of different social ties to each other. However, the analysis of these case study areas can provide general insights into the principle processes of how people live together and the roles water plays in their relationships.

Defining the Household as a Research Unit and Gender

When making a birthday gift, the recipient is one particular person – the one having a birthday that day. In an analysis of a birthday gift transaction, the relationship between this person and the donor is at the centre. Water gifts in the research area are significantly different. If a girl walks to the house of a neighbour asking for water and is granted access by the person opening the door, the transaction is not restricted to the relationship between the two actors who physically implement the gift. The two actors are representatives of two groups. The girl will carry the water to a barrel where she lives and several people will consume this water. Thus, the financial savings does not materialize for the girl physically receiving the gift, but for the group of people consuming the water.

---

50 An overview of all the interviews can be found in the appendix.

The group of people directly consuming from the same storage barrel is defined in this book as a household. The definition combines spatial and social elements. In most cases the household consists of a family whose members – not necessarily only the nuclear family – live together spatially. Some households are not based on kinship as seen in groups of young, male, migrant workers sharing the same plot. However, they rent as a social unit. The spatial unit is mostly a government defined plot of 200 m² that are clearly delineated by walls surrounding all sides of the plot. Sometimes two families share the same plot. They are considered two separate households, if they consume water from different storage barrels.

In this book, the central analytical unit is the household. However, I do not deny the relevance of the individual in the construction of social relations and the gift. The girl knocking on the door, the mother ordering the girl to do so, and the father who is not involved in the water transfers, all have different relationships with the members of the donor household. Through their everyday interaction, they jointly create the social relationship between the two households. I strongly encourage using individual persons as analytical units when analysing water gift transactions. Such an approach would also allow deeper analysis of the relevance of gender embedded in the water gifts; especially since task sharing in water gift transactions are strongly gendered. With the exception of young boys, water is almost always carried by females. Women also tend to be more involved than men in establishing social relationships with neighbours. With more time in the research area and more interviews with members from the same households, the gender aspect could have been explored more intensely.[51]

For the sake of convenience and clarity of the arguments, the households are grammatically equated with individuals. Notions like customer, donor, and recipient refer to a household who purchases, gifts, and receives water, respectively. I will use male-gendered pronouns to describe these actors. Female-gendered pronouns will only be used when the action of a female member of a household is explicitly presented. This choice is uniquely an attempt to increase legibility.

---

51 Working with female rather than with male research assistants, only, would have improved the access to female interview partners.

Interviews

Data was mainly gathered through interviews. In the explorative phase, interviews were conducted completely spontaneously. An interview guide was used for the first interview with each household in the case study areas. This guide did not structure the interview, but merely served as a checklist for the topics to be covered. The interview guide also contained a list of particular statistical indicators, such as how long each person had lived in the area and their reliance on particular water access strategies. In order to maintain the interview's communicative element, statistical questions were rarely asked directly to the respondents. These data were generally filled in from the information provided in respondents' narratives, for example when they were asked to talk about their family history in Khartoum. The collection of some quantitative data during the qualitative interviews strongly supported the relational analysis.

Households considered interesting for understanding water gift transactions were revisited once or several times. Partial interviews were conducted with different members of the same household. Revisits were very important in the research, since they allowed me to integrate information gathered from the neighbours, including those on the relationship between households. Beside households, the social, religious and political elite of the Square and staff of the public water corporation at different levels were interviewed with open interviews, generally in the form of discussions.

Interviews had to be conducted with a translator, which is a significant intermediary actor between the interviewer and the respondent.

> The words and language used by participants often incorporates particular sociocultural meanings and inherent values and beliefs, which need to be understood, translated and transferred to the language of the research team. The translator's role, therefore, becomes an intellectual contribution to understanding the research data within the study context and in seeking equivalence of these understandings in the language and context of the research team (Hennink 2008: 30).

Throughout the research in Square 11, as well as during the three preceding months of field research, I worked with the same field research assistant. In the early phase of the cooperation, we discussed the process of translation as well as the topics discussed in the interviews. The translator became an important actor, contributing to my research with his analytical capacity coupled with his knowledge of the Sudanese context. Nevertheless, the process of translation is always an additional step of interpretation. While some of the interviews were recorded and transcribed, during the majority of interviews, notes were taken by hand and later typed[52]. Quotes presented in the analysis are therefore mainly reconstructed from the notes.

For the interpretation, interviews were coded in the qualitative data analysis software Atlas.ti. In the research, thematic and relational codes where used. Thematic codes ordered the content of the interview. In the research process, thematic codes were continuously redefined and a code hierarchy was established. Understanding the gifts requires understanding practices imbedded in relationships between actors. Therefore relational codes were developed that connected individual actors with statements from other actors.

Technical Measurements and Geographic Information Systems

Geographic Information Systems (GIS)[53] played a crucial role in planning and analysing the research as well as in visualizing the results. Satellite images from Google Earth in combination with a government shapefile containing the water networks, allowed a pre-selection of potential research areas, which were then accessed with a GPS receiver.[54] Registering the coordinates of the location allowed me to return to the same area.

The daily update of the GIS database was an important element in the circular research process. All statistical data from household interviews was continuously entered in the GIS databases. This allowed us to not only determine which households still had to be covered; but also to understand particular spatial patterns in the 'neighbourly waterscapes'. This approach strongly supported a relational analysis of neighbours. Producing maps of water supply performance based on household information on water access served as an important medium in debates with engineers.

---

52 Recording and transcribing the interviews and translating the Arabic passages into English would have allowed a deeper understanding. However, this would have required a translator and the benefits would not have justified the expenses.

53 Throughout the entire process, ArcGIS 9 and 10 were used.

54 The satellite images allowed me to determine whether a particular settlement was formal or informal, to classify the settlement by plot size, which indicates the economic capacities of the inhabitants, and the prevalence of trees gives an indication about the performance of water supply.

Towards the end of the research period, the elevation of the square and of individual household taps was measured by a survey engineer and in several locations water pressure was measured. By combining three types of layers – the natural environment containing a three dimensional location of households, the technical installations in form of water networks, and the social characteristics of individual households – the multiple embeddedness of water gifts could be integrated into the analysis.

Moral Responsibility towards the Actors

Research is not only conducted on actors, but research can also have impact on actors. Weathington, Cunningham, and Pittenger (2010: 33) argue that the most important moral principle in doing research is "do no harm". To protect participants from any negative consequences, all interviews were rendered anonymous. This is especially important to protect those households who illegally altered their water connection. To understand the heterogeneity in water access strategies and the relationship between actors, it is important to illustrate the spatiality of households. In order to allow such illustrations and still prevent specific households from being located, the specific locations of the four case studies in Square 11 are not disclosed in this book and the graphical representation is obscured. It would take much effort to trace the results of my research back to the corresponding houses; the work required would not be justified by the topic and the scale covered. Finally, to ensure perfect anonymity, those households who did make illegal adjustments cannot be located on the maps at all.

5

Fragmentation. A Recent History of Urban Development and Water Supply in Greater Khartoum

This book's main contribution to the water debate is the analysis of water gifts. Water gifts are socially embedded into a relationship between a donor and a recipient, as well as into the socio-natural production of drinking water in the city. Only by understanding this wider framework can water gifts be understood. In the case of Greater Khartoum, where people do not extract water themselves, water gifts must first be purchased from the operators of water supply systems, which transport water from its source to a consumer. The heterogeneity of access to these sources is one of the three elements constituting water gifts. This chapter will concentrate on supply issues that result in such heterogeneity.

After a general introduction to Khartoum and the case study area, Square 11 in Dar Alsalam, with a focus on urban development (5.1), I will concentrate on the public network's water supply. I will show that heterogeneity is prevalent on three different scales: the 'waterscape of the city' (5.2), the 'waterscape of interconnected networks' (5.3), and the 'waterscape of the neighbourhood' (5.4).

5.1. A Short History of Greater Khartoum and Dar Alsalam Square 11

5.1.1. The Urban Transformation of Greater Khartoum and Migration

Greater Khartoum is located at the confluence of the Blue and the White Nile, which divides the agglomeration into three: Khartoum, Omdurman, and

Khartoum North.⁵⁵ Settlements in the Khartoum region date back to prehistoric periods; however, it was only following the Turk-Egyptian invasion in 1821 that Khartoum became an important military, administrative, and commercial centre with some 50,000 inhabitants. The city was eclipsed when the Mahdi destroyed it and developed his capital in Omdurman (El-Bushra 1971: 12). In 1899 the Anglo-Egyptian Army regained power and re-established Khartoum, which remained the capital of Republic of Sudan after attaining independence in 1956.

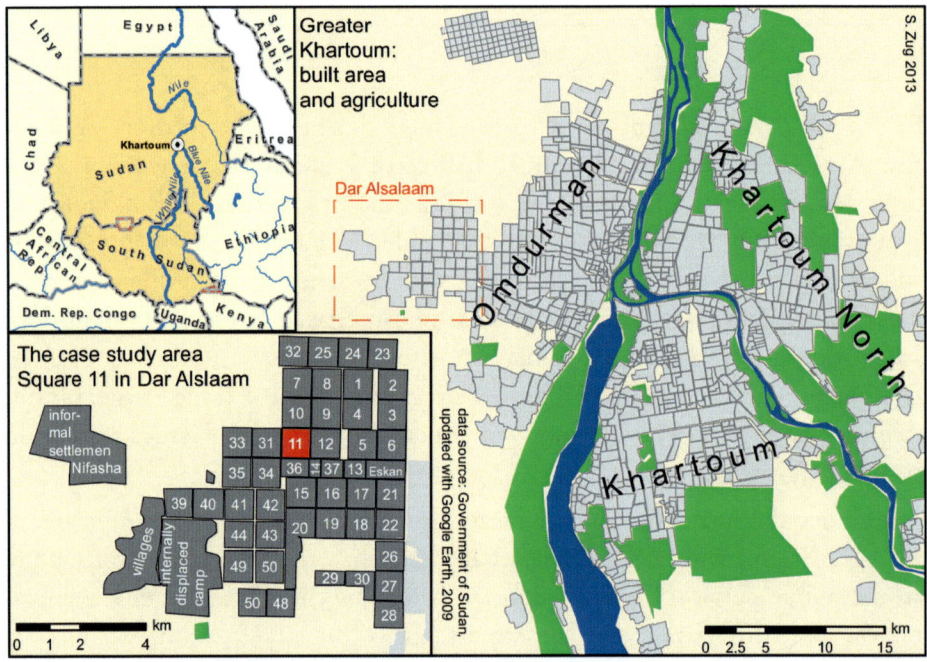

Fig. 9: Khartoum and Omdurman

Today, Khartoum and Omdurman's city centres reflect the historical contexts of their foundations. Khartoum, which was developed by British colonial planners, is characterized by rectilinear streets, which are arranged parallel to the Blue Nile, with prestigious buildings purposely arranged along the waterfront. In contrast Omdurman's urban structure is completely different. The

---

55 The term Khartoum is ambivalent since it is used both for the entire agglomeration as well as for the section located between the Blue and the White Nile. In order to clearly differentiate the terms I will use the term 'Greater Khartoum' to refer to the whole agglomeration.

riverbank has been given much less importance and the urban structure follows no clear geometric patterns. Nevertheless urban development is framed by "conscious planning dictating the creation of the main routes and squares, the location of the marketplace, the Friday mosque, the ruler's residential complex, defensive walls and fortresses and the like" (Ahmad 1992: 28). Khartoum North, the third part of the city, never had the same administrative power as Omdurman or Khartoum, and is today dominated by a central industrial area. The increasing number of bridges between the three parts of the city brings them closer, without modifying their different characters. Today the political and economic dominance of Khartoum is manifest with the construction of a new central business district with prestigious architecture.

Mass Migration and Urban Growth

According to the latest census (2008), 5.3 million people live in Greater Khartoum (Sudan Central Bureau of Statistics 2009: 44). However, this figure is contested and probably ranges closer to 7 million (Pantuliano et al. 2011: 3). In the last few decades, Greater Khartoum's urban growth has only been partially based on the birth rate. The main growth factor is tied to urban migration. While Sudan's total population has increased by 2.2% between the 1983 and 1993 censuses, Greater Khartoum's population grew at a much faster at a rate of 6.9%.[56] Greater Khartoum thus placed among the 5% of fastest growing urban agglomerations in the world for that period (UN DESA 2012).[57] The city cannot be understood with only absolute figures; we must also examine how groups migrating to the city have been integrated into the urban structure.

Greater Khartoum's urban history is strongly linked to human migration. As both rulers, like the Mahdiya and the British, and as inhabitants, migrants have shaped the city. Migrants, be they rulers, like the Mahdiya and the British, or inhabitants, have shaped the city. The bulk of migration is due to po-

---

56 Calculated from Sudan Central Bureau of Statistics (2009). From 1973 to 1983, Greater Khartoum also grew faster (5.1%) than Sudan as a whole (3.9%); but the discrepancy is much less pronounced. For the period between 1993 and 2008, official data shows that Khartoum's annual growth rate (2.8%) was nearly equal to that of Sudan (2.9%). Due to debate over the latest census, this figure has been called into question.

57 Greater Khartoum ranked 605 out of 632 in annual urban growth rate between 1985 and 1990 of all urban agglomerations with 750,000 or more inhabitants in 2011. For the total period between 1970 and 2010, it is still among the 20 % fastest growing cities.

litical conflict and so-called natural hazards. Since the 1970s, people have fled from Ethiopia and Eritrea to Greater Khartoum (e.g. Kibreab 1996: 137) but the accelerated urban growth in the 1980s and 1990s is mainly a result of internal displacement. A drought in several parts of Sudan between 1983 and 1985 as well as the outbreak of civil war in South Sudan and the Nuba Mountains around the same time are the main reasons for mass movements within Sudan (e.g. Assal 2004: 12; De Geoffroy 2009; Pantuliano et al. 2011). The civil war in Darfur, which started in 2003, also led to widespread population displacement; but comparatively few people migrated to Greater Khartoum (Assal 2011b: 4). In 2005 the Sudanese Government and the Sudan's People's Liberation Movement (SPLM) concluded a peace agreement that strongly reduced migration from the South to Greater Khartoum (Assal 2011b: 5). In 2011 through a referendum, South Sudan became an independent country, but the relationship between the two countries remains very tense. It is not yet clear, how independence and the pending debates on the nationality of Southerners living in the North will affect the so far very low return rates of Southerners (e.g. Assal 2011a; De Geoffroy 2011). In the research area, land-prices had already sharply decreased six month before the referendum, which indicates a further reduction of the agglomeration's growth rate.

Re-Planning the City

The government was not able to provide early migrants with adequate housing. While informal settlements had already emerged at the fringe of the city since the 1960s, the strong migratory increase in the 1980s led to a belt of informal settlements around the entire agglomeration, with a purported total population of up to 2 million people (El-Bushra and Hijazi 1995: 508). In the 1990s, the Government implemented two measures to address these informal settlements: 'internally displaced camps' and relocation projects.

Four camps were established in 1992 in Greater Khartoum and others were located elsewhere in the country. People did not choose to settle in these camps, they were forcefully relocated (e.g. Assal 2011b: 5). The camps were supplied with certain services including schools, basic water supply, and health stations, which provided slightly better living conditions than in new informal settlements that did not benefit from any government services whatsoever. However, urban planning in the camps was very similar to that in informal settlements. Rather than government regulated, the camps were in large organized and structured by government appointed 'sultans', tribal leaders representing the ethnic groups living in the camps. After 20 years, most sections in these camps still exist and are characterized by a comparatively high population density and street patterns that resemble those in informal settlements.

While the camps were considered temporary settlements for people returning to the South, the government started providing inhabitants of informal settlements with permanent land titles. Many informal settlements were completely destroyed in order to use the land for other purposes and other informal settlements were rebuilt in the original location. However, in the 1990s, the high population density in the old settlements made it necessary to reduce population. New settlements were established to house this population. While political commitment to resettlement schemes already existed in 1987, progress was very slow in the beginning. Sharif Eldin Bannaga, the former Minister of Engineering and Housing, argues that replanning and relocation of informal settlements increased rapidly in the early 1990s. Within 12 months in 1991-92, 50% of inhabitants of informal settlements were relocated to new settlements, where they received property rights just like other inhabitants (Bannaga 1996: 20).

New settlements were rigidly planned with predefined open squares and rectilinear streets, which were often exactly arranged in north-south and east-west configurations. While the government did not provide any services in informal areas, newly planned areas received basic services such as a health station and schools. Mainly sponsored by international NGOs, boreholes were drilled and water towers constructed. In this system, water was produced by the public water corporation, which had taken over ownership of the water towers. Water is transported from the towers to the households by water vendors with donkey carts, which were given at a NGO subsidized price to poor families in the 1990s (e.g. X27: 93, A4: 69[58]). In this particular biography of water, transportation is the continuous value added to the water, which moves the water into the commodity state.

In resettlement areas, households were allocated plots generally measuring 200 m², which makes the neighbourhoods a third class settlement, the official neighbourhood type with the smallest plot size. In total 274,000 plots were provided mainly to inhabitants of informal settlements and in later years to people from the internally displaced camps (UN Habitat 2009: 22). Most of the new settlements (210,000 plots) are located in Omdurman where the most recent resettlement Al Fatih was also established. Founded in 2002, Al Fatih's

---

58 These references refer to the interviews listed in the annex.

population increased to 300,000 people in 2010 (Assal 2011b: 8). With the resettlement policy, the government has pushed people further out into the peripheries of the city in order to use more central areas for higher class neighbourhoods. Distance to the city centre is a considerable disadvantage of living in the resettlement areas since employment is mainly found in the city centre. Consequently, many plots in the resettlement schemes are still empty or sublet to other families, while people try to stay closer to the city centre. This holds especially true for the recent Al Fatih resettlement, since the original, more central informal settlements of people still exist (Assal 2011b: 8).

5.1.2. The Study Area Dar Alsalam Square 11

The urban history of Greater Khartoum analysed from the perspective of population movements from within the country and within the city also provides an important context for the history of the study area. For this study, one of the very early resettlement areas chosen is officially called Square 11 of Dar Alsalam in Omdurman. Dar Alsalam is located 10 km west of the centre of Omdurman. The area was extended several times and consists of roughly 50 rectangular plots. The majority of squares are laid out following the same design. Amongst them, a few second class housing areas exist that are not part of the resettlement schemes. In the south-west, the Alsalam Camp has been incorporated into the structure, but it has not yet been re-planned. Further west, Dar Alsalam borders certain older villages that have grown rapidly in recent years. A few kilometres further to the west, Nifasha, one of the more recent informal settlements, marks the western limit of the urban agglomeration.

The Urban Design of Resettlements Areas

Dar Alsalam's first squares include Square 11. In late 1991, people from four informal settlements were brought there and received plots. The Shigla settlement in Khartoum North, the Mersouq settlement, and the 6th of April settlement in northern Omdurman were all to be reconstructed in the same location. However, in an effort to reduce density, many people were sent to Dar Alsalam. A fourth group was relocated from a settlement two kilometres north of Souq Libya, which is only few kilometres away from Square 11. The area was completely cleared to prepare for the construction of a hospital.

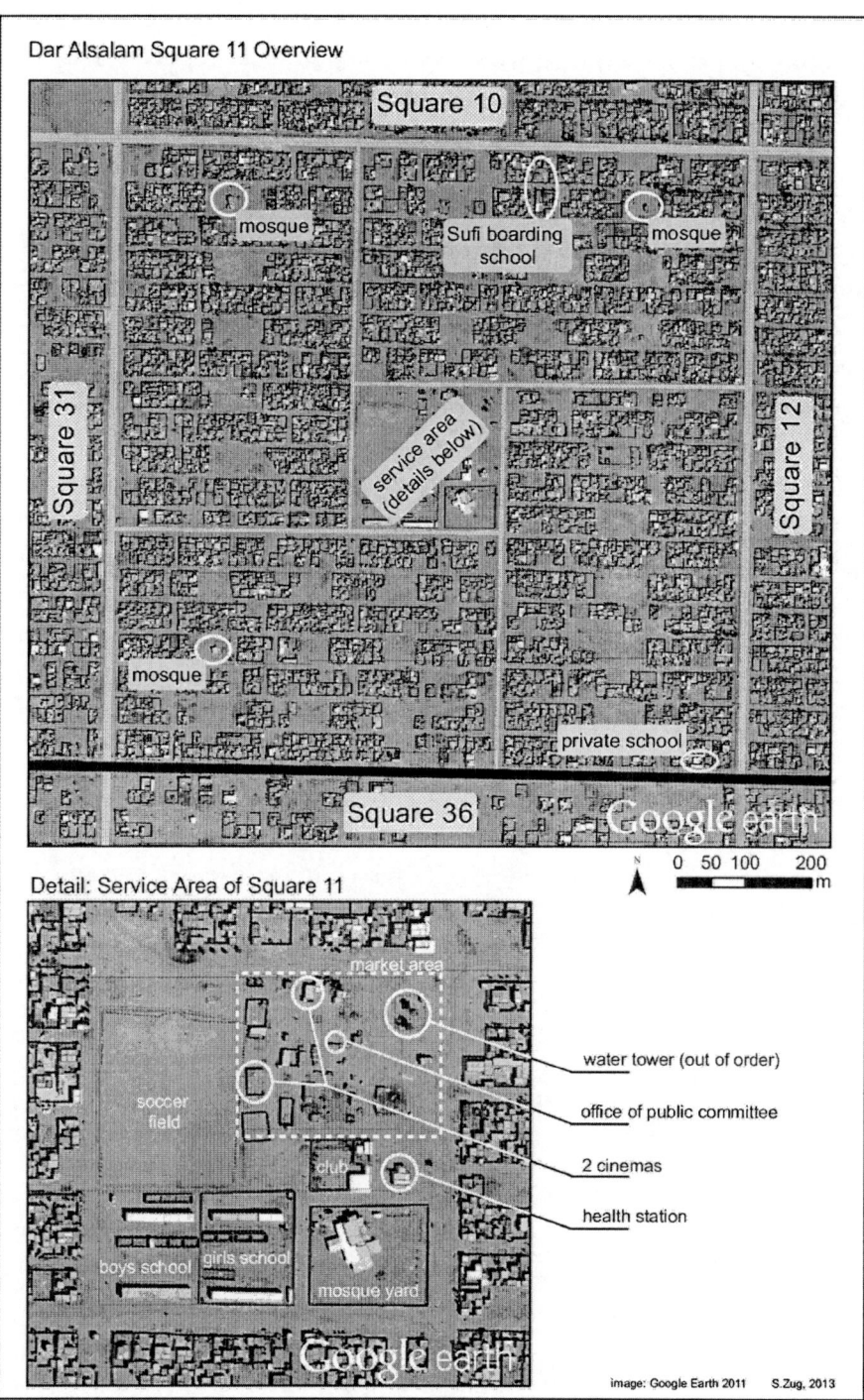

Fig. 10: Settlement Structure and Services in Dar Alsalam Square 11

In the early years of resettlement schemes, people were brought on trucks to resettlement area and plots were distributed on the spot.[59] The trucks stopped in a particular area in the square, and people's names were called from a list. Everyone on the same truck received plots in the same area; however they could choose their plot amongst those on their designated portion of the street (D5: 124). Consequently, those, who were put on the same truck received neighbouring plots (D5: 160; PC1: 215). Since government officials systematically filled the square line by line (EL1: 224), it is more likely that neighbours on the same side of the street had already been neighbours previously than those living on different sides of the street. With this system, the strong ethnic settlement patterns, characteristic of camps for the internally displaced and informal settlements, were disrupted within the square; however, it was maintained to a certain degree at a very small scale. Today, several households from the same ethnic group, sometimes even from the same family, live on several stretches of streets. People originate from all over the country including the Northern Provinces, Northern and Southern Kordofan, Darfur, and the South. It should be noted that due to political restrictions, a square with a Southern Sudanese minority had to be selected. In many other squares, the Southern Sudanese are the majority, which is not the case in Square 11.

Dissolving the ethnically structured neighbourhoods was a welcome side effect of replanning informal settlements and relocating inhabitants. The former minister, when discussing his initiative, stressed the integrative impact of these urban planning measures:

> Many families have moved from old blocks to new ones or from old neighbourhoods to new ones and this process has led to an intermingling of the families, their amalgamation and the diffusion of their habits and traditions and their adaptation towards their new environment and new conditions. New relations have sprouted, new dealings, new social links among all the members of the newly mixed society. Most important among these relations are intermarriages, which have resulted in a new socially knitted fabric of the society (Bannaga 2002: 159).

This statement dates back to a time before the peace agreement; yet it already reflects the fact that the Sudanese Government was interested in maintaining Sudan's unity.

---

59 In present reallocation schemes, plots are distributed by a lottery system, which breaks up the concentration of ethnic groups even more.

Bannaga's reflections do not only reveal that the government had an interest in improving the health and living conditions, but also in bringing migrant population more firmly under their control. Bannaga offers a gloomy description of the informal settlement, Canton Kassala:

> There was a murder almost each week, particularly on Thursday nights and Friday mornings. Large groups of criminals filter into the area, drink themselves into unconsciousness, and bicker over trifles. As is known liquor is the root of grievous sins and leads to the commitment of serious crimes. A misunderstanding begins with words, develops into lashing hands and finally clubbing or chopping with knives resulting in serious harm or killing. Dealing in stolen goods, drugs and narcotics, elopement of women with men resulting in tracing up by relatives, especially among Southern Sudanese, lead to these serious clashes. The intermingling shanties, the narrow lanes, the darkness at night would encourage roaming thieves to prey on the innocent and grasp property through the use of sheer force. Marauders wait by the side of roads leading to the squatter settlement, beat their prey to unconsciousness and run away with money or whatever valuables they can lay their hands on (Bannaga 2002: 131).

In the aftermath of the death of John Garang, the Southern Sudanese leader, in a helicopter crash in 2005, riots spread over the city. In reaction, the government strongly expressed its fear, "government leaders speak fearfully of the 'black belt' that surrounds the city and the threat this demographic majority may pose in times of conflict or democratic elections" (De Waal 2007: 7). The very forceful and strict planning measures strongly underline the Sudanese regime's autocratic approach to government.

The design of the new settlements, both upgraded areas and resettlement schemes, takes these concerns into consideration. Most blocks in Dar Alsalam replicate a standard plan over and over. Square 11 is exactly 900 x 900 metres. Four large streets subdivide it into four sub-squares surrounding a central service area. This central square can be seen from the surrounding streets. Heavy traffic clogs the streets surrounding Square 11. The south of the square is delimited by the most important paved road from central Omdurman heading out west.

Social functions are fulfilled by the central square, but also by many other small, open squares. They are used as playgrounds for children, meeting places for marriages and funeral ceremonies, and during Ramadan, they are filled with men who come to eat and pray after sunset.

Like many other resettlement areas, not all plots in Square 11 are settled. This can partially be explained by the long distances between Square 11 and the areas where people had previously settled. Shigla, the most distant settlement from Square 11, is over 30 road kilometres away. Transportation is time consuming and costly. More convenient options and employment opportunities elsewhere were decisive factors in the decision to not move to Square 11, despite having already received a plot. Members of the local political elite estimate that of the original plot owners one in three sold their titles. Another 15% of plots are not yet inhabited (PC1: 217) and many plots are inhabited by a tenant, instead of by the owner. In total it can be assumed that far less than 50% of plots are inhabited by the households who received it.

After 20 years of existence, hardly any income opportunities exist within Square 11 and most people move to the city's more central areas to find work. Souq Libya, roughly 7 km west of the square, is one of these areas, providing very important opportunities. Unlike other cities, urban agriculture is barely existent and animal husbandry is very rare; both issues are also related to the difficulties with water access. Besides a few craftsmen, such as the cobbler, the tailor, and a family manufacturing stoves from used cans, hardly any employment is available in the secondary sector. Employment opportunities are generally confined to satisfying the direct need of the residential population. Several shops are distributed all over the square, mainly operated as family businesses located on a portion of the residential plot. Some men occasionally find work in the square for house construction. Donkey carts are an important income opportunity. With the carts not only water is transported, but also goods and soil for construction as well as people who want to move in between the squares. The market area is not very intensively used since the market of Square 10 is very vibrant. Still, tea is served and meat, vegetables, and coal are sold in few simple huts made from cloth. A barber offers his service in a brick building.

Social, Political, and Economic Life

UN Habitat (2009: 25) characterises the planning approach as a "sites and services" project. Compared with projects in other countries that carry this label, the services provided in Dar Alsalam are reduced to an absolute minimum. The plots are devoid of any service. When people arrived, there were neither buildings nor toilets, nor access to electricity, drinking water and sewage supply networks. The services were exclusively located in the central area and included the water tower, to be discussed further, a small health centre with a nurse available for consultation five days a week (EL2: 08), as well as separate primary schools for both boys and girls. A private primary school has also recently opened in the square. Additionally a Sufi boarding school is operated.

With only a few Southerners living in the square, Muslims are numerically dominant. The mosque in the central area is the most important landmark of the square. Additionally three simple mosques are located on small yards. Christians go to churches in other squares, but the Catholic Church owns one of the best houses in Square 11, which is inhabited by a priest who works in another square but has strong ties with the local elite.

The central service area fulfils an important social function. Young men intensively use the soccer field in the evening, and once a week a match against other squares of Dar Alsalam within the local league takes place. During the day, men from the square gather in the covered tea stalls. At night, they patronize mobile tea stalls. In two brick buildings men watch television and the social club gathers roughly one hundred men every night to play cards, drink tea, and watch soccer. The club is not only a social institution but also, a highly political one. People discuss general politics as well as the square's local politics. About once a year a public square meeting is held, generally in the club (C10: 117).

Political power in Square 11 is mainly in the hands of the popular committee (*lajna sha'biya*). Officially every two years some 20-30 members are elected by the inhabitants of the square (Hamid 2000: 236). Contrary to the secretary, the president and the members of the committees are volunteers (PC2: 78). Hamid (2000: 236) summarizes the functions of the popular committees:

> The popular committees have numerous responsibilities which can broadly be grouped into: monitoring and supervision of the performance of agencies and service departments operating within their boundaries, provision of certain services, and mobilizing the local community to accomplish specific self-help projects, or to participate in political events such as rallies, collection of donations for the Popular Defence Forces, etc. They also assist the police, through surveillance and regular reporting, in maintaining law and order and in combating various forms of deviance within their jurisdiction.

During my field work, the committee was not very active. The population recognized only the secretary and the president as members of the committee, ignoring all other members. The secretary's main responsibility is maintaining relations with the inhabitants. He spends most of the day in a tea stall at the central square in meetings with people. The president represents the square to the outside. His real profession is an office worker for the locality (*Mahalya*), the next higher level of government administration. His position in the locality provides him with a form of 'political capital', which helps him influence decisions concerning his square.

Fig. 11: Tea Stall Used as Popular Committee Office and Old Water Tower

The popular committees replaced the functions of the sultans in the informal settlements and the internally displaced camps in the 1990s. Sultans still exist, but they are mostly responsible for settling disputes between people from their own ethnic group. Unlike the Sultans, who generally represent their own ethnic group, the popular committee is composed of members from different ethnic groups, but all are members of the National Congress Party (NCP). Due to this affiliation to the ruling party of Sudan, the committee also fulfils important security functions. Considering the president's suspicious views of my work and his initiative to request security services control my motivations and technical equipment, he seems to take these functions seriously (see 4.1).

5.2. Fragmentation of the Water Network at the Scale of the City

Pantuliano et al. (2011: 1) describe Greater Khartoum as "a patchwork of wealth and poverty, demographic density and sprawl, and robust and atrophied infrastructure. It is, in short, a microcosm of the contradictions that mark Sudan as a whole". The histories and characteristics of some neighbourhoods are similar; others like those of informal settlements and the city centre are fundamentally different. The socio-economic fragmentation of the city is reflected by residential land prices, which differ in Greater Khartoum by a factor of one thousand, between certain affluent neighbourhoods in the city centre and the settlements at the urban fringe (Müller-Mahn et al. 2010: 42).

The fragmentation of the city in terms of an urban settlement typology using the socio-economic status of their inhabitants is closely connected to the fragmentation of the water network. Gandy (2008: 126) underlines this relationship:

> The Western model of the 'bacteriological city', with its universal water and sewerage systems, rests on the assumption that urban space is both relatively homogeneous and spatially coherent, which is at odds with the extreme forms of social polarization and spatial fragmentation experienced in the cities of the global South.

Backer argues that "understanding contemporary patterns of fragmentation requires an analysis of the social and technical choices made over time regarding the expansion and distribution of a city's water supply system" (Bakker 2010b: 110). The primary objective of my work is not to explain the fragmented 'waterscape on the scale of the city'. Instead, fragmentation of Greater Khartoum's waterscape will be taken as an empirical reality in which is embedded the everyday practice of people.

The fragmentation of the water supply is not only due to the presence or absence of networked water supply, but it is a comparison between different local waterscapes, which are constituted by different means of water supply and access. Nevertheless, for this subchapter I will restrict my explanations to the fragmentation of the water network rather than of water supply in general, in order to later widen the debate, especially in chapter 7 with water gifts.

I will start with a general overview about water resources in order to later reveal the discrepancies of network supply between different neighbourhoods. This comparison is deeply indebted to Beckedorf (2011), who developed a political ecology of Khartoum's 'waterscape of the city', with a focus on the network.

5.2.1. Water Resources and Water Production

Despite the fact that Greater Khartoum is in the middle of Sahara desert, water scarcity is not an issue. Two major water resources can be used for supplying households: water from the Nile and groundwater.

Greater Khartoum is located at the confluence of the Blue Nile, which originates in the Ethiopian Highlands, and the White Nile, which is mainly fed by Lake Victoria. The Nile's water quality in the city is comparatively high compared to other large rivers in the world (Musa and Musa 1991). Defining a waterscape based on the Nile's 'natural boundaries', its river basin, embeds Greater Khartoum's waterscape within the hydro-political context of multiple countries. While some of these countries, like Egypt and Sudan, are highly dependent for their water consumption on Nile waters, others like Ethiopia contribute much more water to the Nile by precipitation and discharge, than they consume.

The Nile, as it flows today, is the result of multiple social and natural processes. Dams and canals change the flow of the water and large areas are irrigated to produce food. Nile water treaties under different political constellations, prior to and after reaching independence of the countries, led to contested quotas of sharing Nile water. A vast literature has emerged in recent years on the historical and contemporary politics of water in the Nile Basin (e.g. Mason 2009; Taha 2009; Tvedt 2004; Waterbury 2002).

Greater Khartoum's water consumption does not weigh heavily in international political debates about sharing Nile water since the quantities required for feeding the city amount only to about 1‰[60] of the quota guaranteed to Sudan in the water agreement of 1959. The stakes of political negotiations include irrigated agriculture and the construction of dams, which increase evaporation. The city's low water requirements also render international debate not very relevant for the availability of drinking water in the 'city's waterscape'.

The first water treatment plant was constructed in Khartoum in 1924 under the British and cleaned Nile water. The capacity has sharply increased through the construction of new pumping stations and water treatment plants and several extensions of existing ones (Beckedorf 2011: 77).

---

60 The KSWC extracted about 500,000 m^3 per day end of 2010 (Beckedorf 2011: 80), while Sudan has the right to consume 18.5 bm^3 per year (Taha 2009: 190).

The second source of drinking water is stored in aquifers in the Nubian sandstone. Water is pumped to the surface from decentralized boreholes.

Beckedorf (2011: 79) assumes that about the same amount of water is extracted from groundwater as from the Nile. The aquifers are partially recharged by the Nile, but depletion might occur especially in the neighbourhoods that are far from the Nile, if too much groundwater is extracted (Algafar, Abdou, and Abdelsalam 2011; Farah, Mustafa, and Kumai 2000: 672). Abd Alraheem (2000: 263) warns of pollution through infiltration of sewage water, which is directly discharged into the alluvial deposits. In Omdurman two aquifers can be accessed. The higher aquifer reaches a depth of about 120 metres (Farah et al. 1997) with the water table stretching between 10 metres to over 60 metres from the Nile (Algafar, Abdou, and Abdelsalam 2011: 619).[61] While the higher aquifer is partially brackish, especially in several pockets, the lower aquifer at between 150 and 500 metres is of better drinking quality.

5.2.2. Water Distribution in Greater Khartoum: a Network Perspective

The Nile, which both replenishes aquifers and is itself a source of drinking water, provides sufficient water to surpass internationally recommended consumption levels for all households in Greater Khartoum. However, despite this physical availability, not all households are supplied with water within the network paradigm. The lack of access to network water is therefore not based on physical limitations but as Shiva (2002: 119) argues "scarcity and abundance are not naturally given, they are products of water culture". Kulindwa and Lein (2008: 3) define water scarcity as "the result of the interplay between resource availability, consumption patterns and the (mis-)management of the resources". Consequently, two key reasons can explain network water scarcity for a portion of Greater Khartoum's population. On the one hand, there is unequal distribution due to the government's priorities when investing in water infrastructure in general and the performance of these investments. On the other hand, the scarcity is the result of specific spatial patterns of investment that favour certain areas and neglect others.

---

61 We can assume the groundwater table in Square 11 to be at least 50 metres below the surface since the area is 40 metres above the Nile and the table is at least 10 metres below the level of the Nile.

Water networks date back to the colonial period, when the British Administration finalized a network in Khartoum in 1907 and shortly after, another in the Souq of Omdurman (Kennedy 1907, 1908). Beckedorf (2011: 86) compares population growth in Greater Khartoum with the spread of the water network. In the years directly after independence, the network's development generally kept pace with population growth, allowing nearly full coverage. This changed dramatically in the mid-1980s when population increased much faster than before, whereas network expansion stagnated. Almost two thirds of population had no network connection by the end of the 1990s. In the second half of the 2000s, the Khartoum State Water Corporation (KSWC) strongly invested in the networks and the number of connected households doubled within 5 years. Beckedorf estimates the network coverage increased to about 50%.

The development of Greater Khartoum's water supply network is partially based on neoliberal reforms of the agglomeration's water sector. Being politically isolated from the West since the 1990s, Sudan was not forced by the World Bank and the IMF to implement a Structural Adjustment Programme, like many other African countries. Instead they chose to implement neoliberal reforms – especially decentralization, privatization, and commercialization – within the international trend of neoliberalization and under the pressure of substantial budget shortages (Beckedorf 2011: 124). The neoliberalization of Greater Khartoum's waterscape is a process, rather than an abrupt change, in which different actors either push these trends or work against them. Through the 1994 Water Sector reform, the responsibility of providing water was transferred from the national level to the state level, which led to the creation of the KSWC (Beckedorf 2011: 94). The KSWC's history directly mirrors the international debate of whether water should be privately or publicly managed. Until 2000, the KSWC remained a classic public water provider, with managers who "were reluctant to privatize water services, because they considered water supply to be a governmental duty" (Beckedorf 2011: 128). Beckedorf (2011: 133) argues that the neoliberal reforms were strongly connected to the KSWC general manager appointed in 2001, who was very "private sector friendly" and "transformed the KSWC from a governmental water corporation to a governmental entity increasingly similar to a private company". A new accounting system was implemented that tracked profit and loss, total staff was reduced, employee attendance was electronically monitored, and significant tasks were outsourced to private companies (Beckedorf 2011: 135, 183, 190).

Cooperation with the private sector is one of the key factors in the progress of water connections in recent year since it allowed infrastructures to expand without the KSWC directly investing. Construction companies or banks finance both water networks and water treatment plants. Consumers reimburse these investments via the KSWC either through general water fees for water treatment plants or with a specific network charge paid after the establishment of a new network by the newly connected households over a period of several years (Beckedorf 2011: 142, 151). Ultimately, infrastructures become KSWC property.

Beckedorf's evaluation of public-private partnerships in Greater Khartoum's water management is not as positive as the indicator on network coverage might suggest. With the neoliberalization of Greater Khartoum's waterscape new financial sources could be accessed, but "huge amounts of these financial resources were secretly shared between private companies, the KSWC managers and members of the Khartoum State Government, which impeded any comprehensive enhancement of the water supply system" (Beckedorf 2011: 171). A political ecology of water at the scale of Greater Khartoum reveals the strong interconnectedness of political and economic power. Beckedorf (2011: 172) argues, that water privatization has created a new geometry of power with a new elite composed of "political business men, who are at the same time private company directors, party affiliates and political decision-makers in search of new economic opportunities".

The neoliberal reforms in water management did not only have an impact on water coverage, but also on the relation between the water provider and the consumers. Between 1999 and 2005 water prices strongly increased (Beckedorf 2011: 205). Because hardly any fees were collected in the 1990s, the government sourced out money collection to private firms that collect the fees directly at the door of the houses (Beckedorf 2011: 206) and the non-paying are cut from the network (Beckedorf 2011: 213).

There is still leeway to further commercialize water. In Greater Khartoum households do not pay the water they consume since no water metres are installed. According to Beckedorf, the KSWC is reluctant to introduce metres in residential areas. Water in Greater Khartoum is charged at a flat rate tariff, which differs according to the size of the main pipe to the house. Households pay 45 SDG for a pipe of 1 inch diameter and 25 SDG for ¾ inch and 15

SDG for ½ inch, respectively. Household connections in resettlement schemes are exclusively connected by ½ inch pipes.[62]

5.2.3. Network Access: a Question of Social Class

As long as the performance of water networks is not considered, network fragmentation is a binary indicator that differentiates between 'the connected' and 'the unconnected'. A water network is a spatial unity and in Greater Khartoum networks are nearly always constructed for whole neighbourhoods. Fragmentation of water networks at the level of the 'city's waterscape' can be determined by comparing different neighbourhoods.

A community's economic capacity strongly correlates with whether a network is implemented or not. Three categories of neighbourhoods can be roughly established. With very few exceptions, upper and middle class settlements are located in the more central areas of Greater Khartoum and all are connected to water. In newly established first or even second class settlements that are further from the centre, people will only start building houses when their plots are connected to the water network and other services are ensured.

The second category includes the formally planned neighbourhoods constructed since the 1990s to host the former population of informal settlements. This category is internally heterogeneous since it is in process of being connected. While several neighbourhoods are already connected, others are still waiting.

The third category of settlements consists of the remaining camps for the internally displaced and the old and new informal settlements. These settlements are formally excluded from network water supply. A prerequisite for having a network in peri-urban settlements is the completion of a formal planning process. The financial capacities of inhabitants of informal settlements would not be sufficient to establish water networks, nor would such an investment be sustainable since water systems are a long term investment, which are incompatible with the insecurity of land tenure. However, even if people had the capacity to establish a network, they could not since the government prohibits individuals from providing services in informal settlements (e.g. Bannaga 1996: 13). The establishment of informal settlements therefore

---

62 1 Sudanese Pound (SDG) = 0.315 EUR (average exchange rate between August and December 2010)

strongly depends on the existence of water sources in proximity as for example in the informal settlement of Nifasha, which could be established in this location, only, because of existent agricultural infrastructure, where donkey carts can be filled or where people can obtain free water.

The network fragmentation of neighbourhoods in Greater Khartoum follows patterns that are typical for African cities. Water supply favours urban population according to their economic status. The inequality goes beyond a mere lag between network expansion and urban growth in the peripheries. Rather, it is based on a political process in which decisions are taken to build networks in certain areas and not in others. With the same money, central networks can be maintained and improved or new networks can be established for the urban poor.

Beckedorf (2011: 247) demonstrated the KSWC's priority setting and the related political agendas that influence the spatiality of investments with the example of the network extension, closely related to the new water treatment plant Manara on the banks of the Nile. The treatment plant was built by the British company Biwater, and inaugurated in 2010. It was partly financed by the company itself, as well as the Dutch Development Bank. Water fees will reimburse construction over the next 10 years. Purified water is pumped into reservoirs to serve neighbourhood networks (partially as hybrid networks in combination with boreholes). A projected total of 1.5 M inhabitants will be served by the network. The project area includes a military camp and comparatively affluent neighbourhoods in Omdurman close to the Nile, which were already supplied by network water, and two resettlement areas including the northern part of Dar Alsalam and the oldest part of the latest resettlement project area El Fatih.

Beckedorf argues that especially El Fatih was included by the Khartoum State Government under pressure from UN organizations, because of their interest in service provision for the internally displaced. In the course of the project, Beckedorf argues that the KSWC has increasingly shifted priorities from the poor to the richer neighbourhoods and the military camp. The connection of Dar Alsalam and El Fatih was strongly delayed and Manara water treatment plan was only running at 25% of its total capacity during my 2010 research period. The first served areas were those neighbourhoods close to the centre of Omdurman that had already been supplied by network water but which – contrary to peripheral areas – are inhabited by the political and economic elite. The KSWC even considered supplying areas that were not part of the original project because of demonstrations against problems in water supply by an economic middle class.

The decision to allocate recent investments to specific settlements is highly political with different actors interfering different levels. The questions encompassed by these debates are ethical in nature. Fair network access for all inhabitants is compromised by the interests of the upper and middle classes. Even if northern Dar Alsalam becomes fully connected to Manara in the future, the KSWC might divert more and more water to other areas of the city, where people have more possibilities to influence decisions.

5.3. Fragmentation among Neighbourhoods with Similar Socio-Economic Characteristics

The previous subchapter distinguishes three types of neighbourhoods in the 'waterscape of the city' according to the probability of having a network installed. Dar Alsalam is situated halfway between the fully served neighbourhoods of the rich and the neighbourhoods excluded due to the legal status of the settlement. Certain neighbourhoods in this median category – including Square 11 – are already connected while others are not.

In this chapter the analysis of the fragmentation of the 'waterscape of the city' is augmented with an analysis of the 'waterscape of interconnected networks', which contains the neighbourhoods in northern Dar Alsalam where the network is already installed. Heterogeneity on this scale is not analysed with the binary variable of connected/non-connected areas, but within a continuum, which differentiates connected neighbourhoods using the quality of water supply.

Before discussing the fragmentation of the 'waterscape of interconnected networks', I will retrace the history of the transformation of Square 11 from a non-connected to a connected neighbourhood. Finally, I will analyse how fragmentation on this scale is naturally influenced and politically negotiated.

5.3.1. A Water History of Square 11: Transformation of a Non-Connected Area into a Connected One

Square 11 of Dar Alsalam has profited from increased investments in water infrastructure since the mid-2000s. In 2007 a network was installed, which was temporarily supplied by groundwater and which is intended to become connected to the Manara water treatment plant.

Water Supply Prior to the Network

Until 2007, the water consumed in Square 11 would have been classified by the UN as 'unimproved', hence, not fulfilling the Millennium Development Goals. The only water that physically entered the square was extracted from groundwater aquifers and transported by water vendors with donkey carts to the households. Different NGOs financed the construction of boreholes and water towers in the squares of Dar Alsalam. In Square 11 a tower was established in the north-eastern corner of the service area financed by Adventist Development and Relief Agency (ADRA) around 1993, hence, shortly after the first inhabitants arrived. Until that point, sufficient water was available from other towers including the tower of a neighbouring farm (COM2: 23). Tower management was immediately given over to the public water corporation.

The biographies of water delivered through these systems cannot be designated as 'informal', because they are the result of a public-private partnership between the KSWC and water vendors, funded in part by international donors. Not only did the NGOs finance the water towers, they also provided households with donkey carts (WV1: 72; WV4: 93). The water vending system based on donkey carts is part of the water supply strategy for these kinds of settlements that was elaborated between the NGOs and the government. The cooperation between the government, which produces water, and individual entrepreneurs, who deliver the water to the customers, is based on certain agreements and control mechanisms: the price of water at the towers is unified, donkey carts need to be licensed, and regulations about the varnishing of the interior of the barrel exist and are controlled (e.g. WV1: 13; WV4: 104).

The Network

Towards the end of 2006, a contractor constructed a network for the KSWC. Networks in the squares of Dar Alsalam are supplied by different sources, which include the old water towers constructed for the water vendors in the past, new boreholes constructed inside a particular square, and boreholes from neighbouring squares, since the networks are inter-connected.

Like the design of the streets, the design of the network is exactly the same for most of the neighbourhoods. Six inch pipes are installed around the square and on the four main roads which connect the central square to this frame. In every east-west street, a 4 inch pipe is installed. Every house inhabited when the network was built is connected to the street pipe by a ½ inch pipe. Consequently, the empty plots, either never settled or abandoned in the meantime, are not connected unless the later inhabitants negotiated a connection with the KSWC.

The cost of the network is passed on to water consumers through their instalment payments. Households are charged 26 SDG (8.20 EUR), which includes the water fee for a ½ inch pipe of 15 SDG, 10 SDG for repaying the infrastructure, and 1 SDG as tax. The overall cost of the network was set to 580 SDG per household for Square 11. Consequently, after barely five years of regular payment, the monthly payments are designed to reduce to 16 SDG. The total amount to be paid was calculated from the total costs of the network divided by the number of inhabited plots (KSWC 04: 81), which is based on a list of the popular committee. A comparison of network costs with three neighbouring squares, which also received a network at the same time, reveals that per household costs in certain squares can sometimes total twice the price in other squares.[63] This high discrepancy cannot be explained by population density, which is similar across the different squares, but by the establishment of total costs. It might also be connected to corrupted practices within the KSWC and the acceptance of high network costs (e.g. Beckedorf 2011: 166).

The new networks in Dar Alsalam are presently exclusively supplied by local boreholes but they will be transformed into hybrid networks after the squares are connected to Manara. The high capacity boreholes in the area will be maintained and will supplement Nile water with groundwater. The network situation, observed during fieldwork, can be expected to change when Dar Alsalam's networks are connected to Manara. Hence, the present analysis of Square 11 is only the representation of a particular moment in its water history.

---

[63] Square 9: 716 SDG, Square 10: 440 SDG, Square 11: 580 SDG, Square 12: 900 SDG (KSWC04: 82).

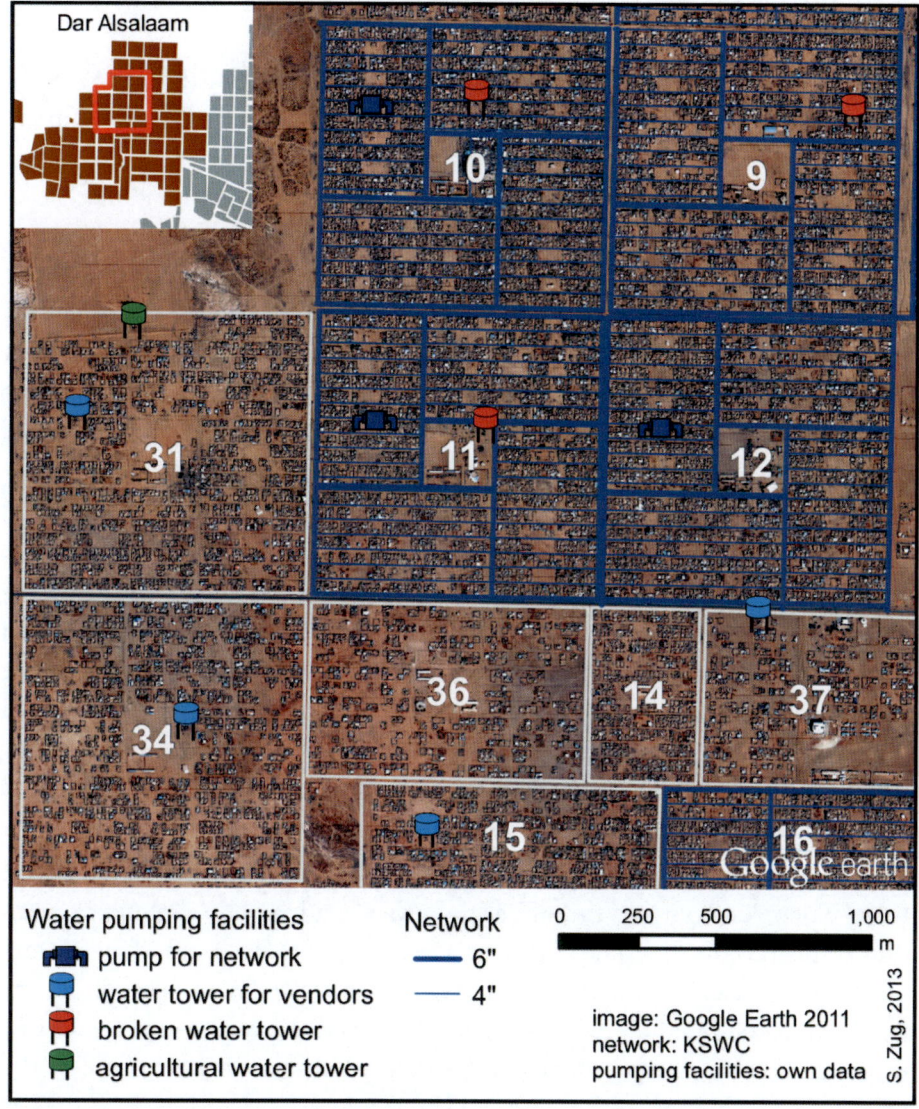

Fig. 12: Water Infrastructure in Square 11 and Neighbouring Squares

5.3.2. Tracking Fragmentation by Tree Canopy

Water networks in Dar Alsalam perform very differently. In this section I would like to compare Square 11's water supply with the network of neighbouring squares (Square 9, 10, and 12). I will also consider Square 31, which does not yet have a network.[64]

I received permission for only one day of research in neighbouring squares. The information presented here on network performance in these other squares is therefore based on data gathered from the KSWC, discussions with actors in Square 11, and satellite images. This is in contrast with information on Square 11 derived from household interviews and direct observations. Water vendors are the most important experts on network performance since they generally work in several different squares and their income is strongly connected to network performance.

In absence of a network, neighbourhoods like Square 31 are strongly dependent on water delivery by vendors. These areas are water vendors' key markets. This is in sharp contrast to Square 9 and 12 where water vendors no longer find customers unless exceptional problems arise and boreholes cannot be operated. Although Square 10 and 11 are connected, water vendors are still very present in these areas. One water vendor (WV1) who lives in Square 11 works exclusively in Square 10. He reports pockets in the latter square where people still do not have water.

Not all aspects of a waterscape are invisible like the underground networks. The way people use water can affect the urban landscape. People in Dar Alsalam plant trees in their courtyards and in front of their houses. These trees give shade and increase the quality of life. They are also status symbols, at the same level as the building material of the walls and the quality of the door of the house. The trees require investments that extend past the purchase of the tree itself, to include regular watering. The tree most planted in Square 11 is locally called 'damas' (*Conocarpus lancifolius*). Baumer (1983: 156) and Booth and Wickens (1988: 52) describe the ecology, distribution and cultivation of these trees: They naturally grow on intermittent watercourses in northern Somalia, but are also cultivated in Sudan (Khartoum and Kassala). Damas trees are evergreen and reach up to 30 metres. They are tolerant of salinity

---

[64] In my analysis I will not consider the squares south of Square 11 since they are less populated than the other squares and much more recently established than the ones in the north, hence, they are less comparable.

and can withstand drought conditions for several months. In a natural environment the tree is dependent on a shallow groundwater table. However, in Square 11 even older trees need to be watered every two to three days with up to four jerrycans since the groundwater table is too low. A local tree nursery (COM6: 22) argues that people prefer the damas tree despite its high water consumption over less water consuming trees like neem (*Azadirachtaindica*) because it is already tall enough to provide shade after only 6 months. Shade is the main argument for cultivating plants, but several houses attribute more value to plants by also cultivating ornamental ground plants, and even in certain cases, lemon trees. Except the lemon trees, urban agriculture in the sense of food production is inexistent in Square 11 as well as in most other settlement areas in Greater Khartoum. Urban agriculture is restricted to large scale projects with their own boreholes and to farming along the bank of the Nile (Franck 2007: 107).

Trees in the city have been analysed in the framework of political ecology and authors revealed that the spatial distribution of trees correlates with social, economic, and ethical characteristics of inhabitants, due to government investment patterns in street trees or people's interest and economic abilities to grow trees on the own premises (e.g. Heynen, Perkins, and Roy 2006; Landry and Chakraborty 2009). In Dar Alsalam the political ecology of trees is strongly linked to the political ecology of the water network. The canopy of trees in different neighbourhoods therefore allows us indirectly to evaluate the performance of the water network. The fast growth of trees in the Sudanese environment supports such an approach since it minimizes the lag between the development of the tree canopy and network improvements.

The tree canopy was determined through remote sensing.[65] The five squares strongly differ in the proportional total of tree canopy. The analysis reveals similar results to the information on water performance provided by water vendors. In the square without a public network (31), hardly any trees are cultivated (0.15%) while in the squares with very good network performance

---

65 The rather small area that was analysed allows a manual approach to remote sensing. Hence, every tree crown was marked with a circle according to the size of the crown. For calculation, open squares including the service area of each square and the smaller open squares were excluded from the data. Tree canopy, consequently, includes only streets and areas planned for housing (including non-settled plots, which are rather homogeneously distributed in all areas). Since the density of inhabited plots is very similar in all squares, the results of different squares should allow a comparison of the water supply in particular areas.

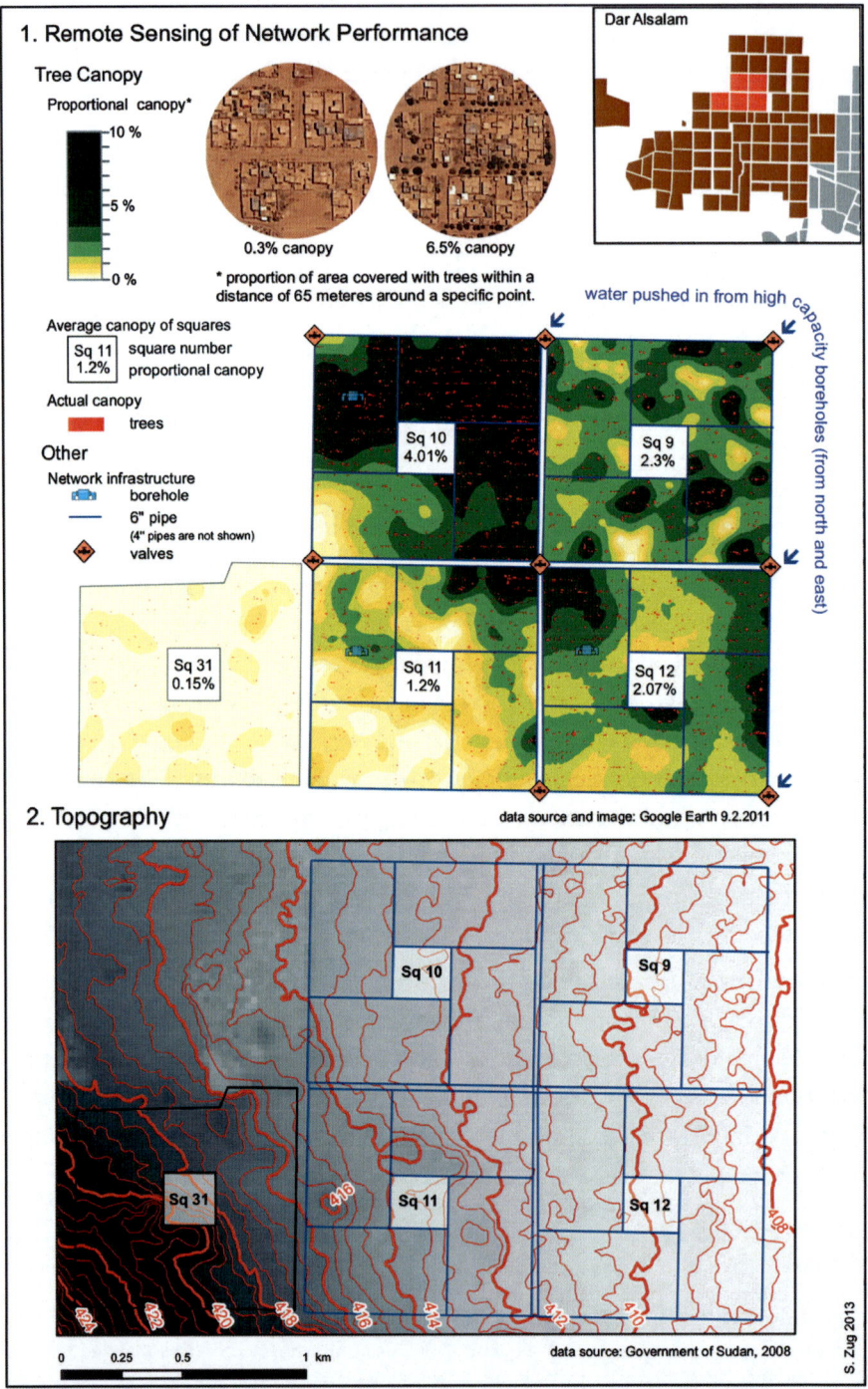

Fig. 13: Tree Canopy and Topography of Square 11 and Neighbouring Squares

(9 and 12) more than 10 times more surface area is covered with trees. In Square 10 the canopy is the densest (4%) but the trees are not equally distributed. Square 11, the square with the weakest network in the area, has significantly lower tree coverage (only 1.2 %).

5.3.3. Explaining Differences in Water Network Performance

The preceding subchapter has demonstrated that different networks in Dar Alsalam more or less satisfactorily deliver water to the inhabitants of connected squares. Explaining the performance of every individual network requires analysing both the particular elements of each network as well as its relationship to other networks. All networks are connected with each other on three levels.

Firstly, they are naturally connected since they are supplied from the same groundwater aquifer and they are elements on a continuous physical landscape.

Secondly, they are technologically connected. By design, every network is a closed system, which can be operated independently form the networks of other squares. However, in the corners of each square valves are installed (see Figure 13.1), which – when opened – allow water to pass from one network to another. In Square 7, to the east, and Square 25, to the north-east of Square 11, two high capacity boreholes are installed. They produce more water than can be consumed in the particular square. The water is shunted towards other networks, like the one in Square 9, which is fully dependent on this 'external' water since there is no operational borehole there. The water also enters those squares with boreholes that do not perform sufficiently to fully supply the square.

Finally the networks are socially, politically, and economically connected. The networks of all squares are operated by the KSWC. The same managers and the same engineers make all the decisions. Consequently, the KSWC institution binds the different networks together. Political negotiations between people of one square do not only influence the network of that particular square, but can also impact several other squares.

In its short history, the network of Square 11 has used very different water sources. In the beginning, the KSWC planned to connect the square's network to the water tower located on the service area, which was used as a filling station for water vendors. However, the borehole ran dry half a year before the network was finished (KSWC 10: 75; PC1: 246) and rehabilitation attempts were not successful (KSWC 04: 27; PC1: 244). Mid 2007, Square 11's network was connected to Square 10, where certain households were still unconnected at the time (e.g. KSWC 10: 80). When all of Square 10's households became fully connected, water pressure in Square 11 decreased. At the end of 2009, a new borehole was established on an open yard in the north-western sector of Square 11 and a generator operated pump has been supplying the square since early 2010 (KSWC 10: 16). Mid 2010 the existing pump was replaced with a higher capacity pump (KSWC 10: 86; KSWC 06:08) but pressure remained insufficient.

The KSWC opened and closed the valves to the neighbouring squares several times, hoping that more water from other squares would enter Square 11 than leave it. To a large degree, valve management in Dar Alsalam is based on trial and error since the engineers cannot exactly define the amount of water that is pumped from a borehole to a neighbouring square because water must first flow through the network of the square where the pump is installed.[66] Consequently, water flows in each square and water pressure in any tap at any given time, are a result of the complex interaction of several elements. Boreholes in different locations with different production capacities and operation times push water into the network from different directions. The given design of the overall network allows water to move more easily in one direction than another. The friction of water in the pipe reduces water pressure in correlation to the distance from the borehole. Water in the pipe is reduced through leakage and the consumption of households, which differs spatially. Finally, gravity impacts flow of the water within the network.

Since the topography is not flat, gravity is a major factor in water flows and the unequal distribution of water amongst the squares. The Nile in the city centre is about 373 m above sea level and Square 11 is about 40 metres higher. While the centre of Omdurman is comparatively flat, the slope increases towards the peripheries. Dar Alsalam is not hilly, and one has to look very closely to see the slope at all, which is some 4 to 8 m per kilometre in the five

---

[66] In the future, when the squares are connected to the Manara treatment plant, each square will be directly connected to the main pipes in order to allow the metering of each square's consumption (Beckedorf 2011: 231). The presently existing connections between the squares will be cut (KSWC04: 127).

analysed squares. The gentle slope is beneficial during the rainy season allowing the discharge of rainwater without leading to major erosion.

Just as rainwater flows towards the east, the water in pipes – if the valves are opened – flows from Square 10 and 11 towards Square 9 and 12. If enough water was produced, the topography would not pose a problem, because the network would be continuously filled from the east to the west until water pressure reaches the highest point of the network in the south-western corner of Square 11. However, water production is insufficient, offering more water to the lower squares than to the higher ones. Disconnecting Square 11 from the other squares would prevent the water produced in the square to flow to the other squares. However, since the most productive boreholes are to the east, it would also restrict additional water entering the square.

The differences in network performance are not only known and experienced by inhabitants of the different squares, who compare their water connection to those of people living in other squares, but also by the KSWC employees, who are aware of heterogeneity of supply. Information flows about the performance of Square 11 to the KSWC are certainly excellent because one of the two KSWC desk officers, who is responsible for recording the complaints of individual household for all of Dar Alsalam, lives in Square 11 (KSWC10).

5.3.4. Lobbying for Square 11. Negotiating Fragmentation

The topography and the law of gravity influence the flow of water but do not determine it. The social interaction with nature finally leads to inequality in access. The KSWC decisions are not only technical; they are also the result of political interactions between several actors within different scales. Infrastructure installations as well as specific management decisions are politically negotiated between the KSWC managers and engineers as well as non-KSWC actors, including the political representatives of the squares.

The example of Square 11 demonstrates that lobbying by the popular committee can to a certain degree successfully change a waterscape. Lobbying does not focus on distributive justice between different types of neighbourhoods. Its concern is not to claim services for low income neighbourhoods instead of for the more affluent neighbourhoods in the city centre. Rather, lobbying focuses on distributing benefits of investment in water infrastructure and allocation of water by valve management between the Squares of Dar Alsalam. The lobbyists of each square – in large part, the political elite – defend the benefits of their square and, consequently, negotiate Dar Alsalam's overall fragmentation. Lobbying for Square 11 on this scale is more likely to be successful than demanding services that would infringe on those offered to the city centre's economic and political elite.

Claiming Infrastructure Improvements by the Popular Committee

The president of the popular committee is the key actor in negotiations between the KSWC and inhabitants of Square 11. He is very proud of his political influence and his lobbying efforts for the square's two major infrastructural projects: electricity and water. He explains:

> When the KSWC said that they will build new networks everybody rushed there. I went 34 times. The people in the KSWC appreciated that. […] Khalid Khalid, the previous head of the KSWC used to have Sundays and Wednesdays as citizen day with open doors from 8 to 8. I used the chance to visit him. I have a very good relationship with him. […] Khalid said to me 'if my secretary tells me that two people from the project area are waiting for me, I will first ask for the one from Square 11' (PC1: 11).

His efforts paid off, especially when repairs to the old water tower were not successful and water from Square 10 was insufficient. Although Square 11's connection to the Manara project was scheduled for the middle of 2010, a new borehole was drilled at the end of 2009. When the president of the popular committee learned that the KSWC would construct seven new boreholes in Dar Alsalam, he took initiative:

> PC1 (28): I always went there and stated our problem. Every day they found me in their office to receive my complaints. […] I just thought it would be a good idea to have the borehole. It's a reserve if something in Manara breaks down. Sometimes maintenance in Manara might take time so it's good to have the borehole as a back-up.
>
> SZ: How did they accept?
>
> PC1: I pressured them with the president of the locality and Khalid Khalid, the General Manger of the KSWC.

The president of the popular committee is referring here to two people who supported his claim. He approached each differently. He paid tribute to the general manager of the KSWC by going into his office and waiting. Whereas, he has close ties to the president of the locality, as he is part of the latter's staff.

A KSWC manager confirms the popular committee president's successful lobbying:

> In a water committee meeting the president of the popular committee from Square 11 raised complaints against the KSWC to the president of the locality about water performance. A political decision was taken despite the engineers' opinion that it did not make sense to build the borehole since Square 11 would be connected to Manara anyway. [...] As a result, the president of Umbadda Locality earned credit with the population (KSWC04: 34).

In the end, the KSWC's investment decision was the result of a complex political constellation, in which the president of the popular committee could use the social capital he had built up over time. These social connections are one element in a complex political system of clientelism and patronage. The president's achievements in the field of local water planning could increase his symbolic capital in the square's political field, leading to a possible re-election. Additional infrastructure for Square 11 comes at the detriment of other squares. From a distributive ethics' perspective, this decision could be strongly criticised and has been by the KSWC Manager. The investment in Square 11 would have more greatly benefited those squares with no plans to be connected to Manara.

Similar political lobbying took place in the current electrification of Dar Al-salam. The secretary of the popular committee reports that they pushed to accelerate Square 11's connection: "There was a plan for electricity to come. We were to receive it after Square 12 and Square 9. We used our connections in not clean ways to get the connections just after Square 12" (PC2: 69).

Interfering in Water Management. The Researcher as a Political Actor

During my research, I analysed the water supply system in the square and interviewed different employees of the KSWC in various offices in Omdurman. Towards the end, I became both an expert for Square 11's water system and a political actor, influencing the square's management practices. This section will outline these experiences to demonstrate a lobbyist's potential influence. I established contact with local KSWC employees through letters signed by their KSWC superiors. Having these letters in my hand encouraged the

KSWC staff to take me seriously. During my research, I established solid relationships with these actors by waiting for them, having tea with them, sharing satellite images, engaging in small talk, and discussing the water network's technical problems. Since the employees themselves have a vested interest in changing the situation, these discussions were highly appreciated and small, management changes were effectuated, generally without any active requests on my part.

My presence in the square concretely changed management on two occasions linked to fuel supply and water exchanges with neighbouring squares. Due to technical limitations, the generator in Square 11 is only allowed to be operated twice daily for a seven hour period each time (KSWC06: 18, KSWC04: 62). In practice the borehole is operated for two periods of four hours due to an insufficient fuel supply. Sometimes fuel runs completely out and pumping stops completely for several days. In mid-December 2010 I wanted to measure water pressure, but the borehole was not operating because no fuel had been delivered (KSWC13: 72). I went to the KSWC manager responsible for supplying the boreholes with fuel. He informed me about the end of year budget shortages and that he would only be able to supply half the usual quantities of fuel over the next several weeks (KSWC05: 40). When I explained that I could not continue my water pressure measurements, he offered to send additional fuel to the square. The additional supply to Square 11 meant, however, that other squares would receive less during that same period. Although my relationship with the KSWC is fundamentally different than that of the popular committee, I too could (slightly) influence the attribution of resources to 'my' square.

With another engineer, I discussed valve management between Square 11 and the other squares. We jointly developed the idea to install two non-return valves that would prevent water flowing from Square 11 to Square 12 while allowing inverse water flows. Consequently, Square 11's water network would have more water available since all water produced in the square would stay within the square while at night additional water would still flow into the square. We agreed to close all valves between Square 11 and the neighbouring squares. In the experimental phase, the valve in the lowest corner would be opened in the morning when water tends to leave the square, and closed in the evening when water starts flowing into the square, to simulate non-return valves. If the experiment was successful, the manager offered to consider installing non-return valves.

The results of the experiment were not immediately conclusive and in the first days at least the situation did not significantly change.67 However, the experiment clarified the interaction between the KSWC, the committee, and the Square's consumers. Controlling the valves could easily have been handled by two workers. However, the KSWC Manager personally travelled to Square 11 with seven of his staff. With such a large team, the KSWC demonstrated their determination to improve water supply, they created a visible symbol. Earlier similar interventions are not proof that the KSWC was convinced that different valve management would benefit the square's water management. Rather, it can be partially understood as proof that the KSWC is showing people they actively improved the situation.

Fig. 14: A Group of KSWC Staff Closing a Valve in a Manhole

The whole procedure is imbedded in rituals of reciprocity. Upon arriving in the square, we went directly to the tea stall the secretary of the popular committee uses as his office. All the KSWC staff was invited for tea. After the

---

67 I could not follow up the experiment since it took place during the last week of my field research.

work was done, we came back for lunch at the expense of the secretary. Certain social rules regulate how water supply is negotiated. Hospitality increases the social capital of the popular committee in reference to the KSWC. "When they finished the borehole, we even slaughtered a sheep for the workers" (PC2: 128).

Although the situations described in this section were strongly influenced by my presence, they demonstrate that the decisions of the KSWC management can be influenced by the agenda of consumers and their representatives. The situation suggests an interpretation of the state of the KSWC. The problematic water situation is a source of pressure for the KSWC's staff. While engineers are used to handling user complaints, a researcher could potentially expose them to additional criticism. The engineers displayed a certain amount of desperation because they were incapable of guaranteeing the network's maximum performance, to the point of considering advice from a social scientist on engineering topics.

5.4. Fragmentation Inside Square 11

Previously, I analyzed the heterogeneity of the network's different fragments (each corresponding to a separate square) in the 'waterscape of the interconnected network'. I will concentrate in this subchapter on the heterogeneity of network water supply within the 'waterscape of a neighbourhood', the technical difficulties to level this inequality, and the social implications of this heterogeneity. As in the previous chapter I will use the tree canopy as an indicator for network performance.

5.4.1. The Spatial-Temporal Development of Tree Canopy and Water Supply

Tree distribution does not only reveal different expanses of canopy in the various squares but also a very strong heterogeneity within each square. The history of Square 11's tree cover can be read as the history of the water network (Figure 15). In 2006, when the square was not yet connected to the network, trees were only scarcely distributed in the square. In the following years vegetation cover strongly increased in the north-eastern corner, along with significant growth in two other sub-squares (NW and SE). Only in the

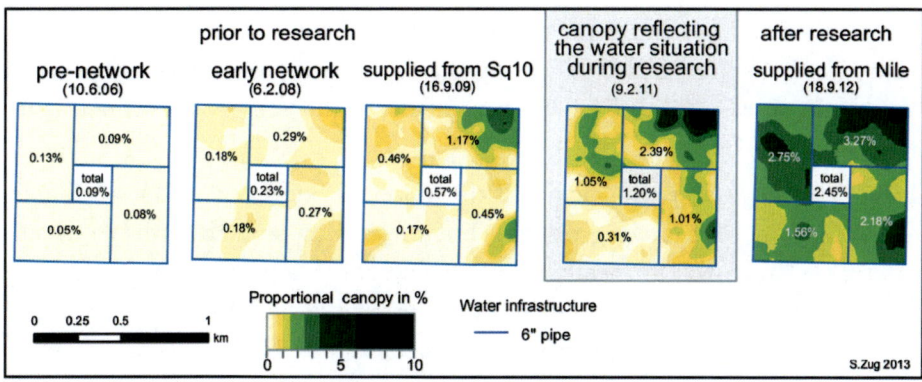

Fig. 15: The Development of Tree Canopy in Square 11 (2006-2012)

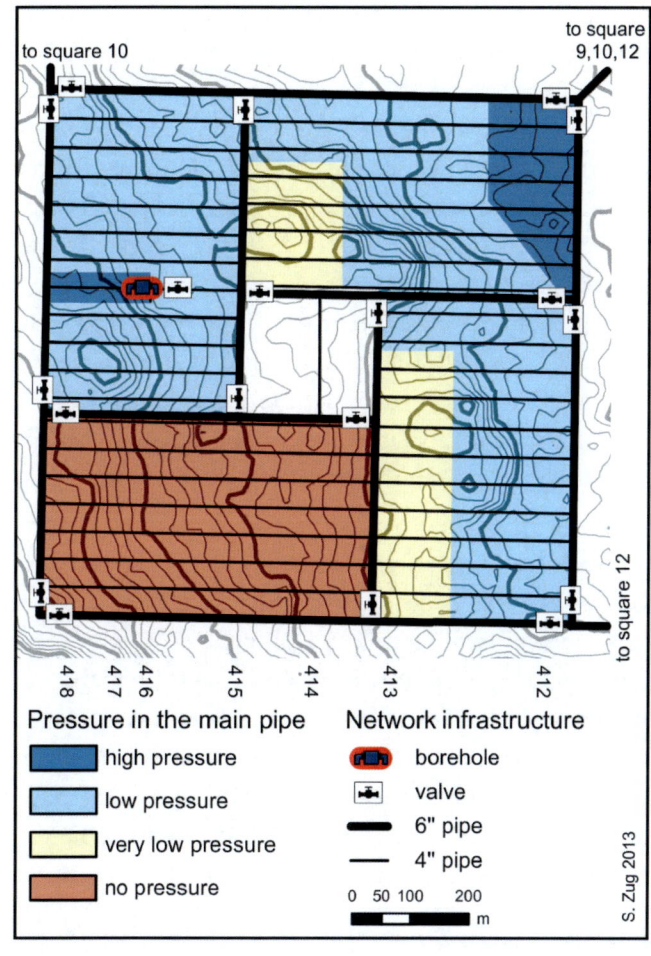

Fig. 16: Internal Fragmentation of Square 11's Network Supply

south-western sub-square was the increase in tree cover marginal (0.31%). In 2011, it was as low as tree cover in squares with no networks.[68] The canopy in the north-eastern sub-square was nearly eight times larger than in the north-eastern square.

Field research took place roughly 2 to 8 months before the 2011 satellite image was taken. Since trees grow fast, but still require some months to develop a visible crown, the images can be considered to reflect the water situation during my research. The results of the canopy analysis correspond closely to inhabitant's perceptions about water availability throughout Square 11 and to various water pressure measurements in several households. The square can be roughly divided into four categories of water pressure available to household taps (Figure 16). In two small areas (dark blue), people enjoyed excellent access and water pressure allows water barrels to be directly filled with a garden hose. The larger area is located in the north-eastern corner, the square's lowest area and the one with the densest canopy in 2011. The smaller area is located in a single street where houses are directly connected to the pipe that connects the borehole to the network. Pressure in this pipe is exceptionally high although the area is located in a relatively elevated area. In the south-western sub-square (red) there is no water access and the taps have remained dry since the network was constructed. On the western edges of the eastern squares (yellow), people could only access water on very rare occasions. Supply was insufficient compared to the total demand of the population. In vast areas of the square (light blue) water access is possible but requires investments, as we will see in the chapter 6.

The last satellite image of September 2012, taken roughly 2 years after the research period, displays a sharp break with this trend. In the north-eastern corner of the square, the tree canopy has hardly increased, while trees grew profusely in those areas with minimum coverage in the past. In the south-western sub-square, vegetation increased fivefold within a mere 18 months. The 2012 change in vegetation growth is due to the Square 11's connection to the new Manara water treatment plant at the Nile in February 2012.[69] Water pressure strongly increased and the areas that had never received water, now had high pressure access. This allowed people to plant new trees, while allowing existing trees to grow faster. This abrupt change in

---

68 In Square 31 the canopy was 0.15% that same year (see Figure 13)
69 Telephone Interview 15.12.2012 with CHR1.

trends demonstrates how closely the development of the tree canopy is connected to the performance of the water network, rather than to heterogeneity of population or soil.

5.4.2. Topography, Network Design, and the Possibility of Managing Water Distribution Inside Square 11

Gravity is not the sole explanation for the heterogeneity of water access in Square 11; network design also plays a role. One solution for more equal distribution of water is implementing an alternating supply schedule for the different areas of the square. This is a common management strategy in Greater Khartoum. Water pressure is increased for several hours in one area, while service is halted to other areas. Within a neighbourhood, inequality is thus minimized.

In Square 11, however, the techno-spatial configuration of the network does not allow for an efficient schedule management since the elevated areas in the west cannot be disconnected from the low lying ones in the east.[70] The KSWC was aware of the problem, but was reluctant to install an additional pipe that would have allowed for the separation.[71]

Nevertheless, the KSWC did implement a schedule, which changed every other day. On Day 1, water is pumped from the borehole towards a rather high point of the square, to the west (A1, Figure 17). In the street from the borehole to the network, water pressure is very high because all the water is pushed against gravity. Most of the water is then channelled through 6 inch pipes directly to the lowest corner of the square (A2a+b). Only a little water is pushed through the outer frame of the network to the south (A2b), because water has many other opportunities to follow gravity. A certain amount of

---

[70] The western part cannot be separated from the eastern part, because the 6 inch pipes, which divide the square from north to south, are connected without any valves to the 4 inch pipes. Even if the 6 inch pipes get disconnected, water can always flow through the 4 inch pipes from the west to the east. The northern squares, however, can be disconnected from the southern sub-squares since no 4 inch pipes are installed north to south. However, such a disconnection would not be beneficial to the water poor southern sub-squares since the borehole is in the north.

[71] A separation of the western squares would require installing a 6 inch pipe parallel to the existing 6 inch pipe, which cuts across the square from north to south. The 4 inch pipes of the western square would be connected to the first 6 inch pipe and the eastern ones to the other 6 inch pipe.

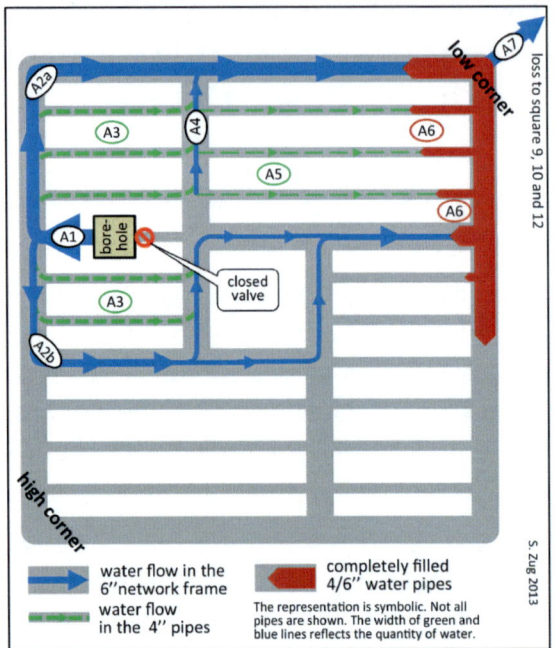

Fig. 17: Daytime Water Flows on Day 1

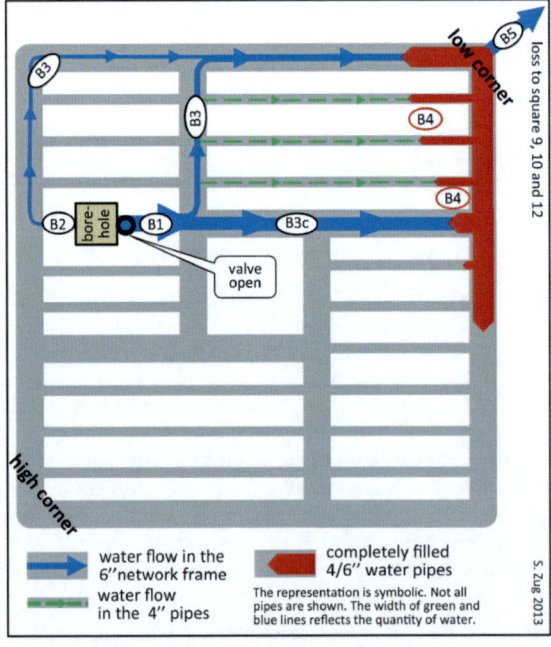

Fig. 18: Daytime Water Flows on Day 2

water enters the 4 inch pipes in the north-western sub-square (A3), but flows through low pressure pipes, and gets drained by the 6 inch pipes (A4). Only very little water enters the 4 inch pipes of the north-eastern sub-square from the west (A5), but the network is filled from east to west (A6). The network fills as long as the loss to other squares (A7) and the consumption in the south-eastern corner are lower than the amount of borehole water reaching this corner. In the opposite, south-western corner, pressure is high (A6) since the water does not only flow through the pipes, they are also continuously filled with water. The higher the water level in the network, the more households can access water in the two eastern sub-squares. In addition, such high pressure and flow conditions access to network water for those households with exceptional supplies in the north-eastern corner.

On Day 2, the valve at the borehole is opened, which allows water to flow directly to the east (B1). People in the street leading east from the borehole (B2) receive water but with much lower pressure than on Day 1 when all water flows through their street (A1). On Day 2, water is pushed in the direction of gravity. Aside from the households in this particular street (B1, B2) no household in the north-western square receives water on Day 2, since water easily drains to the lowest corner (B3a, b, c) and fills the network from the south (B4) or flows out to other squares (B5).

Finally, the only street which benefits from valve management is the street east of the borehole, which would otherwise not receive water at all. However, this street's advantage reduces water availability for the entire sub-square every other day. With one of the two borehole operators living in this street, the street occupies a key position in the field of intra-square water distribution. This is perhaps why the interest of this very small group has been ensured against the interest of a majority.

At night, when the borehole in Square 11 is not operated, the north-eastern corner is still favoured. When water consumption in the eastern squares reduces, but water production continues, water is pushed from the other squares to Square 11 (N1) and fills the network

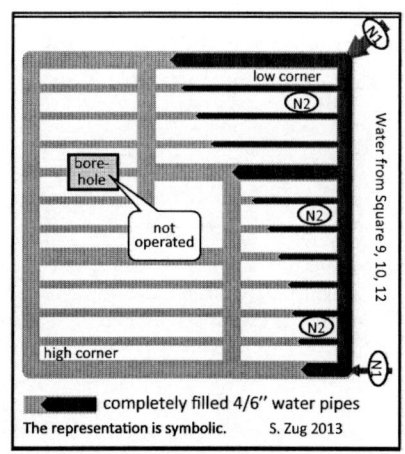

Fig. 19: Nighttime Water Flows

from Square 11's lowest corner (N2). Water rises at night to different levels; however it almost never reaches the western sub-squares. People in the western parts of the eastern squares report that water either does not reach their houses at all, or only very late at night, which renders water access more tedious.

Consequently, the south-eastern corner of the square is favoured by the network night and day. People have water access 24 h a day and the pressure is generally high enough to fill the storage barrels directly with the pipe.[72] Cultivating trees is not only very cheap since water is available in sufficient quantities, but also very easy. A garden hose is simply brought out to the trees and the tap is opened. In other households with lower pressure, people must fill buckets at the tap and carry them out to the tree, requiring time and labour.

The network's low performance not only causes problems for people, but also for the KSWC, who cannot collect water consumption fees from a large number of people who do not receive network water. During my research, the KSWC had registered 1.620 household connections in Square 11, but from February to September 2010 they successfully collected fees from between 28 and 269 of the registered customers per month. In total, only 8% of all bills were paid over the entire period.[73] This figure underlines the substandard state of the network. However, it can be assumed that significantly more than 8% of households could consume tap water during this period. The square's money collector only collects water from those households where she sees that people have water. In the north-east, she knocks on door and enters houses to search for indications of water access such as wet soil around the tap. When she is sure from the outside that people do have water, she quickly walks through the streets and asks for confirmation. For the south-western sub-square she does not even receive bills from her office (MC2: 40).

---

[72] Water pressure was measured at three measurement points along the eastern edge of the square roughly every 90 minutes for 2 days (9 am – 10 pm). In the very corner of the Square (N-E), water was available 24h with a pressure between 40 cm to 160 cm above the tap. While daytime pressure was sometimes low enough to prevent filling a barrel with the pipe, in the evening pressure was always strong (X25:08). At the border between the two eastern sub-squares, pressure disappeared several times a day, but occasionally reached up to 120 cm. In the south-eastern corner of Square 11 water was unavailable during the daytime, but reported to have reached the house only after 2 am.

[73] Data obtained from the KSWC accounting office.

5.4.3. Local Perceptions about Water Justice in the Square

One household (COM6: 78) in the low-lying area integrated their excellent water access into a strategy of capital accumulation. Just after network water began arriving at their house, they started planting trees for themselves. After a while people came to ask for seedlings and they started to sell the little trees. Located not only in the low-lying area but also at a corner of a sub-square, they were able to cultivate roughly 100 m² along two walls of their house. They sell the little trees from their home and twice a week they also take them to the nearby market.

This nursery, as does very high vegetation cover in the north-eastern corner of Square 11, generally signifies that not only do people have good water connections, but that they also use the water from this connection to cultivate trees. This is in opposition to other people in the same square who do not receive water at all and must resort to buying water at great expense from water vendors. From a utilitarian moral viewpoint, watering the trees in low lying areas can be considered immoral, because it favours individual interest over the maximum happiness of the greatest number. This holds true only if we assume that access to drinking water is more valuable than having trees in front of the house.

In a political ecology of Square 11, unequal water distribution can be criticised as a failure of public water governance to technically uniformize water distribution. In such a context, water consumption practices of the local 'water-rich' can also be called into question. This criticism echoes the one concerning the 'city's waterscape', where some people can afford to fill their swimming pools from the network, whereas others are not even connected to it.

This moral critique is, however, not inherent in local debates. In interviews, the undersupplied never contested the situation in a 'meta-pragmatic register' by accusing the 'water-rich' in low lying areas of consuming 'their' water, nor did high-consumers suffer morally over the issue. The 'tragedy of the commons' (Hardin 1968) neither led to disputes – even if the high consuming households are clearly demarcated by the trees surrounding their homes – nor did it lead to a community solution to ensure equal distribution.

Searching for a Scapegoat

Rather than questioning other consumer's behaviour, people restricted their criticism to the network's performance and demanded water production be increased. For many of them, low performance was not only due to the technical configuration of the network under KSWC management. Many people, including certain members of the popular committee (PC2: 93), developed a conspiracy theory that encompassed similar practices, designated in other cities under the label 'water mafia'. In the case of Mumbai, water tanker operators are accused of establishing arrangements with local politicians to delay the construction of water infrastructure in order to ensure their lucrative business (Gandy 2008: 117).

In Square 11, two valves were burnt. A fire in the manhole heated up the steel valve and melted the connected water pipes. Several people argued that the water vendors had burned the valves (and sometimes also closed several valves) so that pipe network would stop operating for a short period, forcing people to purchase water from the vendors. One member of the popular committee even included the KSWC staff in the theory: "Because the KSWC did not take action, I think they are involved" (LS2: 26). He further elaborated:

> The vendors pay those responsible for water to close the valves through which water from Square 25 enters Square 11 [...]. You see, water demand increased during Ramadan. By that time water from Square 25 was closed. The price of two jerrycans increased from 0.5 to 1 pound.

These accusations are strongly based on the fact that water vendors are those most likely to benefit from water cuts. Still, it remains highly questionable whether vendors truly and actively boycotted the network, with or without the help of corrupted KSWC staff. First, a low performing water network is a beneficial to all water vendors. If water pressure were lower than usual, vendors working in other areas would also come to the square. In absence of a mafia-like structure – vendors are neither organized among each other, nor are there influential leaders who own many donkey carts[74] – those sabotaging the network, would not be able to ensure their investment (bribes). In such a context, other vendors would immediately and automatically become 'free-riders'.

---

[74] Gadir (2006: 52) estimates that 80% of Dar Alsalam's water vendors own their donkey cart.

Second, with Sudan's severe police force, burning a valve is highly risky and would only interrupt network functioning for perhaps one or two days, until the KSWC repaired the damage. The economic benefits would not last long enough to outweigh the risks undertaken.

Third, sabotaging the network would not only be punished by the government but it would lead to an internal conflict for the water vendor. A vendor defended his position:

> The accusation is just people talking. I told them I, H., I want this network, because many people are suffering from water shortages. What would be my benefit [of sabotaging the network]? Water is a blessed thing. Nobody would refuse for it to be given to people (WV1: 101).

The water vendor places the argument on a moral level. He situates his personal benefit from selling water in relation with the benefit of network water provided by all. Underlying this argument is a utilitarian perception of morality in which moral acts are good when they benefit the maximum number of people rather than any single individual. If we assume that morality counts as a justification for social action, the overall benefit of the network can contribute to his acceptance of loss.

Fourth, although the water vending business is the main source of income for several households, a strong network would not be the end of business for these families. The water barrels installed on the cart can easily be replaced by a wooden board allowing water vendors to begin transporting people, soil for construction, or goods to the market (e.g. WV3: 76). The water vendors are not necessarily afraid of network providing full service to their areas since other opportunities are available.

Last, there is an alternative explanation to the damage sustained by the two valves. Many manholes are not covered by a lid as intended by the KSWC. More and more are filled with trash, which is then occasionally burnt by the inhabitants.

> I believe trash was placed in this particular manhole and then burned it to clean the area. Despite it being near the water tower, someone brought a little mattress, put it in a manhole, and burnt it. Everyone knew the person who did this; but they denied he was guilty in order to save him (PC3: 19).

The fact that the boy accused of burning the valve is the son of a water vendor only fuels rumours.

Debates about the network's poor performance stigmatize an entire group of actors living in the square, who used to be key actors in rendering life possible in the area. Popular theories, however, also demonstrate that people are strongly implicated in the network and engage in speculations about technical problems.

6

Milking the Network. People's Struggles for Scarce Network Water

The previous chapter presented the fragmentation of Greater Khartoum's waterscape as a trajectory through different scales starting with the city and going down to the neighbourhood. Analysing fragmentation retraces the inequality of network water supplies between individuals living in various locations. We have so far focused on the supply, with the existence and the quality of the water network – for the inhabitants of specific areas – to be an external given. This chapter will shift away from a supply to concentrate on an access oriented analytical approach, and consider how consumers actively shape water infrastructure. This shift of perspective is first conceptualized by contrasting the terms 'fragmentation' and 'access inequality' (6.1). By integrating the supply perspective, this first subchapter also reads as a conclusion of chapter 5. The following subchapter presents different types of network access strategies (6.2), which are later analysed as spatial patterns forming 'neighbourly waterscapes' (6.3). The chapter ends with two conclusions (6.4). First heterogeneity in 'neighbourly waterscapes' are analysed beyond the network, taking into consideration water vendors and water gifts. Second, illegal practices in terms of household access are explained within the city's moral waterscape.

6.1. The Scales of Heterogeneity. Fragmented Supply and Unequal Access

Descriptions of the socio-techno-natural process of water transfers between providers and consumers often use the terms supply and access synonymously. Households that are supplied with water have access to water and those who are not supplied, have no access. Water access is understood simply as a different description of water providers' performances, rather than a consumer activity to gain access to a resource. In the current subchapter, I will strongly argue for a consistent discrimination of the two terms in order to carve out the consumers' contribution to the functioning of the tap. First, fragmentation is presented as a result of inequality in water supply and later confronted with the inequality produced by the differences in access investments of each household.

Fragmentation, a Result of Water Supply

The spatiality of infrastructure networks on the scale of the city is related to urban fragmentation in general. The terminology of fragmentation is very widely used in social science and differently defined. I will mainly refer to 'socio-spatial fragmentation' which focuses mainly on the "localization and concentration of morphological differences, as well as on the transformations of the socio-economic organization that produce these differences" (Navez-Bouchanine 2002: 61, own translation). Jaglin (2005: 76, own translation) summarizes the elements embedded into the notion of fragmentation:

> In urban studies, fragmentation is generally presented as a multidimensional notion that combines several of the following components: a discontinuous and divided morphology, socio-spatial inequalities and a return to existent affinities, polarization of the labour market, politico-institutional dispersion, and multiplication.

She claims that these categories should not be taken for granted, but that the correlation of these factors needs to be empirically analysed to explain fragmentation as a process.

In this book, my aim is not to explain urban fragmentation, like others including Graham and Marvin (2001) with their splintering urbanism hypothesis and Jaglin (2005) with her attempt to translate this hypothesis within the context of the global South. Rather, I consider urban fragmentation to be a description of empirical reality. The empirical reality of Greater Khartoum's fragmentation from a water supply perspective is a combination of the 'technological network fragmentation' and the city's socio-economic fragmentation. Following Jaglin's plea, the spatial correlation of these two categories needs to be revealed.

For network fragmentation of the waterscape, the term 'archipelago' was introduced by Jaglin (Jaglin and Piermay 1996; Jaglin 2001) and by Bakker (2003a) into the francophone and anglophone water debate respectively. The metaphor of the archipelago refers to "spatially separated but linked 'islands' of networked supply in the urban fabric" (Bakker 2003a: 337). The key idea behind the archipelago conceptualizes access to water on a single dimension, which leads to the question of whether certain spatial units are connected to the network or not. The urban history of Greater Khartoum has created a very specific spatiality of networks. Aside from certain exceptions[75], all networked areas are spatially connected. Rather than an archipelago, Greater Khartoum's water network presents itself as a single island with an irregular border that includes non-connected portions of peri-urban Greater Khartoum, with bays and peninsulas. Network extensions, consequently, do not create new islands in the archipelago, but increase the size of the already connected islands.

The urban history of Greater Khartoum traces an outward expansion, starting from the city centre and expanding towards the peripheries. The poor are thus pushed to the urban fringe, both, by the economic realities of land prices that decrease sharply towards the fringe and the government policy to first displace residents of informal settlements from the more central areas to resettlement areas outside the city centre. Second, a strict approach to residential zoning by plot size into three categories was applied, and nearly exclusively third class housing areas were established at the urban fringe. Third, the government made it nearly impossible for informal settlements to emerge near the city centre. Today's informal settlements are consequently located in the far peripheries of the city. As a result of its urban history, Greater Khartoum's neighbourhoods are strongly fragmented by the economic capacities of their inhabitants. The socio-economic fragmentation consequently follows a concentric pattern with the urban rich in the centre and the urban poor towards the peripheries. The exceptional wealthy islands located in the peripheries are mainly restricted to a handful of gated communities in southern Khartoum.

---

75 While exceptions do exist, they are not sufficiently significant to warrant study. The most notable are the first section of the El Fathi settlement area, slated for connection to the network when Manara arrives, and certain decentralized networks – generally community organized – such as in Hag Joussif, two Squares of Dar Alsalam (Crombé and Blanchon 2010) and Serau (Müller-Mahn et al. 2010: 43).

In the 'fragmented waterscape' of Greater Khartoum, network fragmentation and socio-economic fragmentation strongly overlap in a comparison of the government's zonal classification and the existence of networks in the various neighbourhoods. While first and second class neighbourhoods are already connected to water networks, informal settlements have no service at all. The third class neighbourhoods in the peripheries are located in the transition zone, where water supply already reaches certain neighbourhoods, while others are still excluded. It can be argued that the fragmented waterscape's spatiality is the result of the government's investment decisions in combination with the profit seeking displayed by water providers. Consequently, the spatial overlapping of water provision and social-economic characteristics can serve as a basis for the political ecologist's critique of water policy and those actors defining these policies.

As detailed in the previous chapter, network fragmentation is not restricted to "archipelagoization"; the water supply in different neighbourhoods – and even in different parts of neighbourhoods – differs by the quality of water provision. Greater Khartoum's definition of network fragmentation should therefore be qualitatively extended. Similarly to the archipelago, Graham (2000: 185) argues with the "uneven emergence of an array

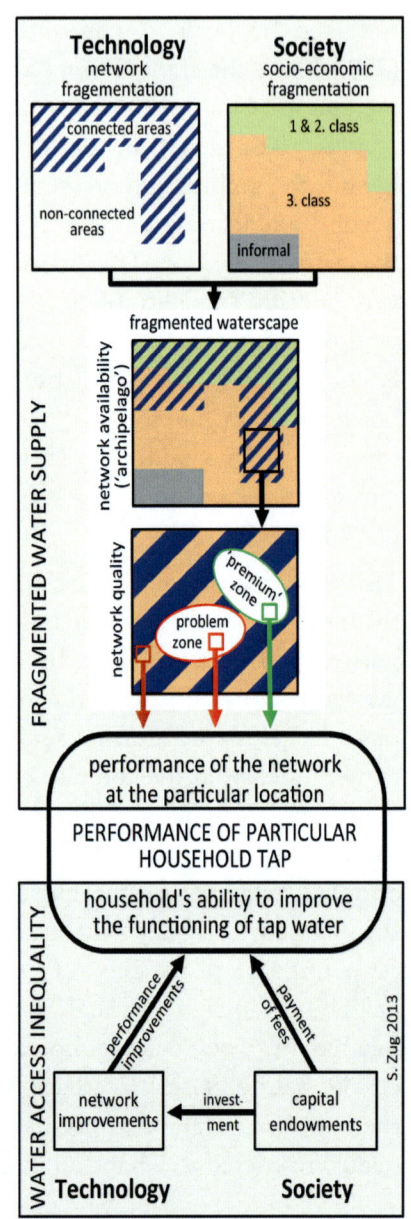

Fig. 20: Conceptualizing Water Supply and Water Access

of […] 'premium networked spaces': new or retrofitted transport, telecommunications, power or water infrastructures that are customized precisely to the needs of powerful users and spaces, whilst bypassing less powerful users and spaces". While the concept of the archipelago differentiates between existence and absence, the notion of premium networked spaces differentiates between premium and standard. Bringing these primarily binary notions together, allows a qualitative differentiation of water networks in a particular location, which ranges from complete absence to 'premium' water supply with different categories of water supply performance in-between.

Differences in network performance in Greater Khartoum are not only a result of the KSWC failing to fulfil their policy objectives but also of a certain heterogeneity that is intentionally defined in the city's water policy. Land classifications overlap pipe classifications. Households in first class neighbourhoods are connected by first class connections with a pipe diameter of 1 inch and households in third class neighbourhoods like Square 11 are exclusively connected by ½ inch pipes, which are third class. Depending on the housing zone, policy dictates that taps deliver different amounts of water.

Beyond the 'government organized' qualitative stratification of network provision along the lines of society's social stratification, an unwanted fragmentation is created through technical limitations as outlined in the previous chapter. Greater Khartoum's social fragmentation, its socio-spatial ordering of the city's population, is only relevant at the neighbourhood scale. Within the neighbourhood, there are no clear spatio-economic patterns. Relatively rich house-holds, as measured against other households in the neighbourhood rather than against those in first class neighbourhoods, have comparatively poor neighbours, leading to a heterogeneous spatial distribution of households by economic capacities. The performance of the network of a particular household consequently is by chance of his location in the square.

So far, analysis has positioned the single household as a consumer and not an actor in the system. In other words, the household is a potential recipient, whose water needs are either satisfied or not. Whether a network in a specific location performs well or not cannot be influenced by the particular action of the individual household living there.[76] Network fragmentation as well as the location of a particular household's plot on one of the fragments, are both givens.[77] Consequently, while the consumer's perspective is important to

---

76 The only exception here would be a general protest, which might lead to an adjustment of network infrastructure or management. This, however, would require mass mobilization, rather than complaints from a single household, only.

77 A household's only leeway in terms of tap quality is the choice of specific neighbourhoods within the city in which to live. The location of one's home is strongly influenced by water,

describe the materialization of the network's fragmentation; it is irrelevant in explaining the phenomena since the fragmentation is produced at a higher scale through power struggles, the focus of political ecology.

The People's Capacity to Access Water

The heterogeneity of people's access to the water network however cannot be explained by equating heterogeneity of tap performance with fragmentation, hence with water supply. Water access also plays its part.

I define water 'access' as the investment of a potential consumer to 'access' the provider's water. Under the modern infrastructural ideal, water access is a very limited consumer activity mainly restricted to establishing a contract, paying the bills, and opening the tap. The water corporation supplies water to the house and takes charge of the entire technological process. In a village, in contrast, people might need to walk for long distances to fetch their water. There, having water at home is much more the result of the activity of 'accessing *water*' by walking and carrying rather than the efforts of an outside supplier. In malfunctioning networks, the aspect of actively accessing network water can be as important as the provider's supply activities in terms of a household's tap performance, because people can try to improve network performances through different technological means. Finally, the amount of water from individual taps is the result of a combined effort of a water provider and the consumer. Depending on the contractual, technological, and organizational definition of the water supply system, there are differences in the degree of consumer participation in making the water flow.

Heterogeneity in water access within a specific fragment of water supply – even if this fragment is characterized by a homogeneous supply – consequently becomes possible, since each individual household has the choice to improve their tap performance. A household in a fragment with a highly satisfactory network can become disconnected if monthly fees are not met, as payments are its access contributions. This study focuses on those fragments of Greater Khartoum's waterscape characterized by poor networks. Hetero-

---

especially for wealthier households. They have the capacity to maintain plots in first or second class neighbourhoods and delay construction until the water network is implemented. This is also perhaps the case for certain families in Square 11, since many plots are still empty. However, for those households that have already settled, their neighbourhood's particular situation is a given.

geneity is produced in these fragments by the different strategies people deploy to improve tap performance. Not all households apply the most successful strategies, since the choice of strategies is a constrained one. While some adjustments require mostly cultural capital – knowing what to do – others require strong economic investments. Since improvements to the network are partially related to economic capacities – and these capacities differ – the spatiality of technological investments within the fragment of water provision are equally heterogeneous.

Heterogeneity in this approach allows a scalar transitional perspective on the spatiality of water inequality due to combining fragmented supply – as a phenomenon of socio-spatial ordering of the city – and inequality of access – as a phenomenon of socio-spatial disorder in a fragment. After analysing fragmentations of the 'waterscape of the city', of the 'waterscape of interconnected networks', and the 'waterscape of the neighbourhood' in chapter 5, the following sub-chapters will analyse the relevance of access for heterogeneity of water tap performance between neighbours, hence, the 'neighbourly waterscape'.

6.2. Appropriation of Pipes through Technical Adjustments

The political ecology of water strongly focuses on the mutual constituency of nature and society by highlighting in particular the interdependence of water and power. Urban fragmentation of Greater Khartoum's waterscape is the result of political relations between actors within and across various scales. The relevant actors are politicians, government administrators, private business men, and also certain community lobbyists, including actors from local political bodies like the popular committee and politically active consumers, such as protesters.

Shifting the perspective from fragmented water supply to inequality in water access in Square 11 reveals a different dimension of the interaction between the water supply network and individuals. The situation here cannot be summed up by the impact of the water network on water consumption of individual households. There are also the people, considered passive consumers by engineers and policy makers, who have actively appropriated the network and changed the technology.

In Science and Technology Studies, the perspective on technology has moved away from a technological determinism of social life towards the incorporation of a "social shaping of technology" (MacKenzie and Wajcman 1999: 2). Mackay and Gillespie (1992: 698) developed the notion of appropriation of technology:

> People are not merely malleable subjects who submit to the dictates of a technology: in their consumption they are not the passive dupes suggested by crude theorists of ideology, but active, creative and expressive – albeit socially situated – subjects. People may reject technologies, redefine their functional purpose, customize or even invest idiosyncratic symbolic meanings to them. Indeed they may redefine a technology in a way that defies its original, designed and intended purpose. Thus the appropriation of technology is an integral part of its social shaping.

A water network is designed by engineers to provide households with water through a tap. In Greater Khartoum, consumer creativity is legally restricted to turning on the tap and to making additional installations inside the house, with the official tap as a source. Only engineers and workers have access to the pipes and the network, located in the KSWC universe, which in turn is protected by the soil cover. The border between the KSWC and the consumer is defined by the exact point where the water pipe enters the house. When the network is performing as expected, this demarcation between the two worlds is consensual amongst the engineers, policy makers, and consumers.[78] With satisfactory access, consumers are not motivated to appropriate the network in ways not intended by those who designed it.

In Square 11 however, the network's performance is insufficient. A tap that provides water when opened is an engineer's vision rather than the consumer's reality. For the households, the hidden world of engineers has become a topic of discussion. People debate the possible reasons for the network's poor performances and who is responsible. People reflect on production processes. In several areas, large stones hindered the laying of underground pipes. This resulted in a convoluted network, leading to speculations by the users on possible damage. Children may have blocked water flow in the main pipe with water bottles or workers may have not have properly bored holes in the main pipe when connecting the individual taps. Other discussions center around management issues, such as the capabilities of borehole operators; while still others speculate on the impact of connections to other squares for Square

---

78 When networks are performing satisfactorily, the only incentive for consumers to interfere with the water provider's universe is water theft.

11's fluctuating water levels (X10: 19). Elevation differences are another widely discussed topic.

Graham and Marvin (2001: 422) argue that large infrastructural networks serve as a black box, "a technological assembly including infrastructure networks whose inner workings are so completely unknown or hidden to its users that its successful functioning is totally taken for granted". In Square 11 the "un-black boxing" (Graham and Marvin 2001: 183) is not only related to consumers no longer taking water access for granted and thus verbally entering the spheres of the engineers; but it is also the result of consumers intensively engaging in technology related debates. They remove the soil that covers the world of the engineers and physically change conducts as well as pressure regimes by installing water pumps. Discussing the technical functions of a water network and actively altering it has no intrinsic interest if the network satisfied consumer expectations.

6.2.1. Pipe Manipulations

Pipe manipulations are a widespread method to increase water tap performance because it requires no expensive investments. These adjustments are based on the assumption of stable pressure in the main pipe; the manipulations therefore aim to improve water flow in the ½ inch connection pipes between the main pipe and the household tap. Local knowledge of water pipes strongly correlates to the physics of movements of fluids in pipes. The final objective of pipe manipulations is to improve water flows, which are related to the force of gravity on water pressure and friction losses in water network installations. To explain the functionality of pipe manipulations, this section will not only present an empirical description of the adjustments but will relate them to basic physics and engineering.

The Elevation of the Tap as a Determinant for Pressure and Flow

In Square 11, the 4 inch main pipes are installed 90 cm below ground level and the taps are installed at the wall inside the house at a height of 60 cm above surface. To reach a standard tap, water consequently needs to be lifted 150 cm above the main pipe. In a network with normal performances, the energy to lift water is generated by a reservoir or a pump, which produces sufficient pressure.

The pressure at the pipe level determines if water can reach the tap or not. Pressure (p) is defined as the force (F) exercised on an area (A): $p = F/A$. In the main pipe, the pressure exerts a force on the water, pushing it 150 cm higher and into the household connection. As the water rises, it gains kinetic energy, and consequently gravity and water pressures exert perfectly opposing forces, creating equilibrium. This equilibrium defines the exact level to which the water can rise and is called hydrological head. The pressure in the pipe consequently can be expressed in relation to this equilibrium.

In international standards, the unit pascal is attributed to pressure, which can be translated into the height to which water is pushed up: $p(h) = \rho g h$. In this formula the pressure (p) is related not only to the height (h) but also to the specific density of the liquid (ρ) and to gravity (g). However, in the analysis of Greater Khartoum's water network, ρ is a constant, defined for water at a particular temperature and the gravity refers to standard gravity. Under the given conditions in Greater Khartoum the inclusion of p and g is merely an arbitrary conversion of pressure into the unit of pascal, allowing the comparison of the pressure of different fluids under different atmospheric conditions. As these conditions can be considered constants, I will denote pressure with the pressure head Δh in this study which is defined as the height of the water column, hence, the distance between the maximum water level that can be reached by the water and the level at which water pressure is measured ($\Delta h = h - h'$). Water pressure Δh is measured as a unit of length, expressed as cmH_2O[79].

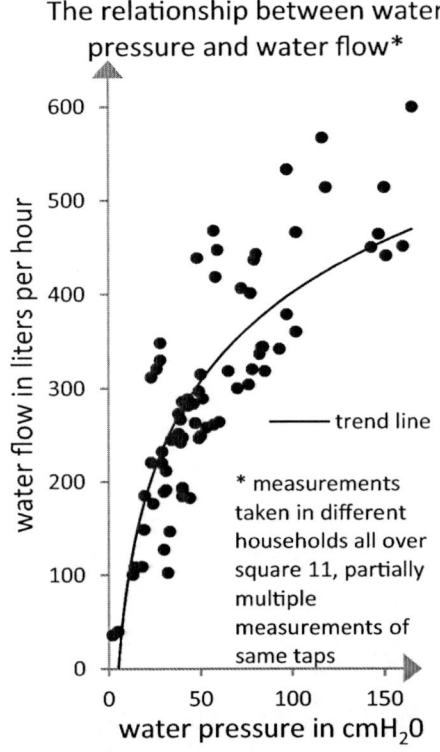

Fig. 21: *Water Pressure and Flow*

---

79 1 cmH_2O equals 98.1 pascal (at a water temperature of 4°C and under standard gravity).

Using cmH₂O rather than pascal as the measurement unit for water offers the advantage of placing pressure and elevation directly in relation with each other. In Greater Khartoum's network, a water tap installed at 150 cm above the network will only receive water if pressure in the network in front of the house is at least 150 cmH20.[80] If water pressure is lower, the water column does not reach the tap and the tap remains dry.

Water pressure does not only determine if a tap receives water, but also the quantity which can be obtained from each tap in a particular moment. Water flow is dependent on the diameter of the opened water tap and the water pressure measured at the height of the tap.[81] By design, the diameter is constant since all households were equipped with identical taps; but the water pressure fluctuates greatly. While obtaining enough water to fill a barrel requires less than 30 minutes when water pressure is roughly 150 cmH₂O, it takes nearly an hour at 50 cm, and 2 hours at a pressure of 25 cmH₂O. Figure 21 demonstrates that water pressure and water flow are not linearly correlated, but pressure differences in the lower range have a much higher impact on water flow than at higher pressure. Many people do not consume from the tap at low pressure rates, since water only dribbles out rather than flowing. The lower the pressure and consequently the lower the flow, the higher the household's cost for accessing tap water in terms of labour and time.

Friction Loss in the Pipe

The above description of water pressure in relation to height and the dependent water flows assumes a system in which no energy loss is experienced in the household connection pipe, hence between the main pipe and the tap. However, there are different forces[82] that resist the flow of water in a pipe, reducing the energy and consequently the pressure and flow of water. Friction occurs between water and the pipe, slowing down water molecules as they come into contact with the surface of the pipe. This effect increases with a decreasing diameter of the pipe and increases with the roughness of the pipe,

---

80 Assuming a frictionless system.

81 The velocity of water can be derived from Bernoulli's Principle: $v = \sqrt{2gh}$ (with g =gravity, h =water pressure in cmH₂O). The flow is calculated with $F = v \cdot t \cdot A$ (with t =time and A = circular area of pipe).

82 The mechanical processes of the loss of pressure in pipes is based on Gupta (2006: 206-230) and Katz (2010: 172-190).

depending on the material. Consequently, the longer the pipe, the more energy is lost. Since the main pipes are not installed in the middle of the street, the houses on the northern side of the streets are connected with 4 m long pipes while the southern ones are connected with 8 m long pipes, theoretically privileging the northern houses. The energy bound in the water that reaches the tap is

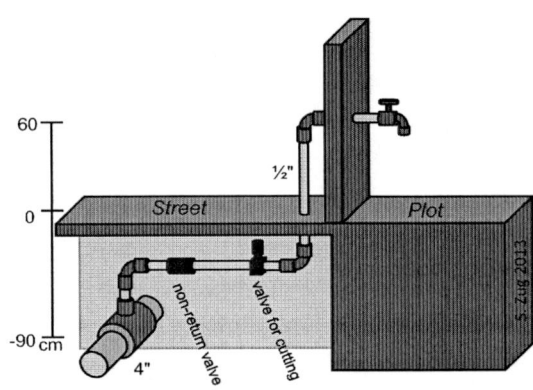

Fig. 22: KSWC Standard Pipe Installation

further decreased by elements built into the pipe. Minimal loss of water pressure is accomplished in a completely straight pipe. The KSWC pipes are not straight. Furthermore, several elements are built into the pipe, which further reduce the water's energy, due to the resistance and turbulences created by decrea-sing diameters and bends. Consequently, at tap level, the water velocity, water pressure, and consequently water flow depend on the specific properties of the pipe and the elements built into the pipe.

Fig. 23: Standard Water Tap with Good Pressure

For a household connection, a tee connector is installed around the 4 inch main pipe. A heated steel rod is used to burn a hole into the 4 inch pipe and a prefabricated ½ inch household pipe is attached to the connector. The KSWC installs tee connectors in such a way that water leaves the pipe towards the surface. Before reaching the consumer, water has to pass three elbows that change the direction of the flow by 90 degrees each, a non-return valve, which prevents water from flowing back from the consumer's house to the main pipe, a built-in valve to help the KSWC disconnect households easily, and finally the tap itself. All these elements offer different degrees of resistance to the flow of water and reduce the pressure and the quantity of water available at household taps in comparison to the water potentially accessible directly at the main pipe.

Tap performance at a given pressure in the main pipe consequently is constituted of two elements. First, the height of the tap above the main pipe, which in a standard system is predefined at 150 cm. And second, friction losses inside the pipe that influences both the water flow in the main pipe as well as having a significant impact on the flow in the household connection.

Addressing Tap Height and Pipe Friction

While households may not fully understand the detailed physical principles of water flows, several of them are aware that the height of their tap and the way the pipe is arranged affects their water flow. People consequently alter pipe installations in three ways: straightening pipes, removing pipe elements to reduce energy losses, and lowering taps from their original installation.

One of the most radical im-provements is presented in Figure 24. People remove all elements built into the pipe including the tap. Inside the plot, people dig a hole to reach the main pipe. For water to flow horizontally out of the main pipe, the ½ inch pipe connected to the 4 inch main pipe must be changed.

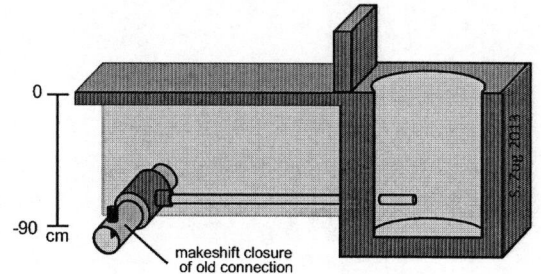

Fig. 24: Maximum Manipulated Installation

The original design connects the two vertically through a hole from the top. A second hole is made next to the original one. To properly close the old hole, the tee-connector needs to remain installed on the 4 inch pipe and closed with a screw (Figure 25). A second tee-connector is required for the new hole, at a cost of roughly 15 SDG. In order to save the sum, people reuse the original tee-connector for the new connection, which however requires an alternate closure for the original hole. One frequently applied method is to close the hole with a round wooden peg wrapped into a plastic bag, which is then hammered into the pipe (Figure 26).

Having removed all elements from the pipe and straightened the pipe, water flow is only limited by the friction of the pipe itself. Several households have even minimized this by reducing the length of the pipe. Instead of building the water hole in the private space delineated within the plot's walls, they chose the front of their house, directly next to the water pipe. By shortening the pipes, these households enjoy maximum pressure.

The degree to which households optimize their pipe differs strongly. Most households try to lower the tap to the ground from its original installation at 60 cm above ground surface. Others go further and place the pipe several centimetres below the surface; while still others reach the maximum depth of 90 cm below the surface. Improvements also differ depending on the degree to which households remove pipe elements and whether they turn the tee valve from vertical to horizontal.

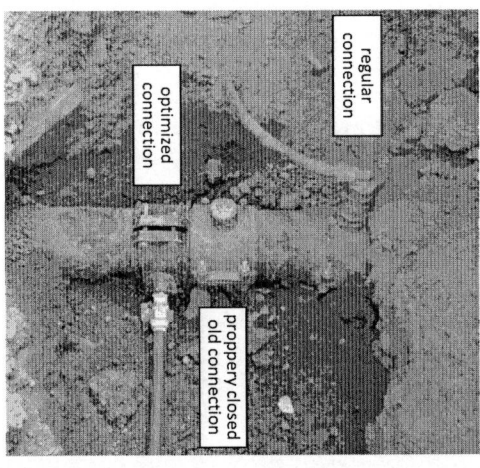

Fig. 25: Optimized and Regular Connection

Fig. 26: Makeshift Closure of Hole in 4 Inch Pipe

Different actors are involved in pipe manipulations. Mostly, people dig out the pipes themselves, but some also pay labourers from the square. For the more sophisticated adaptations, especially if the connection to the main pipe is changed, the households pay either more experienced people from the squares; plumbers, who offer their service at Souq Libya; or even KSWC employees, who perform these adjustments during their free time. Plumber fees range from 15 to 30 SDG, which equals the cost of 7 to 15 barrels of water purchased from water vendors. The one time investment can be highly beneficial financially, if a previously dry tap becomes a family's principle source of water.

By lowering the pipe, the tap becomes less comfortable compared to a conventional connection with sufficient pressure. People must go down into the hole and place a bucket or a jerrycan under the pipe. A handful of households invest even further and build small underground water storage units in concrete that are filled when water pressure is strong. This is a significant improvement, since people do not have to wait for the water to fill jerrycans. They can simply take the water out of the hole, just as from an open well.

Fig. 27: Tap below the Surface

Like KSWC valve management on the square scale, inhabitants' pipe adjustments are trial and error. A local elite (X29: 27), who lives on one of the square's most elevated spots, paid people on four different occasions, to dig underground and straighten the pipes. Despite his investments, he never did access water from his pipe. This failure had nothing to do with the way he made the adjustments. If water does not reach the main pipe at all, because it is too high, even with major adjustments, water remains inaccessible. Some people living in much more favourable areas never improve their connections, or only ever slightly do so; despite the fact that preconditions are much better. The willingness to invest and the belief in technical adjustments differ between people, while the success of adjustments differs according to a particular household's location in the square, hence, by the spatiality of water provision.

Consumer initiatives to optimize connections reduce the number of connected households who do not receive network water. From this perspective, pipe manipulations contribute to KSWC objectives. However, these adjustments have two major negative impacts on the network.

First, the makeshift closure of the hole left when the main connection is shifted 90° can be expected to be highly prone to leakage, especially if the area will later be provided with much higher pressure (KSWC10: 154, KSWC03: 48). KSWC would thus lose significant amounts of water in the future.

Second, pipe adaptations pose a strong health risk, since contaminated water can be sucked back into the network. Water returning into the pipe is possible in systems that are not constantly under pressure. If the pipe is emptied, pipe pressure turns negative. In the KSWC design, non-return valves are built into the system, allowing water to flow only towards the house and not back. Even when valves are not built into the system – which has sometimes occurred due to the KSWC's lack of spare parts – only air is sucked into the system. In the appropriated system, non-return valves are removed and the taps are no longer above ground; but in a hole. Most people leave the water tap open 24 h/day and water often completely fills the holes. If pressure turns negative, the hole's dirty water, rather than air, is sucked back into the system.

6.2.2. Suction Pumps

The second option to improve connection is the installation of an electrical pump, which is connected to the pipe inside the individual plots and greatly increases the water pressure in the house. These pumps cannot be operated successfully in all areas of the square unless water is flowing in the main pipe. Households know when water is available, because they either hear the borehole generator being operated; they are phoned by family members living in areas where water access does not require a pump; or they suck on the pipe to test if water has arrived.

Fig. 28: Suction Pump

The pump allows water access at the level the KSWC chose to install taps, but also to higher points or points outside the plots by pumping water through a garden hose. People generally fill barrels for personal consumption. Pumps render water access much more comfortable than taking water from a hole. More water can be accessed in a shorter time, since the pumps increase the pressure beyond the pressure of the water in the main pipe. Pumping also greatly reduces the workload. People who manipulated the pipe have to wait several minutes until a bucket is filled. It then still needs to be carried to the storage barrel or to the trees. In comparison, the pump merely needs to be switched on.

However, comfort is financially costly. The suction pump alone costs around 100 SDG; then there is the electricity required to operate the pump. Since Square 11 is not yet connected to the public electricity network, electricity needs to be produced by generators. Electricity production has become a business in the square, and some people invested in large generators, to which others are connected. Electricity is mainly produced in the evening and people pay a fee for each bulb and each television connected. However, pump connections are not allowed because they consume too much electricity and they are believed to create voltage fluctuations. Generator operators however use pumps for their own consumption. Operating a pump thus requires purchasing at least a small generator, which costs at least 350 SDG and continuously consumes fuel. The high costs of obtaining water through pumps, hence, makes this access strategy available only to those endowed with high economic capital.

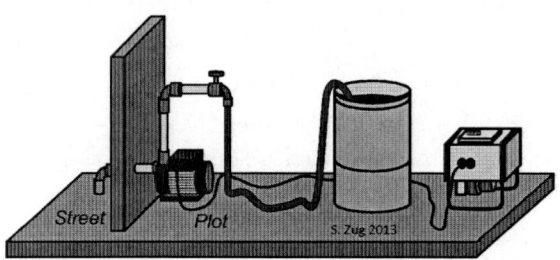

Fig. 29: Generator Operated Suction Pump

Suction pumps are very different than pipe manipulations in terms of water network appropriation. The pump is installed inside the plot and the tap and the household connection does not need to be lowered. Households only lower their pipes down to the surface for practical reasons; they never go below. A suction pump does not require touching KSWC installations and all inbuilt elements can be maintained in a pipe. Since the technical installations all take place exclusively within the plot, suction pumps are fully legal. Where pipe manipulations take the main pipe's water pressure as a given, the operation of suction pumps actively changes the pressure in the pipe.

As a consequence however, water access for other households is lowered on two different scales. Households, who take water from the network, take from the total quantity available in the square. This leaves less for other households to consume. Their direct neighbours experience problems, since suction pumps reduce the pressure in the main pipe and consequently reduce the pressure in their taps (e.g. A6: 33, B7: 39, X10: 29). Arango (2009: 43) reports a similar situation in Daim, an older neighbourhood in the centre of Khartoum. Pumps are a very dominant water access strategy and allow water access any time during the day. The few households, who do not operate pumps, can only receive water late at night, when suction pump consumption is very low. The Daim example shows that suction pumps interfere mostly with the distribution of water, rather than with water availability because the water level throughout the network is constant. To access water at all, people are increasingly forced to install pumps. From the moment all people have installed pumps, the benefit of having a pump is negated as everyone receives the same amount as before any pump was installed.

6.2.3. Conclusion

The appropriation of the pipe unofficially transferred the KSWC's responsibilities to consumers. The separation between provision and access was shifted from the officially designated house wall to the street, where people appropriated the entire pipeline between the main pipe and their wall. The ½ inch pipe was completely brought under their ownership, and even the 4 inch pipe was affected by the changing household connections. The defining point at which the government's network material and intellectual property has been taken over by consumers is fluid over time. From the moment water pressure increases in an area, the households stop debating about their connection and refrain from opening the streets any further. They put the pipeline back into the black box, where it had been placed originally by the engineers. However, consumers may install water tanks on their roofs, which can be filled under a new pressure regime. Their interaction with the water network consequently slips back behind the legal ownership barrier, embodied by the wall of the plot.

6.3. Spatial Heterogeneity as a Result of Water Access Inequality

A fragmented water supply produces spatial homogeneity within which households that have acquired good access through the installation of suction pumps have settled in a particular area, while those who have not invested are located in another 'fragment'. The contrary holds true for the appropriation of water infrastructure. This subchapter aims to analyse the spatial patterns of tap performance as a result of the different forms of investment. Four 'neighbourly waterscapes' will be presented. The four clusters were deliberately chosen in an area where water supply was neither excellent nor impossible. This encompassed the vast fragment of Square 11, in which water access is difficult, but still possible.[83] While two case study areas are completely inside this fragment (A and D), one is located on the border of a fragment where water cannot be accessed at all (B), and another one on the border with an area with abundant water supplies (C). Each cluster contains at least one household with a connection that out-performs those of their neighbours due to either the micro-heterogeneity of water 'supply' or the heterogeneity of the household's specific investments in its water 'access', or a combination of both these factors.

First, a general framework will be developed within which the performance of individual household taps and consequently the heterogeneity of tap performance can be analysed. Then, the four case study areas will be discussed in separate sections. The analysis will take into consideration heterogeneity as a geographic phenomenon and will illustrate empirical data in Figure 30. Households are designated by the letter of the area and a number (e.g. A3, C4). I have turned and mirrored the map to obscure indications of specific

---

[83] Refers to the area marked in light blue in Figure 16.

homes and thus ensure anonymity, thus rendering geographical directions incorrect and useless. The graphic representation will thus be described using the terms: 'up', 'down', 'left', and 'right'. For the same reason there is also no overview of the particular location of the clusters.

6.3.1. Analytical Framework for Household Tap Performance

The analysis is based on the following basic assumption: the better the performance of network supply to a particular plot, and the better the household investments into their water access, the better the performance of their individual tap. Based on this assumed relationship I will explain the heterogeneity of the performance of different neighbouring households for all four clusters. The measurement of the three indicators will be outlined below.

Measuring Performance of Household Taps

The degree of a household's reliance on water from the tap is to a certain degree a proxy for the performance of a household tap. The underlying assumption that households prefer obtaining water from their own tap rather than from other sources holds true and is underlined by local actors especially in regard to cost and convenience.

However, this indicator is only a proxy and needs to be used cautiously. Of two households with a similarly performing tap one household might opt for accessing tap water while the other might be able to afford or prefer paying for the convenience of water delivery. Analysing user reliance on the tap allows a first approximation of a household's tap performance. We have therefore differentiated between households fully supplied[84] by the tap, households who use the tap as a primary water source supplemented with purchases from vendors and/or water gifts from neighbours, and households who do not use the tap at all.

Water tap performance can be technically measured, by determining pressure at the household tap and water flow; a more direct process than deductions based on users' access strategies. These measurements are technically simple. Water pressure can be approximated by a transparent water hose attached to

---

84 Some of the households classified here as fully covered by the network, still occasionally obtain water from other sources, but only in exceptional situations, when the network is not performing as well as usual and they run out of stored water.

the tap and easily measured in cmH$_2$O as the height of the water column in the hose above the tap.[85] Only in low lying areas, where water pressure can exceed 2 metres, is this form of measurement technically limited. In the main focus area however, water pressure remains far below that level. Water flow is measured by the time it takes to fill a water bottle from the tap. This figure can later be translated into a 'litres per hour' flow rate. In the following sections I will refer to both indicators for tap performance.

Measuring Performance of Network Supply

The performance of network supply is defined as the ability of a provider to supply water to customers using the technical means intended by the particular water provider. Hence, a scenario is assumed in which households do not alter their connections, nor do they install suction pumps. A fully performing network would supply sufficient amounts of water to all households in the square, with adequate pressure for taps placed 60 cm above surface, hence, to the level at which taps were designed to be installed. Whether the taps at this particular level are reached by water depends on the overall amount of water produced by the borehole and the way it is distributed in the network. As we have seen the naturally given elevation is a central element that leads to an unequal distribution of the water produced in Square 11.

Water pressure in the network is produced by the pump extracting water from the borehole and reduced by the consumption of those households that can access the water. In an imaginary, simplified network in which air and friction have no impact whatsoever on pipe flow, water pressure produced by the borehole leads to a homogeneous water level inside the network at a particular elevation, which is comparable with the water level of a lake or the water table in an aquifer. All pipes and taps located below this water level receive water; the lower they are located, the higher the pressure available to them.

To compare tap elevation, a zero point was defined at the point where the network is connected to the main pump[86] (the example is illustrated by chart 1b on Figure 30 on the following page). Tap elevation is therefore expressed as the 'height of the tap above source'. Any tap or point in the network below

---

85 Friction in the hose is considered negligible.
86 The zero point is located at 414 m above sea level.

the zero point can theoretically[87] be supplied with water using only gravity. All points above the zero point require pressure in the pipes. A fictive water tap directly at the zero point would be located at 150 cm, the addition of the 90 cm below ground to reach the network and the 60 cm above ground where the KSWC installed the tap. A tap installed on a plot located 80 cm higher than the borehole is 230 cm above the source (150 cm + 80 cm). Consequently, this tap needs more than 230 cmH$_2$O pressure measured at the zero point to deliver water, while the tap at borehole level would already start supplying water at a pressure of 150 cmH$_2$O.

Tap elevation is the major criteria to determine a tap's water supply; but other factors including the distance of the tap from the source, the design of the network that could allow water to move more or less easily to lower areas, as well as the specific topography the main pipe needs to navigate before reaching a household, all affect tap performance. If water needs to climb over a small hill and the main pipe attains a maximum height of 300 cm above the source, the area behind the hill located at 100 cm above source requires at least 300 cmH$_2$O as compared to only 100 cmH$_2$O.

Comparing elevations requires high precision measurements, achieved with differential GPS measurement[88] conducted in cooperation with a survey engineer, which resulted in an accuracy level of less than 3 cm vertically. Elevation of taps was measured for all households with the exception of two households that were not present on the day the measurements were performed and in two areas, where the height of the tap was not required to explain water performance[89].

Measuring the Impact of Household Investments on the Tap

Investments to improve water access of a particular tap through pumps or pipe manipulations are the second explanation for water performance, besides water supply performance.

---

87 Assuming there is no friction in the network
88 Trimble 5700/5800
89 The particular height of taps is irrelevant in the lower part of Area B, which is located on a completely dry main pipe and in the upper part of Area C where water pressure is exceptionally high.

209

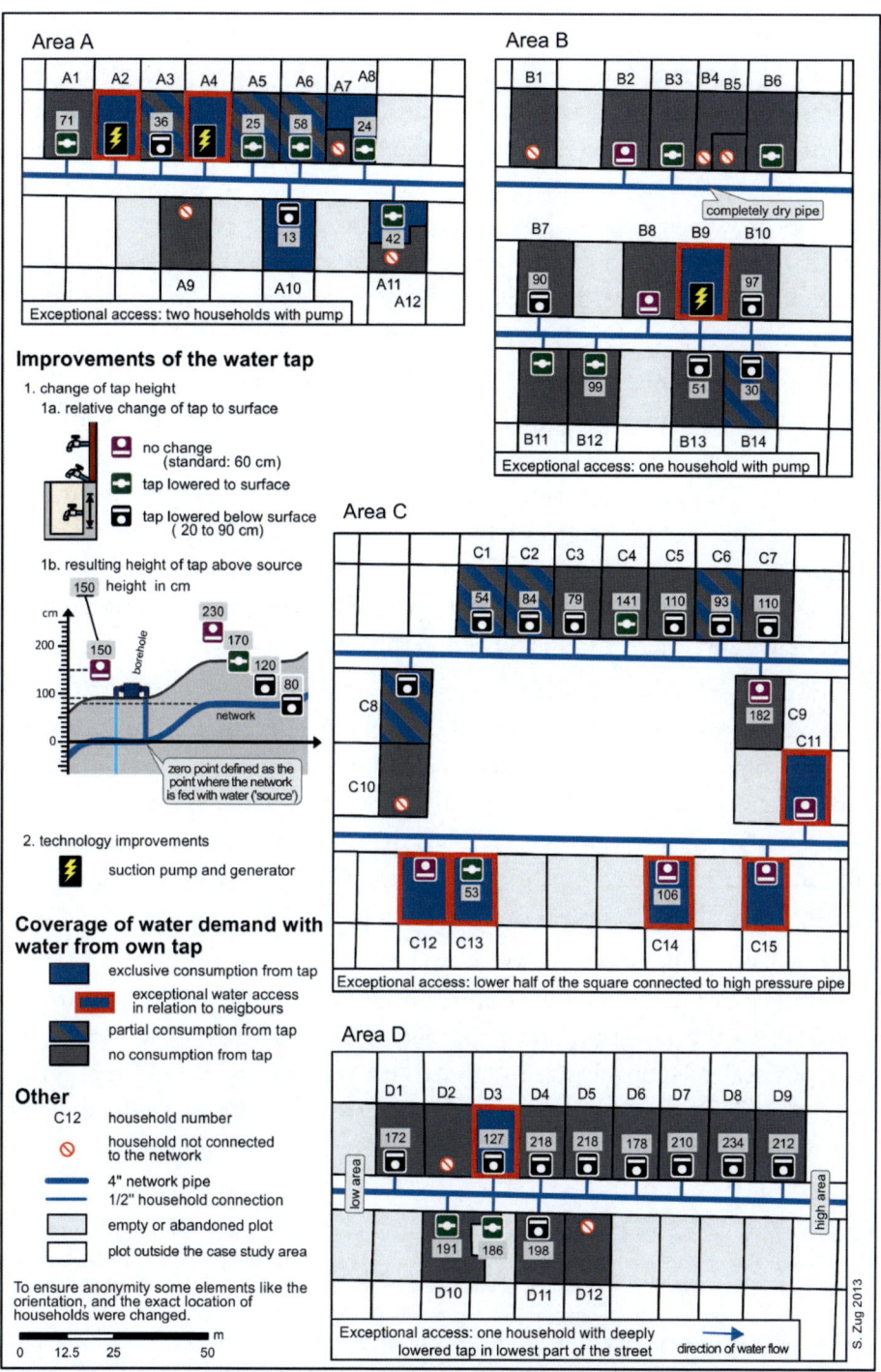

Fig. 30: *Water Access and Supply Inequality: the Heterogeneity of Tap Performance*

All pipe manipulations aim to improve tap pressure. Significant impact can be achieved by lowering the tap (1a on Figure 30). Households can thus alter tap pressure, despite a given network pressure at a particular location. By lowering the tap relative to the surface, the tap is also lowered relative to the zero point (1b), which increases the pressure in the tap. By adjusting the tap's height above surface, households have the ability to reduce the pressure which is required to feed their tap by up to 150 cmH_2O[90]. Consequently, the household's tap pressure depends on the particular elevation of the household's plot and the relative change of the tap's height.

While tap adjustments can significantly improve water access in some areas, they can have no effects in other areas. This holds true for very high areas, like the south-western sub-square, where even a deep hole does not allow households to access water, since no water reaches the main pipe in front of the houses. Beside the height of the tap, other factors play a role in water pressure such as flow restricting devices, the distance to the main pipe, and the way taps are connected to the main pipe. However, major improvements are generally the result of simply lowering the tap.[91]

For those households that access water with suction pumps, the height of the tap above the network in front of the house is less relevant. Pumps suck water out of the pipe even if the water pressure does not reach the pump. Network performance however remains a crucial factor for the possibility to operate a pump. Only when water pressure reaches the main pipe in the particular location, can water be sucked out of the network. Consequently, all access strategies fail if water is not supplied to the main pipe.

With this basic elaborations of water tap performance especially in relation to the elevation of the network in front of the house and the position of the tap in relation to the network, and consequently in relation to the source, the major physical relationships are outlined in order to understand the performance of individual taps in four particular clusters and the spatial heterogeneity of tap performance. In the following sections the heterogeneity of access

---

90 The tap from the previous example which was installed at 230 cm above source can be lowered to 170 cm above source by taking it from the wall and laying it on the ground. It can be lowered even further to a maximum of 90 cm below the surface, which equals the level of the main pipe in front of the house. Consequently, any tap can be lowered by a maximum of 150 cm, which brings this particular tap, originally installed 230 cm above source, down to 80 cm above source.

91 To protect households, I will not disclose any illegal adjustments performed by specific households. The phenomenon is discussed generally for particular streets as a whole, without referring to any one household.

in the 'neighbourly waterscapes' is mapped out according to the combination of water supply and water access.

6.3.2. Area A: Pumping Water to those who can Easily Access Water without Pumps

The first case study area consists of 14 plots located on a stretch of a street with a very typical settlement pattern (see Figure 30). Only ten of the plots were inhabited during the research period. While three plots had always been empty, one plot was recently abandoned. Of the inhabited plots, two plots were further subdivided in two sections by a wall to host two families, each. The KSWC only provides one tap per plot, even if two households live on the one plot. This means that one household on each of these two shared plots did not have their own water tap. A third household in the street did not have a water tap since the house they rented was built after the network was constructed, and the owner had not yet started the necessary procedures to receive a legal tap connection.

The remaining households are all connected to the network. Like all other case study areas Area A receives water every other day, when the valve at the borehole pushes water to the western high grounds for about four hours in the morning and another four hours in the afternoon. Water pressure is closely tied to the operation of the square's borehole, and water pressure stops immediately when the borehole pump is stopped. Water from the other squares, which reaches the low lying areas in the northeast of the square, never reaches all four case study areas.

To access water, people need to invest in their tap since water does not reach the taps at the level KSWC installed them. Two household operate generators and pumps, which allow them to cover their total water consumption from the network. The investment cost for the system is high and requires certain financial capacities. Both households have stable income sources from employment of the male members in the police, workshops, and factories. The household's higher living standards can be deducted from the quality of their belongings as compared to most of the neighbours. All rooms are constructed with baked bricks rather than mud bricks. Decorated steel doors display the households' wealth to the outside world. One of the households even paved his yard. Operating the pump has significantly affected water pressure, which

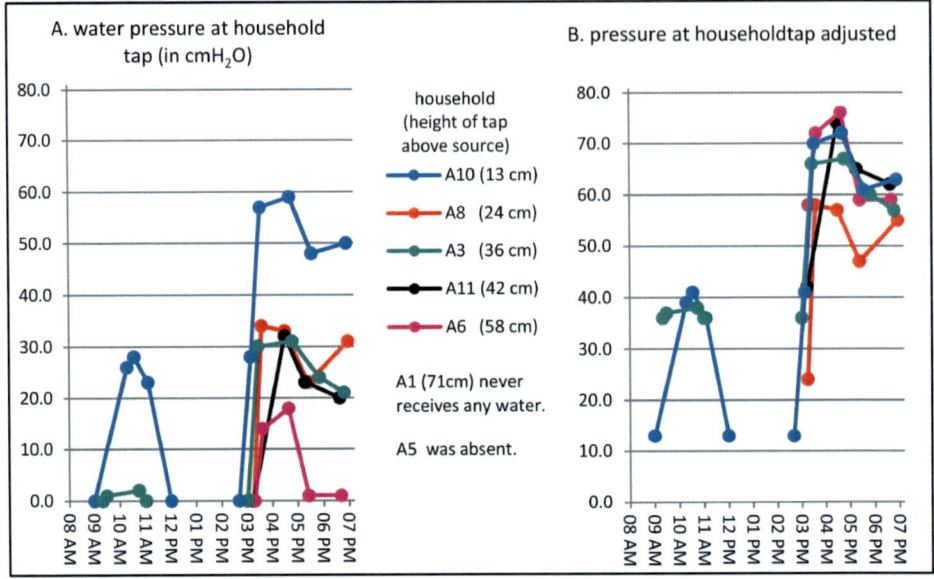

Fig. 31: Water Pressure Measurements in Area A

immediately increased to far above the 250 cmH2O[92] and allowed the barrel to be easily filled. The pumps not only increased the pressure, but also the flow.[93]

In December 2010, pressure of all the taps in the street was measured once per hour.[94] The following diagram (Figure 31.A) reflects the morning and afternoon working hours of the borehole. If the borehole pump was not operated, no water reached the area. On the measurement day, water pressure was stronger in the morning than in the evening, which is however not a general rule. The water pressure measures were very different between the households. While A1 did not receive water at all from the tap and A6 received water with relatively low pressure, A12's pressure was far above average and even allowed good pressure in the morning, when all other taps only dribbled at best (A3). Not only pressure but also water flow was higher in A12, allowing the household to access a maximum of 470 litres per hour while other taps peaked between 120 and 220 l/h.

---

92 Pressure may have been higher, but 250 cmH$_2$O is the highest measurable pressure with the equipment used.

93 In one measurement, the water flow increased from 120 l/h to 800 l/h when the pump was switched on (A4).

94 With the exception of A5, who was absent that day, water pressure measurements were taken in every household that uses water taps without suction pumps.

The major explanation for the differences in tap performance is the difference in tap heights above source. The highly performing tap A12 is located 45 cm lower than the low performing tap A6 and 58 cm lower than the non-performing tap A1. Figure 31.B shows the same data, normalized by the height of the tap above source. With the slight exception of A8, the diagram demonstrates a strong correlation between the height of the tap above source and its performance. The result of these measurements is not a surprise from the perspective of physics, but it underlines the impact of small differences in tap elevation on the possibility for households to satisfy their water needs through simple adjustments.

The differences in tap elevation are only slightly related to the topography, which is rather flat in the area; tap investments had more impact. All households removed the tap from the wall to access water at a level close to the surface and two households even actively brought the taps some 30 cm below the surface, which is a rather small adjustment.

The low degree of users' investment in their infrastructure can partially be explained by the specific location of the area in the 'fragment of weak supply'. It is situated relatively close to the borehole, ensuring good pressure in the 4 inch pipe. In addition, it is located at about 50 cm below the area where the network is located. Consequently, the main pipe in the street is 50 cm below source, hence even lower than the source. The A10 tap reveals that even with very low investments, substantial improvements can be achieved.

The current low investment in the pipe despite the empirical fact that several households cannot fully cover their water consumption from the network, might also be due to the fact that many households have not yet adjusted to decreasing water supply performance. The population of Square 11 widely remarked that water pressure had been good until the end of Ramadan 2010 (early September), which was also the end of the first research phase in the square. Thereafter many taps fell dry and others delivered less water than before.[95] Lowering taps even further is one possible reaction to the water situation. However, households only do so after they are sure that the decrease in pressure is not simply a temporary phenomenon.[96]

---

[95] Interviews with the KSWC did not result in an explanation of this change at the end of Ramadan. No valves were changed, nor were fuel deliveries; consequently, the operating hours of the borehole remained constant. One engineer speculated on the borehole's decreasing production capacity.

[96] The relevance of having access to gifts for underinvestment in water access will be discussed later.

The very high heterogeneity of people's reliance on tap water in the area is generally linked to access issues. Only the absence of a tap for the two households living on a shared plot (A7 and A12) is related to supply. By administrative definition, plots are the property of single households and they are not meant to be shared. The KSWC directive forbids the installation of a second tap on the same plot on legal grounds. Hence, the system of water provision does not allow direct supply of network water to these households. The heterogeneity between the other households is related to different investments in their access strategies. Shortly before the study took place, A10 was not connected to the network. After a while, people took the initiative to get their tap connected and to bring it under supply. A9, who arrived a bit later, did not have access to the network at the time, which is represented on the map. Hence, he was not 'supplied' because he had not invested the required minimum in his 'access'; this investment is represented as either the forms that need to be filed or alternatively paying for a plumber to make an illegal connection.

Households with installed water taps differ in access rates due to their own investments rather than any significant differences in street topography or other provision related issues. The installation of water pumps created superior water access in the area for two households. They can consume water in abundance, while the other households struggle with access. The various installations have varied success rates due to the minimal differences in their ability to lower the tap level.

6.3.3. Area B: Maximum Water Inequality

Area B is centred around two households (B8 and B9). The two neighbouring plots are inhabited by the families of two brothers. The households' receive their main income from two jointly operated general stores. The smaller of the two stores is located on plot B9 facing the wider of the two roads that cut across the case study area. Their other store is one of the biggest in the entire square and is located on a full plot in another area of Square 11. In both locations, they also operate a generator and sell electricity to households located in the surrounding streets. With the electricity B9 also operates a suction pump that allows him to plant trees in an area where trees are very rare. The suction pump provides the household with exceptional access when compared to their neighbours. Among the latter, only one household can partially satisfy their water needs with the network, while all others must rely on alternative sources for all their water needs.

Water access in the Area B is much more difficult than in Area A, since the area is more elevated and much more distant from the borehole. Before reaching the area, a large portion of the water has had many possibilities to drain off towards lower areas in the square. The whole area can be divided into two fragments of water provision along the path of one of the square's major internal roads. In the lower part of the area (B7-B14), investments are needed to access water, while in the upper part (B1-B6), the main pipe is never filled with water. Installing a pump as B9 or digging a deep hole like B14 would not allow the households in the upper area to obtain water.

For the most part of the research, B8 was the only household with any water at all. B14 invested in the improvement of his pipe shortly before the end of the research period in December 2010, by lowering the tap from approximately 30 cm below the surface to the level of the main pipe (-90 cm). The heterogeneity in Area B is very different from that in Area A. While in Area A the performance of the water tap is a gradual phenomenon including many intermediary households, in Area B – with the recent exception of B14 – only one household had water in abundance while the others were completely deprived. Hence, there is maximal inequality in this area.

6.3.4. Area C: the Frontier between High and Low Performance

Like Area B, Area C is located at the fringe between two different fragments. Here the fragment of difficult access borders with a highly supplied area rather than with a non-supplied area. The situation of the lower half of the square is exceptional since it is connected to the main pipe through which all of the square's water supply flows every other day. Consequently, households C11 to C13 have exceptional access every other day. Pressure in C14 reached roughly 150 cmH2O at tap level or 250 cmH2O above source allowing two barrels to be comfortably filled per hour with a hose. Every other day, water pressure strongly decreases, when a valve is opened at the borehole allowing water to flow more directly to low lying areas (see 5.4.2). However, obtaining water from taps at the standard level of 60 cm above surface remains possible, even if people prefer using water stored on high pressure days, since it is more comfortable.

The upper half of the square (C1-C9) greatly suffers from very weak supply. While C9 did not even try to improve its tap, fearing that a lowered tap would dampen and eventually destroy his home's earthen wall (C9: 111), most of the other households invested in lowering their taps. They did not choose to attain the lowest levels possible, but rather chose a partial range of 50 cm below the surface. The water situations for those households connected to the lower pipe worsened dramatically when the network's general water performance throughout the square decreased in the beginning of September 2010. While in August 2010 certain households managed to cover all consumption from the tap, in November 2010 no household could fully satisfy all their needs from the tap and only some households occasionally received water.

The area's heterogeneity is based on highly unequal provision due to its location on two very different fragments of network supply combined with disparate efforts in improving access. The overall heterogeneity in the area is mainly based on supply side inequalities – with the exception of C10 who says he did not have the time for the KSWC's formal procedures to obtain his own tap. The investments in their pipe allowed some households to access water, but this access is still far below the performance of those households (C11-C15) who can rely solely on their water supply.

6.3.5. Area D: Accessing Water by Lowering the Tap under Difficult Conditions

Strong heterogeneity in Area D is produced by supply issues related to elevation, as well as by different investments in access. Street topography is very particular. The slope of the area increases from left to the right, contrary to the area's general slope. Consequently, water flow is restricted by a small hill. The backwater produced by the little hill increases the potential performance of taps in the area in comparison with taps installed on pipes that allow water to flow continuously to low lying areas. This phenomenon might explain why D3 manages to access water with a tap situated at the rather elevated height of 127 cm above source, even though the area is relatively far from the borehole.

The topography favours the left side over the right side of the street. Access is impossible for two households on the highest point of the street (D8 and D9) although they tried hard to lower their tap as far as possible. When water pressure was still strong, most of the households to the left of D8 and D9 received at least a little bit of water. However, this was for most of them only possible thanks to significant investments. One household temporarily operated a suction pump (D7) and two households manipulated the pipe to achieve maximum efficiency by digging a hole directly next to the main pipe, which required them to shift their water tap from the plot to the street. Water could thus be accessed through a connection pipe that was only about 20 cm long, thus minimizing friction and elevation loss to a strict minimum. While accessing water had been possible for houses in the middle section of the street, this became impossible under the new regime. During the period represented on the map, the households in the middle of the street did not have any chance to access water, since water no longer reached the main pipes in front of these particular houses. Of the four lowest households, D2 is not connected and D1 and D10[97] did not invest sufficiently in the depth of their taps although they could potentially reach a depth where their tap would perform.

Pipe measurements offer technical confirmation that under current water provision only the access strategy of D3 could be successful. Measurements taken over two days show that water pressure in the low tap of D3 reached a maximum of 50 cm-H_2O. All other taps are at least 45 cm higher; hence the pressure would have reached a maximum 5 cmH_2O, which hardly allows any flow at all.

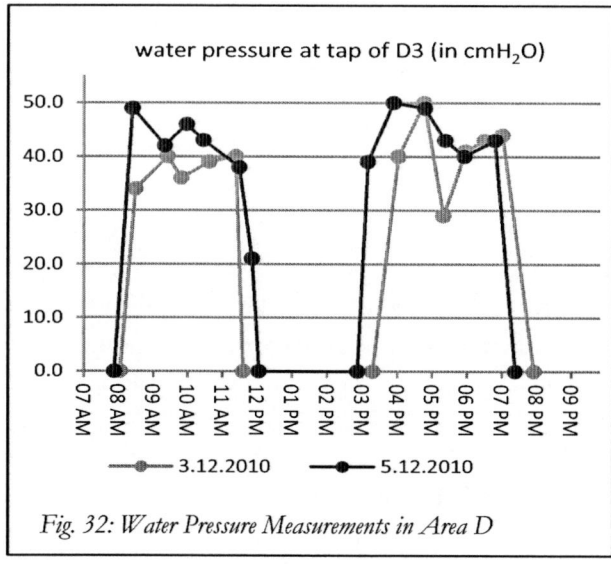

Fig. 32: *Water Pressure Measurements in Area D*

---

97 D10 has two tap connections. One is on his own plot, while the other is on a neighbouring plot where the household built an additional room. The second tap is not separated from the street by a wall. It is on public ground, similarly to the two taps on the street.

6.4. Conclusions

6.4.1. Constructing the Neighbourly Waterscape beyond Network Supply. From Water to 'Waters'

The analysis of the four 'neighbourly waterscapes' reveals highly heterogeneous tap performances amongst direct neighbours. Heterogeneity is either produced by inequality in water supply to the main pipe in front of the house, by different investments in the access to that pipe, or by a combination of both factors.

Inequalities in water supply can either materialize on a north-south axis (Area B and C), hence between people, who are connected to different main pipes that are unequally supplied, or on an east-west axis (Area D) through very local inequalities in elevation of the pipe located under a particular street.

Due to the network's generally weak supply, individual household investments can strongly improve tap performance (Area A, B, and D). Transforming poor water supply into successful water access depends partially on the users' capital endowments. In terms of suction pumps, a high performance tap is generally obtained by investing economic capital. Consequently, disposing of relatively substantial funds is a precondition for installing a pump. At the same time, being endowed with sufficient economic capital, does not necessarily translate into a household investment in a pump. It remains however, an option to achieve a comfortable water supply, even if purchasing from a water vendor might be even cheaper.

Lack of economic capital cannot be the primary reason for people who do not sufficiently manipulate their pipes, since lowered taps quickly pay off plumber's costs with the savings from no longer purchasing water from vendors. Still, empirical data demonstrates that a significant number of households do not invest further in tap improvements, although they are aware that neighbours' taps work better thanks to rather simple investments. A1 could easily access water with just a small hole of roughly 30 cm, but he has left his tap unimproved. Other examples of underinvestment are the D1 and D10 households, which are located in the lowest part of the Area A, where D3 has proven that water access is possible.

Though differences in water supply investment cannot 'objectively' be determined by a household's economic abilities, they are clearly the result of the individual's choice between multiple options in the particular local neighbourly field. Multiplicity of water strategies goes beyond fragmented water supply in the sense that fragments exist within both the water network and within alternative supply options. Water vendors are prominent example in Greater Khartoum. Each individual household can choose between different supply options, hence different socially produced 'waters'.

The Fragmentation of Vendor Water Supply

Analogously to the fragmentation of network supply, the fragmentation of the city's water supply by water vendors can also be analysed. In a classification, areas in which finding water from a water vendor is nearly impossible can be distinguished from areas where water vendors are available. Fragments served by vendors need to be sub-classified by access costs, which include on the one hand the economic cost of water and on the other hand the efforts required to find a water vendor. In general there is a negative correlation between the two types of fragmentation. In the city centre with good network supply, water vendors are completely absent, while in the peripheries, where the network is absent, water vendors are omnipresent.

Differentiating two types of water supply fragmentation is a valuable approach, where fragments of network supply overlap with vendor supply. Square 11 is one of these areas. Due to the malfunctioning public water network, water vendors are widespread, more so in areas with no network water at all, than in those with good water supply. Unconnected households in areas with good network supply will pay more for water from water vendors, since vendors hardly ever travel down their street. Unconnected individuals must therefore walk to other areas, find the vendors, and direct them to their unconnected homes. The vendors' prices might also be higher, since the vendors need more time to find customers.

Competing and Complementary Sources of 'Waters'

The coexistence of water vendors and a water network in the same place, allows households to choose their particular water source. The result is a highly competitive, local water market in which people can access two different 'waters' that differ in cost and comfort.

Water in Square 11's waterscape is much more competitive than in the 'networked waterscape of a city' after neoliberal reforms. Generally, water companies do not compete with each other through their actual performance, through the way in which they satisfy the consumers who choose to purchase water from them. Instead the water network is operated as a monopoly. Competition is restricted to obtaining concessions. Consumers do not choose which network company will supply them. The decision is in the hands of politicians and government administrators. In the waterscape of Square 11 different suppliers compete directly with each other. The Square's consumers therefore do have a choice. One of the explanations for the failure of the neoliberalization of water can be argued from within neoliberal theory. Market access for private companies is not insured by the satisfaction of the consumers on a day to day basis, but by making an offer for a concession, before the company has even performed.

-The competition in Square 11 between commercialized public and private water is the result of the interplay between supply performance of the network and discerning consumers. Consumers decide either to invest in the performance of their access, or to purchase water from a vendor. Their decisions are based on their capital endowments and the evaluation of the cost and comfort of the two supply options.

The constellation can be analysed both in terms of competition and complementarity. The KSWC and various water vendors compete with each other for customers, and consequently for income, obtained from clients paying monthly bills or customers purchasing jerrycans full of water. The objective of a particular household is first to satisfy the 'basic need' for water, which is indispensable, and second to satisfy additional consumption at the lowest overall costs possible. Since the KSWC does not manage to satisfy the basic needs of all households, water vendors automatically complement overall water supply. This second type of water supply, which does not live up to the ideal of modern infrastructure, achieves 'market access' due to the failure of the ideal's implementation.

In the competition between water providers, households are not restricted to one provider, but can and sometimes must obtain water from different sources. Bakker (2003a: 334) generalizes networks with low quality standards in the global South:

> Most households rely on a mix of water supply strategies: for the wealthy, a tank on the roof connected to both a private deep well and the network, supplemented by bottled water for drinking; for the less affluent, a hand-dug shallow well for bathing and cleaning, often in conjunction with a supply of drinking water purchased from neighbourhood water vendors.

221

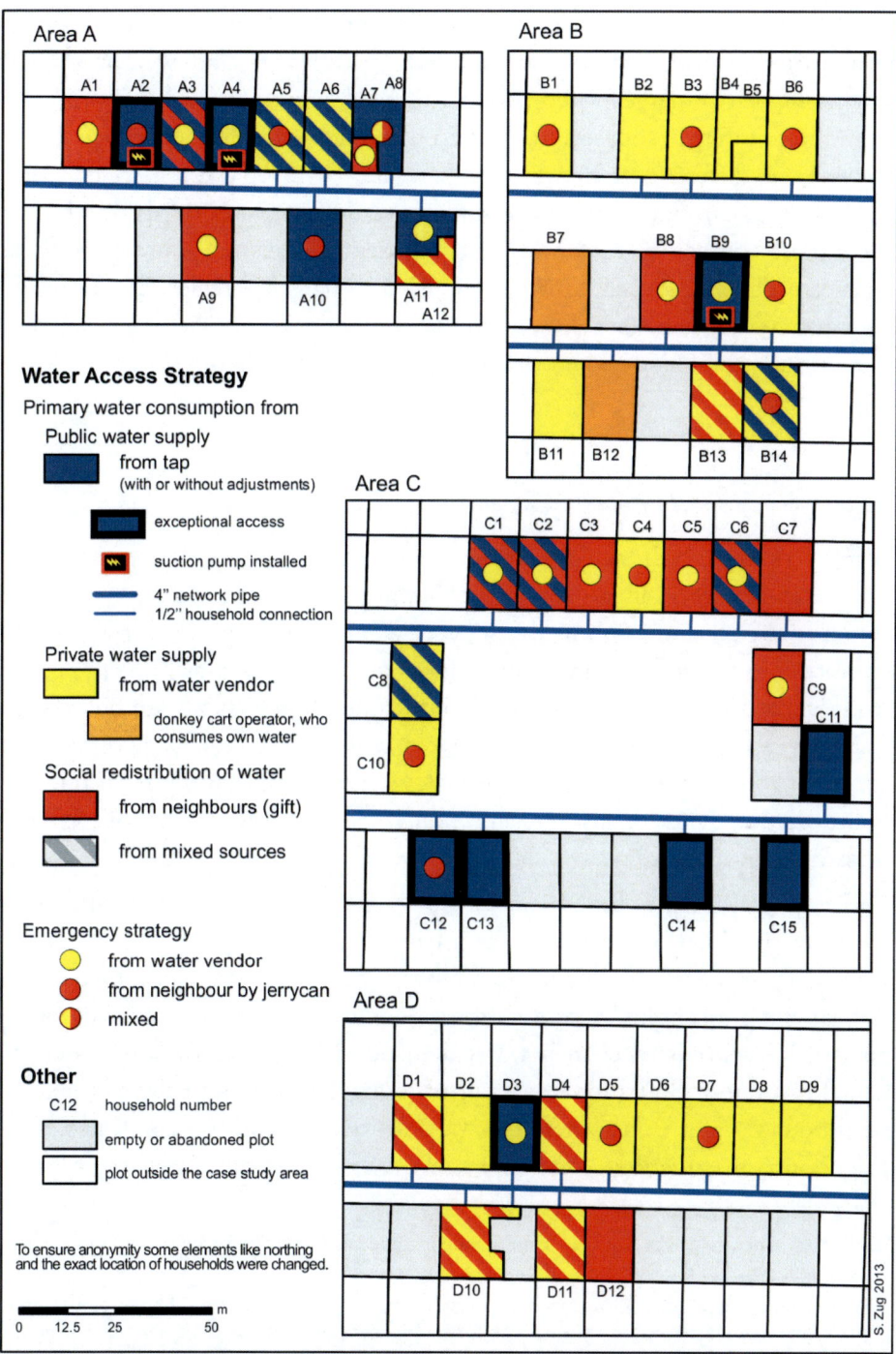

Fig. 33: Multiplicity of Water Access Strategies

In Square 11, households also use multiple water sources for daily consumption, attributing different quality standards to network and vendor water.[98] The multiplicity emerges when people cannot satisfy their water consumption from their preferred source and must complement with another source. In the study, I will differentiate between primary and occasional water sources. Primary sources can but do not necessarily cover all the water needs of a household; these sources however are regularly used. Occasional sources are those sources used by a household when the primary water strategies fail, for example when a water tap stays dry due to temporary problems with water production at the borehole, or when the household does not find a water vendor in the street.

Locating Water Gifts within the Commercial Water Supply

Water vendors and the water network are the only two complete water supply systems in Square 11 in the sense that they augment the total amount of water available for consumption in the square. Water from the network is directly pumped into the square and water vendors deliver water, which they obtained from water towers in other squares. Both water supply types are based on a standard capitalist biography of things, in which water is commodified by a water provider through the added value generated through production, transportation, and finally consumption. The exchange value of water is transferred into use value.

The empirical research in Square 11 shows that households do not rely only on water provided by these two commercial water supply systems. Figure 34 graphically presents the heterogeneity of water supply strategies. Quantification of the households' access strategies sums up the four case study areas: 36% of households meet their water demand at least partially with water obtained from neighbours for free. Half of them (17%) even rely completely on neighbour's water.[99] Another 22%[100] only occasionally obtain water from neighbours, in situations such as when they run out of stored water, when

---

98 Bottled water, which is the only water source people assume to be of better quality, is hardly ever consumed in the Square.

99 The figures are presented to provide an overview of the case study area. They do not claim to be representative either for Square 11 or for its fragment of weak supply, since areas were purposely selected.

100 This figure is not represented on Figure 34. It refers to the 'emergency strategies' presented in Figure 33.

they cannot find a water vendor, or when a neighbour has colder water than theirs. In all, 58% of households at least occasionally consume water from neighbours.

With a few exceptions, water gifts are an extension of the biography of network rather than vendor water. The gift mainly consists of water obtained from a tap that performs better than neighbouring taps due to water supply inequality or different investments in access through pipe manipulations or the operation of suction pumps. In the biography of water, water produced by the public water corporation and delivered via the network to a consumer, becomes decommodified, at least in monetary terms and is given free of charge to neighbours. The neighbour's water is an important source of water to satisfy demand.

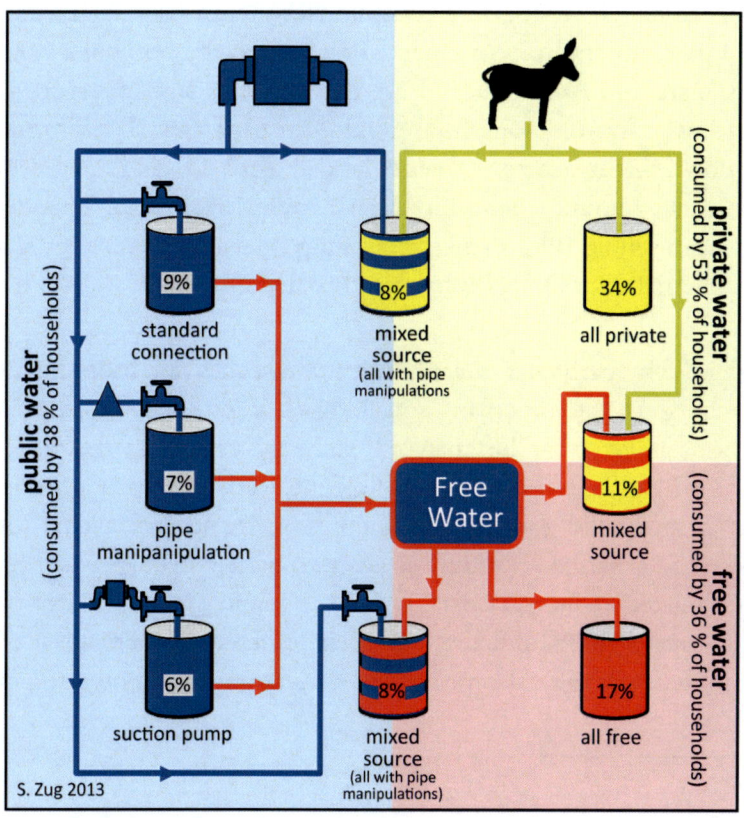

Fig. 34: Quantification of Water Access Strategies

Although water gifts are a source for the recipient, they are not a source of water for Square 11, since no additional water is produced by gift transfers. Instead, existing water is simply redistributed among the households. Every additional drop a household obtains from a water tap to gift to a neighbour reduces the overall quantity in the network, making water access more difficult for other households.[101]

The relevance of gifts as an element of the household's water access strategies strongly differs in the four areas. While in Area A 71%, in Area C 70% and in Area D 45% of all households, who do not fully satisfy their water demand by tap, regularly consume their neighbour's water, the figure for Area B is only 15%. The high flows of gifts in A and C could hypothetically be explained by the quantity of water potential donors receive. In Area A, pressure in the pipes is comparatively strong and two households have installed pumps. In Area C, five households (C11-C15) have exceptional water pressure since they depend on a high performance pipe connected directly to the borehole. Conditions for gift transfers in Area B and D are much worse, since pressure in the main pipe is lower and only one household[102] in each area (B9, C3) has managed exceptional water access. Nevertheless in Area D, 45% per cent obtain water from neighbours whereas in Area B only 15% do so. This despite the fact that household B9 – thanks to a pump – has a much higher water production potential than D3, who has a rather uncomfortable access in a hole 90 cm deep.

To fully understand why particular 'neighbourly waterscapes' are more highly dominated by water gifts, the underlying social logics of gifts and the particular choices of households must be analysed, rather than merely described. Chapter 7 aims to reveal the internal logics of gift transfers by applying Bourdieu's 'economy of symbolic goods'. This theoretical framework allows the local waterscape to be described not only as a water market steered by supply and demand, and related economic costs, but also a market under incorporation of the social constellations of actors and their preferences for water consumption. The existence of gifts also provides explanations to the question of

---

101 Here it is assumed that the square does not lose water through the open valves in the corners of the square; despite the fact that it does.

102 In Area B, B9 is the only household which is in reasonable distance for other households to access water gifts. In Area C households have the possibility to access water two streets away from two holes on the street, which is however only occasionally done, since it requires carrying water for a long distance.

why certain households do not invest in their water access when they could make water from the network accessible at relatively low cost.

6.4.2. Locating Appropriations in the Moral Waterscape of the City

Appropriations of network infrastructure contribute to the enabling of water gift transactions because they increase heterogeneity of tap performance. Beyond the horizontal moral geography within the 'neighbourly waterscape', the appropriations are also linked vertically to the 'moral waterscape of the city'. The second part of the conclusion of this chapter will elaborate on this scalar interrelation, forming an excursus from the general arc of this book. Instead of continuing to focus in on ever smaller scales, we return to the scale of policy makers, hence the 'waterscape of the city'. This section will analyse the discrepancy between the KSWC's legal regulations of the consumer's role in water supply and the KSWC efforts to enforce these regulations.

Legally consumers are allowed to install water pumps to suck water out of the network, but they are not allowed to physically appropriate network infrastructure. Most households are aware that interfering in the technical installations in the 4 inch main pipe and even in the ½ inch household connection pipe, including the built-in elements, is not allowed. The appropriation's illegal nature does not however seem to hinder the majority of households seeking to improve their water connection (e.g. EL1, C1: 44). Likewise, plumbers are aware of the legal restrictions, but they openly offer non-connected households to illegally connect them and to improve their existing connections. Since pipe installations inside homes are very rare in third class neighbourhoods, projects outside the plots are an important source of income for plumbers on the city's peripheries.

Prohibiting private plumbers from working on the network is not an arbitrary regulation to underline the KSWC's the ownership of the pipes. It is a highly reasonable demand since technical changes create two major problems for the network as discussed above (6.2.1). Changing the connection from horizontal to vertical often leaves an improperly closed hole in the 4 inch main pipe that ultimately increases network leaks leading to unaccounted for water and increased water supply problems. Bringing the tap below the surface and removing non-return valves strongly intensifies the risk of network contamination. Consequently, the KSWC is highly vested in preventing people from manipulating their installations.

Appropriation of the network infrastructure outside the plot and illegal connections cannot be done secretly. The soil must be removed to a depth of 90 cm between the house and the main pipe, which takes several hours. For several weeks, unless the project is done during the rainy season, the closed ditch is still visible by the broken soil, which is normally strongly consolidated. Finally, those who dig a hole to gain direct access to water next to the main pipe on the streets, permanently expose their pipe appropriation. Despite the visibility of illegal practices, people are still not afraid that the KSWC will punish them for breaking the law.

The KSWC manager of Umbadda explains what happens to people who illegally connect to the network:

> KSWC11 (124): It is not allowed to connect to the network without following the procedures in our office. They are thieves; it is robbery [...]
>
> SZ: Can you hold the person who did it accountable?
>
> KSWC11: If we come and find the network opened, we just start a police case either against the plumber or the house owner that brought the plumber.
>
> SZ: What happens?
>
> KSWC11: The connection is cut. Both of them are sent to prison for several months.
>
> SZ: Does that happen often?
>
> KSWC11: Only a few cases go all the way to judgement.

The statement demonstrates that bringing people to justice for having appropriated pipes is rarely implemented, despite being KSWC policy. In Souq Libya, several plumbing businesses offer all required parts and many plumbers wait for customers. It is the most important place to find plumbers for all of Omdurman's western peripheries. However, plumbers reported only one case of a plumber sent to prison; he was released when other plumbers intervened (Plumber 1: 35). Plumbers themselves have an explanation for the KSWC's lax enforcement of its regulations: "I know it is wrong to make changes on the pipe, but they know that there are water shortages and many things need to be done. So they pretend that they do not know that people work on the network" (Pl2: 89).

The same manager who stressed that people might be sent to prison for appropriating the pipe explains in the same interview, why they generally tolerate illegal practices:

> What can we do if someone is looking for water, and he is registered with us as a customer? So you just close your eyes. [...] It is different to be hard with people if you are working in electricity or water supply. We are not like the electricity company. We do not stick to our laws. The electricity people are following the law as it is. We have many laws, but the people are not too afraid. [...] Legally we have the same rules. We will cut service to you, and you do not get the service. But we do not do it (KSWC11: 144).

By having similar laws to water provision as those for electricity, yet applying them differently, the KSWC highlights water's moral significance. Another KSWC staff member summarizes the specificity of water in relation to economic profitability: "The work with water is about being water. Water is people's life. Not everybody can work in water, because it is nothing that makes you rich. It is about being water" (KSWC15: 225).

Pipe manipulations lead to a moral dilemma for KSWC staff.[103] On the one hand, being stricter in punishing those damaging the network would in the long run improve performance and the quality of the network. On the other hand, KSWC staff knows that they do not currently fulfil their obligation to provide people with water. Not allowing people to invest in short term access, would be actively denying them access to poorly supplied government water. It would be denying water to people, not just through performance, which can be argued to be related to the KSWC's financial restrictions, but through a conscious decision.

The KSWC's manifest interests enforce the moral tolerance of appropriations. The employees are in a difficult situation as they are aware they cannot fulfil consumers' water demands. At the same time, they must satisfy the government, which does not want people to protest against water provision. This

---

103 A similar moral dilemma has been revealed within KSWC by Beckedorf (2012), who analysed the KSWC employees' position towards water cuts and the installation of water meters. She argues that KSWC is internally divided. Economic interest, which is pushed by the current neoliberal reform processes in KSWC, would justify consequent cutting of services to those who do not pay their bills. The same arguments would justify the introduction of a pre-paid meter system, which allows only those households who pay to consume water. A part of the employees however are strongly opting against both rigid water cuts and water meters. She argues, that "water is particularly essential for life, moral considerations with regard to water supply supersede in some cases the economic principles of current neoliberal reform programmes" (Beckedorf 2012: 10).

would be seen as the expression of the people's dissatisfaction not only with KSWC but also with the government. KSWC staff consequently also tolerates people's appropriations because these appropriations contribute to satisfying user demand for water and to reducing their desire to protest.

The situation takes place in an 'imperfect economy of symbolic goods', in which the KSWC staff's choice is both motivated by interest but also by moral considerations about the specificity of water. The negative impacts of certain people's adjustments are finally tolerated, even though long term consequences should urge KSWC to take much stronger action against these practices.

7

Accessing the Neighbour's Tap. The Gift of Water

Free water transfers are one possible way, among others, to satisfy water demand in Square 11. As the previous chapter revealed, these transfers are quantitatively highly important for a description of water access in the four case study areas. In chapter 2, three elements were developed that impact the likelihood of water gifts: first, the spatial heterogeneity of access to 'conventional' water sources, second, the particular economic and non-economic costs for the donor, which are related to accessing water and supplying the gift, and third the social framework in which the gift transfer takes place.

Spatial heterogeneity in the way people access water on a very small scale is primarily created by the particular performance of individual household taps. It is therefore the result of the combined efforts of the public water corporation and the individual households to increase tap performance. Purchasing water from vendors is another possible way to access water in case one's own tap does not perform sufficiently. Keeping in mind that individual households in Square 11 are in favour of network supply, the water vendors are never the primary choice, but a reaction to the tap's weak performance.

The gift, as the third option for accessing water, needs to be analysed within the particular empirical reality of the heterogeneity of other possible water sources. The four case study areas were purposely selected according to the prevalence of heterogeneity. For the analysis of the gift in this chapter, we can therefore consider different access to the network as a given reality in the particular case study areas.

To analyse the particular gift transfers, I will consequently elaborate on the other two conditions for gift transfers, the economic cost of water gifts and their social embeddedness. Subchapter 7.1 will analyse the different costs and benefits which are created for the donor and recipient within particular biographies of water gifts. The following two subchapters will focus on the social embeddedness of two particular biographies: the gifts that are made by pumping water to a neighbour by hose (7.2) and the gifts that the recipient accesses by bucket (7.3). Selecting these two different gift transactions reveals a difference, not only in the technical and economic transaction, but especially in the social grounding of the gifts, as shown by the relationship between the donor and the recipient.

7.1. Classifying Water Biographies by Economic Costs

SZ: How much do you pay for the water you get from your neighbour?

A3 (74): Money? What are you talking about? No, no.

Merely asking the question about financial compensation for water transfers led to the consternation of several interview partners. It is a 'hard' fact that in Square 11, as in all other areas of Greater Khartoum where water transfers could be observed, water flows between neighbours who are never paid for it. Nevertheless water gifts are economically embedded, since they create costs and benefits for the actors involved in the transaction. The particular economics of a gift are a crucial element in understanding it.

Gift transfers in Square 11 always consist of two very distinct life phases in the biographies of water drops. The first part of a biography contains the passage of the water from the source to the *intended* consumer of the particular provider. In order for the purchased water to become a gift in a second phase of the biography, it has to be moved out of the commodity state. The *intended* consumer does not consume the water, but turns water into a gift and himself or herself into a donor who redistributes water wealth. To allow the transfer of water and the transformation of his position from a consumer into a donor, the potential donor has to pay the costs for purchasing the water under the particular socio-technological characteristics of his water access. Section 7.1.1 will quantify these costs for the donor.

Gift transfers are beneficial for a recipient, since he receives water without paying for it. Still, receiving water is not always for free, even if we do not consider return gifts. As for obtaining water from a water vendor or from the network, the flow of water gifts is made possible by the donor's efforts in water supply as well as the recipient's efforts in accessing the gift. The investments made to access water reduce the recipient's benefit of receiving water for free. The particular costs of the water gift for a recipient will be discussed in section 7.1.2.

The costs for accessing and supplying gifts depend on the specific gift transaction, which differs by the way the water was obtained, and by the method it is transferred to the neighbours. The final section 7.1.3 will incorporate the particular costs into different biographies of water drops from the source to the recipient.

7.1.1. The Economic and Social Costs for Making Gifts

For the donor, gifting leads to several costs that occur in different phases of the biography of water. First, water has to be obtained and paid for and, if necessary; the household needs to cover costs for the improvement of its access to water. These costs emerge in the transaction phase between a provider and a consumer, in which water is treated as a commodity. Since water can be obtained from two different sources (network and a vendor) and can require different access investments, the costs of differently obtained water drops differ. Second, costs emerge in the gift transaction itself.

The Donor's Cost for Accessing Water from a Vendor

Before a household can purchase water from a vendor, value is added to water. Both KSWC and private water tower operators charge 1.00 SDG to fill the tank of a whole donkey cart. Donkey carts in Greater Khartoum are a standard construction. The main cart can be used for the transport of goods or people. For transporting water, a tank is installed on the cart. The tank is constructed from two used oil barrels, which are welded together, and can be filled with roughly 430 litres.

The value of the commodity water increases with its transportation – the service provided by the water vendor. The cost of water increases due to the labour costs of the water vendor, as well as to his investments for the cart, the donkey, the fodder, and licensing (e.g. WV1: 13). The value of the water of a filled cart quadruples from 1.00 SDG to 4.00 SDG.[104] Households purchase

---

[104] The price per m^3 is 9.30 SDG (2.95 EUR). The unit price is constant regardless if small or large amounts of water are purchased. Over time, the price for water only fluctuates if demand or supply changes. Water demand increases when the water network has a problem, making people who are normally supplied by the network purchase water from vendors. Supply de-

Fig. 35: Water Vendor with Donkey Cart

either the water of a whole cart, a half cart, or a certain number of 'pairs of jerrycans', which is the smallest unit by which water vendors sell water.

In order to access water from a water vendor, a household generally does not have to put in much more effort than paying for the water, at least in areas where many people rely on this service and many water vendors are available. The households either arrange regular delivery with a particular vendor, or they just call one of the vendors, who pass through the small streets in the neighbourhood, continuously drumming on their barrel to signal their presence to potential customers. Purchasing water from a vendor includes full service. The vendors stop in front of the plot and fill two jerrycans of 18 litres each, which they carry inside and pour directly either into the customer's storage barrels[105] or into earthen pots, which are used for cooling water.

The Donor's Cost for Accessing Water from the Network

The costs for water obtained from the network are less determined by the market than are the costs of water from a vendor. To obtain water from the network, the household, by contract, has to pay 26 SDG per month. Since it is a flat rate tariff, the household can take as much water as it wants for the same cost, within the limits of water supply. Increasing household consump-

---

creases during the big Muslim holidays, when many water vendors stop working, or when the water towers stop working. In these situations, the price for water can triple.

105 The same barrels as the ones installed on the carts (215 litres) are mainly used.

tion, e.g. for cultivating trees, is consequently free of charge. In an ideal case of water provision, as for example for the households located on the high pressure pipe close to the borehole (C11-C15), or in the low lying areas of the square, households can access much more water than they need for their own consumption. Opening a tap for a single hour could provide enough water to cover the entire day's demand. Instead of leaving the tap closed and abstaining from the water which the tap would still provide, the household can gift the 'surplus' water to other people. Consequently, a household does not have to cover any access costs to gift water from sufficiently performing tap. While the donor is only donating a surplus, which does not have any use value for him, the recipient receives something with a high use value for him. If – and this never happens in Greater Khartoum – water were supplied to neighbours against cash rather than as a gift, the water-poor's use value would define the exchange value. If the water-rich household charged a lower price than the water vendors, the transaction would be profitable for the water-rich household, because it would gain income, and for the 'water-poor', who could save the extra money water from a vendor would have cost. The costs for obtaining water for gifting from the network are consequently significantly lower than the costs for obtaining water from a water vendor.

Depending on the way households access water from the network, the costs for obtaining water for gifting can increase beyond the mere charges. For the gift transaction, however, the only relevant investment costs are those that arise from obtaining additional water, which can be gifted. It is safe to assume that investments in the pump itself, as well as in the hole and the pipe manipulations, are primarily done to improve personal access to water, rather than to supply neighbours. Consequently, the production of water from an ordinary or improved tap does not lead to additional economic costs for the household at all, unless the household's consumption quantity becomes reduced by the consumption of others.

For obtaining network water by a suction pump, not only the fixed costs of the purchase of the suction pump and the generator need to be covered, but also the operating costs, which increase by every additional litre of water obtained from the network, hence by every litre gifted. The cost for pumping water is difficult to determine since generators are not only used for pumping water, but also for operating bulbs and televisions, especially in the evening hours. A4 requires about a litre of fuel per day, which costs 1.50 SDG, allowing him to obtain some 6 barrels of water. Even if pump owners operate their generator exclusively for pumping water, the fuel costs reach, at maximum, 0.25 SDG per barrel. The donor's cost for gifting water obtained from a suction pump is still much lower than the recipient's savings, recipient which equal the cost of a barrel from a water vendor, amounting to 2.00 SDG.

The Donor's Transaction Cost for Gift Transfers

Two technical means to transfer water from one house to another exist in Square 11. First, water is carried manually in a bucket. The bucket is filled from the barrel of the donor, from the running tap inside the donor's plot, or from a hose connected to the tap in front of the house of the donor. Second, water is directly pumped from the network to the neighbour.

In all cases, the transport does not lead to additional economic or labour costs for the donor. Transporting water by bucket from the donor to the recipient is nearly exclusively accomplished by the members of the recipient's household.[106] If water is pumped to a neighbour, no additional running costs emerge for the donor[107], because pumping water into one's own barrel produces the same costs as pumping water into a neighbour's barrel. The costs of pumping consequently are not gift supply cost, but water access costs.

The only financial cost that could be required to supply water to a neighbour is the hose itself. For the pump owner's needs, a 15 metre long hose is sufficient, since it easily covers the distance between the tap and the barrel and trees on the street. The hose is also mostly long enough to supply direct neighbours on the same side of the street. If the water is pumped to households further away, a longer hose is required. In order to supply water from A4 to A7, a hose of some 30 metres is required. The additional 15 metres was purchased by A4 exclusively for A7's use; the 7 pounds spent for the hose is only a small economic cost. Additional costs arise if the hose is damaged, which happens frequently if it is used to supply houses on the other side of the street, exposing the hose to the traffic of donkey carts and also occasionally to minibuses and cars (A9: 269). What is important here is that these additional costs need to be willingly shouldered by the potential donor to render

---

[106] The only exception occurred when the owner carried water from his tap to the house of an old woman (D6: 98).

[107] Here it is assumed that friction in the pipe does not significantly reduce the water flow.

possible another household's consumption. The additional financial and organizational efforts transform the simple gift of surplus of water.

The major costs for supplying water to a neighbour are not direct labour or economic costs related to the transport of water, but transaction costs. These costs are mainly created by allowing other people access to one's own plot. A plot of a household in Square 11 is a very private space, and is protected from the sight of direct neighbours and people passing on the street with a wall – at least two metres high – that completely surrounds the plot. Even rather poor households strongly invest in their wall, which requires compromising on the construction of rooms. My translator strongly advised me to respect this wall, and, after knocking on the door, to position myself next to the door rather than in front of it, in order to show that I was not trying to look inside the plot through the gap between the door and the wall while waiting.

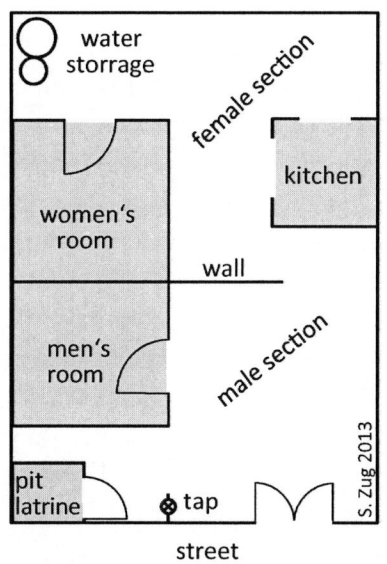

Fig. 36: *Typical Spatial Arrangement of a Plot in Square 11*

Most plots are internally subdivided into two sections with different levels of privacy. The rooms themselves, partly in combination with an extra wall, separate the two spaces. A male section is located towards the street. It generally contains one or several bedrooms for men and, in more wealthy households, a representative room for visitors. Only visitors who have a close relationship with the family are allowed to enter the female section of the plot. Beside the bedroom(s), the female section also contains a kitchen or a place for cooking. The water storage barrels and the earthen pots, which are used to cool down water, are mostly located in the female section, where water demand is highest due to cooking and washing. Obtaining water from a water vendor requires granting him access to the female section of the house so that he can deliver the water. Although several households dislike (e.g. A8: 246; X10: 65) having a man access this very private space, it is accepted since the disturbance only takes a few minutes, allowing the women to cover their hair or to go into one of the rooms while the vendor is inside (e.g. ISL1: 41; WV4: 71).

Allowing people to come inside the plot to get free water is a very different interference in the privacy of the house than that of the water vendors:

> The water vendor just comes and puts his water and goes again. This is not about leaving your door open for anybody to come and go. [For water gifts] it is mainly just kids coming. If male adults would come, that would be an issue for me (D3: 99).

Qualitatively, transfers of free water interfere less with a household's privacy than obtaining water from a vendor. First, men hardly come to ask for water, since water fetching is mainly the work of children and women, and second, the local codes of conduct are respected. Only if households know each other very well do men also enter to take water. The adult son of D11 (74) enters the plot of D4 and D10 to watch television and occasionally also took water, at a time when water pressure was still higher. Since he is a man, he would however never enter the plot of D3, respecting that the female head of household – as she stated above – does not feel comfortable allowing men on her plot.

The place where the transaction takes place impacts how much the donor is disturbed in the process. If water is pumped by hose to the street or directly into the barrel of the recipient, or if the water hole of the household is located on the street, the recipient does not have to enter the plot at all and the gift transaction can be arranged at the doorstep. In order to take water from the barrel instead, the recipient has to enter the very private sphere – or household members have to carry the water to the door. The transaction and the disturbance however are of short duration, since the bucket can be filled very quickly from the barrel. In order to take water from the tap, the recipient only has to enter the male section, but the time to fill the bucket takes much longer, since it is related to the pressure of water in the tap. The social cost of providing water from the tap increases with the duration of time it takes to obtain water.

Highly frequented households like C14 and D3 leave their door open while pressure is available. Young women and children constantly move in and out; they queue at the tap and wait and children play.

> First, I gave the hose to the children so that they could fill their jerrycans on the street. Three times they just put the hose on the ground after they finished and water was running all over the street. Then I stopped that and people have to come in to get water (C14: 76).

Allowing children to take free water requires a certain degree of supervision. Granting people access to their water resource is an effort for the donor household and consequently a cost.

Sharing water from one's own tap does not necessarily mean only sharing one's surplus water – that is granting others access only from the moment when one's own storage facilities are filled. Often households share water even before they have filled their own barrel. A queuing system often regulates access to the tap. If people are queuing on a tap, it takes longer for donors to fill their barrel. If the tap stops delivering water before the barrel is filled, donors can even experience an economic loss, since they might have to purchase additional water from a vendor, even though the water from their taps would have been enough to satisfy personal consumption needs.

While giving water by pump does not entail the major disturbance of allowing people on the plot, operating a generator significantly decreasing the quality life on the plot due to noise pollution, which often makes it difficult even to communicate. If a generator is operated exclusively for gift supply, the disturbance is prolonged.

Gifting mainly creates social rather than economic costs. These costs depend on very different factors, which are related to the particular relationship between the donor and the recipient. The closer the recipient and donor, the less is the cost of having the recipient enter the plot. The cost further depends on the particular location where the household takes water on the plot, and the duration of time that the recipient needs to spend on the plot. These costs of transaction should not be neglected, as the case of hand pumps in a camp for the internally displaced reveals. This example is presented in the following box.

Box 1: The Social Cost of Allowing People on One's Plot to Take Water: The Case of Hand Pumps in Mandela

Mandela is one of the four still existing camps for the internally displaced in Greater Khartoum. It was established some 20 km south of Khartoum centre in the early 1990s. Today it is still mainly inhabited by Southern Sudanese. In 2008 and 2009, more than two months of research were conducted in the camp. In contrast to informal settlements, here NGOs were allowed to install hand pumps, which provide free water to the inhabitants, and which contribute to the production of a completely different local waterscape than those of neighbourhoods.

End of 2008, a section of Mandela was replanned. Houses were destroyed and land was newly laid out with straight streets and clearly demarcated plots – similar to the design of Square 11 – and people received new plots. In the

> new housing pattern, many hand pumps were not on public ground anymore, but rather located inside plots. With the granting of land titles, this public infrastructure officially became privatized and the owner of the plot became the owner of the hand pump. Since plots were distributed by lottery, the new owners could not opt for or against a plot with a pump.
>
> One could assume that those households who received a plot with a hand pump were very happy, since the hand pump would allow them to easily satisfy their water needs not only for consumption, but also for house construction, allowing the household to save significant money because they did not have to buy from donkey carts. However, people were very reluctant to take these plots and several new owners even closed down the pumps.
>
> Why was owning a water pump not perceived as a gain, but as a burden? From the perspective of neighbours, a hand pump does not become privatized but remains public – the neighbours are still granted access rights. Ultimately the private plot turns public again, which strongly devaluates the plot if we take into consideration that the plot is socially conceived as very intimate space. Finally, the social costs of the hand pumps are not compensated by the benefits, leading the owners to close them down. The same social construction of the hand pump had already led to a decay of many pumps in the past, when people did not take responsibility for making small repayments to the pump after the NGOs had left, because the gift of the hand pump was and still is perceived as an unconditional gift.

7.1.2. The Benefits of Receiving Gifts

While the donor of water always has costs for supplying water since he moves water out of the commodity state, the recipient can economically benefit from the water transfer. However, not all water gifts are beneficial for a recipient, since accessing water can also produce certain costs, which reduce the benefit of obtaining water gifts. After quantifying the economic savings from obtaining free water, I will present the costs that emerge for accessing the water gift.

Saving Economic Costs by Consuming Water Gifts

Regardless if the water to be gifted is obtained from a vendor or from the network, the economic benefit of the water gift is to be quantified mainly in relation to the cost of water obtained from a vendor, since a household that does not cover its consumption with water from its own tap only has the choice between consuming water from a vendor or from a neighbour. If a barrel of water is obtained from a neighbour, the household saves the 2.00 SDG that it would pay for water from the water vendor.

The money a household can save by obtaining water gifts is directly related to the amount of water consumed by the household, which depends on the number of people living in the house, but also on the household's consumption pattern. The interviews revealed that households that exclusively consume water by vendor require between half a barrel and two barrels per day, which costs them some 30 to 120 SDG. The economic savings from obtaining water gifts are very significant, especially for those households who have low incomes.

Reduction of the Benefit of Gifts by the Costs of Water Access

The savings from not having to purchase water from a vendor are reduced by a household's costs for accessing the gift, which depend on the way water is accessed. Only those households who receive water by suction pump incur no additional costs. The water is directly filled into the barrel just as if the household had purchased the water from a vendor. It is even more comfortable to receive water by suction pump than to purchase it from street vendor, because the household does not need to search for the vendor on the street, nor do they need to grant him access to the female section of the plot.

If recipients obtain water by bucket, they have to cover significant costs, since access requires time and energy for carrying. Waiting times are increased depending on the way the household obtains the water. Taking water from the barrel is faster than waiting for it to be filled from a tap. The more people queuing and the lower the water flow, the longer the waiting time. Similarly, the larger the distance between the potential donor and the recipient, the higher are the costs of transportation. Members of the D12 household, who rely exclusively on free water from neighbours, carry water roughly 150 metres if the water situation of the close-by D3 household does not allow D12 to completely cover its water needs. Similarly households in the case study areas report that people from Square 11 come to ask for water (e.g. D3: 63, D10: 70). Walking the distance to the donor's water tap and spending time to wait are very relevant costs involved in free water transfers. It is the recipient who needs to decide if the labour costs for carrying are still lower than the costs for the alternative – purchasing water from a vendor. The emergence of gifts consequently is closely related to heterogeneity of tap performance on a small scale, which allows for small distances between potential water donors and recipients.

For some households the costs of waiting and carrying are too high, since they do not have the necessary manpower. Based on my observation, most water is carried by girls and women under 20 years of age. Some boys under 12 also carry water, but less frequently than do girls of the same age. Women above 20 occasionally carry water, while only seldom will men and older boys do so. The waiting time when children are sent can be assumed to be a less relevant cost than if an adult woman were to go and spend several hours.[108] An old woman living together with her adult son would like to cover all her water consumption from neighbours, but she feels too weak to carry the water and only occasionally takes some small amounts of water from neighbours, just for dishwashing (D5: 66). The decision to take water from a vendor rather than to carry it is not necessarily the same every day, but rather depends on a very subjective evaluation of costs in a particular moment in time. C5 (12) states: "I sometimes take water from the vendors, even if water is available in my neighbour's tap. Sometimes I am just too tired to carry".

For other households, it is not merely the physical work that prevents them from taking water by jerrycans. D2 argues: "I never carried water, even in Nyala [Darfur]. There, water came by donkey cart. I have nothing to do with carrying". The reason she does not carry deals with social status. Not exposing the women in the public 'male' sphere has a high value in a Muslim context.

A young mother living in A12 was very used to carrying water in her village. In Square 11, she only takes water from the family she shares the plot with (A11). Although this water is not enough and she has to supplement with water from a vendor, she does not access other free water sources in the street. She argues that she does not carry water in the city, because "the village is different. There, we do not get tired. Here we do nothing, so our body gets tired from everything we do". For her, carrying water is not part of the mode of life in the city. In her home village, she was engaged in physical labour not only for household purposes, but also for agriculture; in Square 11, her role is restricted to work inside the house, while her husband works as a driver.

---

108 A detailed analysis of gender relations and water carrying and of the costs of carrying as a differentiated according to the age and gender of the person doing the carrying is an important factor in understanding why a particular household relies on water gifts, while others do not. Elaborating these questions would have required a deeper analysis of what could be called the 'waterscape of the household', in which the water related tasks, among others, are distributed between different members.

Due to the diverse costs that are incurred from carrying water by bucket, receiving water by hose is a much more comfortable way to receive water. Water gifts by hose consequently are much more valuable than water gifts by jerrycan.

The superiority of water gifts by hose also partially explains why some households do not invest in their water pipe by improving their access. A1 consumes all the water required from his neighbour A2, who operates a suction pump. A1's own tap is hardly improved, although in his location accessing water is possible with simple investments like lowering the tap only some 30 cm below the surface. Obtaining water at this level would however require significant work. One has to wait for the bucket to be filled and carry the water to the storage barrel. Taking the neighbour's gift is just more convenient. If we consider the gift of water to be completely altruistic, accessing water by hose from a neighbour would be the most superior water access strategy, since water access is just as comfortable as the one of a household operating an own suction pump, while no network fees need to be paid.

7.1.3. The Overall Economics of Different Biographies of Water

In the previous section, different costs and benefits of gift transfers were determined, which are on the one hand related to the transformation of the commodity water into a gift, and on the other hand to the transport of gifts to the recipient. Depending on the particular constellation, the economics of these transformations differ. In order to determine the economics of a particular biography of a water drop, different techno-socio-economic elements have to be set together.

The following graph presents four major gift biographies of water, which were observed in Square 11. The donor's costs for providing water gifts (1) as well as the recipient's benefits from receiving gifts (2) are presented. The sum of the donor's cost and the recipient's benefits determines the overall social benefit of the water transfer.

Comparing Different Biographies of Water

The first biography of water (1) in the graph is the transfer of water obtained from the network, but without pump. In absence of a pump, manual carrying is the only possible way to transfer water to a neighbour. The donor's costs in this biography of water are exceptionally low, because he neither has to cover costs for purchasing, since water is charged for by a flat rate tariff, nor does he have any running costs for accessing water. The costs are restricted merely to transaction costs, which are mainly constituted by the costs created by accessing the plot. The costs for transport are carried by the recipient. Consequently, the recipient's economic savings from the gift transfer get strongly reduced due to the work he has to do to carry the water. The transfer is economically beneficial only as long as the perceived costs of carrying are less than the savings. If the cost of carrying is not very high, the joint social benefit of the transaction remains positive.

Water that is obtained by suction pump (2a and b) is more expensive for the donor than water obtained from a normal tap (1), because the donor has to cover fuel costs and is exposed to the noise of the running generator. The cost of pumping a litre of water is equal regardless if the water is pumped into one's own barrel, into a neighbour's barrel, or into the bucket of someone asking at the door. If the donor provides water directly into the neighbour's barrel (2b), even the transaction costs reduce in comparison to manually carrying, since the recipient does not have to enter the plot (2a). Hence, for the owner of a pump, the lowest costs for gifting water obtained with a pump are obtained by delivering water to the neighbour by pump. At the same time, supplying water by hose is also the best option for the recipient, since he does not have to put any effort into carrying water. From this economic perspective, gifting water by jerrycan from a household operating a pump is only reasonable if it is technically unfeasible to supply water by pump due to the distance between donor and recipient.

In all the biographies that are based only on network water (1, 2a, 2b), the benefit of the recipient is higher than the cost for the donor. Gifting consequently is morally good in the sense of Bentham (1823 [1780]), since the sum of happiness of donor and recipient is increased[109], despite the loss experienced by the 'moral' donor. This constellation strongly favours the emergence of water gifts.

The overall profitability of gift transfers is very different for gifting water that has been obtained from a water vendor (3). While network water is free for the donor and inaccessible for the recipient, the economic value of vendor water is equal for both transaction partners, because the water is sold for the

---

109 Here the assumption is made that the loss of income for the water vendor is not relevant.

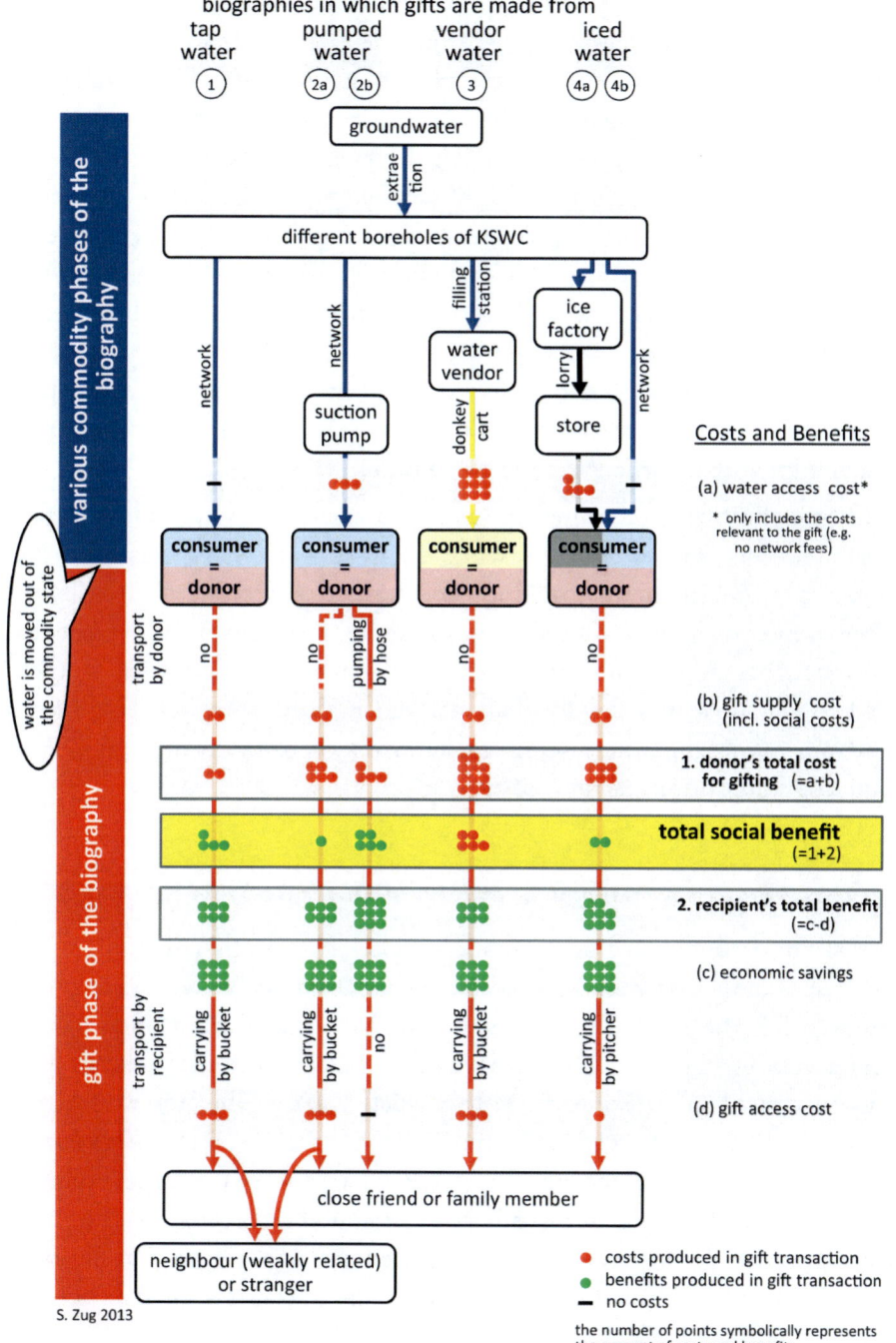

Fig. 37: Water Biographies in Square 11

same price to any customer. If a donor offers vendor water, his financial loss is equivalent to the recipient's savings from this transfer. If we take into consideration that the transfer also produces transaction costs, the overall social benefit of these gifts is negative. This economic constellation strongly explains why gifting vendor water is not a frequent practice. Households are reluctant to ask for water from a neighbour due to the costs that are created for the donor (e.g. D1: 67). Nevertheless, these transfers took place before the network was installed, and they still occasionally take place (e.g. A4: 68, X19: 61). The implementation of a network with poor performance only increased their occurrence. Donating water obtained from a vendor despite the adverse economic constellation becomes reasonable either when the water-poor household cannot purchase water because he is too poor, or when he cannot find a vendor at that particular moment in time.

The last biography (4) presented in the graph is of iced water, which creates rather high costs for the donor[110], while the quantity exchanged is low, since iced water is only used for drinking purposes. Iced water is the result of a combination of two biographies of water. Water obtained from the network (or a vendor) is mixed with water that has been transformed into ice, transported to, and sold in a few local shops. Having iced water at home creates costs from purchasing, but also from the effort of going to the shop. Thus, gifting iced water produces high costs.

The Access to Different Forms of Gifts and the Intensity of the Social Relationship

The decision to gift water to someone – either by actively offering or positively responding to a request – is in the hands of the donor. Legally, any household has the right, and generally also the practical possibility, to deny others access to its water. The household wall clearly protects the tap as an element located in a private and highly protected space. The empirical material however shows that access to different types of water gifts differs for the 'water-poor'. This is on the one hand related to the spatial accessibility of particular water gifts. Only if a spatially close household operates a pump can a water-poor neighbour receive water pumped through a hose. On the other hand, access can be denied due to the particular social relationship between the donor and the recipient.

---

110 Ice bought for 1 SDG will be enough to cool water for 1.5 days (C12: 88).

Iced water (4) is a prime example of a water gift to which access is socially restricted. While members of C12 regularly provide access to their high performance tap to people from the side of the square who are poorly supplied, they provide cold water only to their socially close neighbours (C12: 63, 84). A possible explanation for this restriction is the fundamentally different nature of iced water as opposed to water in general. Water is a basic need; ice water is superfluous. In the other biographies of water presented above, only 'ordinary' drinking water is transferred, which has the same use value. Nevertheless, I will argue in the following two subchapters that different social relationships between the donor and the recipient will determine the access to this type of gift. The underlying hypothesis is that the closer the relationship between the donor and recipient, the higher the donor's investments into the comfort of the water gift to the neighbour. Hence, I will argue that water gifts by hose are only made to close neighbours, while water gifts by bucket – both obtained with or without a pump from the network – can be accessed regardless of the social relationship. Subchapter 7.2 will present water gifts by hose and Subchapter 7.3 will focus on those water gifts by bucket which take place in weak relationships.

7.2. Gifts between Close Friends. Supplying Water by Hose

7.2.1. The Social Embeddedness of Water Supply by Hose

Donating water by hose is only possible for the three households that own a suction pump; hence, only in Areas A and B. In this section, I will present the social embeddedness of water for these two areas.

Water Transfers by Hose in Area A

In Area A, two households own a pump and therefore have the potential to supply water by hose to neighbours. Household A2 only supplies his direct Neighbour A1 with water. They have been neighbours since 1996, when A2 moved to Square 11. Although neither connected by family nor by tribal ties, the two households developed a very intensive relationship with each other. This intensiveness became symbolized by the removal of parts of the joint wall and is verbally underlined: "The moment A2 arrived here, we felt like brothers and sisters" (A1: 137).

A similar relationship, nevertheless without a passage between the plots, exists between A3 and A4, who have lived together since 1993. While A4 is comparatively rich and thus able to operate a suction pump, A3 is rather poor, the result of the death of the husband and of an adult son. Now the female head of household lives with five of her six children aged 8-17 years. Two of the boys work on a donkey cart that transports people, but the main financial resources they receive consist of support from her oldest son, who works for the traffic police, but does not live on the plot anymore. The relationship between A3 and A4 is very intensive and family members of both sides stress the close friendships the two fathers had: "We are neighbours. We are just like a family. Ever since we have lived here, A4 has been a friend of my husband" (A3: 77). Although A3 has an operational tap, they hardly use the water, since they can much more easily access the water from A4.

> When A4 has finished filling his barrel, he sends us the hose. With the hose, we fill our barrel or use the water for washing clothes. Sometimes we refill our barrel a second time in the evening. We can even take water from A4's barrel if there is no water in the pipe. We can take until his barrel is empty (A3: 61).

A strong relationship also exists between A4 and A7, the second household A4 supplies water to. A7, which is only one room on another plot, is occupied by the daughter of A4, who moved there with her new-born child. A7 can take water from A8's tap by bucket, but mostly prefers being supplied by the pipe from her parents' home (A4)

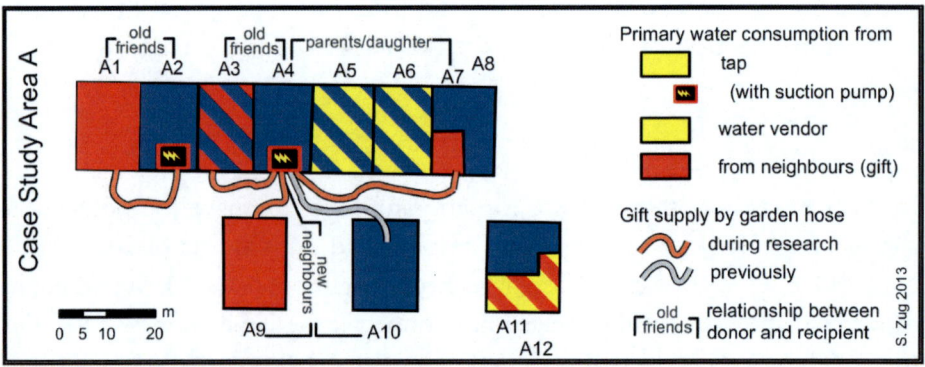

Fig. 38: Gift Transfers by Hose in Area A

Besides supplying these households that A4 is very closely connected to, A4 also supplies water to households that he knew for just a couple of days. A10 had moved to the square about a year before the interviews took place. Until he managed to establish his own connection, he received water by hose from A4. The same situation occurred with A9, who had just lived a couple of weeks on the plot when I first interviewed them. Towards the end of my research, A9 also managed to become connected. A9 recounted the initiation of the gift:

> Our neighbour saw us trying to stop a donkey cart to buy water. He stopped us and said: 'Do not buy water from the donkey cart again. This is the tap and this is the pump. Every day we operate it. Take the water you want.' This was the first time (A9: 254).

This gift of water was not initiated by the members of the recipient household, expressing their need, but by the A4 pump owner, who knew the economic benefit of obtaining water gifts for the recipient. The male head of household explained his motivation in offering water was simply that it is the "Sudanese way to help each other, […] Even Islam advises us to support our neighbours" (A4: 276). The initiative to offer water to a new neighbour can be understood from A4's particular definition of 'neighbour' as a social relationship with clearly spatial boundaries. He differentiates between 'neighbours' and 'social contacts'. 'Neighbours' are only those people living on his stretch of the street[111]; people from other streets – even those with whom he shares the back wall – are only social contacts because they "are too far for everyday communication" (A4: 282). His agenda in providing water to the new families is to include them into the social network as 'neighbours', rather than as 'social contacts' only. By this, he aims to contribute to the very positive perceived overall social situation of the street of which several households, including his, are proud (e.g. A1: 142, A3: 78, A8: 197). For A4, the relevance of a good social relationship with his neighbours is not restricted to people from the same ethnic group. However, he argues that "if neighbours do not come from Northern Kordofan like I do, it is more difficult to connect with them. Then, it is up to communication and the neighbour's personality. But integration is possible" (A4: 286). Households from Nothern Kordofan are slightly

---

111 The spatial margins of Area A were determined according to his definitions. Hence, all households living in Area A are perceived by A4 to be his neighbours in the sense of close contacts.

overrepresented in the area, but two of the households A4 offered water to come from the Northern States (A3) and from Darfur (A10).

Water Transfers by Hose in Area B

Social relationships in Area B are much less stable than in Area A. The core households in Area A have been connected since the 1990s (A1-A4 and A6) and only three households moved in during the 12 months prior to when I started conducting my research (A9, A5, A11). In contrast, the only household that continuously lived in Area B from the 1990s onwards is B8, who only came in 1998. His brother, who operates the only suction pump in the area, followed in 2001. All other households came in the 2000s, with half of all households moving in during the last 12 months (B1-B6 and B10). The high fluctuation of population is strongly related to the high proportion of households who only rent or guard a plot (57%), rather than owning it. Ethnicity in Area B is very heterogeneous, with a high percentage of Darfurian people among the new residents. The two brothers (B8 and B9) had already moved to Square 11 in 1991 with their parents and grew up several streets away from Area B. They are strongly connected to the neighbours there, and much less interested in investing in relationship building in Area B.

B9 is highly selective when providing water by hose to neighbours. He only pumps water into the barrels of two neighbours. His brother B8 is fully supplied, and the two households are strongly interlinked not only by family ties but also spatially, as they have not built a wall between the two plots, and economically, since they share their business. The second household supplied (B13), moved to the area three years ago.

> SZ: Do you have a special relationship with them?
>
> B9 (263): They are the only neighbours with whom I have a relationship.
>
> SZ: How did you build up this relationship?
>
> B9: When any new household arrives, we go to visit them. If they want to continue the relationship with you, they come back. When B13 came, we connected with each other.

The neighbourly relationship developed into a friendship between the women of the two households. They regularly meet with other Muslim women to

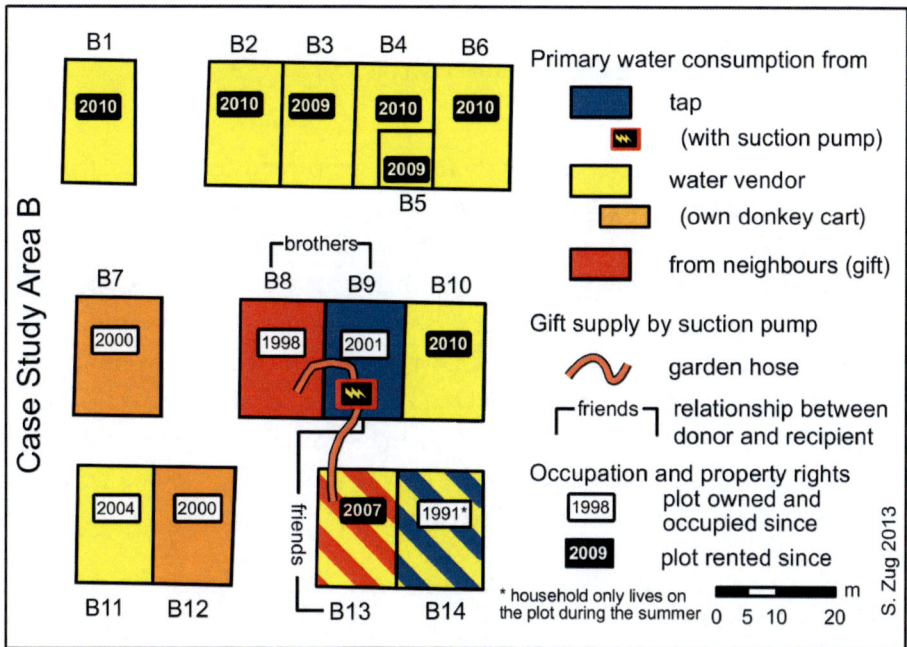

Fig. 39: Gift Transfers by Hose in Area B

have coffee and to chat in alternating houses. Within the context of this relationship, obtaining water from the neighbour's pump was easy. B13 explains how she negotiated receiving water from B9: "It is normal between neighbours. The first time we saw them irrigating their trees [by pumping water from their new pump] we asked them for water. We did this twice. Then they started asking us" (B13: 57). By stating that it is 'normal' between neighbours to receive water, B13 does not refer to the neighbourly relation as only a spatial living together, but as social closeness. It is not 'normal' for the other households living around B9 to receive water by suction pump.

B9 does not supply water by hose to any other neighbouring plot. The female head of household argues that the other households did not follow the initiation rituals of visit and return visit: "They did not visit us back. I went 2-3 times. But they did not come back. So I will not establish a relationship with them" (B9: 267). Furthermore, the male head of household expresses an antipathy against the neighbours:

> SZ: B13 [the only neighbour with whom B9 has an intensive relationship] will move away. So don't you need to build up relationships with some other neighbours?

> B9 (296): There are no good neighbours, so what can we do? We do not want our women to connect to anybody, because there are some who are not good. [...] with them we just connect in Eid and Ramadan. We have Iftar[112] together, but we do not want to have more than that.

His antipathy is first directed at Southerners – who tend to be Christian. B9 states: "I even prohibit my kids from going to some areas, because of things like alcohol. I do not want our kids to be there" (B9: 271). The second type of neighbours he dislikes is any household that consists only of young men. Young, mostly unmarried migrant workers jointly rent plots where they mainly sleep, while they work or search for work outside the square during the daytime. These households can be found all over the square, and two of them are located in Area B. One of these single men households rents a plot that belongs to another brother of B9 and B10, who has not yet settled down on it. B9 explains the relationship to the tenants of his brother:

> B9 (155): We are a family. We do not deal with single men households. We never give them water by hose. [...]
>
> SZ: Why did your brother not rent out to a family instead?
>
> B9: My brother just rented it out. We were very surprised that he gave it to these people.
>
> SZ: What is the problem with single men households?
>
> B9: Single men do not respect others. It is not easy for these people to find a place to rent anywhere in Sudan. Our brother did not take our advice.

The choice of supplying a neighbour with water in Area B is strongly related to the existing social relationship with neighbours, and B9 makes very clear that only those households that he considers eligible because they have a strong social relationship with him – their eligibility is not necessarily determined by their need – can receive water by hose from him.

---

112 *Iftar* is the meal that is taken at sunset during the fasting month Ramadan. In Square 11, men take this meal together with neighbours mainly on open squares, empty plots, or on small streets.

7.2.2. Compensation for Water Supply by Hose

Water transfers by hose – just as gifts of iced water – are always embedded into a family relationship, or into an existent or desired friendship relationship. This relationship is the key to understanding the social logic of the gift transfer. A close social relationship is everyday practice between the households, which extends beyond the mere water transaction. Households cooperate on other occasions. To describe close neighbourly relationships, households frequently cite two sayings. With "the neighbour before the house", they stress the relevance of the social relationship and the obligation to care for the neighbour. There is, however, not only an obligation to support the neighbours – at the same time; one can also count on the neighbour's support. People claim, in slightly different formulations, that "the close neighbour is more important for you than your brother". EL1 (99) explains: "when you cry, who is there to help you? Your brother is far? It is the neighbours who are closest to you".

Having good contacts with neighbours is especially important in case of an emergency, such as health problems at night (e.g. B9: 295, A9: 364). The close neighbours will come and support the family. They will also care for the neighbour by being attentive. If they do not see a person for a while, they will go and check to see if something has happened to him (C12: 100). If people are not there, they will keep an eye on the house. Such an occasion was observed when one day C14 was not at home, but had left the tap open. When network was put under pressure, water started running out of the tap. When the neighbours saw the water reaching the street, they knocked on the door and finally climbed the wall to close the tap. People will support their neighbours in case of accidents; for example, when a house burns down, they will donate money (CHR1: 97). If someone is ill or giving birth, a neighbour will bring him or her to hospital, or take care of the children and do the cooking and cleaning (D3: 193, A12: 52). When building a house, the neighbours can be called for help instead of paying people (e.g. D4: 233, D5: 154), and a household can borrow construction tools from them (B13: 137). In the days before the Eid Festival, many families bake biscuits. C1 (128) borrowed a small machine for forming the biscuits for free from a neighbour, while baking biscuits in the local bakery must be paid for. For local ceremonies like weddings and funerals, a tent is built up in the street to host people coming to congratulate or to console the family, respectively. Neighbours help in these events by cooking (A2: 29). During my research, the father of A12 died. A12

(56) is not connected to the electric grid, but throughout the night the tent was lit with electricity, which they received for free from the nearby generator shop, whose owner is from the same ethnic group. From other neighbours, they received a bag of flour worth 40 SDG in order to make food for the visitors. B13 (139) summarizes: "everything they need, you will give them – except if you do not have it". Consequently, the water gift between close friends is imbedded in multiple gift flows.

The case of the suction pump owner A4 is very useful in analysing capital flows from the recipient to the donor of water. A4 provides water by hose not only to his daughter (A7), but also to three neighbours. Giving water to A3 is one element of the long-lasting relationship the two households have. A3 argues that "since we are neighbours, we do not separate things". During the daytime only women are at home in A4, since the oldest son and the father work outside. The generator is old and dirty and requires physical efforts to start it. The boys of A3 both start the generator and take care of it, including repairing it when necessary (A3: 13). In material terms the relationship between the two households is most likely not fully balanced, but A3 repays their debt with symbolic capital as well. The youngest son of A3 was named after the head of the A4 household, an act that A3 assumes makes his neighbour "happy and proud" (A3: 334). This honour directly translates into a special responsibility for A4, which sometimes is materialized, for example, by paying for the sheep for the name giving ceremony and by gifting the boy little presents during the Eid celebrations (A4: 291). Whether the relationship between the two households is ultimately completely balanced in terms of capital transfers is difficult to determine. However, this example shows that the gift is an imbedded element in the strong social relationships between the two households in which both sides invest into the relationship by transfers of material and non-material capitals.

The relationship between A4 and the new household A9, which had just started in the first days when A4 had offered to provide water by hose, developed in the 3 months between the first and the second interview, especially between the two unmarried young adult daughters of the two households. They meet to chat with each other and once went to the centre of Omdurman to have ice cream together. One of the daughters of A9 now also regularly braids the hair of the girls in A4. And since two of the girls have the same cell phone, they borrow each other's battery if one phone runs out of charge. And finally, "if the shop is closed and you need some matches or something else, we just take it from them" (A9: 30).

On the one hand, there are reciprocal capital flows in the opposite direction of water flows, but on the other hand, A9 tries to minimize their indebtedness to A4 by reducing water flows. Even when A9 had just moved in, they already aimed to have their own water tap, although they were aware that this would be less comfortable than continuing to take water from the neighbour by pump, given the low performance of the network in the area. A9 argues:

> It is better to have one's own tap with all problems these taps have than to take from the neighbour, because it will be our water. When we collect water from the neighbours by pump, they sometimes cannot even fill their barrel. Because many people need the water and even the owners need to fill their barrels (A9: 250).

A10 similarly explains why they also made their own connection rather continuing to take water from A4: "Even if his water is free, A4's family is too big. He needs water for himself and I feel ashamed to take it. Therefore we got our own tap" (A10: 117). The unease to take can be interpreted as the unwillingness to be indebted within a system of reciprocity that thus becomes unbalanced. A Sudanese saying describes a gift situation from the perspective of a predominant recipient: "if your brother turns into honey, do not eat up all of it" (D7: 136). By making their own network connection, the recipients decrease the overuse of the neighbour's hospitality and, at the same time, reduce their indebtedness.

Investing in a particular gift relationship for A4 is not only an investment in the individual relationship between him and the recipient household, but also an element in realizing his particular social vision of the street as a social unit. By the way he socially acts with neighbours in the street – including but not restricted to the water transfers – he was attributed the position of a leader of his street. A3 explains why A4 has this position: "If you engage yourself for the society, they will give you a special place in it. Legally, there are no chiefs in this area, but A4 was put into this position. [...] People come to him to get his advice" (A4: 306).

Having a good reputation can pay out for an actor like A4 in a wider social context. El1 (124) argues that to attain a highly respected position in the square, like being a member of the popular committee or of the school's father's council, people need to have a good reputation. Gifting water can be one element in the creation of such a reputation.

7.2.3. Explaining Supply by Hose in the Economy of Symbolic Goods

Gifts made from water obtained by a suction pump can be explained within an 'economy of symbolic goods' in the sense of Pierre Bourdieu's theory. Water gifts are balanced with flows of different capital. Economic capital in form of return gifts, social capital in the form of being able to count on the neighbours in other situations, as well as symbolic capital in the form of the accumulation of prestige, compensates the donor for his expenses. Knowing that gifting water is morally admirable in the local context, symbolic capital is mainly attributed in the form of 'moral capital', the acknowledgment of the donor's good behaviour.

The social relationship works only if the donor does not feel exploited. Using the terminology of Gauthier, the relationship functions as long as the donor perceives the recipient as a 'constrained maximizer', who takes reciprocity in gift transactions seriously, rather than as a 'straightforward maximizer', who utilizes the support of the neighbour without intending to compensate him in other situations. A straightforward maximizer could be excluded from the benefit of water supply by hose, by not being offered this service anymore. Towards a socially distant neighbour, the donor can behave as a straightforward maximizer, by keeping the benefits of water for himself, with no intention of inviting the neighbour to enter a social relationship of mutual solidarity, which would benefit both.

The reconstruction of the gift transaction in the 'economy of symbolic goods', in which the transfer of water is related to other capital transfers between donor and recipient, is in contradiction to people's explanation of water transfers. Many households stress that water transfers between neighbours are never compensated, neither by money nor by other capital flows related to the gift. BH12 notes: "For water, nothing is given back. Especially for water nothing goes back. The only thing for which you will not get anything back is water".

By applying Bourdieu's theory of practice to analyse social reality, the contradiction between the reconstruction of the gift practice as the interested action of a donor and the actor's perception of water transfers as an altruistic gift can be dissolved. The actor's perceived altruism can be understood as a 'practical logic' that guides individual social action. People are either convinced of this altruism or they actively misrecognize the interests underlying the transaction in order to maintain the fiction of the pure gift (e.g. Bourdieu 1977 [1972]: 171). Bourdieu however argues that one "has to acknowledge that practice has a logic which is not that of logic, if one is to avoid asking of it more logic than it can give, thereby condemning oneself either to wring incoherencies out of it or to thrust upon it a forced coherence" (Bourdieu 1977 [1972]: 109). Consequently, the superior logic is the scientist's reconstruction of the gift as a 'logical logic' of interested gift transactions. The 'neighbourly waterscape' consequently can be understood as an element within the 'neighbourly social field'[113] in which capital, including water, is exchanged. Individual actors have different interests in the particular field and invest differently into improving social relationships. While some try to minimize their social transaction costs for water gifts (e.g. B9), others try to reach high positions in a 'neighbourly social field', which is valorised by their investments (e.g. A4). Restricting the analysis only to gifts by hose to neighbours would not require deep engagement with the moral construction of the waterscape. The following subchapter will provide a different interpretation for a different water gift transaction.

7.3. The Entitlement to Water. Accessing the Neighbour's Water is a Right

Giving water by bucket to a neighbour is technically simpler than transporting water by hose, and the distance between the donor and recipient is not restricted by the length of the hose. In this subchapter, I will argue that gifts by bucket need to be conceptualized differently within the 'economy of symbolic goods', especially for those gifts which are not embedded into a close relationship. In the first section (7.3.1), I will continue to explain water transfers in Area B, which has been discussed before as an example for water supply by hose, but now with a focus on bucket supply. The argument will be supplemented with empirical material from Area C, where buckets are the only possible way to transport gifts. Based on empirical examples from Area D (7.3.2), I will argue that giving water is a social obligation even if an economic loss arises. In 7.3.3 and 7.3.4, the possibility of true disinterestedness will be related to the theoretical elaborations on the morality of the gift.

---

113 A 'neighbourly social field' is not defined primarily spatially, but is defined as the field in which social action between neighbours take place, a field which is spatially restricted, but which does not necessarily need to include all households in this spatially restricted area.

7.3.1. The Social Embeddedness of Bucket Supply

Area B Continued: Water by Bucket

As already outlined above (7.2.1), B9 only supplies water to friends and family members, namely to a friend and to his brothers. He does not supply other households. However, through an alternative gift biography, neighbours still have access to B9's water. Among the four households (B3, B6, B10, and B14) that occasionally consume water from B9 is the household of single men towards whom B9 had strongly expressed his antipathy. To all these households, water is not pumped through a hose, but carried in a bucket. B9 explains that these transfers take place in spite of the absence of an intensive relationship, because "we do not refuse when people want to take water. [...] It is normal, they can take water, and we do not stop them. The hose is outside, we do not guard it" (B9: 281).

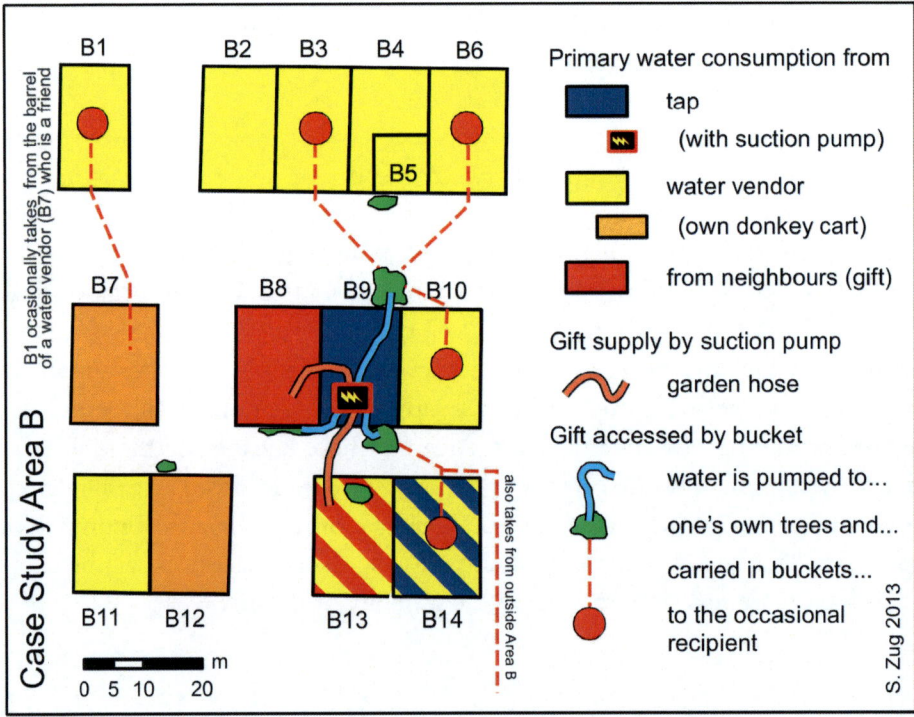

Fig. 40: Gift Transfers by Bucket in Area B

Instead of offering these neighbours water, B9 implicitly allows any neighbour to take water, but only outside, which minimizes access costs produced by having people enter the plot. This is only possible since the pressure in the pipe is augmented by a pump. People can easily take water when the hose is used for outside purposes, hence, either when B9 waters the trees or occasionally when a cousin of B9 washes his minibus in front of the house. These water gifts by bucket do not account for a great deal of overall water transfers in Area B, especially because the time span is very short. The hose is only accessible for some fifteen minutes when it is required for outside purposes, rather than during the whole time the network is under pressure. B6 (52) explains that she hardly takes any water, "because I do not see the hose outside very often. If I saw it more often, I would go more often". In the system, which developed in Area B, households accept the tacit agreement to only take water when the hose is outside.

Empirically separating network water gifted by hose from water gifted by bucket based on the intensiveness of the relationship between the donor and the recipient is supported by B7's analysis of the situation: "If owners of pumps have filled their barrel, they give the hose to the neighbours. That is only when they have a very good relationship" (B7: 85).

Water Transfers by Bucket in Area C

The 'neighbourly waterscape' of Area C strongly differs from that of B, since there are no suction pumps installed. Water gifts are exclusively transported in buckets and never pumped through garden hoses. The households with weak supply, living in the upper side of the square, have a second possible way to access free water, other than from the neighbour's tap. They can walk to the borehole, which is very close. The two guards mostly allow them to access water from an ordinary household tap installed inside the fenced area. I will not take this supply option into consideration[114] for the analysis of water gifts, preferring to concentrate on gifts between households. The predominant donors are the households in the lower part of the area, where water

---

114 In daily practice, taking water from the borehole is hardly different than taking from private households. The borehole is fenced, and access is provided by the guards, just like in normal households. Often it is easier for people to access households, since at the borehole, the guards are not there, they are sleeping, or they complain about children playing inside the borehole ground. The hindrances to entering the borehole are consequently very similar to those to accessing houses.

pressure is very high certain days, and still comparatively high the other days. The recipients in the upper part of the area have a very poor supply.

Households in Area C are not in an intensive relationship with each other, with the exception of a group of five households (C3-C7), who originated from the same area of Sudan and who have lived together since at least 1993. They are even partially connected by family ties. Their relationships with the other inhabitants of Area C, who mostly came much later, are very weak. Their neighbour C11 complains: "They are just connected to each other and they behave as if they were a separate area" (C11: 114).

For water supply, however, most households of this group access water from the households on the lower side of the square. They predominantly access water at C14's tap; a young family has lived for one year on this plot. The high frequentation of this household can be explained by the fact that someone is usually at home (in contrast to C12 and C13), that it is centrally located on the square (unlike C11 and C15, which are located more in a side street than on the square itself (C11: 69)), and the fact that "C14 does not care if children come inside" (C5: 79). Taking water from C14 is however not based on an intensive social relationship between the female household head and the potential recipients.

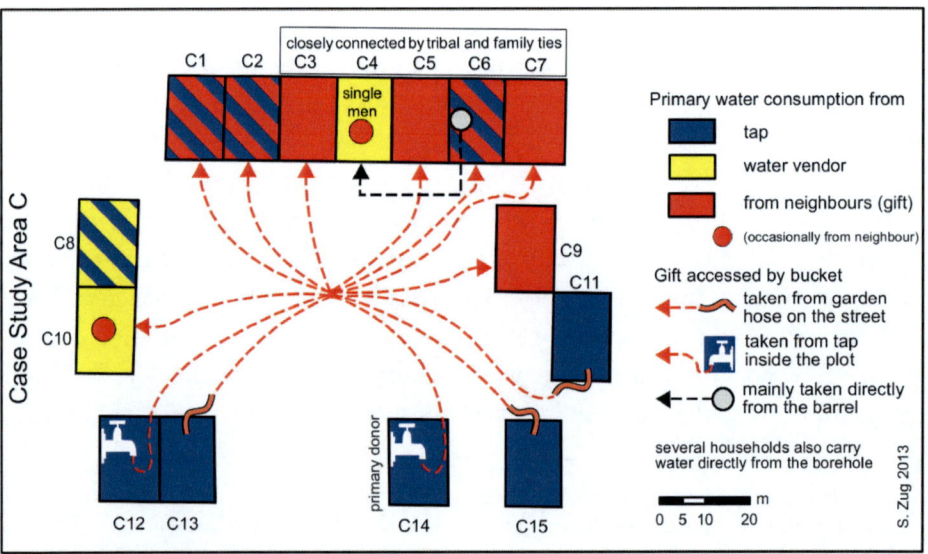

Fig. 41: Gift Transfers by Bucket in Area C

The following passage illustrates the relationship which recipients have with C14:

> SZ: How is your relationship with C14?
>
> C5 (73): It is only the children who go to her. I never go there. Only when they have filled the buckets do they sometimes come and ask me to carry. Then I carry. [...]
>
> SZ: Would anybody give water like C14 does?
>
> C5: Nobody refuses to give water.

C14 herself supports the view that she is not very connected to the households who take water from her:

> SZ: How do relationships normally start?
>
> C14 (100): It is not a normal situation here. Normally, if someone moves to an area the neighbours come. That is normal. But here people did not come.
>
> SZ: Why did they not follow this Sudanese tradition?
>
> C14: It is not a normal situation. And now there are some neighbours who only come if water is running. But few come even if there is no water.

Although she gives water and meets members of most households on her plot every day, she developed a deeper relationship with only a few households that consume her water.

For other water donors in area, water gifts are also not built on an intensive relationship. C15 and C11 are mainly frequented by potential recipients when C14 is not at home or when too many people queue at her tap.

> SZ: How many people come every day to take water from you?
>
> C15 (43): Maybe 3-4 but I do not really know, because I give the hose to the street and people do not make a queue inside my plot. [...]
>
> SZ: Do you know all these people?
>
> C15: No, some I do not know. It is always the children.

The paragraph shows that C15 is neither much interested in the contact with the recipients, nor able to keep track of the people to whom water was given, since they do not meet most of the recipients. Besides these unknowing gifts to people who might be known, gifts to real strangers occur. Several households reported that people come both from more distant streets within Square 11 and even from neighbouring Square 31 (e.g. C11: 64, D3: 63) to ask for water. These people are completely unknown to the donor.

Just as in Area B, where disliked households of single men are granted access to water by bucket, in Area C gifts are given to people the donor would be happy to see leave the area. C11 even expresses a strong negative opinion of one of his recipients, a household who covers all its consumption with different neighbours' water, including the water of C15. Still C11 argues that "even to them one cannot refuse to give water. We cannot, because we have a lot of water. Our behaviour and heart could not accept that" (C15: 110).

In all of these situations, the water transfers cannot be explained with mutual reciprocity within a perfect 'economy of symbolic goods'.

7.3.2. The Minimal Obligation to Grant Access to Water

Area B and C showed that it was seemingly impossible for the 'water-rich' to deny the 'water-poor' access to their water if the latter carry the water themselves in a bucket to their homes. In both areas, the potential donors have access to water in abundance, which mostly excludes the possibility that their own consumption would need to be reduced if a recipient consumed water from their tap. In Area D, the supply situation of potential donors is different. Although the situation was better in the past, when more households were able to access water, even then, most of the taps were only dropping. Discussing water supply under this constellation allows us to draw conclusions on how gifts are provided in situations when water is scarce, hence, when one's own consumption needs to be compromised for the consumption of others.

Gift Obligations in Area D

The very difficult water access conditions in Area D led to very intensive appropriations of the pipe by several residents. Two households moved their water taps out of their plots onto the streets. Digging holes directly next to the pipe increases the possibility that the tap will provide water. In the past, the flow was strong enough to allow them to access some water, even though the quantity was rather small. Together with the tap that is located on a plot partially occupied by D10, three taps are located on 'public space', hence outside the private space protected by walls.

One of the households with a hole on the street argues that despite owning the particular water hole, he does not have full rights to use the water from the tap. In practice, children playing on the street notice first when the tap starts providing water and they immediately start taking water from it and form a queue (D4: 190). Despite owning the tap, the owner of the hole mostly had to buy water from a water vendor. He argues: "If you start first, then they will wait for you. If they start first, they will expect you to wait till they have filled their barrels" (undisclosed: 87). By putting the tap on public space, the tap also becomes public, and water a commons.

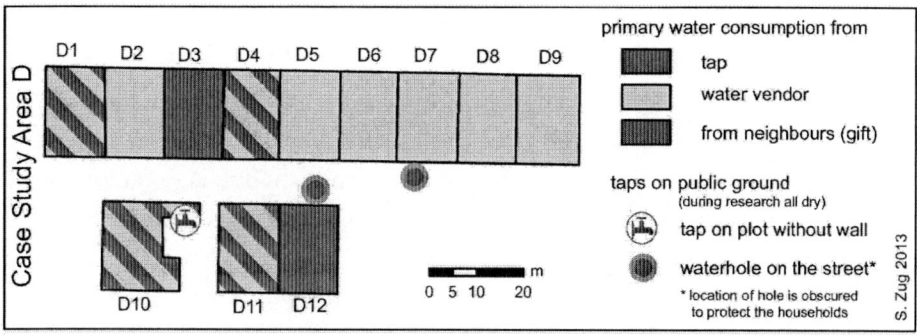

Fig. 42: Water Taps on Public Ground in Area D

The situation is different for taps located inside the plot. Access to the tap of D3, which is the only household that obtained water from the tap in Area D during my research, is regulated by the tap owner. He or she determines the rules for the queuing system. In a group interview with some of the girls taking water from D3, including the daughters of D3, the particular system of accessing water was explained (GD1): the children form a queue by putting their buckets in a line. If water pressure is strong, everyone – including the girls of the tap owner – is allowed to put one single bucket, each, in the queue. With this arrangement, D3 will manage to obtain all the water they require, however, it will take D3 more time to collect their water than if they were to deny others access. If water pressure is weak, D3 will still allow the other children to take water, but they themselves will put three buckets in the line, while the other children still only put one. In this situation, D3 is still able to cover its own consumption from the tap. If the pressure is very weak, the system is again turned back to the system that was applied for high water pressure. The daughter of D3 states that "when water is very bad, we put only one bucket in the queue, so that everybody gets some" (GD1: 55). Hence, when it is most difficult for D3 to satisfy their own water demand, they still do not insist to have all 'their' water from the tap for themselves.

Although households with a tap have slightly higher 'access rights' to their water than those who have a tap on the street, the former do still grant at least a minimal amount to others. A similar situation could hypothetically also be found in Area C. C15 (50) only gives water to neighbours by a hose on the street, hence people do not have to enter the house. If C15's hose were broken, they would still give water from inside the plot to people who asked. However, they would restrict the amount of water people could take to only 2-3 buckets per recipient, rather than allowing recipients to cover their total need.

7.3.3. Justifying Water Gifts to People who do not Reciprocate

The analysis of water transfers by bucket shows that anyone is granted at least minimal access to water, regardless of his relation to the potential donor. Water is given to members of households who are disliked, who are unknown since they live in other streets or in the neighbouring square, or who are not met when they take water. Furthermore, water is given to others even if the donor's own consumption must be reduced and water has to be purchased from vendors instead. These particular transfers by bucket – unless they take place between friends – can therefore hardly be explained as a reciprocal relationship between donor and recipient. They need to be explained differently than water transfers by hose, which are embedded in the perfect 'economy of symbolic goods'. In this section, I will augment the interested Bourdieusian conception of the social, which was applied on transfers by water pump (7.2), with Boltanski's work on justification, by conceptualizing a universal right to water.

Water Gifts – the Cultural Explanation by the People Involved

Interview partners mainly explain the motivation of water transfers as being based in Sudanese culture or in Islam. "Sudanese by nature are not greedy. They want to share. Even if I fill my barrel with water from a vendor and someone asks for it, I will give it to him" (X19: 60). The statement expresses people's high esteem of their own culture, in which social action is not restricted to profit. This positive attitude towards gifting water was highly consensual throughout the whole square. Asking people about the possibility of denying others access to water, as well as about the possibility of financially compensating those who give water or of being compensated for donating water, mostly led to incomprehension of the question itself, because people take the system of water sharing highly for granted.

However, they only take it for granted in their local context. C2 develops the explanation of water gifts into a cultural comparison: "We are good; we are not like white people. We give food and water for free" (C2: 119). With this statement C2 offers culture-based altruism as the underlying motivation for water gifts, and he draws a moral boundary, making water solidarity a distinct element of Sudanese society, rather than an element of human society in general. This moral boundary is stressed with pride, confronting the European researcher with a moral superiority.

7.4. Water Gifts – a Universalistic Explanation

I suggest a different interpretation, which requires again stepping back from the people's 'practical logic' and its religious and cultural explanations. However, although my interpretation will contradict the people's 'practical logic', I will not present a 'logical logic' in the sense of Bourdieu, since I will not restrict myself to hidden economic explanations. Rather, I will extend the assumed locally based morality from a cultural and religious context to a universal one.

In such an approach, water gifts are not explained from the local context in which water is embedded, but by the universality of water itself, which requires qualifying the 'practical logic' of water transfers. People in Sudan can hardly compare Sudanese water morals with European ones, because they do not know European water morals. They can, however, compare their water morals with what the term Europe stands for – which is capitalism. Consequently, their cultural comparison can be interpreted as a comparison between water and goods, which are more strongly embedded in market mechanisms.

Tvedt and Oestigaard (2010: 16) support such an approach and argue that "many notions about water are shared by different religions and different geographical and climatic regions, so specific civilizational or cultural analytical frames are not particularly helpful in this regard". They aim to establish a "history of perceptions and ideas of water", in which water in societies is conceptualized as a "unique [...] element in the sense that it is both universal and always particular. This dual nature of water makes it unique as empirical data because it enables studies of both universal and particular aspects of water at the same time" (Tvedt and Oestigaard 2010: 16).

In such an approach, the universality of water is embedded in particular local interpretations of everyday engagements with water. I will focus in my elaborations not on the universality of water in general, but on the universality of the right to water as one concrete element of water's universality.

Universality of the right to water and the particularity in its implementation can be closely related to Boltanski's conceptualization of different polities to which actors relate their arguments in the 'meta-pragmatic register'. The right to water is universally valid in a specific polity. However, its application depends on the concrete situation. Since social action is not always justified in the same polity, the right to water does not necessarily need to be applied in every situation. However, even if the right to water in a specific situation is not applied, its universality is not called into question.

By defining the right to water as universal, I do not restrict this universality to a specific society as does Boltanski, who claims validity for his polities only for a French context (Boltanski 2012 [1990]: 96). I go one step further for water and suggest that the right to water – as embedded in water gifts to strangers in Square 11 – is a universally valid argument beyond the Muslim and Sudanese context.[115]

The universality of the right to water is grounded in the basic need of water for human life.[116] This basic need is based on human biology rather than on a social construction. As such, water is different from other things that are not basic needs, like electricity. Generator owners in Square 11 charge their

---

115 The right to water is not a separate polity, but it is embedded into a particular polity, which would have to be developed from the philosophical grounding of Sudanese society. In my elaborations, I will not define such a polity, but rather assume its existence. The postulation of the right to water as a universal category valid worldwide is facilitated by restricting this claim to a particular argument in the polity rather than to the whole polity.

116 Boltanski's (2006 [1991]: 74) theory of justifications is restricted to social theories which assume a 'common humanity'. He excludes political constructs which assume the existence of slaves or sub humans. Hence the universality of water only holds true if we assume that actors agree on the right to exist.

neighbours for accessing electricity, and people do not question that customers need to pay for this service. X14 (77) argues: "water is a necessary thing for life. If you do not have water, you will die. Without electricity you will not die". Electricity is fully embedded in capitalism because it is not a basic need. Since water is a basic need, it cannot be just reduced to the status of a commodity like electricity.

When I define water as a universal right, I do not mean in the prescriptive sense of defining a genuine right under international law (e.g. Gleick 1999). International law is rather a codification of the already present right to water. The international debate on the right to water is a process of 'justification' in which the situations are defined in which the right to water needs to be applied. When a country ratifies the right to water, the government takes responsibility for granting its citizens access to water.

In the framework developed in the moral extension of Bourdieu's theory of practice, the right to water translates into a 'capital of moral entitlement to water' in the hands of the 'water-poor', who can command water from the 'water-rich' by this entitlement. As such, the 'capital of moral entitlement' is a rights-based capital and its valuation is therefore strongly dependant on the explicit and implicit moral framework of the particular society.

The Translation of the Universal Right to Water in Islam

In the context of Square 11, the universal right to water is not codified in governmental law, but within Muslim theology and in the local social rules of the neighbourly field. Though people argue with cultural or religious concepts, these concepts represent a translation of the uniqueness of water into cultural or religious concepts.

The 'cultural' embeddedness of water in everyday practice goes beyond the right to water and consumption, but it is also signified by the relevance of water in religious rituals in all world religions.[117] In Islam, water has a very central role in religious practices, especially in the ritual of washing before prayer, in which "purifying oneself shows submission to the will of God and washes away sin, but it also implies physical cleanliness of body and clothes"

---

117 E.g. baptism in Christianity, ritual washing in Judaism, bathing in sacred water in Hinduism, and water symbolisms in Buddhist funerals (e.g. Chamberlain 2008; Pradhan and Meinzen-Dick 2010).

(De Châtel 2009: 288). In Islam, the uniqueness of water is stressed by directly relating water to God. The imam of the central mosque in Square 11 refers to the myth of creation:

> God said we made everything alive from water [...]. Even humans are made from water. The sperm starts out of water, and also the plants need water to start growing. Men take water to live and they use water indirectly to make life (ISL1: 6).

His interpretation reflects the central role of water in the Quran: "Consider the water you drink – was it you who brought it down from the rain-cloud or We?" (Quran: 56.68-70)[118]. By defining god as the creator of water, water is centrally embedded into a religious field, and it is underlined that water is different than other more 'worldly' goods. Human life fully depends on this water and consequently on God's goodness: "Let man consider the food he eats! We pour down abundant water and cause the soil to split open. We make grain grow, and vines, fresh vegetation, olive trees, date palms, luscious gardens, fruits, and fodder: all for you and your livestock to enjoy" (Quran: 80.24-30).

Religion then transfers the myth of creation into particular definitions of water and finally into religious rules. People in Square 11 express one of the religious water rules only by mentioning "grass, water and fire" (e.g. A4: 59), generally without further elaborating on these terms. These three words refer to a hadith which states "Muslims have a common share in [these] three things" (Abu-Dawood 3470, cf. Kadouri, Djebbar, and Nehdi 2001: 91). Water is defined by this hadith as a commons, and access to it consequently turns into a right. The religious rule that defines water as a commons is primarily a religious translation of the universal right to water.

Conflicting Polities and Conflicting Water Rights in Muslim Theology

The 'universality' of the moral entitlement to water as expressed for example in the hadith presented above, does not imply that it is valid in every situation, but only in those situations in which donor and recipient agree on the moral entitlement to water being the most relevant justification for water transfers. Here, Boltanski's different polities come into play. In the 'meta-pragmatic register', people can justify social action in different polities. The moral enti-

---

118 References to the Quran are based on the translation of Haleem (2005).

tlement to water is one justification for a water transfer in a particular moment. A moral-based transfer of water takes place when actors agree that the polity, in which the moral entitlement to water is embedded, is more relevant for the specific situation than the arguments from other polities. If actors agree on a different polity for the situation, the 'water-poor' is not morally entitled and, consequently, can be denied access. However, even though access is not granted in that specific situation, the universality of the moral entitlement remains valid. It is just not applied in that particular situation.

Conflicting polities can even be analysed within the theological interpretations of the right to water in Islam. That water is a common, as implied by the hadith on 'grass, water and fire', is placed into perspective in the theological debate. Kadouri, Djebbar, and Nehdi (2001: 89) argue that most Muslim scholars put water resources into three categories. Only water from rivers, lakes, and aquifers or water in the form of rain is a full public good. The second category contains lakes and rivers on private land and defines water as a restricted public good, to which the owner has privileges to use the water for industrial or agricultural purposes, but to which anyone has access to drink from. The third category refers to water stored in private containers, water extracted from wells or rivers, as well as water obtained from water companies. Water here is defined as a private good, which belongs to the owner.

This categorization shows that the right to water is not absolutely valid. Whereas access to a natural source (category 1 and 2) cannot be denied to anyone, access to water that has been purchased by a potential donor can be denied. This water can be integrated into capitalist accumulation, because "value [was] added to water by labour in the form of retaining it in a recipient and/or through distribution or conservation works [which] may create a qualified right to ownership" (Mallat 1995: 129). Access rights to water, consequently, are defined in a conflict between a right to water and a right of ownership. In the terminology of Boltanski, these two rights are part of two different polities.

The tension between the two rights is solved differently in Muslim theology. In ordinary situations, water of the third category belongs to the person, and does not need to be shared with others. Here the argument of ownership is stronger than the people's universal moral entitlement to water. In situations where a person requires water to satisfy basic biological needs, the justification based on ownership is not strong enough to treat water as a private good even for those people who have obtained water by investment. In the sharia, the right to water is made more concrete to specific situations by the definition of the right of thirst (*chafa*), which is defined as "the right to take water to quench one's thirst or to water one's animals" (Caponera 1992: 70). Hence, even if a household legally – in the sense of sharia – owns water, any other household has the right to use that water for emergency purposes. In a hadith, Muhammad makes this very clear by saying: "amongst the three persons whom Allah will not look at on the Day of Resurrection, nor will he purify them, and theirs shall be a severe punishment, [is] a man [who] possessed superfluous water on the way, and he withheld it from travellers" (Al-Bukhari 3.547 cf. Faruqui 2001: 119). To deny water to someone who asks is an offense against *chafa*, the Muslim translation of the universal right to satisfy basic water needs. Consequently, in emergency situations, the right of ownership counts for nothing against proof from the 'water-poor' of their moral entitlement to water.

Whether free water has to be granted or not, consequently, strongly depends on the ability of the water needy person to make his moral entitlement plausible. In Square 11, the moral entitlement to water is not always a strong enough argument to grant universal free access to water from any source. A consensus needs to be reached wherein entitlement becomes more valuable than other arguments in different polities, such as the right of ownership. Hence, its value strongly depends on the social and economic characteristics of the situation.

The Limits of the Moral Entitlement to Water in Square 11

The existence of commercial water in Square 11, both in the form of the network and in the form of water vendors, illustrates that people are not entitled to free water in all situations. Although local residents agree on the universality of the right to water, vendors can sell water because they have a very valid argument accepted by the residents of Square 11. A water vendor is locally considered to run a legitimate 'business' (e.g. A4: 68, B13: 72), because he has to cover high costs for the production of water. By this acceptance, the water vendor's water transaction is agreed upon in a different polity than the one that contains the moral entitlement to water. A vendor can easily justify not gifting water due to his ownership rights over the water, acquired when he purchased it from a tower and added value to by transporting it. If they did not take money for their service, vendors could not cover their costs and could not make a living from their work. If the vendor's right of ownership was denied, no household would be interested in working in this profession. The system, which is highly necessary to satisfy of water needs of those deprived of network supply, can only exist if water vending is accepted as a business. Moving water into a commodity status is defended by the necessity of providing enough water for human consumption.

The relationship, in which the majority of water gifts – including the ones to strangers – are granted in Square 11, is between network customers and the 'water-poor' with low or no pressure in their tap. On this level, the moral entitlement argument is valid for more than just the satisfaction of the basic need for water. Generally, someone asking for water on a daily basis is not a person close to dying of thirst because he cannot find water in the desert. His survival is already ensured by the vendors, whom he can easily pay to obtain water. His objective instead is to access the water he needs for drinking – but also for taking a shower and for cleaning the house – for free, rather than spending money to purchase it.

A reason for the strength of the right to water argument in everyday practice, despite the 'comparatively low' neediness of the recipient, is not to be found in an exceptionally broad 'cultural' interpretation of the right to water, under which access to water gifts is granted despite low biological need, but in the weakness of the ownership argument. The strength of the ownership of water is correlated with the cost of obtaining water, and these costs under a flat rate network tariff are very low, so the personal interests argument can hardly be defended. Since the sum recipients save from the transfers is much higher than the costs incurred by the donor, denying a water transfer is very difficult to justify.

In Square 11, not being connected to a water network or not having sufficient water in one's own tap is already sufficient to accumulate enough 'capital of moral entitlement' to obtain water from a water-rich person without payment. In everyday practice, the water transfers are habitualized and, therefore, located in the 'imperfect economy of symbolic goods', although the underlying argumentation is reconstructed in the 'meta-pragmatic register'. The donor's disinterestedness is strongly internalized in his water habitus, just as recipients take their moral entitlement to water for granted. The entitled person does not even have to prove that he is endowed with 'capital of moral entitlement to water' – the mere request for water already indicates that his tap does not provide sufficient amounts of water.

The water poor's 'moral entitlement to water' is a very strong argument in the 'meta-pragmatic register', as well as being a motivation in the 'economy of symbolic goods', where it is internalized as market imperfection. Still, in certain situations the ownership argument can become valorised, without however completely invalidating the water poor's entitlement to water. In the 'imperfect economy of symbolic goods', the strength of the moral entitlement to water is expressed by a person's quantitative endowment with 'capital of moral entitlement'. With every bucket a person receives, his perceived neediness decreases and, thus, his argument of being morally entitled to water is weakened. As long as a water-rich household grants a minimal amount of water, like a bucket or two, they make sure that the very basic need – hence, in the worst case scenario, the life of another household – is insured.[119] If this minimal amount is granted, the water poor's 'capital of moral entitlement' to water decreases and the 'water-rich' can deny access to the 'less entitled' 'water-poor', without compromising his moral duty. This compromise between the right to water and the right of water ownership could be found in situations when donors themselves have problems satisfying their water needs and they reduce the number of jerrycans of others in their queue (D3), or when people need to allow others access to their own plot rather than providing them water by garden hose on the street (C15) (see 7.3.2). In both situations, the moral entitlement of a recipient is decreased by granting some water, since both are situations where the cost of water supply and hence the ownership argument of water, have a very high value.

Questioning the Validity of the Universal Right to the Neighbour's Tap

Everyday gift transfers, as described above, are strongly habitualized in social practice. People are very sure about what they can claim in which situation and what they can expect from a particular actor. The moral entitlement to a limited amount of water hardly ever gets contested either by questioning whether the right to water is correctly applied in the form of a 'test of worth', or by questioning the 'validity of the test', hence the choice of polity. In all of my research, only a single situation was mentioned in which an actor denied

---

119 The probability that a household would face serious health problems by not receiving a particular bucket is very low, since there are other options. However, for the donor this minimal donation eliminates this very hypothetical risk, which is already enough to serve as a motivation to give.

other households access to his water. This example allows us to empirically retrace the shift between the 'economy of symbolic goods' and the 'meta-pragmatic register'. The example however takes place not in a situation where a stranger tries to obtain a water gift, but within a street where people know each other and are related to each other, without necessarily defining their relationship as intensive. Consequently, the justification of the situation cannot be thought to be completely independent from social relations and interests between the actors, as could be the justification for refusing a gift to a stranger.

One of the households (donor in Figure 42; undisclosed household) had constructed a hole on the street, in which he had comparatively highly invested, even stabilizing it with concrete. However, the household did not receive much of their own water since other people (recipients) consumed most it. The head of household was strongly dissatisfied with the situation, and he questioned the other people's entitlement to his water (1). He substantiated his claim with his right of ownership, which he felt was denied under the current practice, since neighbours could benefit from his water while he had to cover high costs for purchasing water from a water vendor. He tried to claim his right of ownership, and told the children taking water to wait until he had finished filling his barrels (undisclosed: 89). Hence, he restricted the access of other households by questioning their moral entitlement. By directly expressing that he needed the water for himself, he used the right of ownership as a justification.

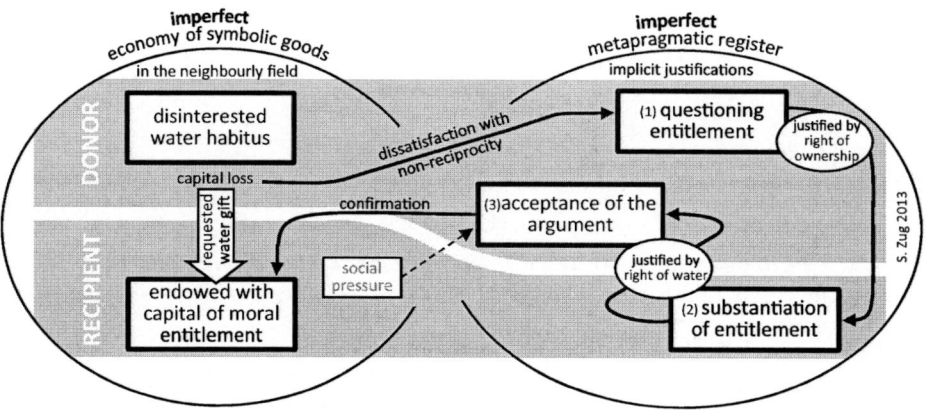

Fig. 43: Example of a Justification: Questioning the Validity of the Moral Entitlement to the Neighbour's Tap

The recipients' reactions were less direct. They did not verbally question that the donor had suspended their right to water, but – according to the donor – the neighbours stopped greeting him and did not contact him anymore. By their actions, they substantiated their entitlement to water (2) and implicitly requested the donor to agree again on the previously valid polity, hence on the argument of the moral entitlement. Here an element of social power has an impact on the 'meta-pragmatic register' in which the donor tried to justify the denial of water gifts. The social donor lost some symbolic capital while gaining economic capital by saving money. However, the donor was not only pushed by the social pressure to adjust his decision, but he also agreed on the validity of the recipients' rights-based argument (3). He states: "here, people think that water is a public good, so it was wrong of me to stop them taking. I cannot do anything [to improve my water situation] unless water comes to all houses". Finally, he accepted that he had to compromise his own consumption due to the moral entitlement of others. By this short detour in the 'meta-pragmatic register', the habitualized justification in the 'imperfect economy of symbolic goods' was confirmed, and the attempt to move the situation of water exchange into a different justification failed.

Claiming Moral Entitlement in a Market Based World

A more successful shift of polities could be observed for vendor supplied water, where the argumentation is shifted inversely, hence from an argument based on ownership to one based on moral entitlement. As presented above, the water vendors are very much accepted as a business. However, in particular situations, even water vendors grant people free access to water and therefore relinquish their ownership right. A water vendor elaborates on such a situation:

SZ: Do you supply people with water for free?

WV1 (81): If someone stops me and says, 'I need water and I do not have money', I give him one or two jerrycans. It happens every week with different people. [...] People say, 'If I get money, I will give it back to you', but I will not follow up to get the money.

In this constellation, the water vendor accepts a loss by agreeing to give water to people who most likely will never compensate him. On these occasions, the vendor agrees that the water poor's moral entitlement to water is more valid as a justification in the particular situation than his interests, or the polity in which contains the ownership argument. Consequently, a 'very' water poor household has a sufficient argument to claim free water from a commercial water provider. Hence, even in a very market oriented water supply system, limited water solidarity can exist.

Granting this moral entitlement is possible without making water vending unprofitable since vendors will only give water to those people who strongly stress being water poor beyond having no water from the tap. Consequently only those who are economically poor and cannot purchase from a vendor have a moral entitlement to free water from the vendors. Since free water is only granted to few people and is restricted to low quantities, solidarity only reduces the overall benefit of water vendors, rather than making the business unprofitable.

Reconsidering the Universality of the Moral Entitlement to Water

Under the assumption of a universality of the right to basic water beyond the Sudanese context, the same concept should be equally applicable to other social contexts. In absence of available research on gift practices in other contexts, I will briefly refer to my personal experience in a European context, in which the constellations of the transfer are very similar to the water gift to a stranger in Square 11. When one runs out of water on a hike or on a bicycle tour, one is in need of water but it is impossible to obtain it by 'conventional' means, that is, from one's own tap or from a shop. One is temporarily 'water poor'. In such situations, I ask unknown people for water, which I see in their gardens. My neediness in the particular moment is strongly signalled to the potential donor since I am holding a bicycle in the one hand and an empty bottle in the other. Hence, I own sufficient 'capital of moral entitlement' to make the universal right to water a valid argument. Without a single exception I received water, whenever I asked.

This example shows that in the European context as well, water from strangers can be easily accessed if the situation is right. The water gift to the stranger, both in a European context as in a Sudanese context, will be granted from the moment a potential recipient is endowed with sufficient amounts of 'capital of moral entitlement'. While a positive response can be expected for water, I would be very hesitant to ask for other things, like a sausage, from people having a barbecue. I even doubt that people would give me a sausage. Unlike water, a sausage is not a 'basic need'.

Conclusions: Water Gifts in an Imperfect Economy of Symbolic Goods

Although the explanation of free water transfers without reciprocity requires looking at the underlying justifications in a 'meta-pragmatic register', water transactions take place nearly exclusively in the 'practical register', which is the 'imperfect economy of symbolic goods', where actions do not need to be reasoned.

That in Square 11 this right is scarcely questioned by bringing forward arguments like the right of ownership from other polities signifies how deep the universal right to water is internalized into the 'economy of symbolic goods'. It is embedded in everyday practice as the structure of the social field and as the moral dispositions of the actors. With morality embedded into the habitus, water gifts can be motivated by moral dispositions of the habitus, which guide the individuals who are acting in a disinterested way.

8

Conclusions

The motivation of this research was to develop an understanding of everyday water practices in Greater Khartoum. Square 11's empirical reality made water gifts its central subject and their conceptualization the primary task. The analysis of these very particular water access and supply practices aims to not only understand processes in the 'neighbourly waterscape', but also to contribute to the comprehensive understanding of urban waterscapes at larger scales. My scientific request to urban political ecologists of water is to integrate water gifts as a central element, among many others, of current debates.

The elaborations outlined three elements that are crucial to the understanding of the existence or absence of water gift transactions in a particular waterscape (2.2.4): the 'spatial heterogeneity of access' to conventional water supply, the social and economic 'costs of the gift', and the 'social framework' in which the transaction takes place.

The empirical analysis of water in Khartoum showed that the heterogeneity of water tap performance is produced on different scales. The 'waterscape of the city' delineates the unequal access to water supply neighbourhood by neighbourhood (5.2). Based on political negotiations and the implementation of particular water production facilities and network technologies in a natural environment (e.g. characterized by the given topography), water inequality is spatial. How total water production is shared between the neighbourhoods is determined at the scale of the 'waterscape of interconnected networks' (5.3). At the scale of the 'waterscape of the neighbourhood' however, we can determine how much water pressure reaches the main pipe in front of an individual household (5.4). This analysis provided a spatial understanding of water supply performance in urban clusters of very different sizes.

Chapter 6 shows that the heterogeneity of tap performance is not only based on water supply but that it is significantly altered by the way people 'access' this supply, hence by their individual investment in their water connection.

These investments differ in the technology used to improve access. While some households reduce the elevation of their tap and eliminate elements that reduce flow, others invest in generators and suction pumps. First, the different investments in the tap alter the heterogeneity of tap performance between direct neighbours, hence within fragments of different water supply, rather than simply between these fragments. Second, the particular access strategy influences the 'cost of the water gift'. Water gifts from high performance, non-optimized water taps are the most cost efficient, since donors donate surplus water for free, due to flat rate tariffs. Donating water obtained from low performance taps can reduce the availability of water for the tap owner, and pumping water to a neighbour through a hose generates fuel costs. The costs for the donor are not restricted to the economic costs of water purchases; they are also influenced by the social costs of the transaction. The overall economic dimensions of water gift transactions also includes the costs of accessing water gifts for the recipient, which include the physical transportation of water and the recipient's potential indebtedness. Understanding the economics of water gifts in the different biographies of water drops is a prerequisite to the conceptualization of how commodified water is moved out of the commodity state.

The analysis of the two forms of water gift transactions (by hose to friends and by bucket to strangers or even the disliked) in chapter 7 showed that not all gift transactions can be explained only through the economics of the transaction; but that the universality of the 'right to water' can produce water transactions that the economics of water provision cannot fully explain. The chapter underlines the 'neighbourly waterscape's' function as a moral waterscape in which the universality of the right to water is negotiated against egotistical interests. In the first part of the conclusions (8.1), I classify the market embeddedness of the two modes of gifts transfers in relation to the other commercial water supply options. This differentiation highlights the utility of morally extending Bourdieu's conception of the social.

Presenting a scalar trajectory of waterscapes from the city down to face-to-face interaction in this book mainly aimed at showing how the water gift is enabled and carried out in a social, moral, economic, natural, and technological environment. In the last two concluding subchapters, I switch perspectives from examining the production of the water gifts to their social impacts. This perspective follows the assumption that water and society are mutual constituents, as expressed by Mosse (2008: 941), who argues that "water systems are not only shaped by, but also themselves shape, social and political relations". In 8.2, I elaborate on the relevance of the gifts for the social security of households, with a spatial focus on the 'neighbourly waterscape', where water gifts are embedded in a direct donor-recipient relationship. In 8.3, the existence of everyday water gift practices in the 'neighbourly waterscape' is linked back to the scale of the 'waterscape of the city'. This underlines the importance of understanding water gifts as an element that tacitly influences the formulation of water supply, despite the absence of gifts in water policies and most probably in debates about these policies.

8.1. The Gift of Water and Decommodification. Social Practice between Moral and Interests

The empirical analysis of the four 'neighbourly waterscapes' in Square 11 resulted in two different explanations of water gifts. Gift transfers by hose (7.2) restricted to relatives and close friends are explained by a conventional application of Bourdieu's theory of practice. These transfers are motivated by interests within a reciprocal conception of the gift. Water gifts to strangers (7.3) and the disliked, in contrast, are explained by moral dispositions in the habitus of people that reflect the universal right to water.

Extending the perspective beyond the analysis of the gift allows the ordering of 'waters' obtained from all access strategies used in Square 11 on a continuum between a commodity and a commons. Water obtained from vendors is most strongly embedded within a capitalist relationship. It is sold in defined quantities for cash. The price is influenced by supply and demand, which is exemplified by increasing prices when water towers are not operating fully. While water vendors are strongly motivated by interest, they are not completely determined by it. In situations when the 'water-poor' are also economically poor and can express their moral entitlement, even water from water vendors can become decommodified.

Network water is less embedded in the market than water purchased from vendors. Although the consumer must pay a network fee, the KSWC is very reluctant in Square 11 to insist on water payment. They even accept household appropriations, which negatively affect the KSWC's water investments.

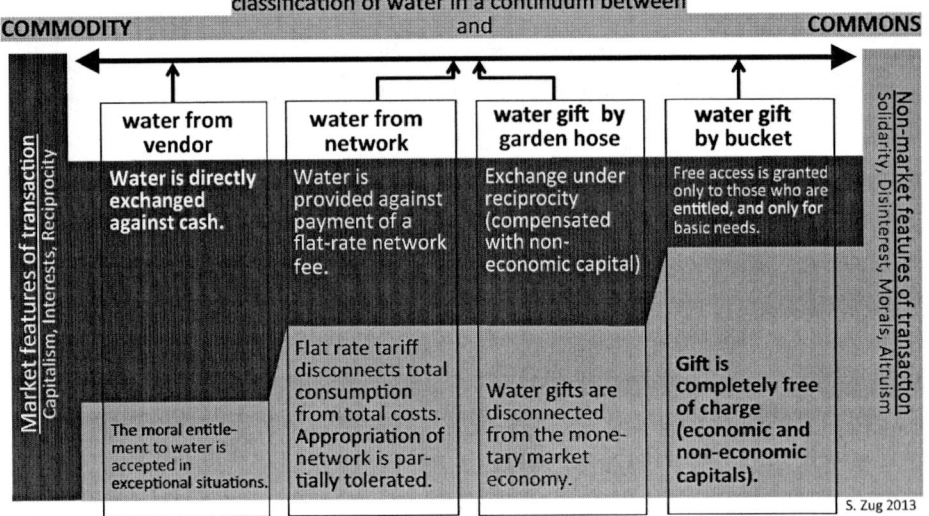

Fig. 44: *A Classification of Water Transfers by their Embeddedness in Capitalism*

Finally, water is not charged by quantity but by a flat rate tariff, which disconnects water price from the water quantity purchased. Introducing social redistribution of water by the KSWC would emphasize even more the place of water in the commons.

The water exchanged by garden hose is only partially commodified. Although it is free of charge, it is mainly guided by reciprocity, and the donor is compensated at another moment with different forms of capital, including moral capital which acknowledges gratitude. Beyond that, even though water gifts by garden hose are embedded in a reciprocal relationship, the 'universal right to water' can affect the relationship, e.g. when the exchange rate of water in the 'economy of symbolic goods' is set lower than the exchange rate of other goods.

Finally, water gifts by bucket to strangers and the disliked are the transfers displaying the most market disembeddedness, since the 'water-poor' are granted free access, based on their moral entitlement to water, without any requirement to reciprocate the water received. Although it is rather easy to claim water from a neighbour, moral entitlements only guarantee a water poor household a minimal amount of water, making the neighbour's tap a 'limited' commons only, which partially guarantees ownership rights.

The classification shows that water in Square 11's different supply regimes cannot be thought of within a binary system of commodity or commons. Rather, water transactions differ by the degree to which they are respectively guided or influenced by the market and by moral considerations. In this book, a theoretical adjustment of Bourdieu's theory of practice was developed, which provides a theoretical framework that allows relationships to be established between interested and disinterested motivations for actions. For such an integration, Luc Boltanski's (2011 [2009]: 62) proposal for a rapprochement of pragmatic and critical sociology was theoretically formulated (3.6).

Combining both approaches is accomplished by supplementing Bourdieu's 'economy of symbolic goods' with the 'meta-pragmatic register', where people justify their action in different polities; hence, where they base their action on theoretic reason. The advantages of such an approach go beyond making morality a possible alternative to interested action. The key benefit is the possibility to theoretically explain how moral motivations can be incorporated as imperfection within an economy of symbolic good. Water gift transfers by bucket in Square 11 are strongly based on morality, even though they do not take place in a 'meta-pragmatic register'. With Bourdieu's concept of habitus, morality can be embedded alongside interest as an equivalent element in the motivation of everyday practice.

From such a perspective, human life becomes disconnected from evolutionary biology, the underlying postulate is Gauthier's (1986: 187) concept of the constrained maximizer, who is good to others while waiting for the materialization of the benefits of cooperation. With the 'imperfect economy of symbolic goods', unbalanced reciprocity can be understood. The evolutionary benefit, however, remains a partial limitation for good acts, since defaulting on reciprocation is only accepted to a certain threshold of tolerance. The 'straightforward maximizers' will only be excluded from the moment they maximize their profit at the expense of others beyond the level that moral entitlements grants to them.

8.2. The Gift of Water and the Community. A Local Basic Lifeline Concept

This second concluding chapter goes beyond the particular donor-recipient gift relation and elaborates on the social function the water gift in the 'neighbourly social field', rather than explaining the gift in the 'neighbourly waterscape'. Both types of gifts developed in chapter 7 lead to a redistribution of water from the 'water-rich' to the 'water-poor', albeit with very different levels of socially embeddedness. Here, the focus is on explaining water 'gifts to strangers by bucket', which are primarily motivated by the right to water and thus most disembedded from the market. Analogies with the debates on water management in the waterscape of the city help this phenomenon.

As elaborated in section 2.1.3, one of the central debates on water management is the debate on the neoliberalization of water. The political ecology debate, as well as the practice of policy making is not restricted to a binary perspective on water provision between the private sector and government water supply. Even when the water supply is privatized, the government can and does influence private sector activities through regulations. Lobina (2005: 13) summarizes:

> The rationale for regulation in water supply and sanitation is provided by the monopoly structure of the industry, implying the risk that the private operator might otherwise abuse its monopoly power. Regulation is thus viewed as an imperfect substitute for competition aiming at safeguarding consumers' interests while providing private companies with the incentives to invest and operate efficiently.

Through regulation, the government has the means to prevent water supplied by private companies or market oriented public water corporations from becoming fully guided by the market. Some forms of regulation directly alter the relationship between the company and the consumer such as establishing tariff guidelines, establishing service and health related quality standards, and contractually binding water corporations to extend water provision beyond the most profitable regions and into unprofitable areas in order to promote social equity (Trémolet and Binder 2010: 21).

Block tariffs are a very concrete regulation to ensure social equity in which the price per unit increases alongside household consumption. By inverting the principle of economies of scale, cross-subsidization can be achieved. A very particular form of block tariffs is the inclusion of a free first block, known as the basic lifeline. The concept is most intensively discussed for South Africa, where every household has a monthly allowance of 6,000 litres of water free of charge (Bond and Dugard 2010; Loftus 2005). The basic lifeline policy is an implementation of the 'universal right to water', which was incorporated into the South African Constitution in 1996.

The KSWC did not introduce a basic lifeline tariff. However, people in Square 11 can always rely on having the possibility to cover basic water needs free of charge. This 'basic lifeline' is insured by neighbours and water vendors. The analogy applies since any of the 'water-poor' can access free – but not unlimited – water by the bucket. As described in section 7.3.2, water-rich households can deny water access to people, but only after they have given them at least a jerrycan of water. The goal of both the South African basic lifeline approach and Square 11's water gift is to ensure basic needs only. The monthly 6,000 litres of free water in South Africa granted by the water corporations find their equivalent in Khartoum in at least a bucket of free water from a Square 11 neighbour upon request.

In both concepts the universal right to water is embedded into water practices, but it is achieved through different means. South Africa's basic lifeline policy is the result of political processes, hence an exchange of arguments in the 'meta-pragmatic register' and the agreement on a particular principle – the universal right to water. The integration of the right to water in Square 11's water practice is instead based on a much longer history. The human right to water as a principle originating in debates in the 'meta-pragmatic register' has been incorporated into the habitus of people and expressed in religious and social rules over generations. Everyday practice in the neighbourly field is guided by this habitus.

The result of both types of regulation is that water is granted to those who have problems accessing water from within the normal water market, without fundamentally calling into question either the legitimacy of the water market itself or the right of water ownership. Water inequality is reduced in societies that have incorporated the universal right to water into everyday practice, whether this is done by a 'governmental' or a socially embedded basic lifeline.

8.3. The Gift of Water and the City. Social Welfare and the Negative Aspects of Solidarity

In the previous subchapter both the gift of water and specific tariffs like basic lifeline are conceptualized as two possible reactions to the inability of certain households to access water under market conditions. In this chapter I intertwine these two processes; the first is located in the 'neighbourly waterscapes' and the second in the 'waterscape of the city'. As a binding concept, the term welfare is used, defined by Guillemard (2001) as follows:

> Welfare is the result of an expanding production of care, financial benefits, or other services for ensuring the material and cultural conditions for the reproduction of humans as biological beings, as economic producers and members of a work force, and as social beings and citizens (the conditions of integration in society and of social cohesion).

Ensuring water access can be considered a welfare service, which can be accomplished by the welfare state. Esping-Anderson conceptualizes the welfare state under the notions decommodification and social stratification. "De-commodification occurs when a service is rendered as a matter of right, and when a person can maintain a livelihood without reliance on the market" (Esping-Andersen 1990: 21). By interfering with the market, the welfare state interferes in "the structuring of class and social order" (Esping-Andersen 1990: 55). In Europe's municipal hydraulic paradigm throughout most of the 20th century, water provision can be considered a welfare service. It did not rely on the ability of people to purchase water, but was motivated by the government's determination of water as 'merit good' essential for the general economic and social interest of society (Bakker 2002: 771). By imposing redistributive tariffs – like the lifeline tariff – governments can promote equity even under privatized or commercialized water supply.

The state is not the only actor, who can actively redistribute or oblige private actors to do so. In the concept of the "welfare society", market actors[120], civil society, and the family autonomously do so as well (Meyer and Hinchman 2007: 147). Water gifts in Square 11 are embedded either within the family, which can be extend here to reciprocal relationships between close neighbours, or in civil society[121], in the sense of a morally regulated redistribution from the 'water-rich' and vendors to the 'water-poor'.

---

120 Market actors in this classification are companies that provide redistribution as a business like insurance companies, rather than companies who incorporated a morality of equity in their business practice. For our analysis in the water sector in Khartoum these actors are irrelevant.

121 In the past, international NGO's also played a significant role as civil society actors in water welfare provision. This is true for the construction of water towers in general, the distribution of donkey carts to the urban poor, and occasional water supply by water tankers like in the early phases of resettlement, when the vendors could not yet serve the urban poor for a reasonable price (O'Neill 1989). Since mid-2000s international NGOs have barely invested in water provision in Khartoum.

Esping-Andersen (1990: 30), classifies welfare regimes of high income countries[122], which are mainly located on the spectrum between market and government welfare provision. For the 'Sudanese welfare society', the two poles should be defined between government investments in welfare and welfare ensured by civil society and the family. The Sudanese welfare state is what Leibfried (1993: 128)[123] defined as a "rudimentary welfare state", in which government welfare provision is very limited and responsibility is mainly taken over by civil society and family.

The approach of the KSWC to ensure the people's right to water is to extend the public water network to the peripheries and provide every household with a tap, allowing them to access water at relatively cheap rates. Since the KSWC is far from achieving universal access to its water supply network, many people do rely on the service of water vendors. On the one hand, water vendors contribute to the fulfilment of people's right to water, since they make it possible for the non-connected in the peripheries to access water, but on the other hand this service comes at a high cost. Consequently, instead of actively promoting equity, Khartoum's present joint system of public network and water vendors leads to inequality of water access between the connected households – a group that includes all of the city's better-off households – and the urban poor living in the unconnected urban peripheries.

If water supply was exclusively based on insufficient network provision and the service of water vendors that are fully embedded in the market, the unconnected, who cannot afford water from vendors, would be fully denied access to water and in the very worst case scenario, they would die of thirst. However, they do not, because their moral entitlement to water ensures their right to water, giving them access to free water from both their close neighbours and sporadically even from water vendors, and unknown people. In a global vision of Greater Khartoum's waterscape, the right to a 'life sustaining' amount of water is fulfilled for all households. However, it is not fulfilled by the welfare state, but by the strongly enforced moral entitlement to free basic water from the water vendors and from the neighbour's tap. Even in areas where no network is available at all, someone will readily grant a very poor person as much water as he or she requires to survive.

---

122 He differentiates a conservative, a liberal, and a social democratic welfare regime.

123 Leibfried builds his argument for Spain, Italy, Portugal, and Greece, where the state does not grant the right to welfare. In these countries, he argues, the older systems of welfare provision exist, which he relates to the Catholic Church.

The positive function of the gift in daily water practices for the urban poor in the 'neighbourly waterscape' negatively impacts the resolution of the problem's root causes. The contribution of non-state actors in granting the right to water to all urban dwellers relieves the KSWC of their moral responsibility to ensure the universal right to water, which makes the gift policy relevant. This relevance most likely does not lead to discussions among politicians and the KSWC about the gift. Rather, the water gift is a constitutive but hidden element in the negotiation of the 'waterscape of the city'.

The gift's absence, however, would require a change in policy. If non-governmental water solidarity did not exist in Khartoum, and people were not able to satisfy their basic needs, the KSWC would be much more prone to moral offense. The KSWC would have to take the responsibility for not fulfilling the universal right to water. Not having this pressure allows the KSWC and the Government to set investment priorities other than supplying the urban poor. People do question the government policy – and indirectly the underlying weak fulfilment of the human right to water – however it can be assumed that they protest less about their rights than if government water supply were their sole source of water. Consequently, the existence of water solidarity in the neighbourly waterscape contributes to the justification of maintaining highly unequal water supplies by pipe network water distribution systems.

This research has underlined the 'universal' character of the right to water. The Khartoum case shows that a minimal basic need for water is always fulfilled; if not by the government, then by neighbourly solidarity.

Bibliography

ABD ALRAHEEM, ABD ALGHAFFAR MAHA (2000) "Pollution in the Water Supply Wells of Khartoum, Sudan". *Bulletin of Engineering Geology and the Environment* 58 (4): 257-264.

AHMAD, ADIL MUSTAFA (1992) "The Neighbourhoods of Khartoum: Reflections on Their Functions, Forms and Future". *Habitat International* 16 (4): 27-45.

ALEXANDER, JEFFREY C. (1995) *Fin de Siècle Social Theory: Relativism, Reduction, and the Problem of Reason.* London: Verso. 231p.

ALGAFAR, MAHA ABD, G. ABDOU, and Y. ABDELSALAM (2011) "Groundwater Flow Model for the Nubian Aquifer in the Khartoum Area, Sudan". *Bulletin of Engineering Geology and the Environment* 70 (4): 619-623.

ALLEN, ADRIANA, JULIO D. DÁVILA, and PASCALE HOFMANN (2006a) *Governance of Water and Sanitation Services for the Peri-urban Poor.* London: DFID. 126p.

——— (2006b) "The Peri-Urban Water Poor: Citizens or Consumers?". *Environment and Urbanization* 18 (2): 333-351.

AMIRALY, AKIL (2009) *Transposition et Appropriation d'un Outil de Gestion dans le Cadre de la Mondalisation: Le Compteur d'Eau en Inde.* PhD Thesis, Économie et Sciences Sociales, École Polytechnique Paris.

APPADURAI, ARJUN (1986) "Commodities and the Politics of Value". In Arjun Appadurai, ed.: *The Social Live of Things: Commodities in a Cultural Perspective*; Cambridge: University of Cambridge. 3-63.

ARANGO, LUISA (2009) *L'Eau Derrière le Tuyau: De l'Homogénéité Apparente, La Diversification Effective et le Partage dans le Changement.* Master Thesis, Département de Sociologie Université Paris 8.

ARARAL, EDUARDO (2009) "The Failure of Water Utilities Privatization: Synthesis of Evidence, Analysis and Implications". *Policy and Society* 27 (3): 221-228.

ASSAL, MUNZOUL (2011a) "Nationality and Citizenship Questions in Sudan after the Southern Sudan Referendum Vote", *Chr. Michelsen Institute.* 15p.

ASSAL, MUNZOUL A. M. (2004) "Displaced Persons in Khartoum: Current Realities and Post-War Scenarios", *A Report for MEAwards, the Population Council Cairo.* 40p.

——— (2011b) "Conflict-Induced Migration in Sudan and Post-Referendum Challenges", *CARIM Analytic and Synthetic Notes 2011/75, Robert Schuman Centre for Advanced Studies.* 13p.

BAKKER, KAREN (2002) "From State to Market? Water Mercantilización in Spain". *Environment and Planning A* 34 (5): 767-790.

―――― (2003a) "Archipelagos and Networks: Urbanization and Water Privatization in the South". *The Geographical Journal* 169 (4): 328-341.

―――― (2003b) "A Political Ecology of Water Privatization". *Studies in Political Economy* 70: 35-58.

―――― (2007) "The 'Commons' Versus the 'Commodity': Alter-Globalization, Anti-Privatization and the Human Right to Water in the Global South". *Antipode* 39 (3): 430-450.

―――― (2008) "The Ambiguity of Community: Debating Alternatives to Private-Sector Provision of Urban Water Supply". *Water Alternatives* 1 (2): 236-252.

―――― (2010a) "Commons Versus Commodities: Political Ecologies of Water Privatization". In Richard Peet, Paul Robbins and Michael Watts, eds.: *Global Political Ecology*; London: Routledge. 347-370.

―――― (2010b) *Privatizing Water: Governance Failure and the World's Urban Water Crisis*. Ithaca: Cornell University Press. 303p.

―――― (2013) "Neoliberal Versus Postneoliberal Water: Geographies of Privatization and Resistance". *Annals of the Association of American Geographers* 103 (2): 253-260.

BAKKER, KAREN, MICHELLE KOOY, NUR ENDAH SHOFIANI, and ERNST-JAN MARTIJN (2008) "Governance Failure: Rethinking the Institutional Dimensions of Urban Water Supply to Poor Households". *World Development* 36 (10): 1891-1915.

BANERJEE, SUDESHNA GHOSH, and ELVIRA MORELLA (2011) *Africa's Water and Sanitation Infrastructure: Access, Affordability, and Alternatives*. Washington: World Bank Publications. 401p.

BANNAGA, SHARAF ELDIN IBRAHIM (1996) *MAWA: Unauthorised and Squatter Settlements in Khartoum. History, Magnitude and Treatment*. Zurich: Habitat Group at the Swiss Federal Institute of Technology. 93p.

―――― (2002) *Peace and the Displaced in Sudan: the Khartoum Experience*. Zurich: Swiss Federal Institute of Technology. 289p.

BARLÖSIUS, EVA (2006) *Pierre Bourdieu: eine Einführung*. Frankfurt: Campus Verlag. 195p.

BAUER, ULLRICH, and UWE H. BITTLINGMAYER (2000) "Pierre Bourdieu und die Frankfurter Schule. Eine Fortsetzung der Kritischen Theorie mit anderen Mitteln?". In Claudia Rademacher and Peter Wiechens, eds.: *Verstehen und Kritik: Soziologische Suchbewegungen nach dem Ende der Gewissheiten*; Wiesbaden: Westdeutscher Verlag. 241-298.

BAUMER, MICHEL (1983) *Notes on Trees and Shrubs in Arid and Semi-Arid Regions: Emasar Phase II*. Rome: FAO. 270p.

BAVISKAR, AMITA (2003) "For a Cultural Politics of Natural Resources". *Economic and Political Weekly* 38 (48): 5051-5055.

BECKEDORF, ANNE-SOPHIE (2011) *Political Waters: Khartoum Governmental Water Management in the Context of Neoliberal Reforms*. PhD Thesis, Lehrstuhl für Bevölkerungs- und Sozialgeographie, Universität Bayreuth.

——— (2012) "Denying Access to Water? Moral Values and Commercialization Policies in Khartoum Governmental Water Management", *WAMAKHAIR Working Papers*. 12p.

BÉNATOUÏL, THOMAS (1999) "A Tale of Two Sociologies". *European Journal of Social Theory* 2 (3): 379-396.

BENDA-BECKMANN, FRANZ VON, KEEBET VON BENDA-BECKMANN, and JOEP SPIERTZ (1997) "Local Law and Customary Practices in the Study of Water Rights". In *Water Rights, Conflict and Policy*; Kathmandu International Irrigation Management Institute. 221-241.

BENTHAM, JEREMY (1823 [1780]) *An Introduction to the Principles of Morals and Legislation*. Vol. 1. London: W. Pickering. 281p.

——— (1839 [1789]) *The Works of Jeremy Bentham*. Vol. X. London: W. Tait. 295p.

BIDET, JACQUES (1979 [1973]) "Questions to Pierre Bourdieu". *Critique of Anthropology* 4 (13-14): 203-208.

BISWAS, ASIT K., EGLAL RACHED, and CECILIA TORTAJADA (2008) *Water as a Human Right for the Middle East and North Africa*. London: Routledge. 191p.

BOELENS, RUTGERD, DAVID GETCHES, and ARMANDO GUEVARA-GIL (2010) *Out of the Mainstream: Water Rights, Politics and Identity*. London: Earthscan. 366p.

BOGUSZ, TANJA (2010) *Zur Aktualität von Luc Boltanski: Einleitung in sein Werk*. Wiesbaden: VS Verlag. 172p.

BOLAND, JOHN J., and DALE WHITTINGTON (2000) "Increasing Block Tariffs versus Uniform Price with Rebate". In Ariel Dinar, ed.: *The Political Economy of Water Pricing Reforms*; Oxford: World Bank, Oxford University Press. 215-236.

BOLTANSKI, LUC (2011 [2009]) *On Critique: A Sociology of Emancipation*. Cambridge: Polity. 200p.

——— (2012 [1990]) *Love and Justice as Competences*. Cambridge: Polity Press. 328p.

BOLTANSKI, LUC, and ÈVE CHIAPELLO (2005 [1999]) *The New Spirit of Capitalism*. London: Verso. 601p.

BOLTANSKI, LUC, and LAURENT THÉVENOT (2000) "The Reality of Moral Expectations: A Sociology of Situated Judgement". *Philosophical Explorations* 3 (3): 208-231.

―――― (2006 [1991]) *On Justification: Economies of Worth*. Princeton: Princeton University Press. 389p.
BOND, PATRICK, and JACKIE DUGARD (2010) "The Case of Johannesburg Water: What Really Happened at the Pre-Paid 'Parish Pump'". *Law, Democracy & Development* 12 (1): 1-28.
BOOTH, F.E.M., and G.E. WICKENS (1988) *Non-Timber Uses of Selected Arid Zone Trees and Shrubs in Africa*. Rome: FAO. 176p.
BORALEVI, LEA C. (1984) *Bentham and the Oppressed*. Berlin: W. de Gruyter. 248p.
BOURDIEU, PIERRE (1977 [1972]) *Outline of a Theory of Practice*. Cambridge: Cambridge University Press. 248p.
―――― (1979 [1965]) *Algeria 1960*. Cambridge: Cambridge University Press. 158p.
―――― (1984) *Distinction: A Social Critique of the Judgement of Taste*. Cambridge: Harvard University Press. 613p.
―――― (1985) "The Social Space and the Genesis of Groups". *Theory and Society* 14 (6): 723-744.
―――― (1987) "What Makes a Social Class? On the Theoretical and Practical Existence Of Groups". *Berkeley Journal of Sociology* 32: 1-17.
―――― (1988 [1984]) *Homo Academicus*. Stanford: Stanford University Press. 344p.
―――― (1990 [1987]) *In Other Words: Essays Towards a Reflexive Sociology*. Stanford: Stanford University Press. 223p.
―――― (1990 [1980]) *The Logic of Practice*. Stanford: Stanford University Press. 333p.
―――― (1991) *Language and Symbolic Power*. Cambridge: Harvard University Press. 302p.
―――― (1996 [1992]) *The Rules of Art: Genesis and Structure of the Literary Field*. Stanford: Stanford University Press. 408p.
―――― (1997) *Les Usages Sociaux de la Science: Pour une Sociologie Clinique du Champ Scientifique*. Paris: Editions Quae. 80p.
―――― (1998) *Acts of Resistance: Against the Tyranny of the Market*. New York: New Press. 108p.
―――― (1998 [1994]) *Practical Reason: On the Theory of Action*. Stanford: Stanford University Press. 153p.
―――― (2000 [1997]) *Pascalian Meditations*. Stanford: Stanford University Press. 256p.
―――― (2000) *Propos sur la Politique*. Lyon: Presses Universitaires de Lyon. 110p.
―――― (2001 [1998]) *Masculine Domination*. Stanford: Stanford University Press. 133p.

—— (2005 [2000]) "Principles of Economic Anthropology". In Neil J. Smelser and Richard Swedberg, eds.: *The Handbook of Economic Sociology*; Princeton: Princeton University Press. 75-89.

—— (2007 [2002]) *Sketch for a Self-Analysis*. Cambridge: Polity Press. 118p.

——, ed. (1999)*The Weight of the World: Social Suffering in Contemporary Society*. Stanford: Stanford University Press. 646p.

BOURDIEU, PIERRE, and LUC BOLTANSKI (1976) "La Production de l'Idéologie Dominante". *Actes de la Recherche en Sciences Sociales* 2 (2-3): 3-73.

BOURDIEU, PIERRE, and LOÏC J. D. WACQUANT (1992) *An Invitation to Reflexive Sociology*. Chicago: University of Chicago Press. 332p.

BOUSQUET, ANNE (2010) "Water and the Poor in Nairobi: from Water Apartheid to Urban Fragmentation". In Helene Charton-Bigot and Deyssi Rodriguez-Torres, eds.: *Nairobi Today: The Paradox of a Fragmented City*; Dar es Salam: Mkuki na Nyota Publishers. 123-166.

BRAADBAART, OKKE (2009) "North–South Transfer of the Paradigm of Piped Water: The Role of the Public Sector in Water and Sanitation Services". In Jose Esteban Castro and Leo Heller, eds.: *Water and Sanitation Services: Public Policy and Management*; London: Earthscan. 71-85.

BUDDS, JESSICA (2008) "Whose Scarcity? The Hydrosocial Cycle and the Changing Waterscape of La Ligua River Basin, Chile". In Michael Goodman, Maxwell T. Boykoff and Kyle T. Evered, eds.: *Contentious Geographies: Environment, Meaning, Scale*; Hampshire: Ashgate. 59-78.

—— (2009) "Contested H_2O: Science, Policy and Politics in Water Resources Management in Chile". *Geoforum* 40 (3): 418-430.

BUDDS, JESSICA, and GORDON MCGRANAHAN (2003) "Are the Debates on Water Privatization Missing the Point? Experiences from Africa, Asia and Latin America". *Environment and Urbanization* 15 (2): 87-114.

CAILLE, ALAIN (1981) "La Sociologie de l'Intérêt est-elle Intéressante?". *Sociologie du Travail* 23 (3): 257-274.

—— (1994) "Don, Intérêt et Désintéressement". *Revue Européenne des Sciences Sociales* 32 (99): 253-283.

—— (2001 [1994]) "The Double Inconceivability of the Pure Gift". *Angelaki: Journal of the Theoretical Humanities* 6 (2): 23 - 39.

—— (2006). "Anti-Utilitarianism, Economics and the Gift-Paradigm" Paper for the *Conference Individual and Society*, 1-3.12.2006, at Dakar.

CAIRNCROSS, SANDY (1990) "Water Supply and the Urban Poor". In Jorge E. Hardoy, Sandy Cairncross and David Satterthwaite, eds.: *The Poor Die Young: Housing and Health in Third World Cities*; London: Earthscan. 109–126.

CAIRNCROSS, SANDY, and JOANNE KINNEAR (1992) "Elasticity of Demand for Water in Khartoum, Sudan". *Social Science & Medicine* 34 (2): 183-189.

CAPONERA, DANTE A. (1992) *Principles of Water Law and Administration: National and International*. Rotterdam: Balkema. 260p.

CARRIER, JAMES G. (1995) *Gifts and Commodities: Exchange and Western Capitalism since 1700*. London: Routledge. 240p.

CASTREE, NOEL (1995) "The Nature of Produced Nature: Materiality and Knowledge Construction in Marxism". *Antipode* 27 (1): 12-48.

CASTRO, JOSE ESTEBAN (2007) "Poverty and Citizenship: Sociological Perspectives on Water Services and Public-Private Participation". *Geoforum* 38 (5): 756-771.

——— (2008) "Neoliberal Water and Sanitation Policies as a Failed Development Strategy: Lessons from Developing Countries". *Progress in Development Studies* 8 (1): 63-83.

CELIKATES, ROBIN (2006) "Zwischen Habitus und Reflexion: zu einigen methodologischem Problemen in Bourdieu's Sozialtheorie". In Mark Hillebrand, Paula Krüger, Andrea Lilge and Karen Struve, eds.: *Willkürliche Grenzen: Das Werk Pierre Bourdieus in interdisziplinärer Anwendung*, Bielefeld: Transcript. 73-90.

——— (2009) *Kritik als soziale Praxis*. Frankfurt: Campus. 272p.

CHAMBERLAIN, GARY (2008) *Troubled Waters: Religion, Ethics, and the Global Water Crisis*. Plymouth: Rowman & Littlefield. 227p.

CHAMBERS, ROBERT (1986) *Rural Development: Putting the Last First*. London: Longman. 246p.

COCHRAN, JAQUELIN, and ISHA RAY (2009) "Equity Reexamined: A Study of Community-Based Rainwater Harvesting in Rajasthan, India". *World Development* 37 (2): 435-444.

COLLIGNON, BERNARD, and MARC VÉZINA (2000) "Independent Water and Sanitation Providers in Africa Cities", *World Bank*. 64p.

CORCUFF, PHILIPPE (2003) *Bourdieu Autrement: Fragilités d'un Sociologue de Combat*. Paris: Textuel. 143p.

CRESSWELL, TIM (2005) "Moral Geographies". In David Sibley, Peter Jackson, David Atkinson and Neil Washbourne, eds.: *Cultural geography: A Critical Dictionary of Key Concepts*; New York: I.B. Tauris. 128-135.

CROMBE, LAURE (2009) *L'Eau Dehors, l'Eau Dedans: Évolutions des Modes d'Accès à l'Eau Dans un Quartier Périphérique du Grand Khartoum, Dar es Salam, Omdurman, Soudan*. Master Thesis, Département de Géographie, Université de Paris Ouest.

CROMBE, LAURE, and DAVID BLANCHON (2010) "Les (micro)-réseaux à la reconquête de la ville : le cas de Khartoum. ". *Bulletin de l'Association de géographes français* (4): 517-533.

DAVIES, H.R.J., and MOHAMED EL HADI ABU SIN, eds. (1991)*The Future of Sudan's Capital Region: a Study in Development and Change*. Khartoum: Khartoum University Press. 272p.

DE CHÂTEL, FRANCESCA (2009) "Bathing in Divine Waters: Water and Purity in Judaism and Islam". In Terje Tvedt and Terje Oestigaard, eds.: *A History of Water*, New York: I.B. Tauris. 273-297.

DE GEOFFROY, AGNÈS (2009) "Fleeing War and Relocating to the Urban Fringe – Issues and Actors: the Cases of Khartoum and Bogota". *International Review of the Red Cross* 91 (875): 509-526.

――― (2011) "The Challenge of Displacement: The Case of Khartoum", *Middle East Institute*. 12p.

DE WAAL, ALEX (2007) *Sudan: What Kind of State? What Kind of Crisis?* London: LSE Occasional Paper 2. 27p.

DELSAUT, YVETTE, and MARIE-CHRISTINE RIVIERE (2002) *Bibliographie des Travaux de Pierre Bourdieu*. Pantin: Le Temps des Cerises. 241p.

DENIS, ÉRIC (2005) "De Quelques Dimensions de Khartoum et de l'Urbanisation au Soudan". *Lettre de l'Observatoire Urbain du Caire Contemporain* 6/7: 21-31.

DERRIDA, JACQUES (1992 [1991]) *Given Time: I. Counterfeit Money*. Chicago: University of Chicago Press. 182p.

DIAZ-BONE, RAINER, and LAURENT THÉVENOT (2010) "Die Soziologie der Konventionen. Die Theorie der Konventionen als ein zentraler Bestandteil der neuen französischen Sozialwissenschaften". *Trivium* 5 (12).

DIRKSMEIER, PETER (2009) "Die kulturelle Übersetzung als symbolische Gewalt: Über die Beobachtung des Kultur/Gesellschaftsverhältnisses in der Kulturgeographie". *Social Geography* 5: 173-197.

DRIVER, FELIX (1992) "Geography, Morality, Politics: Brave new Worlds". In Chris Philo, ed.: *New Words, New Worlds: Reconceptualising Social and Cultural Geography*, Aberystwyth: Cambrian. 61-64.

DYER, SARAH, and DAVID DEMERITT (2009) "Un-Ethical Review? Why it is Wrong to Apply the Medical Model of Research Governance to Human Geography". *Progress in Human Geography* 33 (1): 46-64.

EICHHOLZ, MICHAEL, KRISTOF VAN ASSCHE, LISA OBERKIRCHER, and ANNA-KATHARINA HORNIDGE (2012) "Trading Capitals? Bourdieu, Land and Water in Rural Uzbekistan". *Journal of Environmental Planning and Management* (in print).

EJDERYAN, OLIVIER (2009) *Une Renaturation en Béton!: Comprendre la Participation et la Nature dans les Renaturations de Cours d'eau Suisses au Regard d'une Théorie de la Pratique*. Zürich: Geographisches Institut, Universität Zürich. 303p.

EKEH, PETER. P. (1974) *Social Exchange Theory: the Two Traditions*. London: Heinemann. 237p.

EKERS, MICHAEL, and ALEX LOFTUS (2008) "The Power of Water: Developing Dialogues Between Foucault and Gramsci". *Environment and Planning D, Society and Space* 26 (4): 698-718.

EL-BUSHRA, EL-SAYED (1971) "The Evolution of the Three Towns". *African Urban Notes* 6 (2): 8-23.

EL-BUSHRA, EL-SAYED, and NAILA B. HIJAZI (1995) "Two Million Squatters in Khartoum Urban Complex: The Dilemma of Sudan's National Capital". *GeoJournal* 35 (4): 505-514.

ESPING-ANDERSEN, GØSTA (1990) *The Three Worlds of Welfare Capitalism*. Princeton: Princeton University Press. 248p.

FABIANI, JEAN-LOUIS (2011) "Book Review: Luc Boltanski, De la Critique. Précis de Sociologie de l'Émancipation". *European Journal of Social Theory* 14 (3): 401-406.

FARAH, E. A, O. M. ABDULLATIF, O. M KHEIR, and N. BARAZI (1997) "Groundwater Resources in a Semi-Arid Area: a Case Study from Central Sudan". *Journal of African Earth Sciences* 25 (3): 453-466.

FARAH, E. A., E. M. A. MUSTAFA, and H. KUMAI (2000) "Sources of Groundwater Recharge at the Confluence of the Niles, Sudan". *Environmental Geology* 39 (6): 667-672.

FARUQUI, NASER I. (2001) "Intersectoral Water Markets". In Naser. I. Faruqui, Asit K. Biswas and Murad J. Bino, eds.: *Water Management in Islam*, Tokyo: United Nations University Press. 115-127.

FAVEREAU, OLIVIER (2001) "Complément. L'Économie du Sociologue ou Penser (l'Orthodoxie) à Partir de Pierre Bourdieu". In Bernard Lahire, ed.: *Le Travail Sociologique de Pierre Bourdieu*, Paris: La Découverte. 255-314.

FLICK, UWE (2009) *An Introduction to Qualitative Research*. London: SAGE Publications. 528p.

FOSTER, JOHN B. (2000) *Marx's Ecology: Materialism and Nature*. New York: Monthly Review Press. 310p.

FRANCEYS, RICHARD, and ALMUD WEITZ (2003) "Public-Private Community Partnerships in Infrastructure for the Poor". *Journal of International Development* 15 (8): 1083-1098.

FRANCK, ALICE (2007) *Produire pour la Ville, Produire la Ville: Étude de l'Intgration des Activités Agricoles et des Agricultures dans l'Agglomoration du Grand*

Khartoum (Sudan). PhD Thesis, Département de Géographie, Université Paris X Nanterre.

FRIDELL, GAVIN (2006) "Fair Trade and the International Moral Economy: Within and Against the Market". In Tony Shallcross and John Robinson, eds.: *Global Citizenship and Environmental Justice*; Amsterdam: Rodopi. 81-94.

FUCHS-HEINRITZ, WERNER, and ALEXANDRA KÖNIG (2005) *Pierre Bourdieu: eine Einführung*. Konstanz: UVK Verlagsgesellschaft. 354p.

GADIR, MOHAMED ELAMIN ABDEL (2006) *Small Water Enterprises in Africa. 3: Sudan*. Loughborough: Water, Engineering and Development Centre. 64p.

GANDY, MATTHEW (2004) "Rethinking Urban Metabolism: Water, Space and the Modern City". *City* 8 (3): 363-379.

——— (2008) "Landscapes of Disaster: Water, Modernity, and Urban Fragmentation in Mumbai". *Environment and planning A* 40 (1): 108-130.

GAUTHIER, DAVID P. (1986) *Morals by Agreement*. Oxford: Clarendon Press. 367p.

GEERTZ, CLIFFORD (1972) "The Wet and the Dry: Traditional Irrigation in Bali and Morocco". *Human Ecology* 1 (1): 23-39.

GEMPERLE, MICHAEL (2009) "The Double Character of the German 'Bourdieu'. On the Twofold Use of Pierre Bourdieu's Work in the German-Speaking Social Sciences". *Sociologica* 3 (1): 1-33.

GERTEL, JÖRG (1993) *Krisenherd Khartoum: Geschichte und Struktur der Wohnraumproblematik in der sudanesischen Hauptstadt*. Saarbrücken: Breitenbach. 317p.

GLASER, BARNEY G., and ANSELM L. STRAUSS (2009 [1967]) *The Discovery of Grounded Theory: Strategies for Qualitative Research*. Piscataway: Aldine Transaction. 271p.

GLEICK, PETER H. (1999) "The Human Right to Water". *Water Policy* 1: 487-503.

——— (2010) *Bottled and Sold: The Story Behind our Obsession with Bottled Water*. Washington: Island Press. 211p.

GOWRICHARN, RUBEN (2004) "Moral Capital in Surinamese Transnationalism". *Ethnic and Racial Studies* 27 (4): 607-621.

GRAEFE, OLIVIER (2006) "Wasser, Konflikte und soziales Kapital im Hohen Atlas Südmarokkos". *Geographica Helvetica* 61 (1): 41-49.

——— (2010) "Wasser und Macht: Zur Bedeutung von Machtverhältnissen in der sozialen Konstruktion von Risiko und Sicherheit". In Hike Egner and Andreas Pott, eds.: *Geographische Risikoforschung: Zur*

Konstruktion verräumlichter Risiken und Sicherheiten; Stuttgart: Franz Steiner Verlag. 185-196.

GRAHAM, STEPHEN (2000) "Constructing Premium Network Spaces: Reflections on Infrastructure Networks and Contemporary Urban Development". *International Journal of Urban and Regional Research* 24 (1): 183-200.

GRAHAM, STEPHEN, and SIMON MARVIN (2001) *Splintering Urbanism: Networked Infrastructures, Technological Mobilities and the Urban Condition*. London: Routledge. 479p.

GRASS, GÜNTER, and PIERRE BOURDIEU (1999). "Alles seitenverkehrt. Zivilisiert endlich den Kapitalismus! Der Literaturnobelpreisträger Günter Grass und der Soziologe Pierre Bourdieu im Gespräch.". *Die Zeit*, 2.12.1999.

GUILLEMARD, A.-M. (2001) "Welfare". In Neil J. Smelser and Paul B. Baltes, eds.: *International Encyclopedia of the Social & Behavioral Sciences*; New York: Elsevier. 16416-16420.

GUPTA, JOYEETA, RHODANTE AHLERS, and LAWAL AHMED (2010) "The Human Right to Water: Moving Towards Consensus in a Fragmented World". *Review of European Community & International Environmental Law* 19 (3): 294-305.

GUPTA, S.C. (2006) *Fluid Mechanics And Hydraulic Machines*. New Delhi: Pearson Education Canada. 596p.

HABERMAS, JÜRGEN (1987) *The Theory of Communicative Action: Reason and the Rationalization of Society*. Boston: Beacon Press. 465p.

HALEEM, ABDEL A. (2005) *The Qur'an*. Oxford: Oxford University Press. 464p.

HALL, DAVID (2006) "A Global Review of Multinational Corporations in the Water and Electricity Sectors". In *Beyond the Market: the Future of Public Services. Public Services Yearbook (2005/6)* PSIRU. 179-185.

HALL, DAVID, and EMANUELE LOBINA (2004) "Private and Public Interests in Water and Energy". *Natural Resources Forum* 28 (4): 268-277.

―――― (2006) "Water as a Public Service", *PSIRU Reports*. 48p.

―――― (2007) "Profitability and the Poor: Corporate Strategies, Innovation and Sustainability". *Geoforum* 38 (5): 772-785.

HAMID, GAMAL M. (2000) "Local Level Authorities and Local Action in Greater Khartoum, Sudan". *The Arab World Geographer* 3 (4): 230-248.

HARAWAY, DONNA J. (1991) *Simians, Cyborgs and Women: The Reinvention of Nature*. New York: Free Association. 287p.

HARDIN, GARRETT (1968) "The Tragedy of the Commons". *Science* 162: 1243-1248.

HARK, SABINE (2009) "Reflexivität". In Gerhard Fröhlich and Boike Rehbein, eds.: *Bourdieu Handbuch. Leben-Werk-Wirkung*; Stuttgart: Metzler. 203-205.

HARTMANN, MARTIN (2008) "Rechtfertigungsordnungen und Anerkennungsordnungen. Zum Vergleich zweier Theoriemodelle". *WestEnd Neue Zeitschrift für Sozialforschung* 5 (2): 104-119.

HEMSON, DAVID (2008) "Water for All: From Firm Promises to 'New Realism'?". In David Hemson, Kassim Kulindwa, Haakon Lein and Adolfo Mascarenhas, eds.: *Poverty and Water: Explorations of the Reciprocal Relationship*; London: Zed Books. 13-46.

HENDERSON, GEORGE (2003) "What (Else) we Talk About When we Talk About Landscape: For a Return to the Social Imagination". In *Everyday America: Cultural Landscape Studies after JB Jackson*; Berkeley: University of California Press. 178-98.

——— (2004) "'Free' Food, the Local Production of Worth, and the Circuit of Decommodification: a Value Theory of the Surplus". *Environment and Planning D: Society and Space* 22: 485-512.

HENNINK, MONIQUE H. (2008) "Language and Communication in Cross-Cultural Qualitative Research". In Pranee Liamputtong, ed.: *Doing Cross-Cultural Research: Ethical and Methodological Perspectives*. Springer. 21-33.

HEYNEN, NIKOLAS C., MARIA KAÏKA, and ERIK SWYNGEDOUW (2006) "Urban Political Ecology: Politicizing the Production of Urban Natures". In Nikolas C. Heynen, Maria Kaïka and Erik Swyngedouw, eds.: *In the Nature of Cities. Urban Political Ecology and the Politics of Urban Metabolism*; Abingdon: Routledge. 20-40.

HEYNEN, NIKOLAS C., HAROLD A. PERKINS, and PARAMA ROY (2006) "The Political Ecology of Uneven Urban Green Space: The Impact of Political Economy on Race and Ethnicity in Producing Environmental Inequality in Milwaukee". *Urban Affairs Review* 42 (1): 3-25.

HILLEBRANDT, FRANK (2009) *Praktiken des Tauschens: Zur Soziologie symbolischer Formen der Reziprozität*. Wiesbaden: VS Verlag für Sozialwissenschaften. 270p.

HOBBES, THOMAS (1651) *Leviathan or the Matter, Forme, & Power of a Common-wealth Ecclesiasticall and Civill*. London: Andrew Crooke. 394p.

HOFFMANN, SABINE (2010) *Urban Water and Wastewater Management in Cochabamba (Bolivia): An Ecological and Institutional Analysis*. PhD Thesis, Graduate Institute of International and Development Studies, Université de Genève.

HONNETH, AXEL (1986 [1984]) "The Fragmented World of Symbolic Forms: Reflections on Pierre Bourdieu's Sociology of Culture". *Theory, Culture & Society* 3 (3): 55-66.
────── (1997) "Recognition and Moral Obligation". *Social Research* 64 (1): 16-35.
────── (2010) "Dissolutions of the Social: On the Social Theory of Luc Boltanski and Laurent Thévenot". *Constellations* 17 (3): 376-389.
HOWARD, GUY, JOANNA TEUTON, PAUL LUYIMA, and ROBERT ODONGO (2002) "Water Usage Patterns in Low-Income Urban Communities in Uganda: Implications for Water Supply Surveillance". *International Journal of Environmental Health Research* 12 (1): 63 - 73.
IGNATOW, GABRIEL (2009) "Why the Sociology of Morality Needs Bourdieu's Habitus". *Sociological Inquiry* 79 (1): 98-114.
ILLICH, IVAN (1986) *H2O and the Waters of Forgetfulness*. London: Marion Boyars. 92p.
ISKANDARANI, MARIA (2002) *Economics of Household Water Security in Jordan*. Frankfurt: P. Lang. 133p.
JACKSON, PETER (2002) "Commercial Cultures: Transcending the Cultural and the Economic". *Progress in Human Geography* 26 (1): 3-18.
JAGLIN, SYLVY (2001) "Villes Disloquées? Ségrégations et Fragmentation Urbaine en Afrique Australe". *Annales de Géographie* 619: 243-265.
────── (2005) *Services d'Eau en Afrique Subsaharienne: la Fragmentation Urbaine en Question*. Paris: CNRS éditions. 244p.
JAGLIN, SYLVY, and ANNE BOUSQUET (2011) "Conflicts of Influence and Competing Models: the Boom in Community-Based Privatization of Water Services in Sub-Saharan Africa". In Bernard Barraqué, ed.: *Urban Water Conflicts*; Leiden: Taylor & Francis. 169-193.
JAGLIN, SYLVY, and JEAN-LUC PIERMAY (1996) "Lusaka, de la Ségrégation à l'Archipellisation?". In Jean-Pascal Daloz and John D. Chileshe, eds.: *La Zambie Contemporaine*; Paris: Karthala. 217-258.
JENKINS, RICHARD (1992) *Pierre Bourdieu*. Milton Keynes: Routledge. 129p.
JOAS, HANS, and WOLFGANG KNÖBL (2011 [2004]) "Between Structuralism and Theory of Practice: The Cultural Sociology of Pierre Bourdieu". In Susen Susen and Bryan S. Turner, eds.: *The Legacy of Pierre Bourdieu: Critical Essays*; London: Anthem Press. 1-33.
KADOURI, M. T., Y. DJEBBAR, and M. NEHDI (2001) "Water Rights and Water Trade an Islamic Perspective". In Naser. I. Faruqui, Asit K. Biswas and Murad J. Bino, eds.: *Water Management in Islam*; Tokyo: United Nations University Press. 85-93.
KAÏKA, MARIA (2003) "Constructing Scarcity and Sensationalising Water Politics: 170 Days that Shook Athens". *Antipode* 35 (5): 919-954.

―――― (2004) "Interrogating the Geographies of the Familiar: Domesticating Nature and Constructing the Autonomy of the Modern Home". *International Journal of Urban and Regional Research* 28 (2): 265-286.

KANE, JOHN (2001) *The Politics of Moral Capital.* Cambridge: Cambridge University Press. 277p.

KANT, IMMANUEL (1870) *Grundlegung zur Metaphysik der Sitten.* Berlin: L. Heimann. 351p.

KARIUKI, MUKAMI, and JORDAN SCHWARTZ (2005) *Small-scale private service providers of water supply and electricity: A review of incidence, structure, pricing, and operating characteristics, World Bank Policy Research Working Paper 3727.*

KATZ, JOSEPH (2010) *Introductory Fluid Mechanics.* Cambridge: Cambridge University Press. 456p.

KAUPPI, NIILO (2000) "The Sociologist as Moraliste: Pierre Bourdieu's Practice of Theory and the French Intellectual Tradition". *SubStance* 29 (3): 7-21.

KEENER, SARAH, MANUEL LUNEGO, and SUDESHNA BANERJEE (2010) "Provision of Water to the Poor In Africa. Experience with Water Standposts and the Informal Water Sector", *Policy Research Working Paper 5387, The World Bank.* 61p.

KENNEDY, M. R. (1907) "Sudan Public Works Report", *Public Works Department.* General Reports on Finance, Administration and Condition of the Sudan.

―――― (1908) "Sudan Public Works Report", *Public Works Department.* General Reports on Finance, Administration and Condition of the Sudan.

KIBREAB, GAIM (1996) "Eritrean and Ethiopian Urban Refugees in Khartoum: What the Eye Refuses to See". *African Studies Review* 39 (3): 131-178.

KJELLÉN, M., and G. MCGRANAHAN (2006) *Informal Water Vendors and the Urban Poor.* London: International Institute for Environment and Development. 26p.

KOPYTOFF, IGOR (1986) "The Cultural Biography of Things: Commoditization as Process". In Arjun Appadurai, ed.: *The Social Live of Things: Commodities in a Cultural Perspective*; Cambridge: University of Cambridge. 64-94.

KORF, BENEDIKT (2007) "Antinomies of Generosity: Moral Geographies and Post-Tsunami Aid in Southeast Asia". *Geoforum* 38 (2): 366-378.

KULINDWA, KASSIM, and HAAKON LEIN (2008) "Water and Poverty: The Inextrictable Link". In David Hemson, Kassim Kulindwa, Haakon Lein and Adolfo Mascarenhas, eds.: *Poverty and Water: Explorations of the Reciprocal Relationship*; London: Zed Books. 1-13.

LAFAYE, CLAUDETTE, and LAURENT THEVENOT (1993) "Une Justification Écologique ? Conflits dans l'Aménagement de la Nature". *Revue française de sociologie* 34 (4): 495-524.
LAHIRE, BERNHARD (2011 [2001]) *The Plural Actor*. Cambridge: Polity Press. 280p.
LAMNEK, SIEGFRIED (2005) *Qualitative Sozialforschung: Lehrbuch*. Weinheim: Beltz. 808p.
LAMONT, MICHÈLE (1992) *Money, Morals, and Manners: the Culture of the French and American Upper-Middle Class*. Chicago: University of Chicago Press. 320p.
LANDRY, SHAWN M., and JAYAJIT CHAKRABORTY (2009) "Street Trees and Equity: Evaluating the Spatial Distribution of an Urban Amenity". *Environment and Planning A* 41 (11): 2651-2670.
LANSING, J STEPHEN (1987) "Balinese 'Water Temples' and the Management of Irrigation". *American Anthropologist* 89 (2): 326-341.
LARSON, RHETT (2011) "Holy Water and Human Rights: Indigenous Peoples' Religious Rights Claims to Water Resources". *Arizona Journal of Environmental Law & Policy* 2: 81-109.
LATOUR, BRUNO (1993) *We Have Never Been Modern*. Cambridge: Harvard University Press. 157p.
LAVERGNE, MARC (1995) "L'Aménagement du Grand Khartoum, Entre Planification Autoritaire et "Droit à la Ville"". *Annales de Géographie de l'Université Saint-Joseph* 16: 75-115.
LEE, ROGER, and DAVID M. SMITH (2004) "Geographies of Morality and Moralities of Geography". In Roger Lee and David M. Smith, eds.: *Geographies and Moralities: International Perspectives on Development, Justice, and Place*; Oxford: Blackwell. 1-12.
LEIBFRIED, STEPHAN (1993) "Towards a European Welfare State?". In Catherine Jones, ed.: *New Perspectives on the Welfare State in Europe*; London: Routledge. 121-143.
LEIST, ANTON (2003) "Ethik zwischen Hobbes und Kant". In Anton Leist, ed.: *Moral als Vertrag? Beiträge zum moralischen Kontraktualismus*; Berlin: W. de Gruyter. 1-36.
LEMPERT, WOLFGANG (2010) *Soziologische Aufklärung als moralische Passion: Pierre Bourdieu*. Wiesbaden: VS Verlag für Sozialwissenschaften. 316p.
LÉVI-STRAUSS, CLAUDE (1969 [1949]) *The Elementary Structures of Kinship*. Boston: Beacon Press. 584p.
LINTON, JAMIE (2010) *What is Water? The History of a Modern Abstraction*. Vancouver: UBC Press. 333p.
LOBINA, EMANUELE (2000) "Cochabamba: Water War". *Focus PSI Journal* 7 (2).

—— (2005) "Problems with Private Water Concessions: A Review of Experiences and Analysis of Dynamics". *International Journal of Water Resources Development* 21 (1): 55 - 87.

LOBINA, EMANUELE, and DAVID HALL (2007) "Water Privatisation and Restructuring in Latin America, 2007", *PSIRU Reports*. 60p.

—— (2008) "The Comparative Advantage of the Public Sector in the Development of Urban Water Supply". *Progress in Development Studies* 8 (1): 85-101.

LOFTUS, ALEX (2005) "'Free Water' as Commodity: The Paradoxes of Durban's Water Service Transformations". In David A. McDonald and Greg Ruiters, eds.: *The Age of Commodity: Water Privatization in Southern Africa*; London: Earthscan. 189-203.

—— (2006a) "The Metabolic Processes of Capital Accumulation in Durban's Waterscape". In Erik Swyngedouw, Maria Kaika and Nikolas C. Heynen, eds.: *In the Nature of Cities: Urban Political Ecology and the Politics of Urban Metabolism*; Abingdon: Routledge. 173-190.

—— (2006b) "Reification and the Dictatorship of the Water Meter". *Antipode* 38 (5): 1023-1045.

—— (2007) "Working the Socio-Natural Relations of the Urban Waterscape in South Africa". *International Journal of Urban and Regional Research* 31 (1): 41-59.

—— (2009) "Rethinking Political Ecologies of Water". *Third World Quarterly* 30 (5): 953 - 968.

MACKAY, HUGHIE, and GARETH GILLESPIE (1992) "Extending the Social Shaping of Technology Approach: Ideology and Appropriation". *Social Studies of Science* 22 (4): 685-716.

MACKENZIE, DONALD, and JUDY WAJCMAN (1999) "Introductory Essay: the Social Shaping of Technology". In Donald MacKenzie and Judy Wajcman, eds.: *The Social Shaping of Technology*; Buckingham: Open University Press. 1-49.

MALLAT, CHIBLI (1995) "The Quest for Water Use Principles: Reflections on Shari'a and Custom in the Middle East". In John A. Allan and Chibli Mallat, eds.: *Water in the Middle East: Legal, Political, and Commercial Implications*; London: I.B. Tauris. 127-138.

MARX, KARL (1962 [1867]) *Das Kapital*. Vol. 1, Marx Engels Werke 23. Berlin: Dietz Verlag. 802p.

MASON, SIMON A. (2009) *From Conflict to Cooperation in the Nile Basin*. Zürich: ETH Zürich. 279p.

MAUSS, MARCEL (1966 [1923]) *The Gift - the Forms and Reason for Exchange in Archaic Societies*. London: Cohen & West. 130p.

McGranahan, Gordon, Diana Mitlin, and David Satterthwaite (2008) "Land and Services for the Urban Poor in Rapidly Urbanizing Countries". In George Martine, Gordon McGranahan, Mark Montgomery and Rogelio Fernandez-Castilla, eds.: *The New Global Frontier Urbanization, Poverty and Environment in the 21st Century*; London: Earthscan. 77-97.

McGranahan, Gordon, Cyrus Njiru, Mike Albu, Mike Smith, and Diana Mitlin (2006) *How Small Water Enterprises Can Contribute to the Millennium Development Goals: Evidence from Dar Es Salaam, Nairobi, Khartoum and Accra.* Loughborough: Water, Engineering and Development Centre. 47p.

Mehta, Lyla (2005) *The Politics and Poetics of Water: The Naturalisation of Scarcity in Western India.* Hyderabad: Orient Longman. 396p.

Meyer, Thomas, and Lewis Hinchman (2007) *The Theory of Social Democracy.* Cambridge: Wiley. 279p.

Mills, Kurt (2012) "'Bashir is Dividing us': Africa and the International Criminal Court". *Human Rights Quarterly* 34 (2): 404-447.

Mitlin, Diana (2004) "Competition, Regulation and the Urban Poor: a Case Study of Water". In Paul Cook, ed.: *Leading Issues in Competition, Regulation, and Development*; Cheltenham: E. Elgar. 320-338.

Molle, François (2009) "River-Basin Planning and Management: The Social Life of a Concept". *Geoforum* 40 (3): 484-494.

Mosse, David (2003) *The Rule of Water: Statecraft, Ecology, and Collective Action in South India.* Oxford: Oxford University Press. 337p.

―――― (2008) "Epilogue: The Cultural Politics of Water – A Comparative Perspective". *Journal of Southern African Studies* 34 (4): 939-948.

Müller-Mahn, Detlef, Anne-Sophie Beckedorf, Salma M. Abdalla, and Sebastian Zug (2010) "Wasserversorgung und Stadtentwicklung in Khartum". *Geographische Rundschau* 62 (10): 38-44.

Müller, Anna, and Diana Mitlin (2007) "Securing Inclusion: Strategies for Community Empowerment and State Redistribution". *Environment and Urbanization* 19 (2): 425-439.

Musa, Salah Bashir, and Abbas S. Musa (1991) "Water Supply in Greater Khartoum". In H.R.J. Davies and M.E. Abu Sin, eds.: *The Future of Sudan's Capital Region: a Study in Development and Change*; Khartoum Khartoum University Press. 65-76.

Nauges, Céline, and Caroline Berg (2008) "Demand for Piped and Non-piped Water Supply Services: Evidence from Southwest Sri Lanka". *Environmental and Resource Economics* 42 (4): 535-549.

Navez-Bouchanine, Françoise (2002) "La Fragmentation: Sources et 'Definitions'". In Françoise Navez-Bouchanine, ed.: *La Fragmentation en Question: Des Villes Entre Fragmentation Spatiale et Fragmentation Sociale?*; Paris: Editions L'Harmattan. 45-104.

NEGRE, MICAËL (2004) *ONG et Autoritarisme au Soudan: l'Eau en Question, Collection 15/20*. Cairo: CEDEJ. 111p.

NIEMANN, STEFFEN, and OLIVIER GRAEFE (2006) "Wasserversorgung in Afrika Politik, Bevölkerungsdruck und Machtdefizit". *Geographische Rundschau* 58 (2): 30-38.

NORMAN, EMMA S., KAREN BAKKER, and CHRISTINA COOK (2012) "Water Governance and the Politics of Scale". *Water Alternatives* 5 (1): 52-82.

O'NEILL, ONARA (1996) *Towards Justice and Virtue: a Constructive Account of Practical Reasoning*. Cambridge: Cambridge University Press. 230p.

O'NEILL, THOMAS (1989) "Evaluation of Water Distribution Programme in the Omdurman Area, Sudan", *League of Red Cross and Sudanese Red Crecent*. 30p.

OLIVERA, OSCAR, and TOM LEWIS (2004) *Cochabamba! Water War in Bolivia*. Cambridge: South End Press. 204p.

OLSON, ELIZABETH, and ANDREW SAYER (2009) "Radical Geography and its Critical Standpoints: Embracing the Normative". *Antipode* 41 (1): 180-198.

ORLOVE, BEN, and STEVEN C. CATON (2010) "Water Sustainability: Anthropological Approaches and Prospects". *Annual Review of Anthropology* 39 (1): 401-415.

OSTEEN, MARK (2002) *The Question of the Gift - Essays Across Disciplines*. London: Routledge. 299p.

OSTROM, ELINOR (1990) *Governing the Commons: the Evolution of Institutions for Collective Action*. Cambridge: Cambridge University Press. 280p.

OXFORD DICTIONARY OF ENGLISH (2010). Oxford: OUP Oxford. 212p.

OYEDOTUN, TEMITOPE DARE TIMOTHY (2012) "Urban Water Usages in Egbeda Area of Oyo State, Nigeria". Paper read at 12th edition of the World Wide Workshop for Young Environmental Scientists - Urban Waters: Resource or Risks?, at Arcueil, France.

PAGE, BEN (2003) "Communities as the Agents of Commodification: The Kumbo Water Authority in Northwest Cameroon". *Geoforum* 34 (4): 483-498.

——— (2005) "Paying for Water and the Geography of Commodities". *Transactions of the Institute of British Geographers* 30 (3): 293-306.

PAINTER, JOE (2000) "Pierre Bourdieu". In Mike Crang and Nigel Thrift, eds.: *Thinking Space*; London: Routledge. 239-259.

PANTULIANO, SARA, MUNZOUL ASSAL, BUTHEINA A. ELNAIEM, HELEN MCELHINNEY, MANUEL SCHWAB, YATHRIB ELZEIN, and HANAA MOTASIM MAHMOUD ALI (2011) *City Limits: Urbanisation and*

Vulnerability in Sudan: Khartoum Case Study. London: UKAID, ODI. 44p.

PETER, LOTHAR (2011) "Prolegomena zu einer Theorie der symbolischen Gewalt". *Österreichische Zeitschrift für Soziologie* 36 (4): 11-31.

PEZON, CHRISTELLE (2011) "How the Compagnie Générale des Eaux survived the End of Concession Contracts in France 100 Years ago". *Water Policy* 13 (2): 178-186.

POUPEAU, FRANCK (2000) "Reasons for Domination: Bourdieu Versus Habermas". In Bridget Fowler, ed.: *Reading Bourdieu on Society and Culture*; Oxford: Blackwell. 69-87.

PRADHAN, RAJENDRA, and RUTH MEINZEN-DICK (2010) "Which Rights are Right? Water Rights, Culture, and Underlying Values". In Peter G. Brown and Jeremy J. Schmidt, eds.: *Water Ethics: Foundational Readings for Students and Professionals*; Washington Press: Island Press. 39-57.

PRASAD, NAREN (2006) "Privatisation Results: Private Sector Participation in Water Services After 15 Years". *Development Policy Review* 24 (6): 669-692.

PROCTOR, JAMES D. (1998) "The Spotted Owl and the Contested Moral Landscape of the Pacific Northwest". In Jennifer R. Wolch and Jody Emel, eds.: *Animal Geographies: Place, Politics, and Identity in the Nature-Culture Borderlands*; London: Verso. 191-217.

——— (1999) "Introduction: Overlapping Terrains". In James D. Proctor and David M. Smith, eds.: *Geography and Ethics: Journeys in a Moral Terrain*; London: Routledge. 149-162.

RAWLS, JOHN (1971) *A Theory of Justice*. Cambridge: Belknap Press. 607p.

REHBEIN, BOIKE (2006) *Die Soziologie Pierre Bourdieus*. Konstanz: UVK Verlagsgesellschaft. 270p.

ROBBINS, DEREK (2007) "Sociology as Reflexive Science: On Bourdieu's Project". *Theory, Culture & Society* 24 (5): 77-98.

ROBBINS, PAUL (2012) *Political Ecology: A Critical Introduction*. Chister: John Wiley & Sons. 298p.

RUONAVAARA, HANNU (1997) "Moral Regulation: A Reformulation". *Sociological Theory* 15 (3): 277-293.

SAHLINS, MARSHALL D. (1996 [1978]) "On the Sociology of Primitive Exchange". In Aafke E. Komter, ed.: *The Gift - An Interdisciplinary Perspective*; Amsterdam: Amsterdam University Press. 26-38.

SAINT-VIL, JEAN (1983) "L'Eau Chez soi et l'Eau au Coin de la Rue: les Systèmes de Distribution de l'Eau à Abidjan". *Cahiers Orstom, Série Sciences Humaines* 19 (4): 491-512.

SANSOM, KEVIN, and ANNETTE BOS (2008) "Utility and non-State Water Service Provision for the Urban Poor". *International Journal of Water* 4 (3/4): 290-303.
SAYER, ANDREW (1999) "Bourdieu, Smith and Disinterested Judgement". *The Sociological Review* 47 (3): 403-431.
——— (2005) *The Moral Significance of Class*. Cambridge: Cambridge University Press. 246p.
——— (2010a) "Bourdieu, Ethics and Practice". In Elizabeth Silva and Alan Warde, eds.: *Cultural Analysis and Bourdieu's Legacy*; London: Routledge. 87-101.
——— (2010b) "Class and Morality". In Steven Hitlin and Stephen Vaisey, eds.: *Handbook of the Sociology of Morality*; New York: Springer. 163-178.
SCHULTHEIS, FRANZ (2007) *Bourdieus Wege in die Soziologie: Genese und Dynamik einer reflexiven Sozialwissenschaft*. Konstanz: UVK Verlagsgesellschaft. 166p.
SCHWARTZ, KLAAS (2008) "The New Public Management: The Future for Reforms in the African Water Supply and Sanitation Sector?". *Utilities Policy* 16 (1): 49-58.
SCHWARTZ, KLAAS, and ANTHONY SANGA (2010) "Partnerships Between Utilities and Small-Scale Providers: Delegated Management in Kisumu, Kenya". *Physics and Chemistry of the Earth* 35 (13-14): 765-771.
SEN, AMARTYA (1983) "Development: Which Way Now?". *The Economic Journal* 93 (372): 745-762.
SETTEN, GUNHILD (2004) "The Habitus, the Rule and the Moral Landscape". *Cultural Geographies* 11 (4): 389-415.
SEWELL, WILLIAM H. (1992) "A Theory of Structure: Duality, Agency, and Transformation". *American Journal of Sociology* 98 (1): 1-29.
SHEFFIELD, KAI (2013) "Speak Softly and Carry a Sealed Warrant: Building the International Criminal Court's Legitimacy in the Wake of Sudan". *Appeal: Review of Current Law and Law Reform* 18 (1): 163-175.
SHERMAN, JENNIFER (2006) "Coping with Rural Poverty: Economic Survival and Moral Capital in Rural America". *Social Forces* 85 (2): 891-913.
SHIVA, VANDANA (2002) *Water wars: Privatization, Pollution and Profit*. London: Pluto Press. 156p.
SILK, JOHN (2004) "Caring at a Distance: Gift Theory, Aid Chains and Social Movements". *Social & Cultural Geography* 5 (2): 229-251.
SILVA, ELIZABETH, and ALAN WARDE (2010) "Introduction: The Importance of Bourdieu". In Elizabeth Silva and Alan Warde, eds.: *Cultural Analysis and Bourdieu's Legacy: Settling Accounts and Developing Alternatives*; London: Routledge. 1-13.

SINGER, PETER (1993) *How Are We To Live?: Ethics in an Age of Self-Interest*. Milsons Point: Random House Australia. 303p.
SMITH, DAVID M. (1997) "Geography and Ethics: a Moral Turn?". *Progress in Human Geography* 21 (4): 583-590.
——— (2000) *Moral Geographies: Ethics in a World of Difference*. Edinburgh: Edinburgh University Press. 244p.
SOLO, TOVA MARIA (1999) "Small-Scale Entrepreneurs in the Urban Water and Sanitation Market". *Environment and Urbanization* 11 (1): 117-132.
SOUTHWOOD, NICHOLAS (2010) *Contractualism and the Foundations of Morality*. Oxford: Oxford University Press. 208p.
STEINFATH, HOLMER (2003) "Wir und Ich: Überlegungen zur Begründung moralischer Normen". In Anton Leist, ed.: *Moral als Vertrag? Beiträge zum moralischen Kontraktualismus*, Berlin: W. de Gruyter. 71-96.
STRANG, VERONICA (2004) *The Meaning of Water*. Oxford: Berg. 320p.
SUDAN CENTRAL BUREAU OF STATISTICS (2009) *Statistical Yearbook for the Year 2009*. 465p.
SULTANA, FARHANA (2009) "Community and Participation in Water Resources Management: Gendering and Naturing Development Debates from Bangladesh". *Transactions of the Institute of British Geographers* 34 (3): 346-363.
——— (2012) "Water, Technology, and Development: Transformations of Development Technonatures in Changing Waterscapes". *Environment and Planning D: Society and Space* 30: in press.
SULTANA, FARHANA, and ALEX LOFTUS, eds. (2012)*The Right to Water: Politics, Governance and Social Struggles*. Milton Park: Taylor & Francis. 262p.
SUSEN, SIMON (2011) "Review: Kritische Gesellschaftstheorie or kritische Gesellschaftspraxis? Robin Celikates, Kritik als soziale Praxis. Gesellschaftliche Selbstverständigung und kritische Theorie". *European Journal of Sociology* 52 (3): 447-463.
SWARTZ, DAVID (1997) *Culture and Power: The Sociology of Pierre Bourdieu*. Chicago: University of Chicago Press. 333p.
——— (2004) "From Critical Sociology to Public Intellectual: Pierre Bourdieu & Politics". In David Swartz and Vera L. Zolberg, eds.: *After Bourdieu: Influence, Critique, Elaboration*, Dordrecht: Kluwer Academic Publishers. 333-364.
SWARTZ, SHARLENE (2010) "'Moral Ecology' and 'Moral Capital': Tools Towards a Sociology of Moral Education from a South African Ethnography". *Journal of Moral Education* 39 (3): 305-327.
SWYNGEDOUW, ERIK (1996) "The City as a Hybrid: On Nature, Society and Cyborg Urbanization". *Capitalism, Nature, Socialism* 7 (2): 65.

―――― (1997) "Power, nature, and the city. The conquest of water and the political ecology of urbanization in Guayaquil, Ecuador: 1880 - 1990". *Environment and Planning A* 29 (2): 311-332.

―――― (1999a) "Marxism and Historical-Geographical Materialism: A Spectre is Haunting Geography". *Scottish Geographical Journal* 115 (2): 91-102.

―――― (1999b) "Modernity and Hybridity: Nature, Regeneracionismo, and the Production of the Spanish Waterscape, 1890–1930". *Annals of the Association of American Geographers* 89 (3): 443-465.

―――― (2004) *Social Power and the Urbanization of Water: Flows of Power*. Oxford: Oxford University Press. 209p.

―――― (2005) "Dispossessing H_2O: The Contested Terrain of Water Privatization". *Capitalism Nature Socialism* 16 (1): 81-98.

―――― (2006) "Metabolic Urbanization: The Making of Cyborg Cities". In Nik Heynen, Maria Kaïka and Erik Swyngedouw, eds.: *In the Nature of Cities: Urban Political Ecology and the Politics of Urban Metabolism*; Abingdon: Routledge. 20-40.

―――― (2009) "Troubled Waters: The Public Economy of Essential Public Services". In Jose Esteban Castro and Leo Heller, eds.: *Water and Sanitation Services: Public Policy and Management*; London: Earthscan. 39-55.

SWYNGEDOUW, ERIK, and NIKOLAS C. HEYNEN (2003) "Urban Political Ecology, Justice and the Politics of Scale". *Antipode* 35 (5): 898-918.

SWYNGEDOUW, ERIK, MARIA KAÏKA, and JOSE ESTEBAN CASTRO (2002) "Urban Water: A Political-Ecology Perspective". *Built Environment* 28 (2): 124-137.

TAHA, FADWA (2009) "The History of the Nile Waters in the Sudan". In Terje Tvedt, ed.: *The River Nile in the Post-Colonial Age: Conflict and Cooperation Among the Nile Basin Countries*; New York: I.B. Tauris. 179-235.

TRÉMOLET, SOPHIE, and DIANE BINDER (2010) "The Regulation of Water and Sanitation Services: Literature Review, Insights and Areas for Research in DCs", *AFD*. 112p.

TRÉMOLET, SOPHIE, and CATHERINE HUNT (2006) "Taking Account of the Poor in Water Sector Regulation", *Water Supply and Sanitation Working Notes 11, World Bank*. 75p.

TRIVERS, ROBERT L. (1971) "The Evolution of Reciprocal Altruism". *Quarterly Review of Biology* 46 (1): 35-57.

TUMUSIIME, CHRIS, and CYRUS NJIRU (2004) "Performance of Management Contracts in Small Towns Water Services". Paper read at 30th WEDC International Conference, at Vientiane, Lao PDR.

TVEDT, TERJE (2004) *The River Nile in the Age of the British: Political Ecology and the Quest for Economic Power*. London: I.B. Tauris. 480p.

TVEDT, TERJE, and TERJE OESTIGAARD (2010) "A History of the Ideas of Water: Deconstructing Nature and Constructing Society". In Terje Tvedt, ed.: *A History of Water*, New York: I.B. Tauris. 1-36.

UN DESA (2012). "World Urbanization Prospects: The 2011 Revision" Available from http: //esa.un.org/unup/. (accessed on 20.11.2012).

UN GENERAL ASSEMBLY (2010) "Human Rigt to Water and Sanitation (28 July 2010)", *UN Document A/RES/64/292*.

UN HABITAT (2009) *Urban Sector Studies and Capacity Building for Khartoum State*. Nairobi. 60p.

UN INTERNATIONAL CONFERENCE ON WATER AND THE ENVIRONMENT (1992) *The Dublin Statement on Water and Sustainable Development*. 6p.

UNICEF, and WHO (2012) *Progress on Drinking Water and Sanitation: 2012 Update*. New York. 60p.

VALVERDE, MARIANA (1994) "Moral Capital". *Canadian Journal of Law and Society* 9 (1): 213-232.

VERDEIL, VERONIQUE (2003) *Marchés Locaux de l'Eau. Pratiques et Territoires de l'Approvisionnement en Eau à Metro Cebu, Philippines*. PhD Thesis, Institut Français d'Urbanisme, Université Paris 8.

VERHEZEN, PETER (2009) *Gifts, Corruption, Ühilanthropy: The Ambiguity of Gift Practices in Business, Frontiers of business ethics*. New York: Lang. 321p.

VÉRON, RENÉ (2006) "Remaking Urban Environments: the Political Ecology of Air Pollution in Delhi". *Environment and Planning A* 38: 2093-2109.

WALKER, PETER A. (2005) "Political Ecology: Where is the Ecology?". *Progress in Human Geography* 29 (1): 73-82.

WATERBURY, JOHN (2002) *The Nile Basin: National Determinants of Collective Action*. Yale: Yale University Press. 211p.

WEATHINGTON, BART L., CHRISTOPHER J. L. CUNNINGHAM, and DAVID J. PITTENGER (2010) *Research Methods for the Behavioral and Social Sciences*. Hoboken: Wiley. 647p.

WHITTINGTON, DALE, DONALD T. LAURIA, DANIEL A. OKUN, and XINMING MU (1989) "Water Vending Activities in Developing Countries". *International Journal of Water Resources Development* 5 (3): 158-168.

WHITTINGTON, DALE, XINMING MU, and ROBERT ROCHE (1990) "Calculating the Value of Time Spent Collecting Water: Some Estimates for Ukunda, Kenya". *World Development* 18 (2): 269-280.

WHITTINGTON, DALE, SUBHRENDU K. PATTANAYAK, JUI-CHEN YANG, and K.C. BAL KUMAR (2002) "Do Households Want Privatized Municipal Water Services? Evidence from Kathmandu, Nepal", *Working Paper 02_03, Research Triangle Institute*. 31p.

WILK, RICHARD (2006) "Bottled Water: The Pure Commodity in the Age of Branding". *Journal of Consumer Culture* 6 (3): 303-325.
WITTFOGEL, KARL A. (1957) *Oriental Despotism*. New Heaven: Yale University Press. 556p.
WOLF, JEAN-CLAUDE, and PETER SCHABER (1998) *Analytische Moralphilosophie*. Freiburg: Verlag K. Alber. 221p.
XALI, MTHETHO (2002) "'They are Killing us Alive': A Case Study of the Impact of Cost Recovery on Service Provision in Makhaza Section, Khayelitsha". In John Pape and David A. McDonald, eds.: *Cost Recovery and the Crisis of Service Delivery in South Africa*, London: Zed Books. 101-119.
ZIMMER, ANNA, and PATRICK SAKDAPOLRAK (2012) "The Social Practices of Governing: Analysing Waste Water Governance in a Delhi Slum". *Environment and Urbanization Asia* 3 (2): 325-341.
ZUG, SEBASTIAN (2013) "Transforming Bourdieu's 'Perfect' Economy of Symbolic Goods into an Imperfect One. The Moral Grounding of Water Transfers in Khartoum". *Geographica Helvetica* (in press).
ZUIN, VALENTINA, LEONARD ORTOLANO, MANUEL ALVARINHO, KORY RUSSEL, ANNE THEBO, ODETE MUXIMPUA, and JENNIFER DAVIS (2011) "Water Supply Services for Africa's Urban Poor: the Role of Resale". *Journal of water and health* 9 (4): 773-784.

Appendix: List of Interviews

Interviews with actors in Square 11

Households

A1 - A12	12 households in Area A
B1 - B14	14 households in Area B
C1 - C15	15 households in Area C
D1 - D12	12 households in Area D
X1 - X29	29 households in other areas

Group interview

GD1	girls carrying water in Area D

Popular committee*

PC1	president
PC2	secretary
PC3	member, supervisor during network construction
PC4	female member

*other members are mentioned in their function at KSWC

Commercial actors

COM1	generator operator
COM2	generator operator
COM3	generator operator
COM4	generator operator
COM5	tee stall (used by the popular committee as office)
COM6	tree nursery
COM7	tailor
COM8	shop owner
COM9	owner of a flour mill

Local elite

ISL1	imam of the central mosque
ISL2	head master of Sufi boarding school
CHR1	catholic priest, living but not working in Square 11
EL1	coach of the soccer team
EL2	nurse of the health station

Interviews with KSWC Staff

Umbadda Office (municipality)

actor lives in Square 11

KSWC01	head of office	
KSWC02	deputy head of office	
KSWC03	head of networks (present)	
KSWC04	head of networks (previous)	
KSWC05	head of boreholes	
KSWC06	civil engineer	
KSWC07	accounting officer	

Dar Alsalam Office (administrative unit)

KSWC08	head of office	
KSWC09	officer responsible for customer requests	
KSWC10	officer responsible for customer requests	●

Offices in other administrative units

KSWC11	head of office (Umbadda North)	
KSWC12	officer (Alfetehab)	●
KSWC13	officer (Umbadda South)	●

In Square 11

KSWC14	borehole operator	●
KSWC15	borehole operator, member of popular committee Sq11	●

In neighbouring squares of Square 11

KSWC16	borehole operator Square 10	
KSWC17	boreh. op. Sq12; member of popular committee Sq11	●
KSWC18	borehole operator Square 31	
KSWC19	borehole operator Square 37	

Interviews with actors in the water sector, that are not employed by KSWC

		actor lives in Square 11
Money collection company		
MC1	area manager northern Dar Alsalam	
MC2	money collector Square 11	
MC3	money collector in Umbadda	●
Water Vendors		
WV1	water vendor	●
WV2	water vendor	●
WV3	water vendor	●
WV4	water vendor	●
Plumbers		
PL1	Plumber	●
PL2	plumber	●
PL3	plumber	●
PL4	plumber, Souq Libya	
PL5	plumber, Souq Libya	

Summary

This book examines the 'gift of water' as one way for urban dwellers to access water in the global South. A case study of a peri-urban neighbourhood in the Sudanese capital Khartoum will reveal that households insufficiently supplied by the government water network do not exclusively rely on market alternatives like water vendors. Instead a significant share of these households obtains water for free. This water had been intended for sale by the vendors or purchased by neighbours.

The scientific narratives on urban water – including those in human geography dominated by a group of Neo-Marxist 'political ecologists of water' (e.g. Swyngedouw, Bakker, Kaïka, Linton, Loftus) – hardly acknowledge free water transfers. The absence of water gifts in their debates can be explained by their focus on analysing how social power both shapes and is shaped by network infrastructures. The significant actors within such a perspective are policy makers and those who provide water according to their policies, notably public and private water corporations. The scale of analysis is the 'waterscape of the city'. Policies are made for this waterscape and within it, they are affected by global trends like neoliberalism and under support and pressure from international monetary institutions and donors.

To understand how water is transformed from payable commodity to free gift, I will down-scale the scientific focus to 'neighbourly waterscapes', hence to the scale where free water transfers are produced and negotiated in face to face practices between a donor and a recipient. Such a shift of perspective transforms households – who are conceptualized in most contemporary debates as passive consumers and mere signifiers of water supply inequality – into active actors who contribute to the production of urban water supply beyond purchasing water. Rather than analysing water policy and the political processes that determine who is connected and who is not, individual motivations to give water for free are reconstructed through a 'political ecology of the neighbourhood'.

The various theories on the motivations underlying gifts have been controversially debated, ever since the notion was made popular by Marcel Mauss. Explaining gifts comprises a key ambiguity, which is the relevance of interested and disinterested motivations, hence whether gifts are reciprocal or generous. Empirically, this tension is analysed for water gifts in Khartoum in a detailed reconstruction of both the relationship between the donor and the recipient and the social framework in which the transaction takes place.

Theoretically, the tension between the different motivations underscoring gifts is elaborated by opposing Pierre Bourdieu's theory of practice with Luc Boltanski's work on justification. Bourdieu's relational approach to the social helps translate political ecology's focus on power relations to the local scale, the 'neighbourly social field'. Bourdieu represents these approaches to the gift that highlight reciprocity; hence he explains gifts as an economic exchange in an 'economy of symbolic goods'. Boltanski is one of the scholars who criticised Bourdieu's 'social reductionist' or 'economistic' explanation of social practice. Boltanski argues that people can ground their action on theoretical reason in what he calls in his later work a 'meta-pragmatic register'; but they do not always necessarily do so. I will argue that people in certain situations do refer to a 'universal right to water' that motivates water gifts without striving for individual profit maximization.

This book follows a dual approach. First, it makes use of Bourdieu's and Boltanski's conceptualizations of the social to understand water gifts in Khartoum. Second, based on empirical findings, it elaborates how interested and disinterested motivations can be brought together within a single theoretical framework by supplementing Bourdieu's theory of practice with Boltanski's 'meta-pragmatic register' as an alternative mode of action. Critically analysing Bourdieu's conceptualization of morality, and proposing an adjustment of his theory to allow morality to permeate everyday practice, addresses the economistic critique of the theory of practice without completely rejecting the theory itself. Bourdieu's central concept of the habitus provides a substantial basis for the mediation between morals and interests within particular social fields. Bourdieu's 'perfect' economy of symbolic goods will be transferred into an 'imperfect' one.

The book starts with an overview of political ecology of water with a focus on determining the relevance of considering households as actors who shape the waterscape, rather than merely as water consumers (chapter 2). Shifting the focus from a political ecology of the city to a political ecology of 'neighbourly' and 'moral waterscapes', allows setting the scale and thematic focus required for a conceptualization of water gifts. Using analyses of social science literature on water as a foundation, I demonstrate that the water gift has so far elicited little interest from social scientists as a water access strategy. In the third chapter, I briefly outline the theory of practice as a possible theoretical framework for political ecology followed by an in depth analysis of Bourdieu's conceptualization of disinterestedness and morality. After determining the possibilities of integrating disinterestedness under a conventional reading of Bourdieu, I will unravel some of his assumptions step by step. Extending the Theory of Practice with Boltanski's 'meta-pragmatic register' allows the former to integrate theoretical reasoning and historical habitualisation of morals. After a presentation of the empirical methodology (chapter 4), three chapters discuss the empirical case. Chapter 5 gives a general introduction to water supply in Khartoum and presents the fragmentation of network water supply at different scales. Chapter 6 turns the focus on the households and reveals that direct neighbours have different yet successful strategies to access water supplied by the public water corporation. Fragmentation of supply in combination with heterogeneity in access provides the contexts of water inequality in which redistribution of water by gift transfers takes place. In chapter 7, two types of water gifts are presented. One is explained within Bourdieu's 'economy of symbolic goods', whereas the other justifies the moral extension of his theory.

Zusammenfassung

Dieses Buch behandelt das Phänomen der ‚Wassergaben'. Diese tragen für einige städtische Haushalte in Ländern des Südens zur Deckung des täglichen Wasserbedarfs bei. Anhand einer Fallstudie in einem peri-urbanen Stadtviertel der sudanesischen Hauptstadt Khartum werden Strategien von Haushalten, die nicht ausreichend mit Leitungswasser versorgt werden, analysiert. Neben dem Wasserkauf von Händlern zu Marktkonditionen beziehen etliche Haushalte Wasser kostenlos entweder von Nachbarn, die dieses gekauft haben, oder von Wasserhändlern, welche es eigentlich verkaufen möchten.

Die wissenschaftliche Debatte über städtische Wasserversorgung, die in der Humangeographie von einer Gruppe anglo-sächsischer neomarxistischer politischer Ökologen (Swyngedouw, Bakker, Kaïka, Loftus, Linton) dominiert wird, schenkt der Wassergabe kaum Beachtung. Ihr Interesse gilt vielmehr den Machtprozessen in der Etablierung und im Management von Wassernetzwerken. Der verwendete Betrachtungsmassstab setzt somit die Stadt ins Zentrum. Die relevanten Akteure sind politische Entscheidungsträger sowie die in deren Rahmen agierenden privaten oder öffentlichen Wasserversorgungsunternehmen. Diese ‚städtischen Waterscape' steht sowohl unter dem Einfluss globaler Strömungen wie dem Neoliberalismus als auch unter politischem Druck internationaler Akteure.

Um die Transformation der Ware Wasser zu einem kostenlosen Gut zu verstehen, wird in dieser Arbeit die Betrachtungsebene auf einen niedrigeren Massstab verlegt. In einer solchen ‚nachbarschaftlichen Waterscape' finden kostenlose Wassergaben nicht ausschliesslich physisch statt, sondern sie werden auch zwischen Geber und Gabenempfänger sozial verhandelt. Durch den Perspektivenwechsel von der ‚städtischen' zur ‚nachbarschaftlichen' Waterscape werden Haushalte, die in der wissenschaftlichen Debatte überwiegend auf ihre passive Funktion als Konsumenten reduziert werden, zu zentralen Akteuren. Für das Verständnis von Wassergaben stehen folgerichtig nicht die politischen Prozesse der Stadt im Zentrum. Stattdessen wird in einer ‚politischen Ökologie der Nachbarschaft' die Motivation der lokalen Akteure, die kostenlos ihr Wasser an ihre Nachbarn abgeben, analysiert.

Die Gabe wurde in der theoretischen Debatte, seit Marcel Mauss das Konzept populär gemacht hat, intensiv diskutiert. Die zentrale Kontroverse in der Gabentheorie betrifft den Erklärungsansatz der Motivation der Geber. Dabei wird insbesondere der Bedeutung von Interessen unterschiedliche Relevanz beigemessen. Folglich stellt sich die Frage, ob die Gabe reziprok oder selbstlos ist. Im Kontext dieser Arbeit wird die Funktionsweise der Wassergabe in Khartum rekonstruiert. Dabei wird sowohl die Beziehung zwischen Geber und Beschenktem als auch das soziale Bezugssystem, unter dem Gabentransfer stattfindet, empirisch herausgearbeitet.

Auf der theoretischen Ebene wird die Spannung zwischen den unterschiedlichen Erklärungsversuchen der Gabe anhand einer Gegenüberstellung von Pierre Bourdieus Theorie der Praxis mit Luc Boltanskis Arbeiten zur Rechtfertigung diskutiert. Bourdieus relationaler sozialwissenschaftlicher Ansatz ist der Ausgangspunkt der theoretischen Diskussion dieser Arbeit. Er erlaubt den Fokus der Politischen Ökologie, der Machtbeziehungen ins Zentrum stellt, vom städtischen Kontext in das ‚nachbarschaftliche soziale Feld' zu übertragen. Bourdieus Theorie gehört zu den Ansätzen, welche die Relevanz von Reziprozität in der Erklärung der Gabe hervorheben. Boltanski zählt zu den Wissenschaftlern, die Bourdieus Theorie ‚Ökonomismus' und folglich eine ‚Reduktion der sozialen Realität' vorwerfen. Boltanski argumentiert hingegen, dass Akteure ihr Handeln in ausgewählten Situationen auch auf ‚theoretische Vernunft' stützen können. Diese Handlungen finden in vollem Bewusstsein in einem Handlungsmodus statt, den er in seiner späteren Arbeit als ‚meta-pragmatisches Register' bezeichnet.

In der vorliegenden Arbeit wird erst der Versuch gemacht die Wassergabe innerhalb der Theorie der Praxis zu erklären. Da sich einige Wassergaben jedoch nicht ausschliesslich durch Interessen der Geber erklären lassen, wird in einem nächsten Schritt ein Konzept erarbeitet, in welchem die Gabe interessenbasiert und/oder selbstlos motiviert sein kann. Dazu wird Bourdieus Theorie der Praxis mit Boltanskis ‚metapragmatischem Register' erweitert. Eine kritische Analyse der Bourdieuschen Konzeptualisierung von Moral und die daraus folgende Modifikation seiner Theorie erlauben nicht nur die Erklärung von bewusstem Handeln, sondern auch einer kontinuierlichen moralischen Durchsetzung alltäglicher Handlungen. Diese Erweiterung der Theorie stellt somit eine konstruktive Reaktion auf die Kritik an Bourdieus ‚Ökonomismus' dar. In dieser Erweiterung nimmt der Habitus, als ein zentrales Konzept in Bourdieus Theorie, eine wichtige Funktion ein. Mit dem Habitus lässt sich die Vermittlung zwischen Moral und Interessen verstehen. Durch die Integration von Moral in Bourdieus Theorie, wird seine perfekte ‚Ökonomie der symbolischen Gütern' zu einer unvollkommenen ‚Ökonomie der symbolischen Gütern'.

Die Arbeit ist wie folgt aufgebaut: Nach der Einleitung wird im zweiten Kapitel eine Übersicht der ‚politischen Ökologie des Wassers' dargestellt. Dabei liegt der Schwerpunkt insbesondere auf der Analyse der Funktion von Haushalten als aktive Akteure in der sozialen Konstruktion der Waterscape. Der Perspektivenwechsel von einer politischen Ökologie der Stadt zu einer politischen Ökologie ‚moralischer' und ‚nachbarschaftlicher Waterscapes' erlaubt eine Bestimmung des thematischen Fokus sowie der Massstabsebene für eine Konzeptualisierung von Wassergaben. Eine Übersicht über bisherige Arbeiten zeigt auf, dass die Wassergabe wenig Beachtung in der sozialwissenschaftlichen Auseinandersetzung erfahren hat. Im dritten Kapitel wird die Theorie der Praxis als ein möglicher theoretischer Ansatz innerhalb der politischen Ökologie umrissen, um anschliessend intensiv die Funktion von Moral und Selbstlosigkeit innerhalb der Theorie herauszuarbeiten. Nachdem dargelegt wird, inwiefern bereits unter einer konventionellen Lesart von Bourdieus Werk Selbstlosigkeit theoretisch gedacht werden kann, werde ich nach und nach einige von Bourdieus Annahmen aufgeben. Die Erweiterung der Theorie der Praxis mit Boltanskis ‚metapragmatischem Register' erlaubt die Integration theoretischer Vernunft und deren historische Habitualisierung in die Theorie. Nach der Darstellung der angewendeten empirischen Methoden (Kapitel 4) folgen drei Kapitel, in denen die empirische Studie ausgeführt wird. Im fünften Kapitel wird die Fragmentierung des Wasserversorgungssystems von Khartum auf verschiedenen Massstabsebenen aufgezeigt. Im sechsten Kapitel wird die waterscape aus der Perspektive der Haushalte analysiert. Damit wird gezeigt, dass Haushalte unterschiedlich erfolgreiche Strategien im Zugang zu Leitungswasser haben. Fragmentierung der Wasserversorgung in Verbindung mit den spezifischen Fähigkeiten einzelner Haushalte Wasser für sich nutzbar zu machen, führt zu einem ungleichen Zugang zu Leitungswasser. Dadurch wird die Gabe ein relevanter Wasserversorgungstyp. Im siebten Kapitel werden zwei Arten von Wassergaben präsentiert, von denen die eine innerhalb Bourdieus ‚Ökonomie der Symbolischen Güter' erklärt werden kann, während die andere die moralische Erweiterung seiner Theorie rechtfertigt.